Medieval Philosophy

This book presents a new, contemporary introduction to medieval philosophy as it was practiced in all its variety in Western Europe and the Near East. It assumes only a minimal familiarity with philosophy, the sort that an undergraduate introduction to philosophy might provide, and it is arranged topically around questions and themes that will appeal to a contemporary audience.

In addition to some of the perennial questions posed by philosophers, such as "Can we know anything, and if so, what?", "What is the fundamental nature of reality?", and "What does human flourishing consist in?", this volume looks at what medieval thinkers had to say, for instance, about our obligations toward animals and the environment, freedom of speech, and how best to organize ourselves politically. The book examines certain aspects of the thought of several well-known medieval figures, but it also introduces students to many important, yet underappreciated figures and traditions. It includes guidance for how to read medieval texts, provokes reflection through a series of study questions at the end of each chapter, and gives pointers for where interested readers can continue their exploration of medieval philosophy and medieval thought more generally.

Key Features

- Covers the contributions of women to medieval philosophy, providing students with a fuller understanding of who did philosophy during the Middle Ages
- Includes a focus on certain topics that are usually ignored, such as animal rights, love, and political philosophy, providing students with a fuller range of interests that medieval philosophers had
- Gives space to non-Aristotelian forms of medieval thought
- Includes useful features for student readers like study questions and suggestions for further reading in each chapter

Andrew W. Arlig is Associate Professor of Philosophy and Program Coordinator of Studies in Religion at Brooklyn College, City University of New York. He is the editor of *On What There Was: Parts and Wholes* (projected 2023) and coeditor (with Christina Van Dyke) of *Medieval Philosophy* (2019), which is part of the Critical Concepts in Philosophy series published by Routledge.

ROUTLEDGE CONTEMPORARY INTRODUCTIONS TO PHILOSOPHY

Series editor:
Paul K. Moser
Loyola University of Chicago

This innovative, well-structured series is for students who have already done an introductory course in philosophy. Each book introduces a core general subject in contemporary philosophy and offers students an accessible but substantial transition from introductory to higher-level college work in that subject. The series is accessible to non-specialists and each book clearly motivates and expounds the problems and positions introduced. An orientating chapter briefly introduces its topic and reminds readers of any crucial material they need to have retained from a typical introductory course. Considerable attention is given to explaining the central philosophical problems of a subject and the main competing solutions and arguments for those solutions. The primary aim is to educate students in the main problems, positions and arguments of contemporary philosophy rather than to convince students of a single position.

Recently Published Volumes:

Philosophy of Social Science
2nd Edition
Mark Risjord

Philosophy of Psychiatry
Sam Wilkinson

Philosophy of Emotion
Christine Tappolet

Ancient Philosophy
2nd Edition
Christopher Shields

Medieval Philosophy
Andrew W. Arlig

For a full list of published *Routledge Contemporary Introductions to Philosophy*, please visit https://www.routledge.com/Routledge-Contemporary-Introductions-to-Philosophy/book-series/SE0111

Medieval Philosophy

A Contemporary Introduction

Andrew W. Arlig

NEW YORK AND LONDON

First published 2024
by Routledge
605 Third Avenue, New York, NY 10158

and by Routledge
4 Park Square, Milton Park, Abingdon, Oxon, OX14 4RN

Routledge is an imprint of the Taylor & Francis Group, an informa business

© 2024 Taylor & Francis

The right of Andrew W. Arlig to be identified as author of this work has been asserted in accordance with sections 77 and 78 of the Copyright, Designs and Patents Act 1988.

All rights reserved. No part of this book may be reprinted or reproduced or utilised in any form or by any electronic, mechanical, or other means, now known or hereafter invented, including photocopying and recording, or in any information storage or retrieval system, without permission in writing from the publishers.

Trademark notice: Product or corporate names may be trademarks or registered trademarks and are used only for identification and explanation without intent to infringe.

ISBN: 978-0-367-36675-9 (hbk)
ISBN: 978-0-367-36674-2 (pbk)
ISBN: 978-0-429-34802-0 (ebk)

DOI: 10.4324/9780429348020

Typeset in Times New Roman
by codeMantra

For Christina

Contents

Acknowledgments   ix

1 Introduction   1
    1.1 Some Initial Questions   2
    1.2 Defining Medieval Philosophy   3
    1.3 Genres and Tips for Reading Them   9
    1.4 History Matters   16
    1.5 Philosophy, Religion, and Philosophy of Religion   17
    1.6 Let Us Begin   24
    Suggestions for Further Reading   26

2 Science, Certainty, and Skepticism   28
    2.1 Varieties and Uses of Skepticism   30
    2.2 Certain Knowledge   32
    2.3 Ghazali's Encounter with Global Skepticism   37
    2.4 Degrees of Certainty   47
    Study Questions   53
    Suggestions for Further Reading   55

3 The Building Blocks of Reality   56
    3.1 Hylomorphism for Beginners   57
    3.2 Universality and Individuality   65
    3.3 The Plurality of Forms Debate   76
    3.4 Universal Hylomorphism   83
    3.5 Are Forms Extended?   88
    3.6 Alternatives to Aristotelian Hylomorphism   91
    Study Questions   100
    Suggestions for Further Reading   102

4 What Are We? — 104

- 4.1 Am I but a Soul? — 106
- 4.2 Persistence in This Life and the Next — 112
- 4.3 Mystical Union and the Alleged "Annihilation" of the Self — 121
- 4.4 Individual Humans, Persons, and Moral Standing — 131
- Study Questions — 136
- Suggestions for Further Reading — 137

5 Happiness and the Meaning of Life — 139

- 5.1 The Greek Background: Eudaimonism and the Emphasis on Virtue — 141
- 5.2 From Aristotelian *Eudaimonia* to Heavenly Bliss — 155
- 5.3 Humility, Emptying Oneself, and Going beyond Virtue — 162
- 5.4 Resurrection and the Afterlife: Philosophy Encounters Scripture — 171
- Study Questions — 179
- Suggestions for Further Reading — 181

6 Love Thy Neighbor — 182

- 6.1 Self-Love — 183
- 6.2 Can We Love God? Can God Love Us? — 187
- 6.3 Loving Your Neighbor and Tough Love — 193
- 6.4 Bad Company — 197
- 6.5 Love for All Creation — 203
- Study Questions — 210
- Suggestions for Further Reading — 212

7 The Philosopher in Society — 213

- 7.1 Al-Farabi on the Perfect State — 215
- 7.2 The Critique of Democracy — 224
- 7.3 You Can't Handle the Truth: How the State Talks to Its Citizens — 229
- 7.4 The Freedom to Be Wrong — 233
- 7.5 The Philosopher as Stranger in the World — 253
- Study Questions — 262
- Suggestions for Further Reading — 264

8 From Here, Where? — 266

- 8.1 Why Study the History of Philosophy? — 267
- 8.2 Why Study Medieval Philosophy? — 273
- 8.3 What Now? — 274

Appendix: Timeline of People and Events — 277
Bibliography — 284
Index — 299

Acknowledgments

I came to medieval philosophy by a long and circuitous route. As an undergraduate, I took an elective in medieval philosophy taught by Josef Stern and I was fascinated by what I encountered. But when it came time for me to write an undergraduate thesis, I initially wanted to write on Nietzsche, Heidegger, or someone else from that Germanic tradition. It was only after my first choice for an advisor turned me down that I turned to Professor Stern and proceeded to work on a thesis about divine eternity. It was by reading the classic paper "Eternity" (1981) by Eleonore Stump and Norman Kretzmann that I discovered Boethius, who would eventually become one of my favorite philosophers. I loved every minute of that project, and Professor Stern was the best adviser that one could possibly have wished for. In retrospect, then, I ought to thank that other professor (who shall remain unnamed) for declining to mentor me.

While I had those first enticing tastes, my undergraduate experiences were not enough to propel me immediately into graduate-level study of medieval philosophy. For that I owe thanks to Barbara Fillon, who first introduced me to Julio Cortázar and Jorge Luis Borges. During the several years between my time at the University of Chicago and my graduate study at The Ohio State University, I worked in a bar and a bookstore, and in my free time, I read Latin American literature. I believe it was Carlos Fuentes who led me to the Spanish author Juan Goytisolo. I read Goytisolo's *La Cuarentena* (*Quarantine*), and I was blown away. In many of his writings, Goytisolo was resisting a narrative of Spanish history and culture that was started by the winners of the wars between Christian and Muslim states (wars that came to be known as the "Reconquest") and bolstered by Franco's nationalistic myth. Through his novels, I began to uncover another history of Spanish art, literature, and culture, and in particular, the Islamic and Jewish contributions to Spanish and Western European culture. The vibrant multicultural mosaic of al-Andalus was of course situated in the Middle Ages. It was this that finally inspired me to apply to graduate schools and to assert that I wanted to study medieval philosophy, philosophical theology, and mysticism.

One cannot do it all, especially when a graduate student is expected to narrow down, carve out a special niche, and make a substantive contribution to the field. Under the guidance of Tamar Rudavsky and especially Peter King, I completed a dissertation on twelfth-century Parisian theories of parts and wholes. (See what I mean about specialization?) That set other things in motion, and before I knew it, most of my published work was in a very specialized area in medieval metaphysics. Yet, I always wanted to return to some of those figures and themes that had initially captured my imagination and fired up my spirit. In a way, this book has allowed me to fulfill that wish.

In addition to my old teachers and mentors, to whom I owe an incalculable debt, I want to thank John Marenbon, Irène Rosier-Catach, Gyula Klima, Claude Pannacio, Scott MacDonald, and Robert Pasnau for opening up many opportunities to me as a young scholar.

Some of the material in this book has been tried out on audiences at Lafayette College, the University at Konstanz (Germany), Columbia University, and a meeting of the Midwest Society for the Study of Medieval Philosophy, hosted that year by the University of Notre Dame. I thank the organizers and members of those audiences for the opportunity to experiment with often ill-formed thoughts.

Brooklyn College provided me with my first tenure track job, and it is still the place that I call home. I am thankful to my colleagues in the Department of Philosophy for providing me with encouragement and assistance over the years. I also want to praise my colleagues and friends from our college's interdisciplinary faculty working group in Late Ancient, Medieval, and Early Modern studies (LAMEM), and especially the tireless work of the group's first and sustaining cause Prof. Lauren Mancia. Over the past few years, LAMEM has provided me with several opportunities to bounce ideas around, often in very rough and provisional forms. The seeds for several chapters in this book stem from presentations I gave to that group while we all sat around the grand wooden table in the Costas Classics Library.

And then there are my students. They are a wildly diverse bunch, and their energy inside and outside the class is infectious. Time and time again, they have challenged me and provided a multitude of new perspectives. They have taught me how to teach better and to think more clearly about philosophy. One of my former students Arooj Alam, who is now pursuing a doctorate in Islamic studies, was kind enough to read several draft chapters of this book. Her keen insights and suggestions helped make this book better than it otherwise would have been.

This book would not be possible without the work of too many scholars to name. Several of them took the time to review this book in either its proposal stage or once I had a full first draft. I benefited tremendously from the detailed comments of the two readers enlisted by Routledge. They rescued me from numerous errors, some small, but several quite serious. I hope I have addressed all the shortcomings that they found while not importing any more. One of the reviewers identified himself. So, I get to thank by name Jeffrey Hause for his extremely sage advice and his gentle, but firm fraternal correction on several points. Of course, any errors that remain in this book are mine and mine alone.

Finally, I want to thank my spouse Christina Van Dyke. She urged me to take the leap when I was first approached by Andrew Beck about writing this book. I know it is quite common to see writer's expressing thanks to partners and family, but there is a reason for that. Contemporary scholarship can often be a solitary, even alienating experience. It helps to be pulled out of one's shell by those who share the same house, even if it is only for a cup of coffee, a brief, sweet kiss, or a reminder to eat something. Over the years, I suffered through several dark moments of doubt about my scholarship. Without Christina's love, encouragement, humor, and fiercely glowing presence, I might have thrown in the towel on several projects that are now seeing the light of day. With my heart far too full of love and gratitude to adequately convey with words, I dedicate this volume to her.

1 Introduction

1.1	Some Initial Questions	2
1.2	Defining Medieval Philosophy	3
1.3	Genres and Tips for Reading Them	9
1.4	History Matters	16
1.5	Philosophy, Religion, and Philosophy of Religion	17
1.6	Let Us Begin	24

Welcome to this contemporary introduction to medieval philosophy. Like all the books in the *Contemporary Introductions to Philosophy* series, I will be assuming that you, my reader, are a university student who has recently completed an introduction to philosophy. I will try not to assume much more than that in what follows. Even if you have not taken an introductory course in philosophy, I think that you will get something significant out of this book. In some ways, this book could serve as your introduction to philosophy, since I will be emphasizing many of the ways in which medieval philosophers address the so-called perennial questions.

It is my hope that there will be something in this book for more seasoned readers as well. As you will see below, the medieval period as it is typically construed is vast and it spans several linguistic and intellectual traditions. Not even "experts" in medieval philosophy are conversant with every tradition and every topic. They are, however, often asked to present a survey course of the period. Perhaps this book will give them some ideas for where to begin when expanding their courses beyond their own areas of specialization. And if you are looking for some evidence of what Professor Arlig's (sometimes) expert opinion is about this or that issue, you will see me showing my hand throughout this survey. Given that this is an introduction, I will take measures to be evenhanded and generous, and yet, there is no way to eliminate thoroughly my perspective. This an "opinionated" introduction.[1]

DOI: 10.4324/9780429348020-1

2 Introduction

You should be aware that these opinions do not appear only with respect to specific positions and arguments. My own views about what should count as *philosophy* and what should count as *medieval* philosophy have guided me as I determined what to include and what to skip over in this introduction. I take my charge to write a *contemporary* introduction quite seriously. Academic philosophers are presently thinking very hard about our history, what should be included in the canon of Western philosophy, and even whether there should be a canon. We do not agree on everything. (Professional philosophers *rarely* agree!) But there are a number of us who believe that the canon and the curriculum need to be much more inclusive than they traditionally have been. There are plenty of introductions to medieval philosophy already on the market, and many of them are absolutely worth reading. But one significant limitation of many of these older introductions is their almost exclusive focus on philosophy as it was practiced in Western universities between roughly 1200 and 1400 in the Common Era. This is the philosophy of the "schoolmen" or "scholastic philosophy." To be sure, other voices are typically included. Earlier Western figures like St. Augustine (354–430), Boethius (c. 475–c. 526), St. Anselm of Canterbury (1033–1109), and Peter Abelard (1079–1142) are often discussed, and there is usually some coverage of significant thinkers from the Arabic philosophical tradition, including especially Abu ʻAli al-Husayn ibn ʻAbd Allah ibn Sina (aka Avicenna, 980–1037), Abu Walid ibn Ahmad ibn Muhammad ibn Rushd (Averroes, c. 1126–98), and Moses ben Maimon (Maimonides, 1138–1204).[2] But these additional voices are generally considered in so far as their ideas intersected with and helped to shape philosophical debates in the European schools.

There is, of course, a lot of good philosophy that comes out of the Western universities. If you have been trained by a teacher in the so-called "analytic" philosophical tradition – a tradition that places great emphasis on rigorous definition and argumentation – scholastic philosophy will feel very familiar. But I want to push you to explore philosophy that comes from outside the universities as well. This will require that I say a bit more about how we might go about developing an ample understanding of what counts as medieval philosophy.

1.1 Some Initial Questions

Each subsequent chapter in this book will end with a set of study questions as well as some recommendations for where you can begin to read more about the topics covered in the chapter. For this chapter, however, it seems best if I pause now and ask you to reflect on some of your initial assumptions about the Middle Ages and medieval philosophy. Try writing your answers down and then return to them once you finish this book. Remember: These are your first impressions. There are no right or wrong answers.

1. When you hear the words "Middle Ages" or "medieval," what immediately jumps into your mind?
2. Roughly *when* do you believe that the Middle Ages begins, and when does it end? You can think of this in terms of time or in terms of major events, whether these be political, scientific, or something else.
3. What makes a work of literature a *philosophical* work? Does it have to conform to a specific genre or style of writing and thinking? Are there clear boundaries between, say, philosophy and religious writing, or between philosophy and poetry? (Incidentally, you should not misunderstand me here. I am not suggesting that philosophy *must* be written down. While it is true that historians of philosophy usually are compelled to find their evidence in texts, it does not follow that these texts were in fact at the center of the traditions that we study. Because books were so expensive and rare, even philosophy as it was practiced in the Western scholastic tradition was largely centered around live discussion (see Section 1.3).)
4. What makes something a work of *medieval* philosophy? Is it merely a work created during those Middles Ages that you already have defined, or are there other characteristics of a philosophical work that make it "medieval"? In other words, could someone write a medieval philosophical work in the seventeenth century or perhaps even the present day? If you are already familiar with a medieval philosopher – perhaps, for instance, Anselm or Thomas Aquinas (1225–74) – consider using them as a model. What are the distinctive characteristics of their works?

1.2 Defining Medieval Philosophy

The first order of business is to arrive at some workable definition of medieval philosophy. To accomplish this, we will need to consider both elements in the label. Start with the first of the two. What makes something "medieval"? This turns out to be a very difficult question. I am inclined to think there is no unique correct definition. But something needs to be said, and some workable definition must be in place.

This much should be indisputable: Periods, eras, ages, and so forth are artifacts created by historians, and they are assigned only once the events have passed. (For that matter, days, years, and centuries are arguably artifacts as well, but that is another investigation altogether.) Thomas Aquinas, Ibn Sina, and Catherine of Siena (1347–80) would not have referred to themselves as "medieval" thinkers, nor would they have situated themselves in the "Middle Ages." From their perspective, they were living in the present. In fact, there are numerous discussions in which medieval philosophers will explicitly distinguish the "old" ways practiced by the "ancients" from the "new" ways practiced by "modern" thinkers. I have come across such writings in my own research on material written in *the 1100s*.

Still, serious historians do not carve up the events of the past into periods of time haphazardly. They have reasons for marking out a set of events and labeling them the "Middle Ages," even if it becomes increasingly odd to think of the Middle Ages as a period that falls in the *middle* as more time passes. Let's begin by seeing where historians of medieval philosophy usually start and where they usually end. Then we will see whether we can discern why they pick their starting and ending points.

A casual survey of widely available anthologies and histories of medieval philosophy suggests that the period begins with Augustine and Boethius and ends sometime in the fourteenth or fifteenth century, depending upon whether the book stops with figures like John Buridan (1295/1300–1358/61),[3] a master of the Arts faculty at the University of Paris, or with someone like Nicholas of Cusa (1401–64). But why do these books start and end where and when they do? If we do a little digging, I think we can begin to see what is underneath the dates and representative figures.

Begin with Augustine. Arguably, he is someone who belongs to another historical period, namely, "Late Antiquity." Indeed, the subtitle of one study of Augustine as a philosopher is "Ancient Thought Baptized" (Rist 1994). Augustine is trained in classical literature, particularly Cicero (43 BCE), and he was familiar with a form of Platonism espoused by Plotinus (270 BCE). He sees himself as being engaged in his era's attempt to reconcile pagan Greek and Roman learning with what is still an emerging consensus on what Christianity amounts to. The same could be argued for Boethius, although he is looking to the future in ways that are markedly different from Augustine. Boethius explicitly sees part of his project as preserving the best of Greco-Roman thought for subsequent generations. Arguably, then, he sees himself as the beginning of some future tradition. But how Augustine and Boethius thought of themselves and the position of their work relative to traditions of thought seems to be largely irrelevant for why we place them where we do in our histories of philosophy, nor are they included in medieval anthologies because they are situated in the "middle" of historical time. Rather, the reason why they are included is because, whether intentionally or not, they profoundly influenced intellectual developments that occur during the years that scholars generally agree on being part of the Middle Ages.

This same sort of reasoning might be why Nicholas of Cusa is often *not* included in anthologies. The *Cambridge History of Medieval Philosophy* describes Nicholas as an "innovative philosopher and theologian, often regarded as a key precursor to modern thought" (Pasnau and Van Dyke 2014, vol. 2, 931). Nicholas's theories about infinity inspired another precursor to modern thought, Giordano Bruno (1548–1600), but I know of no anthology or history of medieval philosophy that treats Bruno with anything but a cursory mention. Instead, Bruno and Nicholas are often relegated to histories of "Renaissance" philosophy, which as it turns out is another deeply problematic periodization in the history of philosophy. For one thing, if you read around enough, you will see scholars referring to several distinct "rebirths" of philosophy in the West, including one that allegedly happened in twelfth-century France. But let us do our best to avoid that Pandora's box. The salient point here is that if you examine Nicholas of Cusa's writings, you will quickly see that he is enmeshed in the "medieval" traditions of his day. He draws on the same authorities. He covers most of the same topics. He uses the same technical jargon. And he adopts many of the assumptions of schoolmen from the thirteenth and fourteenth centuries. But like Augustine and Boethius, historians often focus on Nicholas's legacy. Viewed in terms of his influence and impact, he seems to be a man "before his time," so to speak.

By thinking about influence, and cause and effect more generally, we can begin to break the link to time at least in this way: We need not worry about the start and end dates of medieval philosophy. But to track the effects that a philosopher has on later developments, we need to find ways to individuate medieval philosophical trends, themes, and approaches. Perhaps a way to begin that search is to see whether we can identify a distinctive set of themes, terminology, and methods of investigation that start with Augustine and Boethius. And, as it happens, a number of scholars suggest that what makes medieval philosophy distinctive is the way that it pursues a set of questions primarily laid down by ancient Greek thinkers using the terminology and starting principles found in Aristotle's (322 BCE) corpus. So that we do not preemptively exclude medieval philosophy from other linguistic traditions, the emphasis on terminological and conceptual affinity with Augustine and Boethius per se will need to be softened. But there are clear ways to do this. Augustine and Boethius themselves are part of a broader late ancient tradition or way of studying Platonic and Aristotelian philosophies, a tradition whose fruits were assimilated and adapted by intellectuals in the Arabic-speaking world, especially during the period when there was a state-sponsored effort to translate Greek scientific and philosophical works into Arabic (see Gutas 1998).

By focusing on effects, influences, and ways of approaching philosophical puzzles, we can even posit that medieval philosophy can temporally overlap with other traditions. For instance, certain philosophers who are often counted as belonging to "medieval" philosophical traditions, such as Francisco Suarez (1548–1617) and Mulla Sadra (Sadr al-Din al-Shirazi, 1641), lived and sometimes even interacted with philosophers from the so-called early modern tradition. René Descartes (1650), for instance, was taught at a Jesuit institution where he would have read books by Suarez and other late scholastics.

So, here is the current proposal: Medieval philosophy is defined as philosophy that focuses on a set of questions raised by a close reading of Aristotle, using a set of categories and technical discourse that also ultimately derives from his work and other ancient sources, and which is subsequently refined by preceding generations of scholars and commentators. While I think this way of trying to determine the parameters of medieval philosophy has much to recommend it, certain implications of the proposed definition should give us pause. Despite universal acknowledgment that Descartes was trained in a scholastic tradition, there is still a tendency to emphasize Descartes's *break* from the medieval tradition. In conjunction with this, notice that there is another implication often at work in the word "middle" (*medium*), from which, of course, the word "medieval" is derived. A *medium* is often a stage or state through which we have to pass in order to get to a state that we deem to be important. Thus, to describe a body of philosophy as occurring in the middle is to suggest that it is philosophy that is done between two important periods. And this is in fact how the history of Western philosophy is often written and taught. We are told about the Greek giants, Plato (347/8 BCE) and Aristotle. We then learn that there was this long period of time between them and the "modern" giants, including Descartes, John Locke (1704), David Hume (1776), and Gottfried Leibniz (1716).

While I think that there are interesting and important differences between the works of someone like Aquinas and those of Descartes, emphasizing the differences leads to what I see as a pernicious myth of the "quantum leap" in the histories of philosophy as well as the suggestion that the philosophy of the Middle Ages is a valley between two peaks. I think that a careful examination of the history of philosophy, one that is not prejudiced by a certain ideology perpetuated by the "moderns," will reveal that philosophy, like most intellectual developments, tends to be continuous, and only rarely defined by hard, sharp breaks. Once you get down to the business of examining what people actually say and how they say it, I think you might begin to find it hard to discern sharp, clear lines that demarcate a *medieval* way of doing philosophy from a modern one. You might even come to agree with John Marenbon's suggestion that

> there is much of importance in Descartes and Leibniz that is comprehensible only when it is seen at the end of a tradition of Latin philosophy, and in Spinoza that reads as both a culmination of and reaction to earlier Jewish philosophy.
>
> (2007, 350)

At certain points in this book, I will pause to make note of some of these continuities. But often I will build my case without comment, trusting that after careful reflection you will see both the differences and the affinities for yourselves. Hopefully, you will also come to see that the philosophy created between roughly 600 CE and 1700 CE is not mediocre or merely preparation for the achievements of Descartes, Spinoza, and Leibniz.

I want to express one more concern about the notion that medieval philosophy is a specific way of approaching philosophical questions that is heavily influenced by late ancient ways of studying Plato, and especially Aristotle. The suggestion that medieval philosophy is a kind of Platonic–Aristotelian philosophy risks missing a whole lot of important philosophical literature that is produced during the Middle Ages. Take the case of Abu Hamid Muhammad ibn Muhammad al-Ghazali (1111), who wrote a book entitled *The Incoherence of the Philosophers*. As you will see, in this book, I treat Ghazali not only as a critic of philosophy but also as a *philosopher*. Why? The short answer is that if we are going to get an adequate picture of medieval philosophy, we need to look beyond the people who get that label. When Ghazali talks about "philosophy" (*falsafa*), he is referring to those who elaborated a system based on principles found in the Platonic and Aristotelian works that had been translated into Arabic. In other words, his target is precisely the sort of people who are allegedly the paradigmatic representatives of a *medieval* way of doing philosophy. Yet, in the Islamic world, which includes Jewish intellectuals living under Muslim rule (and often writing in Arabic), *falsafa* was not the only game in town. One prominent competitor was *'ilm al-kalam*. *'Ilm al-kalam* literally means "the science of the word," where the crucial sense of "word" is ultimately the divine word or the Quran. So, *'ilm al-kalam* or *kalam* is theology (or as some translators render it, "dialectical theology"). Ghazali thought that the proper task of this science is to defend the faith by showing how the opponent's own assumptions lead to contradictions or an affirmation of Islamic truth (al-Ghazali 1980, 59–60; Watt 1994, 27–9). His criticism of *kalam* as it was practiced in his day and age is that its practitioners often strayed beyond this apologetic purpose in an attempt to build and defend a positive speculative edifice. And indeed, when scholars have looked at actual works in the *kalam* tradition, what we find is something that we nowadays would – and I say *should*... call philosophy. Moreover, scholars have begun to appreciate the impact of *kalam* on Aristotelian Arabic philosophy and vice versa. So, once again, we see more continuity than fissure.

To be clear, much of what I have just said is not news to scholars of medieval philosophy. It has long been appreciated that if we studied only books labeled as philosophy by medieval thinkers, we would be overlooking many of the central texts of scholastic philosophy, such as Thomas Aquinas's *Summa Theologiae* (*Summary of Theology*). And my claim that works produced in the *kalam* tradition are philosophical is not original or much disputed by experts of Arabic philosophy. But what I now will say is, I suspect, somewhat more controversial. From our vantage today, we professional philosophers often privilege texts in which a certain pattern of presenting and defending claims occurs. In particular, a lot of emphasis is given to thought that can be regimented into a premise-conclusion format. We expect a work to have arguments, or more specifically arguments that follow a certain format, in order to count as "philosophy." I feel the pull of this way of viewing things. I was trained to view things this way. But I want to resist it, since I worry that it marginalizes a lot of important material, relegating it to an amorphous category of "wisdom literature," when it ought to be considered part of a more expansive and inclusive conception of philosophy. A lot of this so-called wisdom literature has traditionally been labeled as "mysticism" which then is contrasted with "philosophy," the former often being considered to be vague and "airy," whereas the latter is "rigorous" and "clear." By doing this, scholars have excluded *without a hearing* practically all the philosophically relevant literature produced by women in the medieval European and Islamic worlds. In this book, I will suggest that individuals like Marguerite Porete (1310), Catherine of Siena, and 'A'ishah al-Ba'uniyyah (1517) have plenty to contribute to philosophical reflections and discussions.

What may have seemed to be an innocent question, "What is medieval philosophy?", has led us into some very deep waters. And perhaps you can now see why debate about periodization and the canon has been so robust and inconclusive. If even experts have not settled on a consensus, what are we going to do?

Having raised these difficult questions, I am going to suggest something that might appear to be a dodge. But I will do this precisely because attempting to settle on a perfect solution is, in my view, a fool's errand. I propose that we start with some of the standard figures and move outward from them. You, after all, picked up this book presumably because you had *some* notion of when the Middle Ages were and who might be covered in such a period. For instance, you might have read or heard about Anselm's or Thomas Aquinas's arguments for the existence of God in an introductory course in philosophy (the former being the infamous "ontological argument," the latter often mentioned as Aquinas's "five ways"). (If you did not, don't worry.) Perhaps your exposure to such figures piqued your interest and prompted you to want to learn more about them and other individuals in this period. Or perhaps you have encountered a portrayal of medieval life in either a movie or a book and you now want to discover what people in that time and place thought from a philosophical perspective. Or, sadly, you might have heard "medieval" used in a derisory fashion to mark out some practice or set of beliefs as old-fashioned and repugnant. In particular, the views of certain present-day religious groups are sometimes derided as being "medieval", "backwards", and in short brutal and cruel, especially by those who think of themselves as being compassionate, "modern", "enlightened", and "progressive". You then might be intrigued by the fact that someone would bother to write a book encouraging you to read more medieval philosophy and to take it seriously as *good* philosophy.

I will start, in short, by introducing you to many figures who are commonly described as being medieval philosophers or as belonging to the Middle Ages. I will put these figures into conversation with one another and I will attempt to make some of what these people take for granted intelligible to you. On occasion, I will use as a starting point certain claims made by Descartes and other so-called early moderns, since they often consciously define themselves in contrast to the individuals who are the focus of this book and they will insist that what they are doing is new and decisively breaking away from the past. As you might have already guessed, at times, I will suggest that these thinkers are not as innovative as they pretend to be. This is not to say that there are no ways in which the medieval and the modern mind differ. There is sometimes a difference over principles and frameworks. Other times, there is a difference in something more intangible, such as temperament or sensibility. It is okay if you don't quite see what I mean yet. As we proceed through this book, I will stop to point out some of these likenesses and differences.

1.3 Genres and Tips for Reading Them

One way to expand our understanding of what counts as medieval philosophy is to appreciate the fact that philosophical literature comes in a variety of genres.

Some of the genres that medieval philosophers adopt might be already familiar to you as ways in which philosophers present their ideas. Perhaps the most common genre is, broadly speaking, the treatise, wherein an author systematically presents a series of propositions that are defended with arguments and evidence. These can be compendious treatments of a subject (say, the natural world) or they can be devoted to a single topic or question (such as whether the world is eternal).

A second genre of philosophical writing that you might have encountered is the philosophical dialogue, which is the preferred format by which Plato works out his philosophical ideas. The dialogue is a very common form in the Middle Ages. Augustine, Anselm, and Abelard, to name only a few notable examples, employed this medium.

A great deal of medieval philosophical material comes in the form of a textbook, that is, a text designed for use by students as they attempt to master a subject. Medieval textbooks come in several forms. There are summaries and overviews. These can be summaries of a famous book that is studied in detail at later stages in a medieval curriculum, such as Aristotle's *Metaphysics*, or they can be systematic introductions to a certain topic or field. Examples of the latter include Abu Nasr al-Farabi's (950/1) short summaries of logic (trans. Dunlop 1955–59) and Boethius's summaries of parts of late ancient Greek logic, such as his *On Topical Differences* (trans. Boethius 1978) and *On Division* (1998). After studying a summary introduction, a student often moved on to the primary texts. But Aristotle, in particular, can be notoriously hard to understand. To guide students to a fuller comprehension of the primary texts in the curriculum, medieval lecturers produced line-by-line paraphrases ("glosses") as well as more substantial commentaries, including commentaries on textbooks. For instance, Albert the Great (1280) commented on Boethius's *On Division* (alas, not available in translation), and John Buridan's *Summulae de dialectia* (trans. 2001) is a detailed line-by-line commentary with frequent deeper investigations on the most popular textbook of logic in his age, Peter of Spain's (fl. 1230s–40s) *Summulae logicales* (trans. 2014).

The more complex commentaries often include digressions where students and teacher reflect on a problem that the text seems to generate in a more sustained way. These *quaestiones* ("investigations") developed into a separate genre. In some cases, what has come down to us are whole books that consist of a series of investigations of questions that arise from a close reading of, say, Aristotle's *Metaphysics* or *On the Soul*. The most well-known "summaries" (*summa*) of philosophy and philosophical theology, such as Thomas Aquinas's *Summa Theologiae* and *Summa Contra Gentiles*, are also often composed using the *quaestiones* format. (More on that below.)

As you would expect, the *quaestiones* present a wealth of close, rigorous argumentation. But you shouldn't overlook the more introductory material. The line between glosses, commentaries, and *quaestiones* are not always clearly drawn. Especially in earlier Latin and Arabic "commentaries," there is usually a combination of paraphrase, commentary, and deeper investigations of select topics. The famous discussion of the problem of universals by Boethius, which we will examine in some detail in Chapter 3, is one of these break-out sessions that is embedded in a larger commentary on an *Introduction* (*Isagoge*) to Aristotle's logic composed by the late ancient Platonist Porphyry (c. 305). These "introductory" books are enormously valuable, because they give us insight into what students found difficult about the ancient material as well as how innovations in logic and interpretation occurred. They are also useful because what medieval students might have taken as obvious, given, or introductory is not necessarily obvious or introductory for us. For instance, it might come as a surprise to learn that Aquinas's most famous works are intended as textbooks (albeit for what we might nowadays call graduate students). Contemporary professionally trained individuals have spent entire academic careers studying these works precisely because what Aquinas and his students take as given and the terminology that they use to describe their thoughts are sometimes very alien to us.

In addition to treatises, dialogues, textbooks, and commentaries – many of which are designed for school-like settings – there are several other noteworthy genres. Some authors, for instance, have written books that are ostensibly autobiographical. The two most notable examples of this phenomenon are Augustine's *Confessions* and al-Ghazali's *Deliverance from Error*. I have deliberately hedged with the word "ostensibly" because these autobiographies are not full accounts of their authors' lives, and there are some reasons to suspect that at least parts of the story are not historically accurate.[4] The interest of these books as philosophical texts lies primarily in how they develop an intellectual itinerary, that is, they provide vivid portraits of the reasoning that leads to this or that philosophical outlook. Augustine tells us why he moved from a dualistic conception of reality called Manicheanism to skepticism, then to Platonism, and finally to Christianity. Al-Ghazali describes his beginning as a curious young man who is unable to accept things merely based on authority. His curiosity eventually leads a skeptical "sickness", which he needs God's aid to resolve (see Chapter 2, Section 2.3). Once cured, he continues his journey through *kalam* and Aristotelian philosophy, until finally he arrives at mysticism.

Related to autobiographical stories with an instructive bent, we also have one of the masterpieces of medieval literature – and I don't just mean philosophical literature, I mean *literature*, period – Boethius's *Consolation of Philosophy*. This book was composed while Boethius was in prison and awaiting his execution. And while it starts with these facts for its dramatic setting, I think it is safe to say that Boethius is not literally visited by Lady Philosophy, nor should the elaborate series of arguments that commence be taken to be a transcript of Boethius's dialogue either with someone else or with himself. In addition to tropes established in the ancient letters of consolation, at least one scholar detects elements from an ancient kind of *play*, a satire (Relihan 2007).

Boethius's masterpiece is not the only medieval philosophical work that has dramatic and poetic elements in it. Perhaps one of the most astounding examples is Marguerite Porete's *Mirror of Simple Souls*, where we have Love conversing with Reason, the Soul, and several other personifications. Reason even "dies" and walks off stage as the drama unfolds. But this is only the tip of the iceberg. Many contemplative works draw on literary tropes and forms that are borrowed from troubadour poetry and romances. We also possess some longform medieval philosophical tales, which we might even call novels. Perhaps the most famous examples come from the Islamic world, including Abu Bakr Muhammad ibn Tufayl's (c. 1110–85) *Hayy ibn Yaqzan* (discussed in several chapters of this book) and a tale entitled *The Case of the Animals versus Man Before the King of the Jinn* (discussed in Chapter 6).

Finally, medieval authors inherited from late antiquity the mode of wisdom transfer known as the didactic poem. A well-known late ancient poem in this mode is Martianus Capella's *De nuptiis Philologiae et Mercurii* (trans. Stahl et al. 1977). We also see theory set to verse in Boethius's poetic interludes between the prose arguments of his *Consolation*, Alan of Lille's (c. 1203) *Anticlaudianus* (in Alan of Lille 2013), and Ibn Sina's poem on the soul (Madelung and Mayer 2016).

For most of these works, all you need to do is to read closely and to bear in mind things that you would need to do to interpret any work belonging to the genre. So, for instance, in a tale or a poem, you will need to be especially sensitive to metaphor and other forms of figurative or allegorical allusions to truths. In dialogues and dramas, you should be aware that the author may use several characters as his or her mouthpiece, and even in the case where it seems that one character is primarily the mouthpiece for the author, not everything said by that character is necessarily definitively held by the author. The dialogue form allows an author the chance to moot ill-formed, uncertain, or otherwise provisional ideas precisely to test them.

There is, however, one genre that is specifically medieval, indeed specifically scholastic, and thus some pointers to the uninitiated are warranted. I have here in mind the format of the scholastic disputation, which is the dominant way in which ideas are presented not only in *quaestiones* but also in the more elaborate commentaries and *summa* of Latin university masters from the late twelfth century all the way up to the seventeenth century.

The disputation mimics the format of a standard university lecture. So perhaps a quick word about the nature of scholastic education and the literature that emerges from this setting is in order. As Anthony Kenny and Jan Pinborg once observed, "The fact that the sources available to reconstruct the intellectual life of the Middle Ages are written records tempts us to forget that university learning was widely determined by oral teaching" (1982, 16). As they proceed to point out, the centrality of oral teaching was the product of necessity. Prior to the printing press, the cost of labor and materials as well as the sheer amount of time required to transcribe a text meant that books were very scarce. Moreover, when books were produced, they were not always to the standards that we have come to expect.

> This preponderance of the oral aspects within the medieval transmission of learning [...] also helps to explain the fact that the written texts that were used for studies are often in a shockingly corrupt state. It is frequently difficult to understand how such faulty texts could be of any use to students. But if we remember the facts associated with an oral tradition – which imply that the students had a large number of formulas, quotations, stock arguments, and standard moves stored in their memory – it becomes much easier to understand. They used the texts not as their only sources, but rather as abbreviations, reminders of what they had heard. They used written sources mainly as a source of useful arguments or distinctions, not as texts to be relied on for reconstructing the thoughts of others. The written records as we have them are only a limited reflection of a much richer oral culture.
> (Kenny and Pinborg 1982, 17)

The more you read from primary sources, the more you will see what Kenny and Pinborg have in mind. The arguments often are heavily compressed and elliptical. Sometimes the scribe even tells us that he is omitting something the teacher said because the scribe thought it was boring or useless. The more I read many of these written products from the schools, the more I wish I had a time machine so that I could go back, sit in my author's lectures, and take my own notes.

One common book in the medieval school setting would be the course books (*littera*). These would be the basis of the *lectiones* ("lectures" or "readings") that the school's masters (or as we would call them, professors) were expected to engage in. The basic form of a lecture is this (Kenny and Pinborg 1982, 20):

1 The reading aloud of a section from the *littera*.
2 A division of the section into smaller parts.

3   An exposition of the parts. Sometimes there were mere paraphrases of the parts, sometimes they consisted of a relatively thorough interpretation of the assigned reading.
4   *Dubia* ("doubts"): real or fictitious disputations inspired by the assigned reading.

In addition to the lectures, masters engaged in highly formalized public disputations. Such disputations lasted at least two days (see Kenny and Pinborg 1982, 21–2; Marenbon 2007, 215–8). On the first day, the students and the master would meet, usually in the morning. The master would give an introduction, often including a suggestion of the order of the topics to be discussed. Then one of the students, with the standing of a "bachelor," would be appointed to entertain arguments presented by members of the audience. The bachelor would then offer replies to the objections, sometimes with the assistance of the master. On the second day, the master would summarize the arguments for (*pro*) and against (*contra*). Finally, the master would give his own *determinatio* to the question being disputed.[5]

A record of the proceedings would be documented by a secretary. Proceedings of the meeting were published either in the form of notes taken at the meeting (a *reportatio*) or in a revised and expanded version by the master (an *ordinatio*) (Kenny and Pinborg 1982, 22 and 35–6). It is crucial to note that "the number of texts transmitted to us in the author's own original version or in a copy directly authenticated by him is very small" (35). Even in cases where autographs exist, there are other problems with the state of the manuscripts. Aquinas's handwriting is notoriously hard to read. And then, as every writer knows too well, even authorized copies can have errors that the master did not catch.

These disputations determined the format of commentaries that have come down to us. They have also heavily influenced the style of works written in other genres, such as Aquinas's *Summa*, which was "designed from the outset as a manual to be read by students" (Kenny and Pinborg 1982, 26; also Marenbon 2007, 216) There is, however, some question as to how much of what we possess is a transcript of actual debates held in the classroom. "We do not know to what extent, if any, such *quaestiones* were staged as disputations. Certainly from the fourteenth century onwards we have testimony that they were only read aloud by the master" (Kenny and Pinborg 1982, 20–1). And as Marenbon observes, "in much of the most sophisticated theological writing it had become something of a formality even by the end of the thirteenth century" (2007, 217).

Nevertheless, it remains true that many of the scholastic writings that have survived mimic the structure of the classroom setting. For this reason, when reading a "question," I suggest you imagine that you are reading a transcript from a lesson. The basic format of a written disputation is as follows.

1. There is an introduction of a topic and a specific question to be investigated. Usually, this investigation is posed as a "yes"/"no" question. For instance, "Is knowledge acquired by natural means possible?" or "Can God's existence be proved?"
2. A series of preliminary reasons for answering "yes" and "no" are presented, often in a very abbreviated or summary manner. I say "reasons" since not all of them are arguments per se. Often, the affirmative or negative position is supported by appeals to a secular authority, such as Aristotle or "the Commentator" (i.e., Ibn Rushd), a church authority, or a passage from the Bible.
3. Next, we get the "corpus" or "body." This is where the master states in *propria persona* his views on the question. Quite often, the master concedes that both initial positions get certain matters right and that the initial question is not posed with enough nuance. This is where we see one of the most well-known features of scholastic reasoning, the distinction. In later centuries, this tendency to make distinctions is criticized and even lampooned. Think about the negative connotations of our turn of phrase "hairsplitting" or the criticism that one is making "a distinction without a difference." In such cases, we are suggesting that a person is being unproductively subtle and that their attempts to clarify are in fact obscuring our view of the heart of the matter.
4. Once the master presents his position, he then turns and addresses the initial arguments. These are often referenced with the Latin preposition "ad" ("to"); hence, "ad 2" is referring to so-and-so's reply to the initial second argument. Sometimes the master's responses to the specific objections are quite elaborate. Other times, the master will merely note that the objection has been sufficiently answered in the *corpus* or that the answer can be worked out by the careful reader on her own time.

I should stress that this is the *basic* format. In practice, especially as the genre matures in the late thirteenth and fourteenth centuries, things get much more complicated. For instance, certain arguments *pro* or *contra* are so complex that the master may feel the need to add several digressions. Perhaps, there are several legitimate ways to disambiguate a part of the initial question. Or perhaps a key premise in one of the arguments needs to be thoroughly investigated before we can see clearly how to proceed. These digressions can themselves involve what are effectively disputations within a disputation. ("This key premise seems to be defensible. Here are the main arguments for it. But here are the main reasons to be hesitant about endorsing it.") Exhibits of disputations within disputations can be found throughout the writings of many of the great scholastic thinkers, and especially in the works of John Duns Scotus (1308) and William of Ockham (1347).[6]

Often editors and translators will help you by marking out the main components of the investigation. Look for text in [brackets] or sometimes <pointy brackets> which are standard ways that editors and translators signal that the words enclosed are interpolations that are not present in the original text. In some cases, a translation will have several kinds of brackets, which are used to distinguish different reasons why the English words are present on the page. Perhaps the words are there because the translator felt that an equivalent of the English word should have been present in the original. Other times, the English words are bracketed because while the phrase in the original language makes perfectly good sense, a literal rendering would be unintelligible. A good translator who uses brackets will provide a key in the introduction to the translation.

You should make sure that you read not just the *corpus* but also the responses to the initial objections. The responses are often where the author elaborates on some of the implications of his position that remain only implicit or imperfectly developed in the *corpus*. Therefore, you skip these at your own peril. For that matter, you skip the initial arguments at your peril. These provide crucial contextual information and they illuminate many of the otherwise unspoken assumptions that frame and motivate the debate.

In short, I recommend that you think of scholastic disputations as *dialogues*. This will require some mental limberness on your part. It is crucial that you keep your wits about you and that you are always aware of precisely where you are in the overall dialogue that is developing between the author and his real and imagined disputants. The pay-off, however, for all this taxing mental effort can be quite rewarding. An investigation undertaken by one of the scholastic greats is about as thorough and rigorous an investigation as one could hope for.

1.4 History Matters

It is essential when studying philosophy, and especially historical philosophies, to remember that all philosophy is embodied philosophy. I don't intend anything mysterious by this claim. All I mean is that all philosophers practice their art in a specific time, place, and intellectual context. We, therefore, run the risk of gravely misunderstanding a philosopher if we fail to appreciate the ways in which their upbringing, education, and culture shaped their perspective on what questions to ask and what solutions were viable. We cannot automatically assume that they are thinking about problems in the way that we are, even if they seem to be using familiar terms and formulations. For that matter, we cannot assume that they are even thinking about the same problems. However, this does not mean that we cannot have conversations with historical figures, just as the differences between you and I do not mean that we must fail in our attempts to communicate with one another. This book assumes that such conversations are possible – although I hope you will be convinced that this assumption was warranted once you look at the details. We will need to exercise caution, just as we need to patiently listen to one another, allow one another to speak, ask one another to clarify what we mean, and to not jump to conclusions, assuming that we know how someone will finish their sentence. If we do this, we have much to gain, not only from conversations with our contemporaries but also from people living in other times and places.

We will return to some of these issues in Chapter 8. For now, let me merely reiterate the importance of context, especially since my presentation of medieval philosophy does not follow a linear plot through periods and traditions but is rather organized around topics and themes. The topical approach has certain advantages that, to my mind, warrants the jumps between times, places, and cultures that I make in what follows. In particular, by organizing the material in this way, we can begin to see some of the common sensibilities of philosophers who often had no awareness of each other or their works. Besides, if you want a linear history, we already have John Marenbon's excellent introduction to medieval philosophy (2007). My aim is to not supersede that work but rather to complement it.

To help you keep track of everyone and to begin to place them in time and space, I will provide scholars's best guesses as to when our protagonists lived at the first instance when they appear in a chapter. (All dates are to the Common Era (CE), unless otherwise indicated. A single date indicates the year when a philosopher died.[7]) In addition, I have included a skeletal timeline as an appendix to this book. There you will find the major protagonists in my story arranged on a temporal continuum along with some but by no means all the significant historical and culture transformations that were happening around them.

1.5 Philosophy, Religion, and Philosophy of Religion

One pervasive stereotype is that medieval philosophy is focused on religious questions. A closely related stereotype is that medieval philosophers often lean too heavily upon appeals to authority and, in particular, religious authority. There is some basis for these impressions. For one thing, many of the books that we nowadays examine for their philosophical content are in fact books developed in and used in schools of *theology*. Look no further than Thomas Aquinas's most famous work; it is the *Summary of*

Theology, not philosophy. Hence, it should not be at all surprising that the central focus of the book is theological concerns. Moreover, in theological discourse, appeals to scripture and other foundational texts are not only legitimate, in many cases they are expected. That said, I wish to argue that the notion that medieval philosophy is overly obsessed with religion and inordinately deferential to religious authority fails to do justice to what is in fact a highly nuanced attitude toward religious questions.

Theology, as medieval scholastics tend to construe things, comes in two versions. There is the sort of theology that one can do merely with the cognitive tools available to us given our biological makeup, or as they often put it, our "nature." Following a well-established tradition, we can call this way of tackling religious topics "natural religion" or "natural theology." Natural theology is placed in contrast with what we can call "revealed theology." Revealed theology stems from revelation, which as Aquinas and many others see things, is a direct intervention by God. At the very beginning of his *Summa Theologiae*, Aquinas asks whether any teaching in addition to philosophy is necessary (1, q. 1, art. 1). In effect, he is asking whether there is any need for revelation. Isn't human reason on its own up to the task at hand? Hasn't Aristotle shown us that we can know that God exists, what God is like, and what our purpose in the greater scheme should be, at least to some acceptable degree? I add "to some acceptable degree" since even Aristotle seems to hold that getting a full, complete grasp of an infinite being is beyond the capabilities of a finite mind.

Aquinas's answer is interesting for what it uncovers about a very common medieval understanding of our human limits. First, Aquinas notes that God's purpose for humans is that they will return to Him and know Him. But this creates a problem, since God "exceeds reason's grasp." In particular, if we don't know that God exists and that He wants us to return to Him, we will have no motivation to make any progress in that direction. And even if we do know that God is and that we ought to return to God, if we don't know any of the specifics as to how to go about doing that, we will not be able to form the right intentions and do the right actions.

Even for those things that are within reason's capacity to grasp, revelation is still necessary.

> It was necessary that God provide divine revelation to humans even for those things concerning God that human reason can investigate. This is because when a truth about God is investigated by reason, things proceed for a human little by little, and it takes a long time, and many errors are mixed in. Yet, a human's whole salvation, which is in God, depends upon the cognition of such a truth.
>
> (*Summa Theologiae* 1, q. 1, art. 1; my translation)

Notice what is working in the background here. Aquinas is assuming that God is good and that, as a consequence of this, He would not set us up to fail. If some information crucial for human salvation is either impossible to discover using innate human capacities or very difficult for most of us to acquire, God will not fail to provide us with that information in some other way. We could even put it this way: In some sense of "had to," or "must", God had to provide us with prophets and other forms of direct guidance. (Don't ask me to precisely specify in what sense God "had to" do this, as God's freedom makes discussions of necessity very tricky. All we need for the moment is the fact that Aquinas claims that it was "necessary.")

If you read Aquinas's question carefully, you will see that he does not specify precisely where human reason must fail. Indeed, in his reply to the second of two initial objections, he emphasizes the idea that there are some things that can be discovered *either* by means of the "light of natural reason" *or* by means of the light of divine revelation. It may be that some of us can, after much effort, arrive at quite a bit of knowledge about God's nature and plans. As I read Aquinas, he seems to be one of those who *does* have a generally optimistic view about the powers of natural reason. Other philosophers in the Middle Ages take a much more pessimistic attitude. For some, a great emphasis is placed on the divide between God's infinity and our finitude. This way leads to *apophaticism*, that is, the claim that God's nature is ineffable and unknowable. A classic statement of the apophatic position can be found in the first part of Maimonides's *Guide of the Perplexed*. As we will see in later chapters, it is also typically associated with the so-called mystics. One important thing to note, however, is that the dispute between optimists like Aquinas and apophaticists is over the *degree* to which human reasoning is limited. No one to my mind expresses the thought that human reason is entirely sufficient on its own.

Moreover, as Aquinas has pointed out, if we consider humanity as a whole, revelation is even more in need. Humans are born with different dispositions. Some of us, no matter how good we are at concentrating, do not have the intellectual gift of thinking rigorously and abstractly. Some of us are better than others at keeping distractions at bay and concentrating our minds on the structures of reality and the divine plans that they actualize. We'll also see in several of the later chapters that there is an appreciation of the idea that we are not all born with the same opportunities (see especially Chapter 7). Some – indeed many of us – will be born into flawed communities, with flawed understandings of the divine plan. In some of these communities, people are encouraged to live no better than brute animals, chasing bodily pleasures and material wealth. Thus, even for those who have the requisite intellectual gifts, the chances of success are small. Too many contingencies are stacked against too many of us. And yet, God is good and God wants all creatures to flourish. God, therefore, chose to make His thoughts known to us through charismatic individuals who have a knack for conveying difficult truths in earthier, simpler formats.

Given that revelation is useful, if not necessary, the study of theology as a speculative endeavor must include the study of revealed texts and the opinions of those who were thought to have a special gift for understanding revelation. Hopefully, this will explain the ubiquitous appeal to scripture and religious authorities in medieval works studied for their philosophical content. At the very least, scripture puts a check on human reason, which on its own might go astray. For some, it also is the only way to get some crucial starting points for any speculation on God and God's plan for creation.

Given that medieval philosophers take scripture and its claims seriously and then proceed to provide complex, rigorously argued systems from these starting points, it would seem that a book like the one I am giving you here ought to emphasize this. I hope that after completing the book you will see that I do just that, throughout. But what I have not done is provide a separate chapter devoted to what we now often call philosophy of religion. This might come as a shock to many of my colleagues, as well as to many of you. After all, isn't philosophy of religion one of the domains where medieval philosophy has left a distinct and still to this day vital impact?

I have in effect already noted my main reason for not including a chapter devoted solely to philosophical questions pertaining to religion. The fact that God exists, arranges the world according to a benevolent plan, and demands that we eventually return to Him means that for your average medieval philosopher, all of philosophy is at bottom religious philosophy. They do not have a curriculum that separates metaphysics, political philosophy, ethics, and so on from philosophy of religion, as though the latter were a separate philosophical science. Of course, some of the philosophical topics that we examine in this book will seem to be distant from or logically separable from this theistic outlook, but others we cover will directly touch upon how we understand God's revelation. It seemed best to have such moments arise organically within their wider setting.

Still, you might wonder, why do you start off with a discussion of the limits of human knowledge and the basic building blocks of reality? What about establishing first and foremost that God exists, and then perhaps that there is only one such God, and that He is simple, and good, and all-knowing, and so on and so forth? After he discusses "sacred teaching," what it is, and why it is needed, Aquinas devotes the next several questions to the existence and attributes of God (*Summa Theologiae* 1, qq. 2–11). Why not follow Aquinas's curriculum?

Here are two replies to that question. First, in my view there are already a number of good introductions to arguments for God's existence and the traditional properties ascribed to a perfect being. Many of these draw heavily upon the classic arguments given by Aquinas and others. But second, and relatedly, I think the *way* that those arguments are treated in a contemporary introduction to the philosophy of religion is different from the way that Aquinas and many other medieval thinkers are thinking about these arguments.

In both introductions to philosophy and introductions to philosophy of religion, one often will find Anselm's "ontological argument" or Aquinas's "Five Ways." These are typically presented as cases of natural theology, specifically, proofs for the existence of God that use only tools and principles available to the natural human mind. As such the ontological argument and the Five Ways seem to be the reasons that one would provide to an agnostic or an atheist. I think this goes a long way toward explaining *our* present-day interest in them and why they often appear in theistic apologetics.

I don't think that this explains their appeal to the *medieval* writers who offer them, for I find it hard to believe that there were hosts of atheists in the mold of a Christopher Hitchens or a Richard Dawkins roving about in the medieval world. When Anselm, for instance, addresses his ontological argument to the "fool" (*Proslogion* 2), I don't believe that he has an actual person or group of people in mind.

This is not to say that there may have been some who *were* worried about atheism. Nasir al-Din al-Tusi (1201–74), for instance, begins one of his theological treatises with a chapter devoted to a "refutation of the argument of one who denies the Creator," which begins as follows:

> If, God forbid, someone should voice his denial of the Creator, the Sublime, the Exalted, he should be asked: "Do the things of this world [exist] by themselves or through something else?"
>
> (Tusi 2005, 16)

Al-Tusi and others in his milieu are aware that some of the ancient Greek philosophers were atheists. In the brief history of Greek philosophy that al-Ghazali provides in his *Deliverance*, he refers to a class of philosophers whom he labels as the Materialists. They denied that "the world has existed from eternity as it is, of itself and not by reason of a Maker." These philosophers are "godless in the full sense of the term" (1980, 61). Al-Ghazali tells us that this was the first group of philosophers, and that they had been decisively refuted by the "theistic" Aristotelians. Nevertheless, perhaps there were some among the educated elite who were attracted to these older forms of Greek wisdom. Perhaps al-Tusi is working in a time and place where there is a concern that at least some among the intelligentsia are crypto-atheists. While they might have been true, there are some complications to this picture. For one thing, al-Tusi's chapter advertises that it is also addressing polytheism, and there clearly were polytheists living in places that had economic ties with al-Tusi's Persia, even if none were living in his immediate community. This points to a deep problem with interpreting al-Tusi and others who compose similar defenses of the existence of God, for it seems that al-Tusi all too easily slips between the question of whether there is a god (that is, the problem of *atheism* proper) and whether there is only one God (that is, the question of the *unicity* of God). Furthermore, I wonder whether al-Tusi is using the names "Creator," "Sublime," and "Exalted" as Quranic names for Allah, the one true God, and not in some more abstract, generic sense. If that hunch is right, then in the passage quoted above what al-Tusi is *really* concerned about is whether someone believes in the *correct* god, not whether someone might deny that there is a divinity of any sort.

I think in the case of Anselm (and also Aquinas), it is even clearer that the worry is not that there are atheists or agnostics out there who need to be saved from their error. If we start our reading of Anselm in Chapter 2 of the *Proslogion*, where the "fool" is introduced, we may be tempted to overlook something important that happens before this. Anselm begins the *Proslogion*, which is the only place in Anselm's vast *oeuvre* where he presents the ontological argument, with a prayer. In this prayer, he asks God for understanding, since he *already* has belief.

> I acknowledge, Lord, and I thank you, that you have created in me this image of you so that I may remember you, think of you, and love you. Yet this image is so eroded by my vices, so clouded by the smoke of my sins, that it cannot do what it was created to do unless you renew and refashion it. I am not trying to scale your heights, Lord; my understanding is in no way equal to that. But I do long to understand your truth in some way, your truth which my heart believes and loves. For I do not seek to understand you in order to believe; I believe in order to understand. For I also believe that "Unless I believe, I shall not understand."
> (*Proslogion* 1; Anselm 1995, 99)

Anselm also makes it clear that he is addressing this book to an audience that already believes, even if they fail to understand. Read in its proper context, then, Anselm is attempting to deepen his faith, not to arrive at or justify it. It is one thing to believe in God and another to have a complex, abstract understanding of God. The latter takes patient, rigorous exploration of the sort exhibited by the *Proslogion* and its predecessor the *Monologion*. Once one gets this intellectual vision of what one already trusts in and loves, that love and perhaps now also a sense of awe become more intense. The intellectual ascent to divinity, which starts by examining the rational basis for the belief that there is such a thing, is therefore very much worthwhile as an endeavor.

But this is not how Anselm's argument is often treated in contemporary discussions of the ontological argument. Our contemporary discussions of the ontological argument are more in line with Descartes's use of an ontological argument in his *Meditations on First Philosophy* (Meditation 3). For when Descartes marshals his version of the ontological argument, he is in a radical state of doubt. He can only believe with absolute certainty that he exists. To secure confidence in anything else, he needs the guarantee of an omnibenevolent divinity. Medieval thinkers at points do have serious doubts, and as we will see in several places in this book, for several of them, faith is very much in tension with reason. But the places where these doubts and tensions arise is not always where Descartes or we moderns see them. Indeed, for many modern thinkers, the claim that we must believe in order to understand seems to get it backward. Don't we want to understand something *before* we believe it?

Anselm is not going through the meditations in the *Proslogion* in order that *he* may believe that there is a God. Moreover, the people he addresses in his dedication are his fellow brothers, and presumably, they too are believers seeking understanding. Does this mean that he thinks that *no one* needs an argument in order to believe that God exists? Here I am less certain. Earlier in the first chapter, Anselm does speak about humanity's fall.

> How wretched human beings are! They have lost the very thing for which they were created. Hard and terrible was their fall! Alas! Think what they have lost and what they have found; think what they left behind and what they kept. They have lost the happiness for which they were created and found an unhappiness for which they were not created. [...] When will you give yourself to us again? Look favorably upon us, O Lord; hear us, enlighten us, show yourself to us.
> (Anselm 1995, 97–8)

It is not entirely clear what Anselm is asking when he prays that God will "show his face" once more to humanity. Perhaps Anselm is thinking that there are some who are so fallen, so mired in the pains and toils of material existence, that they fail to even believe that there is a God. Perhaps they mouth the words, but in their hearts they don't really believe. Perhaps. But it is not certain that this is so. Nor, again, is it clear that the argument developed in *Proslogion* 2–4 is meant to alleviate that kind of fallen person's suffering. Would such a person, so beaten down and obsessed with merely eking out an existence, be receptive to the conclusion of such an argument? Or would a being so great that nothing greater is conceivable be too abstract and distant to goad such a fallen soul to a return to God and true happiness?

There is a lot, then, that is extremely interesting in Anselm's *Proslogion*, of which the ontological argument and subsequent meditations on God's perfection and attributes are crucial and integral parts. But to appreciate it properly, I think we would need to have a fuller appreciation of the sensibilities and overarching framework within which these arguments are developed, one that I think I can begin to gesture at by approaching medieval philosophy in the way that I do in the rest of the book. It is not clear to me that shoehorning medieval attitudes to natural and revealed theology into one chapter would be the best way to gain such an appreciation.

1.6 Let Us Begin

At this point, I think we are ready to begin. I have divided material up in a manner that might be familiar to you from your introductory course. We will begin with some foundational stuff about our ability to know reality and what reality is like – in other words, metaphysics and epistemology. Medieval philosophers often describe investigations into what there is as "first philosophy." Once we survey some of what medieval thinkers had to say about these topics, we will turn to ethics and political philosophy. As one of my students recently observed, ethics would seem to deserve (more than metaphysics, at any rate) the label "first philosophy." Given that the overarching goal for human beings is to return to God, this student's thought strikes me as being on the mark. If you read the chapters in order, I think you will see that all the difficult material in the first few chapters has a point. It gives medieval philosophers the tools they need to get an accurate fix on what our return to God will be like and what we need to do to make such a return. The book ends with political theory because as many medieval thinkers argue, humans are generally not equipped to make the arduous return to God by themselves. The support of one's friends and neighbors is vital.

While there is a discernable overarching narrative in this book, each of the chapters can stand on its own, which means that you and your teachers can jump around or in and out as much as you like. This means that there is some overlap in content between chapters. I need to sometimes return to an idea or question in order to weave together the miniature narratives that I offer. Hopefully, any repetitiveness that you come across is not too distracting.

Of course, I cannot cover everything that might be of interest to you or your instructor. Nor will I be able to go into any specific topic too deeply. Consider what follows, then, as something like a tasting menu. A tasting menu is where a chef offers you small bites designed to show off what she does best. Of course, she can cook any number of things in addition to what she presents on the menu. But this is her chance to entice you to come back for more, again and again. Hopefully, in this book, you will sample enough tasty morsels of medieval philosophy that you will want to come back to it again and again.

Finally, let me say a few words about translations and transliterations.

I have tried as much as possible to use medieval works that are widely available in English translation. When that was not feasible, I have offered my own translations. All such cases have been noted.

I also need to mention my method for transliteration of non-Latinate alphabets. Scholars in the field of Arabic philosophy, for instance, have developed several systems for transliterating Arabic letters into the Latin alphabet that English and many other Western languages employ. If you start reading around, you will see these systems and you will notice that many of them make heavy use of special diacritical marks. (At the beginning of a book that uses these systems, there should be a table which explains the system in place.) I have attempted to minimize the inclusion of foreign words to places where it is absolutely essential in order to make the argument intelligible. In such cases, I have resorted to a very simple system of transliteration, one which tries to minimize these diacritical additions. I trust that neither beginners nor experts will need the diacritical marks to use this book. If you wish to do more research, be aware that there is no single standard for transliterating Arabic, Hebrew, and other languages that do not use the Latin alphabet. Many of the more accessible introductions to Arabic and Hebrew thought also simplify things, although not necessarily in the same manner that I have. Moreover, when searching on the worldwide web, many of the diacritical marks get dropped. This will take some getting used to. Be patient, and if at first your search comes up empty, try other permutations or common spellings of a term or philosopher's name.

Notes

1 One of my models is the wonderful introduction to the problem of universals by David Armstrong (1989).
2 On dating, see Section 1.4.
3 As you can see, scholars are not always sure about precisely when some of the figures we study existed. Medieval record keepers were not always concerned about birthdays – perhaps understandably, given the mortality rate of infants in this age – and sometimes even the death of an individual is shrouded in mystery.

4 There are also examples of straightforward biographies, such as the composite autobiography and biography of Ibn Sina (Gohlman 1974), which, while not lacking in value, are not primarily concerned with presenting and defending a philosophical position.
5 As you can see, the format for lectures and disputations are highly ritualized. But lest you conclude that they would have been drab affairs, you should know that there is evidence to suggest that "disputations did not proceed as solemnly as the written redactions might make us believe." In particular, scholars have discovered statues prohibiting hissing, making noise, or even stone throwing (Kenny and Pinborg 1982, 24).
6 Some readers might notice that I do not discuss Scotus and Ockham much in this book. One reason for this is that their works are so difficult to dissect and summarize. It is hard to say anything about how they tackle an issue without having to say a lot of things.
7 In some works, you will also see references to the Muslim dating system, often signaled by the abbreviation "AH," which counts forward from the Hijra, or "emigration," of Muhammad and his companions from Mecca to Medina.

Suggestions for Further Reading

In the succeeding chapters, I will provide suggestions for resources that are directed specifically to the topics covered. At present, I want to recommend some books that will supplement this necessarily brief orientation to the study of medieval philosophy and its history.

It is extremely important to situate medieval thinkers in their historical contexts. I have only mentioned this in passing in this Introduction and the appendix to this volume only offers the briefest of sketches as to what was happening when the authors I cover were writing. To really do historical contextualization justice, I would have to say a whole lot more about the history and historiography of the Middle Ages, but for that, I would have had to write a separate book. Fortunately, we now have Matthew Gabriele's and David M. Perry's overview of how scholars are reconceiving the history of the Middle Ages. *The Bright Ages* (2021) is an engaging, up-to-date book, written for a lay audience but with a bevy of suggestions for where to start making deeper dives into the scholarly literature.

When it comes to the study of medieval philosophy, I have already noted John Marenbon's marvelous book (2007). In addition to developments in the Western universities and its antecedents, Professor Marenbon gives overviews of non-university traditions, both in Western Europe and in the Byzantine, Islamic, and Jewish worlds. The book works through the material temporally, interspersed with some brief case studies where certain philosophical issues are treated in a bit more detail. It is in many respects an excellent complement to this book.

Perhaps the most ambitious attempt to provide a comprehensive introduction to medieval philosophy is a podcast series by Peter Adamson entitled *History of Philosophy without any gaps* (https://historyofphilosophy.net). This is an ongoing project, covering philosophy from ancient times to the present, across not only the Western and Middle Eastern traditions but also African and East Asian philosophy. Some of the podcasts have been adapted and released as books. The two most relevant for our period are Adamson 2016 and Adamson 2019.

In addition to these two surveys, there are several handbooks, companions, and encyclopedias out there that may be consulted as you begin to research specific individuals and topics in more detail: Cross and Paasch 2021, Gracia and Noone 2003, Lagerlund 2011, Marenbon 2012, Pasnau and Van Dyke 2014. Finally, do not forget to search for up-to-date information in the Stanford Encyclopedia of Philosophy (https://plato.stanford.edu/index.html). This online encyclopedia is continually adding new entries and updating older ones. All articles are written by experts and reviewed by professional philosophers. Pass over Wikipedia; this and Adamson's website should be your first points of entry on the internet.

2 Science, Certainty, and Skepticism

2.1 Varieties and Uses of Skepticism	30
2.2 Certain Knowledge	32
2.3 Ghazali's Encounter with Global Skepticism	37
2.4 Degrees of Certainty	47

Epistemology is the systematic study of knowledge. What can be known, if anything? What is the difference between knowledge and mere belief or opinion? If something can be known, how can it be known? For instance, what sorts of cognitive equipment and powers must we have to get it? Will we need help "from the outside," say from God? Are there other conditions that must be met? Is my position in the universe or within a society relevant?

In contemporary Anglo-American philosophy, there has been considerable interest in a separate, albeit related, set of questions (Fricker 2007). Given that much of our knowledge seems to be secondhand and based on transmission via authorities, it is crucial that we ask who has epistemic authority and why they have this authority. Given that our standard criteria for determining that this or that person has authority might be based on unsupportable biases, we can see how epistemology quickly brings in normative concerns. Who *ought* to be an authority? And more broadly, what *should* be the case for someone to count as being "rational," that is, receptive to *proper* or *virtuous* reasoning.

Incidentally, these questions about authority have medieval parallels. In particular, the medieval thinkers we are focusing on in this book all are embedded in religious traditions that are based on scriptures, that is, records of either divinely inspired writings or, in the case of the Quran, records of the words of God Himself. Medieval thinkers, therefore, are deeply interested in knowledge based on the authority of these texts and situating it relative to knowledge that one might be able to obtain using "natural" human faculties and means.

DOI: 10.4324/9780429348020-2

Relatedly, thinkers embedded in all three of the major Abrahamic faiths had to come up with views about "traditions." The holy text does not always explicitly deal with cases that arise hundreds of years after the revelation. Guidance, therefore, had to come either from a concerted effort to interpret the holy text or from some other means where one could be confident that these means are divinely inspired. In Islam, for instance, medieval individuals (and individuals even to this day) look to the example set by the Prophet Muhammad and his early companions. Presumably, these first believers were living their daily lives, in all their fine detail, in a divinely inspired and divinely sanctioned way. Therefore, even if the Quran is silent on a particular issue that arises, there may be guidance that one can glean by looking to the authoritative word or action of one of these divinely inspired individuals. Of course, medieval individuals (like us) have access to these exemplars only through oral and written reports. (In Islam, the words and deeds of the Prophet and his companions are referred to as the Sunna, and the written reports as *hadith*.) And they were profoundly aware of the fact that some of these reports were fabricated or at least distorted. Sorting through these reports requires skill and time. Authenticating and interpreting these reports in tandem with the holy scripture is a full-time occupation. By the time we get to the people we are studying in this book, all three Abrahamic faiths have institutionalized this occupation and there are individuals in all three traditions who are claiming a special sort of authority based on their study of scripture and tradition. Again, however, it is one thing to *claim* to know the way to right living and ultimately salvation, it is another to actually know the way. Thus, in medieval contexts, like now, there is vigorous debate about *who* should be given proper deference and what made a report or an individual espousing an interpretation authoritative.

We will return to the issue of authority on several occasions in this book, but in this chapter, I want to start with what is perhaps the primal question of epistemology, if not of philosophy altogether: Can we know anything? As you may have discovered in your introductory course to philosophy, the answer to this question is not clear, and indeed, there is a long history of challenges to the notion that humans can know anything at all. Medieval philosophers tend to not go to such extremes – although, see Section 2.3 – since as we have already noted, most of them believed that there was *some* knowledge to be had, namely, from revelation. But even if God sometimes helps us out, we also seem to have other means for acquiring knowledge. Perhaps God even gives us tools so that we do reliably track the world around us. In this chapter, we will focus our inquiry on so-called "natural" knowledge, that is, knowledge acquired by using the capacities and organs that we possess in virtue of being a certain kind of biological organism. The question, then, is whether we can know anything naturally.

This inquiry will proceed as follows. In Section 2.1, we will introduce philosophical skepticism, taking care to distinguish between skepticism taken on as a philosophical position and skepticism used as a means for testing our alleged knowledge and clarifying the rules by which we determine whether something really is knowledge. One commonly held notion, both now and in the Middle Ages, is that what really matters is that we are aware of and confident that we know. Roughly, we don't just want to have correct beliefs, we want to know that our beliefs are correct. It is often asserted that in order to know that we have knowledge, we must be *certain* that we know. In Section 2.2, we explore this idea. If we cannot be certain that we know P (where "P" stands in for any proposition we are presently entertaining), a pernicious form of skepticism about P seems to threaten. To see how damaging the lack of certainty can be, in Section 2.3 we turn to the remarkable reflection on certain knowledge by the great Muslim philosopher and theologian Muhammad al-Ghazali. Ultimately, al-Ghazali thinks that he can save himself from a radical form of skepticism. He, however, will claim that we ultimately need divine intervention. But perhaps there is another way to ward off the threat of skepticism, or at least contain it so that our doubts are manageable and not destructive. In Section 2.4, we turn to the Latin-speaking world and examine the proposal that certainty can come in degrees. If it does, then perhaps we can be confident about some beliefs even if it remains possible that we are wrong.

2.1 Varieties and Uses of Skepticism

It is quite typical for epistemologists to develop criteria for determining whether we know and whether we can be confident that we know something. But once we set a standard for what counts as knowledge and insist that every putative case of knowing meets this standard, this invites *skepticism*; for skepticism is just the expression of doubt as to whether anything that we allegedly know actually meets those standards (Pasnau 2014a, 359–61).

Skepticism either can take the form of a philosophical position or it can be utilized by a philosopher for methodological purposes (Perler 2014, 385). Skepticism as a philosophical position has a long history which medieval writers had some inkling of. The first generations of Muslim theologians, for instance, seem to have come across in one way or another the skeptical positions espoused by several Greek schools. Here is a report from one of those practitioners of *kalam* mentioned in Chapter 1, al-Baghdadi (1037).

> On this point the opposing views are those of the Sceptics. Of the several sects of them one held that things have no reality, that there is no knowledge of them; these are the *Muʻanidun*. [...] The second sect of

Sceptics, the *ahl al-Shakk*, assert: "We do not know whether things and knowledge have reality or not." [...] The third group assert that things have their reality as a result of beliefs, and hold that whenever a man believes a thing his object-of-belief is as he believes it to be.

(Watt 1962, 5–6)

These broad ways of thinking about knowledge, or the lack thereof, are recorded in Greco-Roman sources. The so-called Academic skeptics, so named because they dominated the Platonic Academy in Athens from the third to second centuries BCE, are said to have held the position that the only thing we know is that we know nothing. The rival Pyrrhonist school, named as such because of their founder Pyrrho (mid-fourth century BCE), proclaimed that this position is self-defeating. If I *know* that I know nothing, then I know something. But if I know that I know nothing, I know nothing. Therefore, I both know nothing and I know something. I cannot have it both ways! Whether the Academics really are in trouble is a matter we will put to one side. The Pyrrhonists maintain instead that we do not even know whether we don't know anything.[1] The Pyrrhonist maintains a state of "equipoise": Everything is still up for grabs. For every position about what really is the case, there seem to be equally strong reasons in favor and reasons against maintaining the position. Now, it might so happen that tomorrow more reasons will come along that will break the tie, but at present we are not in a position to know whether this will happen or not. All we can do at present is realize that we are in a position neither to assert anything about reality nor to deny anything about it. Pyrrhonism is, therefore, less a denial of the possibility of knowledge as a studied agnosticism about its possibility. The third position mentioned is one that is associated with Protagoras (around 490–420 BCE), who allegedly held that man is the measure of all things.[2] Notice that the Protagorian position does not strictly deny that we have knowledge. Instead, it reduces knowledge to a radical form of subjectivism or relativism. If I believe P is true, P is true. Knowledge is a form of true belief. Hence, if I believe P and P is true, then it seems that I can also claim that I "know" P. In the rest of the chapter, we will put this form of "skepticism" to one side and focus instead on positions that maintain that we don't know or don't know whether we can know things as they really are.

Traditional Greek skepticism appears to be quite *global*. Consider the position of the Pyrrhonist again. Even a cursory view of Sextus Empiricus's (second or third century CE) surviving works will reveal that he advises us to maintain a state of equipoise in practically every domain, not only in the natural sciences and theology but also the mathematical sciences, ethics, and the practical arts. But it should be observed that skepticism can be restricted to a specific domain. For instance, a philosopher could maintain that we can know some things about the natural world, but when it comes to moral facts, we have no way of knowing what is true or false. We would call such a person a moral skeptic. This more *localized* brand of skepticism will be something that we observe in a number of medieval debates. Most notably, we will see a number of medieval thinkers expressing doubts about our ability to know anything about God's inner nature or plans. Some also express doubts about whether we can know the core natures of created things.

Especially once we admit that there are forms of local skepticism, we can see that there are many philosophers who have taken on some form of skepticism as a philosophical position. But perhaps even more philosophers have taken on skepticism as a method. Probably the most famous example of a philosopher using skepticism for merely methodological purposes is René Descartes's (1596–1650) famous use of skepticism in the first two chapters of his *Meditations on First Philosophy*. You might have encountered Descartes in an introductory course on philosophy. Indeed, for a time, Descartes was a ubiquitous character on philosophy syllabi, and he has often been cast as the "father" of "modern" philosophy and the archenemy of much "postmodern" philosophy (especially on the Continent). His inclusion on introductory philosophy syllabi is not without some merit. If you have not read his *Meditations*, I encourage you to do so. It is an engaging read, and it will help you to understand how much of subsequent European and American philosophy is framed and developed. The claim that Descartes is the initiator of a new form of philosophy is a bit more dubious. After reading this book, following that up with some of the other sources I point you to, and then comparing how Descartes goes about things – even the technical notions that he employs – I think you will see that Descartes's relation to earlier European philosophy is, let us just say, much more complicated.

Descartes considers a radical form of global skepticism ("what if there is absolutely nothing that I can know?") because he thinks that we must clear everything away before we can start over and build up a sturdy and secure edifice of knowledge. Global skepticism is not the conclusion of his project, it is only an instrument that he employs to arrive at claims that we can say with absolute confidence that we do know. The first and probably most famous of these, which Descartes discovers in the second of his *Meditations*, is that he can be thinking only if he exists. Descartes argues that he can only be entertaining the thought that he does *not* exist if he exists.

2.2 Certain Knowledge

Skepticism arises when we set a standard and then insist that all true instances of knowledge meet it. So, what is the standard? Contemporary philosophers have typically held that in order for me to know some proposition, P:

1   I must believe P.
2   P must be true.
3   I should be justified in believing P.

Contemporary epistemologists also tend to insist that certain other conditions must be met, since as Edmund Gettier famously argued, it seems that in some cases I can meet all three of these conditions and yet fail to have knowledge (Gettier 1963). Gettier's alleged counterexamples have not convinced everyone, but they convinced enough contemporary epistemologists that something more is required, and this in turn has led to a vast and concerted effort to identify those extra conditions that must hold. (On this, start with Ichikawa and Steup 2018.) We, however, will sidestep that particular debate, as attempts to defuse "Gettier cases" and their descendants is a concern that, to my knowledge, has no parallel in medieval philosophy. Instead, we will turn to an issue that both is medieval and still resonates with us today. This is the notion that to have knowledge of P – or perhaps more accurately, complete or perfect knowledge of P – one must have *certain* knowledge of P.

The notion that knowledge must be certain does not appear to be of primary concern for many of the ancient Greeks, and especially for Aristotle, but it is definitely present in the Middle Ages. We see it emerge early in the Latin tradition when Augustine reframes skepticism in terms of doubt (*dubitatio*) and links doubt to certainty (Lagerlund 2020, 58). It also comes to the fore early in the development of Islamic philosophy. Indeed, as scholars have pointed out, linking knowledge to certainty was almost a foregone conclusion given that the Arabic translation of Aristotle's *Posterior Analytics* – the book where Aristotle lays out his understanding of knowledge, or *scientia* – liberally employs the word *yaqin* ("certainty"), where Aristotle's Greek merely refers to knowledge or demonstration (Black 2006). Once Aristotle's *Posterior Analytics* and the Arabic commentaries on it arrive in the Latin world, the link between knowledge and certainty is so fixed that it seems that certainty is constitutive of knowledge in its ideal form, or what someone like John Buridan, a fourteenth-century master in the Arts faculty at the University of Paris, will call knowledge in its strictest and most proper sense.

> Furthermore, most strictly, we restrict the name "knowledge" to a steadfast intellectual cognition with the certainty and evidentness of a necessary and demonstrable speculative conclusion.
> (John Buridan, *Summula de dialectica*, 8.4.3; trans. Buridan 2001, 706)

Buridan goes on to point out how this definition excludes "understanding," "art" (the know-how that artisans and medical doctors have), and "prudence" (that is, an understanding of how to act in a given situation). This strictest of definitions precludes "understanding" (which is an operation of the intellect), because understanding involves "first principles," or what we might nowadays call axioms. For while these are "steadfast" and certain, we don't prove that axioms are true. We grasp that they are true and then proceed to use them in proofs or demonstrations. It also precludes the results of demonstrations involving practical know-how, since while these results are necessary and evidently demonstrated, they fail to be "steadfast" and certain in the right way.

Certainty is an attractive feature for determining whether we know. Speaking somewhat loosely, we do not want to merely know, we want to *know* that we know something. More precisely, we do not want to merely be tracking the truth – this is something that we could be doing already – we want to be *aware* that we are getting things right. When we hit upon a truth, we want it to present itself to us in a special way. And it seems that one good sign is if the putative truth that we believe is something that we find it hard to give up or deny.

> Another thing is required on our part, namely, that our assent be firm, i.e., without doubt or fear of the opposite side; and this is also required for knowledge, since a doubtful and fearful assent does not transcend the limits of opinion. For if someone assents to a proposition fearing that the opposite [may be true], he would never say that he knows that it is true, but rather that he takes it or believes that it is.
> (Buridan, *Summula*, 8.4.4; 2001, 707)

Now, this might at first make it seem that knowledge is merely a function of the firmness of the belief, or perhaps more accurately a firmness on our part with respect to a belief. But surely certainty is something more than a mere firmness in our conviction to believe something. After all, like me, you have probably met people who stubbornly believe all sorts of things that strike you as being obviously false. Suppose I am unsure about whether P is true, whereas my associate firmly believes that it is. I can concede that I do not know P. But does the strength of my associate's conviction by itself indicate that P is true and that he knows it? If this is all that it takes to know something, then perhaps something like that aforementioned Protagorean subjectivism should be back on the table.

I suspect, however, that many of you do not want to take that path. And here Buridan has some helpful clarifications to offer.

> But firmness of assent is that whereby we adhere and assent to a proposition without fear of the opposite and this can take place in three ways.

> In one way, [it proceeds] from the will, and in this way Christians assent and adhere firmly to the articles of Catholic faith, and even some heretics adhere to their false opinions, so much so that they would rather die than deny them, and such is the experience of the saints who were willing to die for the faith of Christ.
>
> (Buridan, *Questions on Aristotle's Metaphysics*, book 2, ques. 1; trans. Klima et al. 2007, 145)

This seems to describe what is going on with my associate. He wants his belief to be true. But as Buridan notes, while this act of will is something that the faithful do, it is also something that heretics often do as well. In a second way, Buridan says, "firmness proceeds in us from natural appearances by means of reasoning." This is getting us on the right track, since certainty appears to require more than merely wanting what we believe to be true. For that matter, it seems that certainty must stem from something more than the fact that what we believe is actually true. The saints believe in something that is actually true. But what they don't have when their firmness of assent stems from a sheer act of will, and what Buridan suggests we need, is a firmness that stems from the fact that someone has *reasoned* their way to the belief.

While we are on the right track, this second form of firmness is still not enough. A firmness that comes merely by reasoning from "natural appearances" still allows room for cases where we firmly assent to false things.

> For many people believing and holding false opinions take themselves to have firm scientific knowledge, just as Aristotle says in Book 7 of the [*Nicomachean*] *Ethics* that many people adhere to what they opine no less firmly than to what they know.
>
> (idem)

Even if we reason well (which is a condition that fallible humans sometimes fail to meet), the results of our reasoning are only as good as the material that we start from. But it is precisely here that we often do go astray. Many smart people believe false things, because as Buridan (alluding to Aristotle) notes, many things that people take to be commonsense are false. To have the right kind of firmness, the belief under inspection must be "evident."

> In the third way, firmness proceeds in us from evidentness. And it is called the evidentness of a proposition absolutely, when because of the nature of the senses or the intellect man is compelled, though without necessity, to assent to a proposition so that he cannot dissent from it. And this is the sort of evidentness that the first complex principle

[the principle of non-contradiction] has, according to Aristotle in the fourth book of this work [viz. the *Metaphysics*].

(idem)

Of course, something that strikes us as commonsense could be said to be "evident" in some sense. But the reflective individual will appreciate that what is apparent and what seems at first to be straightforward and obvious must be pressed and tested. Only after closer inspection should we take the obviousness of the belief in question to be evident in the sense that Buridan is after.

Notice that to be evident in the sense that Buridan is interested in the belief must "compel" me to believe it. It must be for me extremely difficult, if not inconceivable, to deny it. The strained way that I am putting the point is prompted by Buridan's qualification that the "compulsion" that he has in mind does not "necessitate" that I believe it. Here I take it that Buridan is trying to emphasize that an evident belief is not an automatic, necessary result of some cognitive process. After all, we are considering a firmness of *assent*. True assent requires that I weigh the two options and then make a *free* choice to assent or withhold my assent. In other words, there is a sense in which I could refrain from assenting to a "compelling," "evident" thought or proposition. It is within my power. But if the proposition is evident in Buridan's preferred sense, then it will seem to me that the only reasonable option is to affirm it.

Here is another thing to note about Buridan's description of this third type of firmness of assent: The evidentness and hence compelling quality of the belief does not have to stem from the fact that we have *reasoned* in the right way to that belief. Some evident beliefs, it seems, might just pop into our heads. Of course, as we have already noted, for that belief to count as *knowledge*, reasoning of a proper sort might indeed be required. But here we have been fixing our gaze on one of the qualities that the beliefs have. Knowledge in the strictest sense must be a belief that is the product of reasoning of a specific kind, which Buridan calls "demonstration." But the process is only one of the necessary components. We must also consider the proposed belief and (freely) assent to it firmly. And finally, this firm assent must stem from a quality that the proposed belief has. The proposed belief must be compelling, indeed so compelling that we find it very difficult if not inconceivable to reject it. Thus, evidentness or the compelling quality of the proposed belief is a crucial part of Buridan's account of knowledge in the strict and proper sense, but nothing here in what he says rules out the possibility that some proposition or belief might be evident, but not strictly speaking knowledge.

You may have picked up on Buridan's tendency to identify "absolute," "strict," or "proper" senses of a notion and to distinguish these from qualified senses of the same. If so, perhaps you have already observed that in the description of evidentness that we have studied, Buridan is describing an "absolute," or unqualified, kind of evidentness. You, therefore, will not be surprised to learn that Buridan quickly adds *two more* kinds of evidentness, ones which apply to certain restricted classes of beliefs or propositions. These grades of evidentness will play a crucial role in how Buridan deals with skepticism. But before we go there, let us pursue the thought that instances of certain propositions and certain knowledge are marked by the fact that one cannot help but assent to them, or to put it negatively, that it is inconceivable for us to deny them. At first glance, there seems to be something right about this idea. Certain knowledge should be so unshakeable that it will not be given up, no matter what. Yet, remember that once a standard is set, we need to see whether anything measures up to it. It may in fact turn out that the sort of firmness which is allegedly required for certainty will make it impossible for us to know anything with certainty. To see how this might go, let us turn to the Islamic world, where we will see a striking example of how the insistence that knowledge requires absolute evidentness can lead to skeptical troubles.

2.3 Ghazali's Encounter with Global Skepticism

Abu Hamid Muhammad al-Ghazali (1058–1111) is sometimes called the second greatest Muslim after the Prophet Muhammad and "the Proof of Islam" (*Hujjat al-Islam*), largely because of his voluminous *Revival of the Religious Sciences*, which even to this day is considered by many Muslims to be essential reading. The *Revival* contains much of interest for philosophers, but perhaps the most fascinating work of all is his *Deliverance from Error*.[3] It is not only philosophically rich but also dramatically riveting, for it purports to be an account of not one but two intellectual and spiritual crises that Ghazali had. The second crisis occurred while he was a successful teacher with high-ranking political connections in Baghdad, which at that time was the capital of the remaining vestiges of the Abbasid Caliphate. It had become clear to him from his investigation of the way to truth that his "only hope of attaining beatitude in the afterlife lay in piety and restraining [his] soul from passion." And, yet, when he surveyed what his life had become in Baghdad, he realized that he had strayed.

> I also considered my activities – the best of them being public and private instruction – and saw that in them I was applying myself to sciences unimportant and useless in this pilgrimage to the hereafter. Then I reflected on my intention in my public teaching, and I saw that it was not directed purely to God, but rather was instigated and motivated by

the quest for fame and widespread prestige. So I became certain that I was on the brink of a crumbling bank and already on the verge of falling into the Fire [of Hell], unless I set about mending my ways.

(al-Ghazali 1980, 79; Watt 1994, 58–59)

Like many who have made New Year's resolutions only to then procrastinate and backslide, Ghazali says that he "put one foot forward, and the other backward." But finally, God called him out on his unfulfilled promises. God "put a lock on my tongue so that I was impeded from public teaching." Soon Ghazali was unable to eat or drink, and unsurprisingly he fell ill. So, he retreated from Baghdad and ultimately arrived in Damascus, where he eventually recovered and started writing his *Revival*. Scholars generally believe that this part of Ghazali's story is true to the facts, although there is some speculation that he withdrew from public life not only for spiritual reasons but also because of political intrigues at the center of the empire, including the assassination of his patron and protector Nizam al-Mulk (al-Ghazali 1980, introduction, 21 and especially 24–37).

This is the *second* of two big intellectual and spiritual crises that Ghazali reports. The first is the one that we will turn to now. While it is not entirely clear when this first crisis appeared in time, it is without question the *logically* prior crisis, since it involves the lack of confidence in the existence of all certain and stable knowledge. Before Ghazali could even be in the position to suffer his second crisis, Ghazali had to confront and defeat a severe version of global skepticism.

Ghazali tells us that ever since he was a boy, he was unremittingly inquisitive. He was dissatisfied when his elders told him that he should believe something is true just because they said it is true. Ghazali, however, could not embrace the way of *taqlid*. (Translators have had a tough time picking out one word to render this Arabic term. What it often means, and what Ghazali in particular has in mind, is an uncritical submission to authority. Hence, it is sometimes rendered as "blind submission to authority.") As he observed, believing something is true merely based on authority will not work if one is interested in getting at what is really true, since there were contradictory authorities. Merely following authority meant that "the children of Christians always grew up embracing Christianity, and the children of Jews always grew up adhering to Judaism, and the children of Muslims always grew following the religion of Islam" (1980, 55; Watt 1994, 19). But surely only one of these religions could be the true religion. Thus, he had to find other way to secure what he was after, which was the true and the real. Interestingly, Ghazali insists that he didn't choose to be this way. None of his relatives, schoolmates, or teachers encouraged him to be an uncompromising seeker. This was his God-given nature (1980, 54–5; Watt 1994, 19).[4]

Ghazali lived in tumultuous times, much as we are here in the first few decades of the twenty-first century. In addition to theological challenges posed by Christians and Jews, Muslims were literally at war with one another. In particular, a Shi'ite principality based in Egypt was challenging the Sunni rulers in Baghdad. Moreover, as Ghazali notes in several of his works, even within Sunni Islam, there was much debate over theological and legal matters. These debates could become so heated that partisans of different sides often accused their opponents of heresy. So, there was an overwhelming abundance of competitive, contradictory worldviews, each of them insisting that it was the sole picture of what is true.

What was a man thirsting to know the truth to do? Ghazali thought he had hit upon a surefire method by characterizing certainty and certain, stable knowledge in terms of indubitability.

> Then it became clear to me that sure and certain knowledge is that in which the thing known is made so manifest that no doubt clings to it, nor is it accompanied by the possibility of error and deception, nor can the mind even suppose such a possibility.
> (al-Ghazali 1980, 55; Watt 1994, 19–20)

It is important to pause and make it clear precisely how strong this criterion is. On this account, if I have certain knowledge of P, it is not just that I don't actually have doubts about P, it is also the case that there is no *possibility* that I could be wrong about P. Thus, when I am testing P for sureness and certainty, I have to think through all the possibilities. If it is even *remotely* possible that P could be false, then I cannot be certain of P, and, accordingly, I cannot have certain knowledge of P.

You should not take me to be suggesting that Ghazali invented this particular characterization of certainty in terms of indubitability. We have already noted, for instance, that Augustine develops his notion of certainty in terms of doubt. And while there is no reason to think that Ghazali was at all aware of this North African Christian's writings, this need not worry us. For we can find this notion in the books of the philosophers that Ghazali probably did know. Here, for instance, is Abu Nasr Muhammad al-Farabi (950):

> Certainty means that we are convinced, with respect to the thing to which assent has been granted, that the existence of what we are convinced about with respect to that thing cannot possibly be different from our conviction. Moreover, we are convinced that this conviction about it cannot be otherwise, to the point that when one reaches a given

> conviction concerning this initial conviction, he maintains that it [also] cannot be otherwise, and so on indefinitely.
> (Al-Farabi, *Book of Demonstration, On Assent and Conceptualization*, n. 2; trans. McGinnis and Reisman 2007, 64)

Here we see a way of working out the indubitability requirement in terms of iterations of inconceivability. In order to be certain that P is the case, I cannot see any way that I could be wrong about P, and the conviction that I cannot be wrong about P is itself so strong that it too cannot be undermined by doubt, and so on and so forth. This iterative approach is not something that we see in Ghazali's set-up for the problem of global skepticism. And, thus, while it would be worthwhile to reflect on it more, we won't do so here.

The salient point is that Ghazali has found and taken on as his own a criterion of indubitability: Certain knowledge is knowledge so secure that it is impossible that one can be wrong about it. However, what Ghazali immediately says afterward might seem to muddy the issue.

> Furthermore, safety from error must accompany the certainty to such a degree that, if someone proposed to show it to be false – for example, a man who would turn a stone into gold and a stick into a snake – his feat would not induce any doubt or denial. For if I know that ten is more than three, and then someone were to say: "No, on the contrary, three is more than ten, as is proved by my turning this stick into a snake" – and if he were to do just that and I were to see him do it, I would not doubt my knowledge because of his feat. The only effect it would have on me would be to make me wonder how he could do such a thing.
> (al-Ghazali 1980, 55; Watt 1994, 20)

At first, this might seem to be a strange non-sequitur. Why would anyone think that transformations of stone into gold or sticks into snakes would compromise our belief that ten is greater than three? The simple answer, and Ghazali's primary point, is that a proposition like *ten is greater than three* is so firm that the magician cannot undermine one's assent to it. Ghazali is imagining that the individual challenging the proposition is a true magician and that the transformation (for all he knows) is real. His point is that even in this case, the evident-ness of the proposition that ten is greater than three will not be compromised. Contrast this with other propositions that Ghazali might be entertaining at the time, such as, will this medicine cure him? If the magician told him that it will, Ghazali might be swayed to trust him. But that is because the proposition *this medicine will cure me* is not certain.[5]

We can draw several other lessons from Ghazali's example. First, the imagined case shows us that we need to be aware of what can count as counterevidence. The reason why it might seem silly to us that a magic trick – or even a case of real magic – could shake our confidence in the truth of ten being greater than three is that sticks and snakes seem to have no relevant connection to the properties of numbers. Whether snakes can come from sticks or not has no bearing on the truths of mathematics. We can easily see this in the case of the sticks-snakes and their lack of connection to mathematics, but there might be other cases where it might be easier for a trickster to confuse us into thinking that something is relevant, when in fact it is not.

Second, and piggybacking on this first point, Ghazali might be indicating that the certainty of one proposition is (at least in many cases) independent from the certainty of another. And thus, if someone undermines my conviction about one proposition, this by itself does not undermine my conviction in others. Initially, we might think that *sticks cannot become snakes* and *ten is greater than three* are equally obvious and secure. Then, the magician puts on his show. This evidence might force me to concede that sticks can turn into snakes. But just because my certainty has been shaken about sticks, my certainty in mathematical truths need not be undermined.

Finally, it is also worth pointing out that the examples that Ghazali chooses might be far from accidental. The proposition *ten is greater than three* is a claim about intelligible objects, and as Ghazali will soon go on to suggest, such truths seem to be reducible to some basic first principles, like the law of noncontradiction, or more immediately and relevantly, *the whole is necessarily greater than its part*. By contrast, both *sticks cannot become snakes* and *stones cannot become gold* are claims about the sensible world, and they seem to be based on experiences that we have had of sensible objects. But as Ghazali famously argues in the *Incoherence of the Philosophers*, these beliefs, and in particular, the claim that these transformations are impossible are not warranted (al-Ghazali 2000, 170 ff.). God can do anything that does not involve a logical contradiction. There is no logical contradiction in the claim that something that was a stick is now a snake, especially once we concede that God can be the cause of the transformation. Therefore, a stick *can* become a snake.[6]

This distinction between beliefs founded in sense experience and beliefs vouchsafed by reason alone is crucial. For after Ghazali defines certain knowledge as knowledge that cannot in any way be doubted, he immediately turns to these two sets of beliefs as the likeliest candidates.

The candidacy of beliefs based on sensory experience is short-lived, and the reasons for casting doubt upon such beliefs are reasons that many of you are probably already familiar with. First, we are familiar with cases of optical illusions – such as the straight straw appearing to be bent when submerged in a glass of liquid. But it goes deeper than this. Distortions of sense experience are routine and indeed natural consequences of our physical makeup and position. Ghazali's example is especially instructive (1980, 56; Watt 1994, 22). A star appears to be the size of a coin, even though we think – nay, we exclaim that we "know" – that it is much, much larger than that in actual fact.

Why do we think that a star is not really the size of a coin? It is because our sense experience is organized and judged by reason, and in particular, it is guided by such allegedly necessary truths as the same thing cannot be both F and not F (at the same time and in the same respects). Since stars are hard to examine up close, take another example of perceptual distortions. From afar a tower appears to be flat and rectangular. But now let us walk toward the tower and examine it up close. From this vantage, the tower appears to be cylindrical. Sensation has provided us with two bits of data: the tower is cylindrical and it is rectangular. It is *reason* that intercedes and proclaims that the tower cannot be both, since the very same object cannot be both really rectangular and really cylindrical. (Bearing in mind those parenthetical caveats to the rule about contradictory properties, we also have reason to think that the tower itself does not change its shape as we walk toward it.) Further data along with subsequent adjudication by reason leads us to posit a more general theory of optics, which includes a rational, systematic account of these shifting appearances. It is through the application of this theory of optics that we come to believe that stars are really much, much bigger than the size of a coin.

So far, so good. We can only be certain of something if we cannot doubt it. In the case of beliefs founded solely on sense experience, we have identified a host of reasons why we cannot trust their reports. These reasons stemmed from the fact that they led to violations of seemingly indubitable rules of reason, or as Ghazali puts it, they fall afoul of the "reason-judge." But what about these fundamental rational principles, the "primary truths"? At this point, Ghazali personifies the senses and has them challenge reason.

> Then sense-data spoke up: "What assurance have you that your reliance on rational data is not like your reliance on sense-data? Indeed, you used to have confidence in me. Then the reason-judge came along and gave me the lie. But were it not for the reason-judge, you would still accept me as true. So there may be, beyond the perception of reason, another judge. And if the latter revealed itself, it would give the lie to the judgements of reason, just as the reason-judge revealed itself and gave the lie to the judgements of sense. The mere fact of the

nonappearance of that further perception does not prove the impossibility of its existence."
(al-Ghazali 1980, 56; Watt 1994, 22)

Ghazali doesn't leave it at this. It is one thing to *say* that something is possible, but he knows that he needs to give reason some motivation to take this seriously as a possibility. Thus, the senses continue.

Don't you see that when you are asleep you believe certain things and imagine certain circumstances and believe that they are fixed and lasting and entertain no doubts about that being their status? Then you wake up and know that all your imaginings and beliefs were groundless and insubstantial.
(al-Ghazali 1980, 57; Watt 1994, 23)

Several centuries later, Descartes also makes an appeal to dreams, to famous effect. But there is a crucial difference: Descartes uses the possibility that he is caught up in a dream in order to undermine the belief that his experiences map on to a world outside of his mind. But he, nevertheless, concedes that his appeal to the dream possibility will not undermine his faith in rational first principles.

For whether I am awake or asleep, two and three added together are five, and a square has no more than four sides. It seems impossible that such transparent truths should incur any suspicion of being fake.
(Descartes, *Meditations on First Philosophy* 1; Descartes 1984, vol. 2, 14)

This is why Descartes introduces the possibility of an extremely powerful, supernatural deceiver (his "evil genius"). It is only then that Descartes thinks that he can undermine his confidence in such beliefs as that ten is greater than three.

Ghazali does not countenance the possibility of a supernatural deceiver, be it God or a demon. Instead, he takes the primary lesson to be one of perspective. When you are in the dream, you take what you are presented with *as if* it were real. Think about an especially vivid nightmare involving a monster. While you are having the nightmare, you react with fear and you attempt to flee. If it is an especially vivid nightmare, the chase can be extremely terrifying. But it is terrifying precisely because your mind is treating the dream monster as if it were real. It is only upon waking up and gaining the vantage point of someone who is awake that you are then able to sigh with relief and say, "That monster wasn't real." But could it be the case that, even now in your "waking state," you are perceiving things from the wrong vantage? Is it not possible that all of the things that you assume to be secure or impossible are in reality not as they seem to be? Ghazali is not just talking about whether there are monsters or not, he is talking about the rules that the monsters behave by. Go back to the nightmare. As you were fleeing, perhaps you tried to move in a straight line across the room, but as you did, maybe the distance still appears to be the same: No matter how fast you run, you make no progress. Or think about any number of other seemingly "illogical" aspects of dreams. Again, why do we confidently assert that these are in fact illogical? The answer surely is that we judge the rules that operate or fail to operate in the dream from the vantage of the mind that is awake. But if rules can change as the vantage changes, and if it is possible that the human mind can achieve a higher vantage than that of reason, then how confident should we be in the rules that *reason* deems unbreakable?

Ghazali does not have to leave the possibility of such a higher vantage as mere speculation. He notes that there are people walking around who claim to have achieved such a higher vantage point.

> It may be that this state beyond reason is that which the Sufis claim is theirs. For they allege that, in the states they experience when they concentrate inwardly and suspend sensation, they see phenomena which are not in accord with the normal data of reason.
>
> (al-Ghazali 1980, 57; Watt 1994, 23)

Just how "not in accord with the normal data of reason" are these experiences? Well, some of them claimed that when they achieve this state of bliss, they are "annihilated." Taken literally, this means that they cease to exist. But how can they cease to exist and yet return to the living to report about this? As we will see later, Ghazali is not convinced that annihilation really happens (Chapter 4, Section 3). But even relatively "sober" mystics report that the laws of noncontradiction bend, if not brake, in the realm of the divine. And they do so precisely because our basic, seemingly immutable logical principles are tailor-made to this plane of existence, and not for the higher one.[7] Ghazali also adds that the words of God and His prophet seem to support the possibility that what we take here in this life to be logical, rational, and certain, is still distorted and veiled. For instance, the Prophet Muhammad purportedly said that "Men are asleep; then after they die they are awake," and the Quran at one point states, "But We have removed from you your veil and today [sc. now that you are dead] your sight is keen" (50: 21–22).

But the key point is this, and it should not be overlooked: Ghazali is not claiming that these reports of the mystics are true or that the scriptures must be read in the way suggested above. He is merely showing that there are reasons to allow that the existence of a higher state with different rules is possible. And this is all that he needs, the mere *possibility* that the rules of logic and the first principles of reason might not really hold. Once that is conceded, the trap has sprung. For as Ghazali notes, reason cannot save itself.

> The objection could be refuted only by proof. But the only way to put together a proof was to combine primary cognitions. So if, as in my case, these were inadmissible, it was impossible to construct the proof.
> (al-Ghazali 1980, 57; Watt 1994, 24)

It is an established principle of "waking state" logic that you cannot prove P by using P as a premise. This would be the fallacy of *petitio principi*, or to put it a little more colloquially, such reasoning would be circular. But this is precisely where reason now finds itself. It must find a way to justify its starting principles without resorting to these very principles. But no such way exists. Reason is stuck.

Remember, Ghazali wants nothing more than to know the truth. But it appears that there are no certain truths to be had. Once this realization sinks in, Ghazali reports that he was "a skeptic in fact, but not in utterance or doctrine" for nearly two months (1980, 57; Watt 1994, 24). That is to say, when it came to stating what is true and real, he could take no position. But this did not mean that he ceased to go about his daily life, eating and drinking and going to the mosque. In effect, he seems to have practiced what the ancient Pyrrhonian skeptics recommended, that one live solely "by appearances" (Sextus Empiricus, *Outlines of Pyrrhonism*, 1.10–11 and 1.33).

What restores him from this "malady" is not a proof. Rather, God directly intervenes by casting a "light" into his breast. The truths of reason take on a new sheen and he is able treat them as the indubitable, stable starting points that he needs.

This is another noteworthy difference between Ghazali's treatment of global skepticism and Descartes's more famous one. Descartes thinks that reason can save itself by discovering a principle upon which not even an evil genius can cast doubt: I can only be deceived if I exist and I am thinking. Hence, given that I am thinking a thought about which I might be deceived, I exist. Descartes's ancestor when it comes to this move is not Ghazali, but Augustine, who argues that "If I doubt, I exist" (*si fallor sum*) (*On the Trinity* 15.12.21).[8]

Why didn't it occur to Ghazali to make this kind of move? For one thing, it is not clear that Ghazali would allow it. Descartes's inference adheres to the rules and first principles of logic. Ghazali frames his argument in much more general terms, so that it covers all the potential starting principles, including the law of noncontradiction. Second, given Ghazali's appeal to the Sufi tradition, he might have thought that such an appeal to a stable and persisting self is not indubitably warranted. As we already noted, many of the Sufis suggested that the self (*al-nafs*) ceases to exist and is "unified" with God's essence when it makes its trip to the divine realm. And, as you might have already encountered in your philosophy lectures, there are any number of commentators who have attacked Descartes on this point. At most, they argue, Descartes is entitled to this claim: There is some deception; therefore, there is some thinking. But Descartes makes the unwarranted move from *there is thinking* to *there is a* thing *that is thinking*. And even if we were to grant that much, one could also ask whether Descartes is entitled to infer that *he* exists from the fact that a thinking thing exists.

We will end our tour of Ghazali's fascinating foray into global skepticism with this observation. Ghazali describes the direct intervention of God on his mind and soul as if it were like light. This image picks up on a long tradition that can be traced back to Plato, if not earlier. (See, for instance, Plato's famous analogy of the Form of the Good to the sun in *Republic*, Book 6.) This Platonic notion that the divine makes it possible for the finite, embodied human mind to think is quite common in the Middle Ages, both in the philosophy developed in the Islamic world (including much of Jewish philosophy) and in the Latin West. In the West, what comes to be known as the doctrine of "divine illumination" is put forth by Augustine, and indeed it is part of Augustine's complete solution to the problem of skepticism (Lagerlund 2020, 48–9). His position was adopted and elaborated into an epistemological theory that was developed and defended by a number of thirteenth-century thinkers, including Bonaventure and Henry of Ghent (Noone 2014). In the case of these later thinkers, the theory gained credence because the rival "empiricist" and "naturalist" theory of cognition derived from Aristotle's books seemed to be incapable of furnishing the human mind with immutable, necessary intellectual first principles. Intelligible objects are unchanging and necessary. But everything that the human mind is immediately acquainted with is changing and contingent. Therefore, it seems to be impossible to derive intelligible objects from the material immediately available to the human mind. Moreover, and following a line of reasoning that can be traced back to Plato, even if we derive an intellectual representation of things from our experience, we are in no position to determine whether this representation is an adequate model of the real, necessary, and unchanging paradigms that produce this world (Plato *Meno*, 80d–e; *Phaedo* 74a–75c).

I am not suggesting that these arguments are impregnable. There are also considerable differences between the Latin theory and Ghazali's utilization of this light imagery. But from a high enough vantage, we can see that Ghazali is on the side of those who think that human cognition requires an extra helping hand from above. We will return to this issue in a little bit. But first, let us finish this chapter by returning to the issue of certainty. Perhaps there is another way to defuse global skepticism.

2.4 Degrees of Certainty

Ghazali's *Deliverance* was not translated into Latin in the Middle Ages,[9] and so thinkers in the Latin-speaking parts of Europe were not exposed to his striking encounter with global skepticism. This, however, does not mean that Latin thinkers were blissfully unaware of skeptical challenges to the foundations of epistemology. They had plenty of potential exposure to skeptical challenges. They could learn about Hellenistic versions of skepticism from Cicero and Augustine. And while it is still unclear how widely studied it was in Europe, a late thirteenth-century translation of Sextus Empiricus's *Outlines of Pyrrhonism* is extant in manuscripts traceable to three major medieval university centers, Paris, Venice, and Madrid (Perler 2012, 548 and 562, note 3; Lagerund 2020, 54). Moreover, and perhaps most significantly, medieval thinkers in the Latin-speaking tradition were keenly aware of the possibility that they were being deceived either by a demon or even God.

Latin medieval thinkers were especially impressed by the possibility of external world skepticism. They worried that what they perceived is not an accurate representation of what there is in the world outside of their minds. This inaccuracy or deception could come in two varieties. One could be deceived about some of the features of the thing being perceived. For instance, I could think that the voice I was hearing was God's voice when it, in fact, was the Devil speaking. But I could also be deceived about whether something is currently existing out there in the world. It could appear to me that there is a tree in my yard when, in fact, there is no tree. Both of these were possibilities because for an Aristotelian, knowledge of the external world is mediated through the senses, and it was thought that both demons and God could manipulate our sensory apparatus in such a way as to present to us false representations (what they usually call "species") (Perler 2012, 549–54). Indeed, sufficiently powerful supernatural forces could create a facsimile of a sense impression that is so vivid that we would not be able to discern the fact that there is nothing at all behind it.

> The senses can be deceived, as it is commonly said, and it is certain that the species of sensible things can be preserved in the sense organs in the absence of these things, as it is stated in [Aristotle's] *On Sleep*

and Waking. And then we judge that which is not there to be there, and that is why we err on account of the senses. And the difficulty is greatly increased by what we believe in our faith; for God can form in our senses the species of sensible things without these sensible things, and can preserve them for a long time, and then [, if He did so,] we would judge those sensible things to be present. Furthermore, you do not know whether God, who can do such and even greater things, wants to do so. Hence, you do not have certitude and evidentness about whether you are awake and there are people in front of you, or you are asleep, for in your sleep God could make sensible species just as clear as, or even a hundred times clearer than, those that sensible objects can produce; and so you would formally judge that there are sensible things in front of you, just as you do now. Therefore, since you know nothing about the will of God, you cannot be certain about anything.

(Buridan *In Metaph.* 2.1; trans. Klima et al. 2007, 143)

Notice how Buridan starts off with the observation that species detached from the object that they represent can occur naturally, as is often the case in dreams. But he quickly moves beyond this, presumably because he is thinking that dreams really only deceive when they are especially vivid, and even then, only momentarily. It is also quite striking that Buridan passes over the case of demons altogether. He immediately moves to the greatest threat to our knowledge of the external world: *God* could be deceiving me and sustaining this deception for a considerable amount of time.

The thought that God might deceive is striking. Descartes only humored the possibility that God would deceive for a moment before he quickly backtracked. God is thought to be absolutely good. But deceit is an evil action. Therefore, God would not deceive. This is why Descartes immediately replaces the thought that God is deceiving him with the supposition that the deceiver is some very powerful malicious entity. But Buridan does not hesitate, and he does not retract the possibility that God creates counterfeit sense impressions. We can see hints of his reasoning in the passage just quoted: We can't assume that deception is always evil. God does lots of things that are hard for us to understand. For all we know, God might have good reasons to deceive us.[10] That is, it might be good for us that He deceives us, at least on some occasions. To warm us up to the notion that deception *might* be benevolent, think about the half-truths and "white lies" that we tell those we love, especially if we think that they are too young, or otherwise incapable of understanding. It might also be legitimate for states to tell half-truths or outright lies to their citizens (see Section 7.3).

Buridan is also relying on what by his time is a well-established distinction between "ordained power" (*potestas ordinata*) and "absolute power" (*potestas absoluta*) (Lagerlund 2020, 79; Perler 2012, 548). Ordained power respects the laws of nature set down by God. Absolute power, however, is only bound by the law of noncontradiction. In other words, by Buridan's time, Latin philosophers commonly make the distinction between what is naturally possible and what is logically possible. Even if it would be a violation of the natural order for there to be a sensible species in my soul of a tree when there is no tree presenting in front of me, it is logically possible that such a state of affairs obtains. Thus, God could create a counterfeit sense impression of a tree when there is no tree in front of me, and He "can" do this both in the sense that it is within His power to make it so and in the sense that it might even be for the good that He does this.

How does Buridan address this potential threat to our confidence that the world is really out there and possesses the features that it appears to have? Buridan starts by distinguishing two senses in which we might grasp a truth. In one sense, grasping a truth is merely a matter of whether a true proposition exists in the soul. But as Buridan correctly perceives, this minimal notion of grasping a truth is not what we are most interested in. We want to know whether we should "assent" to propositions that we have in our souls, and whether we can do so with any certitude. As we noted earlier in the chapter, I don't just want my picture of the world to be correct; this could happen by accident. I want it to be the case that I am confident that my picture of the world is accurate.

On Buridan's analysis, the firmness of my conviction is due to two elements: First, there is the firmness of the truth in question. Is it necessary and stable in itself? This will depend on what grounds it. This explains why Buridan here uses as his example the proposition that God exists (*In Metaph.* 2.1; Klima et al. 2007, 145). He is not suggesting that a person cannot express doubts about this proposition. Many indeed do. Rather, Buridan means that the proposition about the world is grounded in something objectively unshakeable. There is no way at all that it could not be true that God exists.

Second, there is a subjective element. Here the will and judgment based on reasoning and evidence come into play. As we noted above in Section 2.2, sometimes firm assent is merely a matter of the will. This is where Buridan sees what we commonly refer to as "faith" at work. This is the way that "Christians assent and adhere firmly to the articles of Catholic faith". Alas, it is also the sort of firmness of assent that "heretics" have as they cling to "their false opinions". (*In Metaph.* 2.1; Klima et al. 2007, 145). Hence, we should hope that for at least some propositions, we can assent to them because we are justified in doing so. And Buridan thinks that in some cases reasons justify our assent to a proposition. In some cases, this reasoning stems from "natural appearances." which means that error can still creep in. The strongest form of assent is one that we make when the proposition is "evident." Here we find something that echoes Descartes's recommendation that assent should only be given to propositions that are clear and distinct.

As this point we have arrived at the heart of the matter, and the distinctions that Buridan proceeds to make will provide him with the tools he needs in order to undercut our worries about global external world skepticism. The evidentness of a proposition comes in degrees. Some propositions are so evident that the human intellect "is compelled, though without necessity, to assent to a proposition so that he cannot dissent from it" (*In Metaph.* 2.1; Klima et al. 2007, 145). Buridan's example of such an "absolutely" evident proposition is the principle of noncontradiction. As we have already seen, this principle could be challenged. So, the proposition is not "compelling" in the sense that it is metaphysically impossible that the human intellect refuses to assent to it. But the principle is nevertheless very hard to resist.

But for most propositions, evidentness comes in a lesser degree. And these are the more relevant cases. There are the propositions that are evident to a degree that is sufficient for inquiry into the workings of the natural world.

> Evidentness is taken in another way not absolutely, but with the assumption that things obey the common course of nature, as was said earlier. It is in this way that it is evident to us that every fire is hot or that the heavens are moving, although the opposite is possible by God's power. And this sort of evidentness is sufficient for the principles and conclusions of natural science.
> (Buridan *In Metaph.* 2.1; Klima et al. 2007, 145–6)

Finally, there is an even lesser degree of evidentness that is nevertheless good enough that if we have it, we may occasionally assent to what we think.

> Indeed, there is an even weaker kind of evidentness that suffices for acting morally well, namely, when someone, having seen and investigated all relevant facts and circumstances that man can diligently investigate, makes a judgment in accordance with these circumstances, then his judgment will be evident with the sort of evidentness that suffices for acting morally well, even if the judgment is false, because of some insurmountable ignorance of some circumstance. For example, it would be possible for a magistrate to act well and meritoriously in hanging a holy man because from testimonies and other legal evidence it sufficiently appeared to him concerning this good man that he was an evil murderer.
> (*In Metaph.* 2.1; Klima et al. 2007, 146)

Buridan's example of a magistrate coming to a particular verdict is instructive. For a judge to come to an appropriate verdict, she does not need to think about all the logical or even natural possibilities. She only needs to consider all the evidence that could be reasonably gathered and that seems to be most pertinent to the present case. For this reason, she could make a mistake. It is possible that despite all the evidence before her, she could miss the fact that the person on trial is innocent. Yet, this error is excusable so long as she practiced due diligence, that is, she did her best to uncover all the available evidence given the constraints on her time and other resources.[11]

Buridan calls these lesser degrees of evidentness "conditional" evidentness, and he proceeds to argue that their existence is enough to push back against those who want to "destroy the natural and moral sciences on the grounds that their principles and conclusions are often not absolutely evident" (*In Metaph.* 2.1; Klima et al. 2007, 146). Here he seems to be worried about the position of his colleague at Paris, Nicholas of Autrecourt (1369), who endeavored to undermine Aristotelian natural science precisely by pointing out that many of its inferences were not warranted by immediate sense evidence in combination with the principle of noncontradiction.[12] For instance, Nicholas challenged the necessity of the inference from perceptible qualities to underlying substances. I am looking at a snowball. I immediately see the spherical shape and the whiteness. I also feel the coldness in my fingers. But what I cannot perceive is any underlying thing in which these properties inhere. Moreover, there is no violation of the principle of noncontradiction to suppose that the whiteness, coldness, sphericity are presently hovering there in the world without anything – the snow itself – underneath them. After all, in the case of the Eucharist, God is able to detach the bread's shape, texture, smell, and color from the bread.[13]

Buridan denies Nicholas's central claim that everything that counts as certain knowledge must conform to his single, very high standard. In many domains, the kind of evidence that we can reasonably expect humans to find and consider given constraints on their powers and resources is sufficient. In the natural sciences, our experiences combined with intellect suffices, and crucially, Buridan thinks that the human intellect can "discern beyond the discernment of the senses." Thus, in the case of possible deception from God, Buridan has this to say:

> In response I say that if the senses are naturally deceived, then the intellect has to investigate whether there are people there or not, and it has to correct the judgments of illusion; but if God absolutely miraculously intervened, then we should conclude that he can do so; therefore

there is only conditional evidentness here, which, however suffices for natural science, as has been said.

(*In Metaph.* 2.1; Klima et al. 2007, 146)

The senses can occasionally deceive us. We can experience optical illusions or even hallucinations. In such cases, Buridan believes that we can and often do detect the error by using our intellects, just as Ghazali observed happens with what the senses tell us about the size of stars. We look at things from different angles. In the case of whether there really is a tree present, perhaps we verify what we see with other witnesses. In short, the intellect is what we use to triangulate and rule out the deceptive information. Yet, once we do this, we need not go further. It is logically possible that God is currently deceiving us. But if this is not something that we can detect, then is it something that we need not consider, unless and until further evidence arises that suggests God is in fact deceiving us. This is why our assent is *conditional*, even though it is warranted.

Buridan's strategy is attractive, but we might ask whether it is justifiable. Nicholas of Autrecourt provides a simple, universally applicable standard of knowledge (Perler 2014, 395). To be sure, it is strict and, thus, it eliminates a lot of what we initially thought were cases of knowing. But one could say that this is just the cost of doing philosophy. Philosophy may start from commonsense, but philosophy cannot stop there; for commonsense is messy and inconsistent. Once the philosopher is done, even a philosopher like Aristotle who tries to preserve much of the "appearances" will find that some aspects of the commonplace are no longer rationally tenable. While we might hope that there are ways to soften our criteria for knowledge in order to preserve more of what we normally take to be knowledge and justified beliefs, the trick is to see whether we can do so in a principled manner.

Here is a place where, as Perler observes, we see some of the metaphysical assumptions at work in scholastic thought, and in medieval thought more generally (2012, 554–5 and 559–61). Scholastics in general assume that cases of deception, even divine deception, will be at most "local" or exceptional cases. The world as a whole is not only lawlike, but also intelligible to the rational human mind. Both of these are consequences of the fact that the world is the creation of an all-powerful and omnibenevolent God. It is assumed that God's goodness will entail that the world behaves according to rules and that God creates His creatures in such a way that they can discern in some measure these rules. Otherwise, they would not be able to achieve their ultimate end, which is to flourish both in this life and, at least for humans, in the life to come. Since God does not create things in order that they suffer, our powers of sensation and intellection must be generally good at tracking the world as it really is. Thus, the possibility that we could be deceived about everything is in a real sense inconceivable from the scholastic framework. It is only when the possibility of a powerful supernatural deceiver is raised without these underlying metaphysical assumptions that the sort of global skepticism countenanced by Descartes becomes feasible.

This might explain why the closest parallel to Descartes's flirtation with a truly global skepticism appears in the medieval world from someone like Ghazali. Ghazali comes from a theological tradition, namely, the Asharite tradition, which started from the fundamental assumption that God's omnipotence means that He is absolutely unconstrained. This leads the Asharites to a number of remarkable conclusions, such as (1) that only God causes things; (2) that while God causes a person to believe or not believe in Islam, the blame falls on the unbeliever and not God; and (3) that there is no independent standard of the good and the bad, and hence, no one can compel God to reward her, even if she is saintly in all her dealings. We will return to some of the metaphysical assumptions that are grounding the Asharite position (Chapter 3, Section 6). For the moment, merely observe that such a picture seems to undermine that aforementioned Aristotelian premise about *intelligibility*. God seems to be so utterly unconstrained that He could be from our perspective utterly capricious. If we combine this with the mystic's claims that the divine realm could behave in ways that are absolutely incomprehensible to our rational intellects, we now have the right metaphysical frame within which global skepticism can gain traction. It also underscores a point that we have already mentioned, namely, that the only way out for someone like Ghazali is divine grace.

Study Questions

1) Try running through a number of scenarios to see how stringent al-Ghazali's indubitability criterion for certain knowledge is. (When you use a knife to carve a slice of bread, can you be certain that your action was what created the slice? When you flick the light switch, was this what caused the light to go on? And so, and so forth.) Given how tough the criterion is, is this an indication that al-Ghazali made a mistake by adopting it? Is there an obvious alternative?
2) Suppose that Ghazali does not receive aid from God on high. Is there any other escape from the "sickness" that someone who has followed and assented to Ghazali's line of reasoning may have?
3) Who do you think has the stronger position, (a) Ghazali or Nicholas of Autrecourt with their strict, universal criteria for certain knowledge, or (b) John Buridan with his more nuanced, contextualist approach?

54 Science, Certainty, and Skepticism

4) Skepticism in a variety of forms, but especially skepticism of the external world, seems to gain an enormous amount of momentum if we assume that God could be deceiving us. Is there any way we could block this assumption? Is there any way that we can be confident – perhaps not absolutely certain, but at least reasonably confident – that God would not deceive us?

Notes

1 For reports of the Pyrrhonist view in Greek sources, see: Diogenes Laertius *Lives*, IX.74–9; Sextus Empiricus *Outlines of Pyrrhonism*, 1.33, Section 226. Watt thinks that the *Mu'anidun* are "almost certainly the Pyrrhonists, as stated in Redhouse's *Turkish Lexicon*" (1962, 6). It may well be the case that Muslim authors thought that Pyrrhonism took the view that we have linked to the Academics. This could be because of the sources that were used by Muslim authors. But given that we don't know what they used, it is hard to make a determination. More research needs to be done about the sources and understanding of skepticism in the medieval Islamic period.
2 For the surviving evidence of Protagoras and his positions, see Laks and Most 2016, Chapter 31.
3 There are several serviceable translations of this work. I will be quoting from Father McCarthy's translation (1980), but I will also provide references to the widely available translation by W. Montgomery Watt (1994).
4 Another book that is often assigned in introductory courses is Plato's *Apology of Socrates*. Even if you have not read this book, you might have heard about Socrates, a self-described "gad fly," and his infamous trial and execution for corrupting the young by practicing philosophy in the marketplace. In Plato's fictionalized account of Socrates's defense speech (the Greek word *apologia* means "defense"), Socrates tells the jurors that he was merely following the will of the gods and that he was not querying the citizens of Athens in order to be a nuisance or to show off, let alone to corrupt the young and set them against their elders. By pointing you to this parallel, I am not suggesting that Ghazali was modelling himself on Socrates per se. Ghazali knew that there was a Greek "theistic" philosopher named Socrates, who was the teacher of Plato. But Ghazali indicates no familiarity with any of the details of Socrates's life or Plato's *Apology*. What it does show (at the very least) is just how pervasive and perennial the suspicion of free thought, long associated with philosophy, is.
5 I must thank one of the anonymous readers for the press for helping me to appreciate this point and for the example of someone pondering whether to take a particular medicine.
6 For more on Ghazali's famous "proto-Humean" challenge to the notion of a necessary connection between cause and effect and more broadly essentialism, see Lagerlund 2020, 65–8.
7 See, for instance, Ibn Tufayl (2009, 82). We will encounter Ibn Tufayl in several later chapters.
8 See also Lagerlund 2020, 46. When I talk of ancestors, I don't mean to imply that Descartes actually got his idea directly from Augustine. Although, it is quite possible that Descartes did. It is less likely that Ghazali had any direct or even indirect influence on Descartes, as the *Deliverance* was never translated into medieval or early modern Latin.

9 The only works of Ghazali that appear to have been translated or circulated to any extent are his *Maqasid*, a summary of the positions of the philosophers, and his *The Incoherence of the Philosophers*. The existence of the former meant that Latin philosophers often cited Ghazali as a philosophical authority on a par with Ibn Sina and al-Farabi, an ironic result given that Ghazali is now usually regarded as a fierce opponent of these individuals. The *Incoherence* was translated into Latin along with Ibn Rushd's point-by-point rebuttal, entitled the *Incoherence of the Incoherence*, in 1328. See Lagerlund (2020, 67), for some brief remarks on the possible impact of the latter book by Ghazali in later medieval Europe.

10 See Lagerlund 2020, 80, and Perler 2012, 555. This seems to be a view that developed later in the thirteenth century. Aquinas, for instance, does not seem to countenance the possibility of divine deception (see *Summa Theologiae* 1.25.3 ad 2).

11 In later periods, this third grade of certainty comes to be known as "moral certainty" (Pasnau 2014a, 367–8).

12 See Pasnau 2014a, 367, and Lagerlund 2020, 81–90. Nicholas was not, however, a skeptic. "He rather adopts a foundationalist position by looking for an infallible foundation for all knowledge – a foundation he locates in the first principle and in immediate sense perception. Consequently, Nicholas rejects all knowledge claims that are not firmly based on this foundation. This does not, however, amount to a denial of the possibility of knowledge" (Perler 2014, 395). In fact, using this foundation, Nicholas developed an atomistic theory of the natural world. See Lagerlund 2012, 480–1, and Pasnau 2011, 412–4 and 665–71.

13 Some philosophers thought that God had to find some subject to put the perceptible qualities of the bread in. But by Nicholas's and Buridan's age, and especially given what the Condemnation of 1277 said about God's power, it seems that this is no longer necessary. According to the Condemnation, one had to assert that any effect, E, caused by some proximate cause, C, can be immediately caused by God without the existence of C. Thus, even though an instance of whiteness usually exists in virtue of some snow in which it inheres, God could make it such that the whiteness exists without the snow or any other natural subject. See Lagerlund 2020, 79 and 84.

Suggestions for Further Reading

For some primary texts on knowledge and skepticism in English, see Klima et al. 2007. For useful overviews and starting points for further research on topics covered in this chapter, I recommend following up on the references that I have made to Lagerlund 2020, Pasnau 2014a, Perler 2012 and 2014. In addition, see Pasnau 2017. For a careful reconstruction of Aquinas's theory of human cognition, which touches on the problem of how we can be sure that our faculties are properly tracking the world, see Stump 2003, Chapters 6 and 7. For a classic exploration of skepticism from a contemporary vantage, see Stroud 1984.

3 The Building Blocks of Reality

3.1 Hylomorphism for Beginners	57
3.2 Universality and Individuality	65
3.3 The Plurality of Forms Debate	76
3.4 Universal Hylomorphism	83
3.5 Are Forms Extended?	88
3.6 Alternatives to Aristotelian Hylomorphism	91

The issues covered in Chapter 2 are not the only ones pertaining to knowledge that will be covered in this book. But before we delve into more investigations of knowledge and its limits, we first need to take a tour through some medieval metaphysics; for as we have begun to see, medieval theories of cognition and knowing are often grounded in a specific set of shared metaphysical assumptions. Accordingly, challenges to a philosopher's understanding of science and cognition often are due to challenges to some of their underlying metaphysical assumptions.

This chapter examines in broad outline the metaphysical framework that underlies both scholastic metaphysics and its correlates in the Arabic-speaking milieu. Specifically, it will give an overview of the synthesis of certain Platonic and Aristotelian elements that contribute to the consensus that the world consists of forms, matter, and their combinations (Section 3.1). The chapter then turns to some of the puzzles that arise as different medieval thinkers begin to work out the details within this framework. One of the first orders of business is to determine which of the components, the form or the matter, is responsible for making an individual thing like others but also different from them (Section 3.2). We will then cover in a cursory fashion the issue of whether a complex composite thing, such as an animal, consists of one or many substantial forms (Section 3.3). Turning to the material side of things, we will ask whether *every* created being must not only have form but also matter (Section 3.4). As we will see, some

DOI: 10.4324/9780429348020-3

philosophers thought that every created being must have some sort of material component or aspect, since matter is what grounds potentiality and possibility. We will then consider the manner in which a form inheres in a body (Section 3.5). For instance, does it exist wholly in each part of the body (that is, "holenmerically") or does it exist partially in one part and partially in another. Finally, we will briefly study some challenges to the matter + form, or hylomorphic, framework both by medieval atomists and by some of the so-called mystics, who seem to have positions that emphasize Platonic metaphysical notions more than Aristotelian ones (Section 3.6). The atomist and mystical doctrines, in particular, will challenge the Aristotelian assumption that some created things are substances that persist in their own right.

3.1 Hylomorphism for Beginners

The dominant theory, or rather family of theories in not only scholastic but also Byzantine, Islamic, and Jewish philosophy is hylomorphism. The word "hylomorphism" derives from two Greek words, *hule* and *morphe*. Thus, "hylomorphism" refers to any theory which posits that the basic building blocks of things are *hule* and *morphe*.

"Hule" is the Greek word that Aristotle chooses to pick out one of his important metaphysical building blocks. We translate this Greek term as "matter." The standard Latin translation of Aristotle's terms is "materia," but there is another late ancient Latin translation of the word, namely, "silva," which in its basic meaning signifies "wood." This alternative translation makes it into the medieval world by means of Calcidius's (mid-third to fourth centuries CE) commentary on Plato's *Timaeus*, which incidentally is one of the few works of Plato in wide circulation in Latin during the Middle Ages. Why would Calcidius do such a thing? Well, it just so happens that the Greek word that Aristotle chose for his metaphysical component has as its root meaning "wood," and if you go back to Aristotle's introduction of his concept of matter in his *Physics* (book 1, chapters 7–9), you will see that many of the objects that he uses to illustrate the concept are artifacts like chairs and beds, which generally are fashioned out of wood. Aristotle intends for us to use the examples of chairs and beds to get at the more basic notion of some malleable element, part, or perhaps aspect of a thing which is brought together and shaped and arranged into a particular object belonging to a recognizable kind. Thus, Aristotle is not like those pre-Socratic philosophers, whom you might have heard about, such as Thales (roughly seventh to sixth centuries BCE), who allegedly posited that everything is made out of water. Aristotle thinks that people like Thales have their finger on something important. Many, if not most, things that we encounter in the material world are made *out of* something. But Thales is wrong to assume that everything is made out of a specific kind of stuff, one with a well-defined, perceptible nature. Indeed, as we will see below, Aristotle and his medieval readers tend to think that matter in its most basic form lacks *most* of the positive characteristics that we perceive in things.

Now turn to the second of Aristotle's basic building blocks. "Morphe" is one of several words that Aristotle uses to talk about the "shape" or "form" of a thing. The more common word that Aristotle uses for referring to forms is "eidos," which Latin translators rendered by either "forma" or "species," depending upon the context. The Greek noun is itself derived from a verb that can mean both "to see" and "to know." Thus, an *eidos* is something either visible or intelligible. But in metaphysical contexts, Aristotle and his medieval interpreters primarily use the term to designate something intelligible.

Aristotle gets his notion of an *eidos* from Plato, who used this term as well as the Greek word "idea" to refer to those abstract, eternal, immutable items that are the foundation of the existence and intelligibility of everything else. You might have already encountered Plato's description of forms, or Platonic ideas, either in your introductory philosophy course or in your wider reading. (It is a famous notion.) As I have also noted, Plato also seems to have developed in broad outline the notion of matter in his *Timaeus*. Nevertheless, speaking very generally, it is Aristotle's particular characterization of form and matter that had the most impact on medieval thought, and it is in Aristotle's hands that matter and form are identified with some key properties.

Form, as we have already said, is aligned with what is visible and, more important, intelligible. Aristotle puts this item *in* the thing and he identifies it as the element, part, or aspect of the thing that is responsible for making that thing what it is and the sort of thing it is, or as medieval thinkers will put it, form is largely if not solely responsible for a thing's *quiddity* (from *quid*, i.e., "what") and its *quality* (from *quale*, or "what kind"). (I add this caveat about responsibility because in the Middle Ages, there is intense debate over whether the matter also enters into an account of a thing's quiddity. There is also considerable debate about whether the matter contributes to any of the qualities that a thing possesses. You will begin to see why these debates arise in what I say next, but bear in mind that we will only make a quick pass at them. Medieval metaphysical debates can be quite complex and subtle.)

One way in to thinking about form's role in determining a thing's quiddity and quality is to reflect on Aristotle's examples of artifacts. Consider a chair, for instance. A chair starts out as, say, some wood. But the wood cannot become a chair until the carpenter imposes a shape and structure on the wood. It is this shape and structure which makes this wood become a certain kind of thing, a chair and not a chest or door. The form imposed by the carpenter is also responsible for the appearance of the chair, its qualities. Each particular chair has a particular shape, a particular color, and so forth. Of course, some of these qualities are partly determined by, for instance, the color, grain, and hardness of the wood. Aristotle and his medieval readers appreciated this fact, and they made sure to accommodate this in their physics and metaphysics. Nevertheless, for the present, the key point is that without the imposition of form (the shape and structure of a chair) on the matter (the wood), this particular chair would not actually exist. It could exist; this wood has the potential to be a chair. But the form must be present for the chair to actually be present. Likewise, if we were to take a hatchet to the chair and chop it to pieces, the wood would lose its shape and structure. It would cease to be a chair. In short, we can now see that for Aristotelians:

- Matter has the *potential* to be F (where "F" stands for some kind of thing, e.g., a chair or a human being)
- Form is responsible for making something that can potentially be F, *actually* be F.

These key features, intelligibility, quiddity and quality, and actuality, are central starting points in the medieval Aristotelian's account of the formal contribution to the construction of objects.

Of course, our actual, particular chair cannot exist without the wood. And in general, particular physical things cannot exist here and now without that out of which they are constructed. Thus, the actuality of the chair, in a sense, is due to not just its form but also to its matter. Indeed, it might go even deeper than this: To have an actual chair existing here and now, you might need to have *matter of a special sort*. It may not need to be wood, but it will have to be a material that has some specific properties. For instance, it is hard to make a chair out of marshmallow, since chairs need to be able to maintain their shape even when pressure is applied to them. This leads many medieval Aristotelians to conclude that what a chair is – the chair's quiddity or *essence* – is to be a certain form combined with a certain kind of matter. Here, for instance, is Aquinas in chapter 2 of his rightly famous little essay *On Being and Essence*:

> In the case of composite substances, then, form and matter is familiar, e.g., soul and body in human being. However, it cannot be said that either one of them alone is called the essence [of the composite substance].
>
> (Thomas Aquinas 2014, 16)

60 *The Building Blocks of Reality*

Aquinas first points to the facts that we have already covered above.

> Indeed, it is obvious that the matter alone of a thing is not the essence. For a thing is both cognizable and ordered in a species or genus by its essence. But matter is not a principle of cognition. Nor is something determined to a genus or species according to its matter, but rather according to what the thing actually is.
>
> (idem)

Matter is only potentially F; the wood is only potentially a chair. Thus, matter by itself cannot make it so that we can know that this thing is a chair, or to allocate this wooden thing to the class of objects that we identify as chairs (that is, to give its "species," *chair,* and the higher category, or "genus", that chairs, tables, couches, and so forth belong to, namely, *furniture*). But Aquinas goes on to stress that form alone cannot do the job either.

> Also, neither can only the form of a composite substance be called its essence, although some philosophers try to assert this. For it is clear from what has been said that the essence is what is signified by the definition of a thing. But the definition of a natural substance contains not only the form but also the matter, for otherwise natural and mathematical definitions would not differ. Nor can it be said that matter is put into the definition of a natural substance as something added to its essence or as a being outside of its essence. For this kind of definition is more proper to accidents, which do not have a perfect essence, and as a result accidents must admit into their definition a subject that is outside their genus. Therefore, it is clear that the essence of a composite substance includes both matter and form.
>
> (idem)

There are several subtleties in this passage which we need to elucidate.

First, notice the argument that the essence needs matter since otherwise a definition of a composite natural thing would not differ from a "mathematical" definition. What does this mean? Here, Aquinas is drawing on a distinction that he receives from Boethius, who in turn ultimately receives it from Plato and Aristotle.[1] In his short, but extremely important, treatise on the Holy Trinity, Boethius tells us that "speculative" thought is divided into three parts: natural science, "mathematical" science, and theological science (*On the Trinity*, chapter 2; Boethius 1973, 9). Theology deals with objects that are separable and entirely removed from the realm of change. In particular, Boethius names God's substance, which is entirely void of matter and change. (Whether there are any other things that are void of matter and change is an interesting question, but it is one which Boethius does not take up here. See our reflections on whether everything else apart from God has matter in Section 3.4.)

We may put theology aside for the moment, since it is the distinction between natural and mathematical science that is of primary concern at present. Natural science, or what is often translated as "physics" (from the Greek word for nature, "phusis"), considers objects in so far as they are changing and combined with matter, or as Boethius goes on to clarify, "it considers the forms of corporeal things along with matter" (idem). Mathematical science, by contrast, also considers changing objects, but it examines these forms of corporeal things in isolation from their matter. In other words, even though corporeal forms cannot in fact exist without being in matter, they can be focused on and studied without any consideration whatsoever of the material elements of the thing.

To see what Boethius and Aquinas have in mind, go back to our example of a chair. In fact, let us add more specificity and detail about the precise kind of chair we will be speculating about. I was once pleased to discover that the furniture and housewares maker Ikea named a line of their products "Arlig." A casual search on the internet suggests that the line has been discontinued, so I cannot confirm what I am about to propose, but let us suppose that, as part of this line of products, Ikea offered an Arlig chair. Now, of course, Ikea produces many, many instances of this one kind of chair. Nonetheless, every *Arlig* chair would conform to a specific formula or recipe, a formula that is different from the specifications for an Ikea *Lak* chair, for instance. This formula would not only specify the shape that each Arlig chair must have in order to be an Arlig chair, it also would include details about what kind of material each Arlig chair must be made from. Perhaps Arlig chairs must all be made from a specific kind of pine that has been treated in a specific sort of way. The formula, then, for an Arlig chair is *a form + pine of a specific kind that has been treated in a specific manner*. If we were to use a different material, say oak or aluminum, what we would produce would be something other than an *Arlig* chair. It is this general formula, a formula that can be repeated over and over to produce many Arlig chairs, that is our analogue for what Aquinas has in mind when he is thinking about an essence. My chair, the one that I am sitting in, has a certain pattern or form exhibited in particular pieces of pine that have all been treated in the specified way. My Arlig chair is an individual instance of the Arlig chair essence.

Thus, a particular Arlig chair is a pattern or form manifested in a certain kind of wood. If we study the chair as physicists, we will study both its pattern and the wood it is realized in. All of this will need to find its way into our account, or scientific story, of Ikea Arlig chairs. But we could also consider the pattern of the Arlig chair by itself and in isolation. When we do that, we will focus only on its geometrical properties, the ratios between the parts in the pattern, and so forth. Aquinas claims that the "mathematical" account or definition that we come up with from such an investigation will be a definition of the pattern only, not of Ikea Arlig chairs.

It is crucial to notice that Aquinas is here drawing a distinction between the matter considered as part of a thing's essence and the matter that is part of a particular, concrete instance of a thing of a certain sort. Our particular Ikea Arlig chair is a particular kind of chair. What it is to be a particular kind of chair is the chair's essence, and this is something that all instances of that kind of chair share. Thus, for any instance of this kind of chair, to belong to that kind of chair, there has to be a certain form combined with a certain kind of matter. But now consider a particular Arlig chair, such as *my* Arlig chair, the one I am sitting on as I write these words. My Arlig chair belongs to a kind of chair, the kind to which all Arlig chairs belong. To be *this* Arlig chair, the one under my body, the form and the matter both need to be particularized even further. How this particularization occurs turns out to be a deep and thorny issue, and it is one that we will return to in Section 3.2.

Notice that after all these twists and turns, we have only managed to fully address the *first* of two reasons why Aquinas thinks that the form alone does not constitute the essence of a composite substance. As a reminder, here is the second argument.

> Nor can it be said that matter is put into the definition of a natural substance as something added to its essence or as a being outside of its essence. For this kind of definition is more proper to accidents, which do not have a perfect essence, and as a result accidents must admit into their definition a subject that is outside their genus.
>
> (Aquinas 2014, 16)

Here Aquinas is utilizing another key Aristotelian distinction, this time between a thing's essence, or core being, and anything that is incidental and peripheral to it. Go back to my particular Arlig chair. Some of the qualities that the chair has seem to be the sorts of qualities that the chair must have to be an Arlig chair. Such characteristics belong in the Arlig chair's definition, which as Aquinas notes, identifies the Arlig chair's essence, the core of what it is to be an Arlig chair and that Arlig chair. But there are other qualities that my particular Arlig chair actually has which it might not have to have – for instance, its color. Ikea furniture has a tendency to come in very neutral browns, grays, whites, and black. But if I assemble my Arlig chair and then paint it bright red, have I compromised its

Arlig-chair-ness? If you think that it has, that is perhaps due to the fact that we are working with an artifact, and not a *substance*. (More on *that* soon!) But I am inclined to think that I still have an Arlig chair, but now my chair is bright red. If that is right, then what I have discovered is that the color of my particular chair is an "accident" of my chair. It is not crucial to the being of this Arlig chair.

With this roughly drawn picture of the distinction between essence and accident, hopefully you can now see why Aquinas thinks that a composite substance's matter cannot be "outside" or added on top of the core of that composite substance. To do so would amount to the claim that the Arlig chair pattern *is* the Arlig chair. The pine could come or go without affecting the core of the Arlig chair. Or, more accurately – since for Aristotelians there is a sense in which matter can "come or go" without the core that is the chair being undermined (see Chapter 4, Section 4.2) – the pine need never have been present for the Arlig chair to exist. But that does not seem to be right. Patterns of chairs are not chairs. Chairs must be some material (again, perhaps even material of a specific sort) that is configured according to the pattern on the blueprint.

Here incidentally is a way in which Aristotelianism diverges from a dominant reading of Plato. On Plato's view, it seems that the chair pattern is the chair. But that is because the Arlig chair is something over and above any of the material things that we call Arlig chairs. What we call Arlig chairs are merely ephemeral "participants" in the Arlig chair. They are "images" of the true Arlig chair and not substances in their own right.

Now is as good a place as any to emphasize that for Aristotle and medieval Aristotelians chairs are *not* substances. No object fashioned by humans is. For Aristotle, the primary reason is that artifacts lack an internal nature. Chairs don't maintain themselves or produce other chairs. Medieval Aristotelians also point to a distinction between God's power and what humans can do. God creates in the strict sense. Humans only manipulate the things that God creates. There is a tendency for medieval Aristotelians to associate creation with the coming to be and passing out of existence of substances, the fundamental items in the world, or as they would put it, with substantial "generation" and "corruption." Once this association is made, certain propositions are entailed that we nowadays might find particularly odd. So, for instance, you will find Aristotelian philosophers in the Middle Ages maintaining that when we put sand and other materials in the furnace, we merely provide the conditions for substantial change. It is God, in fact, who makes one substance (the sand) into another substance (the glass). (This might also seem odd to us, that glass is a substance. But I don't think that there is anything that I could quickly say that would convince you that this view is intelligible.) You will also find Aristotelians maintaining that it is not your mother and father who create you. Your parents provide the conditions. But it is God who is acting in the womb and who really created you.

All of this is just to say that Arlig chairs are not substances. And since they are not substances, for Aquinas and other Aristotelians, they don't have an essence in the proper sense of the term. Why did I allow us to pretend that Arlig chairs might be substances for so long? I did so in part because Aristotle also uses artifacts to motivate hylomorphism. I think he did so for a reason. In artifacts, it is easier to see the two basic elements of things at work and to keep track of them. In true substances, things quickly get much subtler, much more abstract. The Arlig chair is, thus, a heuristic. You must pay attention to the key characteristics of matter and form at work in this case and then analogically extend these characteristics to the cases where medieval Aristotelians think that matter and form are doing their core work.

You may at this point be thinking, "Wait? The Arlig chair case is supposed to be the *easy* case? That was pretty tough going!" I am sympathetic. Metaphysics, and especially medieval metaphysics is quite complicated. I would never dream of subjecting you, fresh out of an introduction to philosophy, to metaphysics in all its subtlety. But for you to get an adequate feel for medieval thought, some metaphysics is essential. I will do my best to guide you through it, because it will only get subtler from here through the end of this chapter (as well as the next). But at the end of the day, yes, metaphysics is hard.

If it is any consolation, medieval readers of Aristotle often felt the same way. Ibn Sina (1037), for instance, reports that he read Aristotle's *Metaphysics* numerous times without any comprehension until finally he chanced upon al-Farabi's (950) exposition of it (Gohlman 1974, 33–5). Only then, he claims, did the scales fall from his eyes. There is a lot of disagreement over the specifics of Aristotle's system. Al-Farabi was leaning on readings of Aristotle by late ancient scholars like Alexander of Aphrodisias (late second to early third centuries). All three of the figures just mentioned have their own understandings of how to interpret and systematize Aristotle's thought. To medieval eyes, Aristotle's pronouncements about form and matter were ambiguous. Accordingly, we find an energetic and concerted attempt by many generations of students and masters, both within the universities and without, to develop this broad but underdetermined framework into a detailed, coherent system. In what follows, we will take a quick survey of some of the most important ambiguities in Aristotle's framework and how medieval thinkers attempted to fill in and develop a full-fledged theory of the construction and composition of the objects that we encounter.

3.2 Universality and Individuality

So far, we have been talking about the patterns, shapes, essences, and even a certain kind of "matter" as if they were general and repeatable *things*. But can there really be any such things? Without question, our language and thought easily accommodates generality. Indeed, if anything, most of our language is about generalities. Most of our nouns and adjectives (as well as their corresponding concepts), like "chair," "dog," "human," not to mention, "green," "triangle," and so on are words (and concepts) that apply to many numerically different instances. Plato and Kamala Harris are both humans. This and that are drawings of triangles. That car and this tree are both the same shade of green. But can it really be the case that there is a *thing*, the green (or, perhaps, green-ness) that is really present in (or otherwise somehow related to) both that car and this tree? If so, then this portion of concrete, mind-independent reality behaves in a manner quite unlike anything else that we encounter. Neither I, nor that tree, nor that car can be present in more than one place at the same time. But if these parts of us, the ones that make it so that we are humans, cars, trees, and green things, are universal things, then it appears that they can behave in this way.

Now, of course, you could just shrug and say, "Yes, that is how things like these behave." In other words, maybe that is just what it is to be a universal thing: it is to be something that can be present in more than one place at the same time. If you asserted something like this, you would be what metaphysicians call a *realist*. Realism has several attractive features. Notice, for instance, that realism easily explains why we apply the same word to many numerically distinct things. It also helps us to explain why it appears that the world naturally breaks down into kinds of things. It seems that Plato, Kamala Harris, and I all belong to the same kind of being. We are naturally grouped together. Indeed, it seems that we apply, or "predicate," the word "human" to all of these things precisely because they all belong to the same kind of thing. These facts about group membership and predication are due to the fact that we all possess as a part of us a thing, the human or humanity.

Sounds pretty good. But here is a rule of thumb that many metaphysicians – and philosophers and scientists, more generally – live by: Only posit a new kind of being if you cannot do without it. This is a formulation of the principle of parsimony, or what is sometimes referred to as "Ockham's Razor." The fact that the Razor is named after the fourteenth-century philosophy and theologian William of Ockham (1347) should be your first clue that not all medieval philosophers were willing to stick with realism. This is because they thought we can explain predication and our habit of grouping things together into natural kinds without having to make any appeal to a special kind of thing. Such philosophers are often referred to as *nominalists*, since they did not deny that universality is a phenomenon of our language and thought. (The word "nominalist" comes from the Latin word for a name or noun, "nomen.") What medieval nominalists denied was the notion that there were any universal *things*.

Here, incidentally, is a place where we need to look beyond the labels that scholars use and to pay attention to what the positions actually are. Oftentimes, especially in contemporary metaphysics, "nominalism" is construed as the denial that there are any "abstract" things. This is a related but importantly different way of construing nominalism. Consider, for instance, the number 1. This number, if it is a thing, would be individual. There is only one number 1. (Of course, there are things that have number, that is, a quantity. But put that to one side.) Thus, the number 1 does not violate the medieval nominalist's position that no thing can be present at more than one place at the same time. But, in point of fact, where is this number 1? It appears that it is nowhere and at no time. Hence, it is said to be "abstract." Some, however, have thought that it is a condition for being a thing that it be somewhere and at some time. Thus, the number 1 cannot be a thing. This would be that anti-abstractionist version of nominalism. No medieval thinker whom I know of is anti-abstractionist.

The principle of parsimony says that if we can do without universal things, then we should not posit that there are any such things. But the trick for nominalists is to show that they can explain all the phenomena that requires explanation. In the seminal medieval discussion of the problem of universals, Boethius mentions the fundamental challenge to nominalism. First, Boethius observes that everyone agrees that universals exist in the understanding. That is, our thoughts and words contain or refer to such generalities. Do these thoughts and words give us an accurate picture of reality or not? Indeed, it would seem that our thoughts and words are derived from our experience of the world out there. So, if our thoughts and words can be universal, doesn't this mean that they arise from the things to which they refer "as those things are disposed"? If the answer is "yes," then universality is a property that belongs to some of the things out there in the world; there are universal things. But now suppose, as the nominalist does, that universality is not a property that things out there possess.

> On the other hand, if the understanding of genus [i.e. a kind of universal] and the rest is taken from the thing, but not in such a way as the thing subjected to the understanding is disposed, then that understanding must be empty. It is taken from a thing, granted, but not as the thing is disposed. For what is understood otherwise than the thing is false. So, therefore, because genus and species do not exist, and the

understanding of them when they are understood is not true, there is no doubt but that all this careful arguing over the five predicables [i.e., kinds of universal, including genera and species] is to be discarded. It is not enquiry about a thing that exists, or about a thing about which something can be understood or stated.

(Boethius, *Commentary on the "Isagoge,"* version 2,[2] book 1, ch. 10; trans. Spade 1994, 23)

If you think that your friend Daniel has brown hair or you say, "Daniel has brown hair," but Daniel does not have brown hair, then as Boethius would put it, your thoughts do not arise as the subject thing is itself disposed. That is, you are thinking and saying something about Daniel that has no basis in reality and hence is not true. Likewise, if you think that whiteness is in both this table and that snowball, but there is in fact no universal thing, the whiteness, out there, then it appears that your thought is not based in reality and that what you are thinking is false.

Recall the format of scholastic disputations that we outlined in Chapter 1 (Section 1.3). Boethius's presentation of the problem of universals can be traced back to Aristotle and it is called "aporetic," since it centers around creating what appears to be an *aporia* (an "impasse"). Aristotle is considered to be the master of attempting to find a "middle way" through an apparent impasse. It is called a middle way, because Aristotle tries his best to acknowledge that each side in the debate has something going for it.

Once we appreciate the Aristotelian, aporetic structure of Boethius's break-out investigation (as it were, a proto-*quaestio*) we can easily see that his challenge to the nominalist is intended only to be provisional. It is part of a series of preliminary arguments both for and against, and like the scholastic disputations that this particular excursus will inspire, Boethius then proceeds to try to find a middle way through the problems that seem to bedevil both the realists and the nominalists.

Boethius does so by immediately acknowledging that the challenge to the nominalist is not refined enough. Of course, our thoughts can present things in ways that are different from the way that they are out there, and indeed, there is a sense in which they must. My friend Daniel is flesh and blood and weighs 210 pounds. But my *thought* of him is neither flesh and blood nor does it have any weight. Closer to the point at hand, Boethius also observes that our minds are able to isolate and consider things as separate, when in fact they are not separable. I can, for instance, consider the blondness of Daniel's hair in isolation from Daniel or even his hair, even though this color cannot in reality be separated from his hair. That is, you cannot find any disembodied blondness floating around in the external world.

Medieval and earlier modern philosophers call the mind's capacity to isolate and consider properties of things without their subject's "abstraction," and as both Boethius and nominalists argue, abstraction is the key to any solution to the problem of universals. Abstraction is attractive, because if done properly, it seems to provide an accurate representation of some aspects of reality. If I consider Daniel's blondness in abstraction, I can learn all sorts of truths about this particular color even though this color exists in my thoughts in a manner different from the way in which it exists in reality. As long as I fixate on aspects of the color that are intrinsic to it, I am on safe footing. I only start to err if I think that this blondness can, say, exist without any body in the external world. I would also err if I thought that there is a unicorn with blonde hair. This is an error brought about, as Boethius observes, by the fact that our minds can decompose and recombine the elements of a complex mental picture (*Commentary on the "Isagoge,"* book 1, ch. 11; Spade 1994, 23–4). The elements of that blonde unicorn are derived from real things, namely, animal horns, horses, and Daniel's blond hair. The error comes when these are recombined and then presented as the thought that there is such a composite object out there in the world beyond my mind.

Abstraction is the key, but there is still more work to be done. Several scholars have observed, for instance, that Boethius's own solution seems to punt when it gets to the difficult part.

> For this reason, when genera and species are thought, their likeness is gathered from the single things they exist in. For example, from single men, dissimilar among themselves, the likeness of humanity is gathered. This likeness, thought by the mind and gazed at truly, is the species. [...] And so these things exist in singulars, but are thought of as universals. Species is to be regarded as nothing else than the thought gathered from the substantial likeness of individuals that are unlike in number.
>
> (*Commentary on the "Isagoge,"* 1.11; Spade 1994, 24–5)

At first, this seems to be a theory friendly to nominalists. The species humanity seems to be a representation of something, a "likeness," that has been abstracted from particular humans. But press just a little further and the proposed solution becomes less clear. What is the nature of this *likeness* that has been gathered from all those human beings? Boethius tells us that this likeness "becomes sensible when it exists in singulars, and it becomes intelligible when it is in universals" (idem; Spade 1994, 25). But that does not answer the question. Again, what is the nature of this likeness in and of itself? It seems to be a reality that transcends both the mind and the sensible world. Now, this might well be the case. Ibn Sina (known in the West as Avicenna) seems to have held such a view, as he famously maintained that horseness is singular in corporeal objects, universal in the mind, but by itself horseness is just horseness.

> For the definition of "horseness" is not the definition of universality, nor is universality included in the definition of "horseness". For "horseness" has a definition that is not in need of the definition of universality, but is [something] to which universality accidentally occurs. For in itself, it is nothing at all except "horseness"; for, in itself, it is neither one nor many and exists neither in concrete things nor in the soul [...] "Horseness", however, is in itself only "horseness".
> (Avicenna, *Metaphysics of 'The Healing'*, book 5, chapter 1, paragraph 4; Avicenna 2015, 149)

This, however, seems to be a collapse into a sort of realism, since now these likenesses, or as later philosophers talk about them, "common natures," seem to be realities with weird properties. No wonder philosophers like Peter Abelard (1142) and Ockham balked!

There is another way in which Boethius's solution seems wanting. These likenesses would appear to be (1) either *derived from*, or (2) the *basis of* the resemblance that one object has to another. If we go in the latter direction, as I think Boethius in fact does, we seem to fall back into Platonism/Avicennism. But suppose Boethius, if pressed, chooses the former path. This way also is treacherous. Remember, we were searching for something out there in the world that serves as the basis or ground for our judgments that this and that belong together and deserve the predication of the same word. So, exactly what is this real basis for such classifications and predications? Boethius doesn't really tell us.

Nominalists like Abelard and Ockham saw that any answer that tried to appeal to anything other primitive resemblance between individuals collapsed into some form of realism.[3] If I and Daniel are both human because we resemble each other in certain respects and this resemblance is due to the fact that I have X and Daniel has X, then it seems impossible to resist the inference that this X – whatever it is – is a thing that is present in more than one place at the same time. The only thing left to say is that Daniel and I are "indifferent." That is to say, I am or have as a constituent X, Daniel is or has as a constituent Y, and X and Y resemble one another in such a way that entitles someone to say that we are both human.

In actual fact, medieval nominalists had a bit more to say. Many of them believed that the mind of God contained the blueprints for all created things. Hence, the X in me and the Y in Daniel are both copies of a blueprint for humans in the Divine mind. (See, for instance, Abelard *Glosses on the Isagoge*; Spade 1994, 41–5, where he discusses the "common cause" of the application of names to things.) This appeal to a paradigm in the Divine mind guarantees that the brute resemblance that we find in X and Y is objective. Medieval philosophers, therefore, could avoid a charge that many realists have lodged at resemblance nominalists, and nominalists in general, namely that they cannot account for the fact that some groupings or classes are natural, whereas others are gerrymandered. David Armstrong, in particular, prefers to frame the problem of universals as the problem of explaining the naturalness of some groupings (2018, see esp. chapter 1). Abelard and others who follow suit seem to have an answer to that challenge.

Let that suffice as an overview of how medieval philosophers attempted to account for the commonality of things. But there is also the flipside to this phenomenon. How do we explain the numerousness of things?

Go back to our homely example of the Ikea Arlig chairs. We observed that they all had something in common which made them Arlig chairs, and not Lak chairs or Arlig tables. But there is also something else true of them, they are all numerically distinct from one another. This Arlig chair is not that Arlig chair. This is the other side of the metaphysical coin: How do we explain the fact that there are two Arlig chairs as opposed to merely one? This is known as the problem of individuation.

Our nominalists have a ready answer to the problem of individuation: It is not a *problem* at all. Everything, in their view, is already particular and individual. Nothing's particularity needs explaining. Realists, on the other hand, need to explain how a common essence, for example, the common essence of the Arlig chair, becomes many instances of it.

Before we proceed any further, take heed: In this Introduction, I will be treating "individual" and "particular" as synonyms. However, you should be aware that if you dare to scratch the surface, subtleties await. To give one example, some metaphysicians think that while all individuals are particulars, the converse is not true. In their eyes, there is something more that must obtain for a thing to be an individual. For instance, one might think that an individual is a complete, independently existing particular. Hence, Socrates is an individual, since he is a particular human being, but Socrates's hand or his paleness, while also particular, are not themselves individuals. For many of the subtleties that come with the problem of individuation, I recommend that you seek out and read Jorge Gracia's *Introduction to the Problem of Individuation in the Early Middle Ages* (1984/88). However, I think that we can put such nuances to one side and consider in broad terms how realists think about causes that make things many instances of one kind.

A realist account of individuation that was quite popular early on started with the observation that, while individuals are the same with respect to the essence, or "substance," they differ from one another with respect to many of their other properties. Daniel and I are both human. We have the same substance. But Daniel is blond and I have gray hair. Daniel is six foot five inches and I am only six feet tall. We have different weights and different bodily proportions. He is a violin maker and I am a professor of philosophy. Now, considered one at a time, none of these properties is essential to either one of us. I could have been a garbage collector, not a professor. Daniel could have been an accountant and not a violin maker. He and I can both lose and gain weight. At one point, my hair was also blond. And so on and so forth. These properties are ones that we happen to have, and if we lost any of them and gained another, it seems that nothing about us has essentially changed. That is why medieval philosophers call such properties "accidents" (from the Latin word *accidere*, "to happen to").

These accidents, when taken in isolation, may not be significant. But when we consider them collectively, they seem to be sufficient to distinguish Daniel from me.

> Socrates is called an individual, and so is this white thing and the one who is approaching, the son of Sophroniscus (if Socrates is his only son). Such things are called individuals because each of them consists of characteristics the collection of which can never be the same for anything else. For the characteristics of Socrates cannot be the same for any other particular. But the characteristics of human – I mean, of human in general – are the same for several things, or rather for all particular humans insofar as they are humans.
> (Porphyry, *Isagoge*, "On species"; Spade 1994, 6–7, here slightly modified)

Think of it this way: If you consider all of the properties that Daniel and I have at this moment in time, there will be at least one accident that he has that I do not. Indeed, in our cases, there are a whole host of them. Thus, a comprehensive list of my properties and a comprehensive list of Daniel's properties seem to be the difference maker. Might they, therefore, be the metaphysical cause of our individuality?

Boethius flirts with this idea of accidents being the principles of individuation. At first, it appears that he merely echoes Porphyry and suggests that it is a collection of accidents that does the trick.

> But a variety of accidents make numerical difference. For three humans differ with respect to their accidents, not with respect to genus or species.
> (Boethius, *On the Trinity*, 1.56–63; my translation)

72 The Building Blocks of Reality

But notice that Boethius immediately proceeds to something a bit deeper.

> Even when the mind separates all [other] accidents from them, there is still a distinction among them with respect to place, which is something we can in no way pretend to be one. For two bodies cannot occupy one place, which is an accident.
>
> (idem)

Boethius is thinking about spatial location but translated to a contemporary mode of thought, we could venture to say that the individuating principle is spatio-temporal location. The thought is well motivated. Suppose that Daniel and I were identical twins. Imagine further that he and I had the exact same sets of experiences. As hard as it might be to pull this off in actual fact, it seems that we could make it so that we are absolutely alike in our properties, save but one: we cannot occupy the very same location in space at the very same time. Perhaps the point is even easier to see in the case of our Ikea chairs. They might have every accidental feature in common, but they cannot be the same in every respect. One was made a little bit before the other, and even if that is not true, they nevertheless occupy different places.

As compelling as this proposal might be, many medieval thinkers see a fatal flaw. Abelard, for instance, admits that when it comes to perceptual discernment, accidents help us to pick out individuals and then reidentify them later. But the accidents cannot be the metaphysical cause of the individuality of numerically distinct substances like Daniel and me. This is because accidents are taken to be things that depend upon their substances. This they took to be an intrinsic part of the metaphysical framework that they inherited from Aristotle. Indeed, it was usually held that an individual accident depended so much on the individual substance in which it "inhered" that it was impossible for *it* to transfer to another individual substance. The importance of this claim will be something that we return to in the next chapter (Section 4.2, where we call it the No Transfer Thesis). Abelard utilizes this feature of accidents to launch a devastating attack on the theory that things are individuated by their accidents.

> We, however, wish to say that, if individual humans such as Socrates or this human are made by accidental properties, then the accidents that have completed the individual are naturally prior to the individuals that they belong to, just as rationality is to a human or whiteness is to a white body. But then accidents cannot be present in the individual.
>
> (Abelard *Glosses on the "Isagoge"*; Abelard 1919, 64, lines 7–11; my translation)[4]

There is a lot of technical language in this passage. The central point that Abelard is trying to make is that the thesis under examination gets the order of nature backward. According to Aristotle, it should be the case that substances come "first," so to speak – not necessarily earlier in time, but first in a metaphysical sense. It is by existing that they make it so that accidents can exist. The thesis that accidents make individuals seems to reverse the story of what comes first in this metaphysical sense. To drive this point home, Abelard immediately adds the following corollary.

> Moreover, since the name "Socrates" denotes a certain accident, how will this be *present in*, that is, be an *accident of* Socrates, for whom this cannot come or go without causing corruption? The reason is this: Since Socrates is said to be "this sort of human", when the accident that causes the existence of the "this sort" is removed, the "this sort" cannot remain. But then *Socrates* cannot remain when the accident is destroyed, just as no human, in that he is human, can persist if the rationality through which he exists is removed.
>
> (idem, 64, lines 14–19; my translation)

Remember, an accident is supposed to be the kind of property that can come and go without any consequence to me in so far as I am this human being. Rationality, on the other hand, is a property that is essential to me. If I were to cease to be rational, I would cease to be human (maybe – see Chapter 4, Section 4.4). But if accidents make me the individual substance who I am, it seems that they longer can come and go so innocently. Rather, my blondness and my weight now seem to be as important to me being me as my rationality is. As we will see in a bit more detail soon enough (Section 4.2), my persistence might in fact be that tenuous. But if we go down this path, we seem to be blowing up the Aristotelian framework in the process. Abelard believes – and not without some justification – that his opponents will not want to dispense with the Aristotelian framework, a framework that clings to a strict distinction between essence and accident.

At this point, you might be squirming in your seat, thinking, "Isn't it obvious? It is the *material* that individuates." This certainly seems like the right move if we return to the Ikea chairs. The blueprint is the same for all the Arlig chairs, but the pattern or form inscribed in the blueprint is realized in different bits of matter. This chair here is made out of this wood; that one out of another pile of pine. Yet, the way that I just made the point only serves to push the question back one step. What individuates the piles of pine? Suppose we persist until we get to some sort of material substrate underneath it all. Maybe there is something like a shapeless, colorless, malleable substance that is ready to be shaped and formed into any old thing. Something like this metaphysical clay seems to be countenanced by Plato in the creation story that he works up in his *Timaeus* (50b–51c), which Latin metaphysicians would have been aware of thanks to Calcidius's partial translation and commentary. In late antiquity, a number of Platonic and Aristotelian thinkers made use of the image of a signet ring, that is, a ring that had a particular pattern carved into it and which an authority figure then pressed into softened wax to form a copy of the image. Forms, it was suggested, were like the pattern in the ring. Concrete material things were like the copies of the pattern impressed in the malleable wax.

Of course, we need to tread carefully at this point. Just *how* featureless must this matter be in order to do its job as individuator? Based on the pressures that got us to this point, it would appear that matter ought to be devoid of *every* feature that is repeatable and thus itself in need of an explanation for how it is individuated. For instance, matter cannot have as one of its intrinsic, essential properties any specific color, since color is a universal, whereas in order to transmit individuality to other things matter must be fundamentally individual. And yet, any form that we can think of seems to be repeatable. Aquinas held that prime matter was so featureless – so devoid of any actuality (since, after all, actuality is due to form) – that it was not even essentially extended or spread out.[5] This may be one reason why Aquinas famously maintained that individuation is caused not by prime matter but rather by something that he refers to as "designated matter" (*materia signata*) (Aquinas, *On Being and Essence*, chapter 2; Aquinas 2014, 20–1). Hence, it would stand to reason that matter intrinsically and in essence is absolutely featureless.

This conclusion, however, brings in its own puzzles. If matter has *no* features, how can it exist at all? In other words, why have we not gone all the way to a radical form of Platonism, where everything that exists is the effect of some emanation from the One true, immaterial, and supra-intelligible being?[6] Why do we not conclude that everything that exists is some kind of spiritual substance? (See Section 3.6, for more on some of these versions of Platonism.) Medieval Aristotelians did often agree that pure or "prime" matter is at the very limit of being. But this by itself did not deter some of them from holding that prime matter *is* in some low-level way, and that it is one of the fundamental components of the universe. Here I quote Marsilio Ficino (1499), because while he presents his philosophy as an exposition of Platonism (note, specifically, the title of his work), his discussion of matter is quite Thomistic.

> For matter is simple, because neither is it composed from matter and form, since it is the prime and formless potentiality, nor does it require

a specified mass of parts for its existence, since in its natural origin it precedes the dimensions of quantity. [...] Matter cannot be changed from what it is except by being changed into nothing.
(*Platonic Theology* 5.4.9–10; Ficino 2002, 25–7)

Prime matter is. It is not nothing at all; it is a step – but only one step – above nonbeing. However, because it is intrinsically form*less*, considered as it is by itself, matter is "potentiality" pure and simple (compare, e.g., to Aquinas *Summa Theologiae* 1.76.1, with discussion in Hughes 2002).

If you have a hard time wrapping your head around a thing that has no actuality at all, you are not alone. Numerous scholastic philosophers following in Aquinas's footsteps expressed concerns about prime matter as he had construed it. Since we are primarily concerned in this section with matter's alleged role as the *individuator* of things, here is one way to pose a problem for the notion of matter as pure potential: Purely potential stuff, stuff lacking any sort of characteristic at all, would not be capable of marking out this instance of a universal form from another.[7] Matter has to intrinsically possess some sort of individuating marks or designations before it can be the ground for subsequent individuation. There are other reasons as well why many later scholastics pulled back from the edge and concluded that even formless matter had some very low-level kind of actuality. We will not pursue those twists and turns in a debate which, as some scholars have argued, ultimately leads to early modern, "corpuscular" theories of matter.[8] However, it is worth noting that by giving matter its own low-level actuality, we may have opened the door to problems pertaining to the identity or material things both at a moment in time (Section 3.5) and across time and change (Section 4.2).

Note another potential problem that haunts any attempt to identify matter as the cause of individuality. Some individuals do not seem to have matter. For instance, Aquinas and many others think that angels are purely spiritual substances. Of course, they could be wrong. Indeed, the very fact that angels are individuals might entail that angels have matter after all (see Section 3.4). Aquinas's own solution in *On Being and Essence* is to propose that each angel is its own unique species, that is, the essence of each angel is not repeatable (*On Being and Essence*, ch. 5; Aquinas 2014, 29). But this is not the only way out of the problem of explaining the individuality of immaterial beings. One could, for instance, posit that in addition to universal substantial forms, accidents, and matter, there are also special metaphysical entities whose sole job is to individuate. These are John Duns Scotus's (1308) famous *haecceities* (or "thisnesses").

But at this point, we have probably ventured as deep as we dare for a first foray into this particularly subtle terrain. Instead, let us turn to another issue pertaining to forms that exercised the minds of the greatest medieval metaphysicians.

3.3 The Plurality of Forms Debate

In addition to the question of whether the formal components of things that we find outside of the mind are individual or universal, medieval thinkers tried to determine just how many forms a complex mundane object, like a stone, a tree, or especially, a human, has.

In one sense, practically everyone believed that a complex mundane object has a multiplicity of forms. For, as we have noted already, Aristotelians maintain that an everyday particular object has both an essence, which at least in part consists of a substantial form, and accidents. But there are compelling reasons to think that when it comes to the core of a thing, its essence, here too there is a plurality of substantial forms. There are also reasons to resist this thought.

The view that an object has a multiplicity of substantial forms occurs quite early in medieval thought. It is encouraged by a reading of Aristotle's logical works, especially in tandem with Porphyry's *Isagoge*. For in the *Isagoge*, we get the suggestion that a thing's specific form is a composite of a generic form with numerous substantial differentiating forms.

> Just as things consist of matter and form, or have a structure analogous to matter and form – for instance a statue is made up of matter (the bronze) and form (the shape) – so too the specific man in common consists of an analogue of matter (the genus) and of form (the difference). The whole, rational-mortal-animal, is man – just as for the statue.
>
> (Spade 1994, 9–10)

In his commentary on this passage, Boethius stresses Porphyry's use of the term "analogous," and thus he concludes that "for a species the genus is a kind of matter and the difference a form that is something like a quality" (*In Isag.* ed. 2, book 4, ch. 11; Boethius 1906, 268.21–2). But even so, Boethius concedes that the structures of a hylomorphic composite and an incorporeal species are similar enough that it is proper to speak this way, and indeed, nothing he says here or in other places in his commentary on the *Isagoge* would suggest that such mereological terminology as "whole" or "conjoining" is wrong or misleading when applied to the structural analysis of these forms. Thus, it is not surprising that many later medieval thinkers saw nothing wrong with thinking of the composite structure revealed in a definition as a kind of true whole.[9]

Now, given that (1) a concrete human being such as Daniel is a composite of a specific substantial form (humanity) plus matter plus an array of accidental forms, and that (2) Daniel's humanity itself seems to be composite, it would stand to reason that (3) Daniel has a set of substantial forms, layered one on top of the next to arrive at one complete, concrete human being. The conclusion identified as (3) is a popular early realist account of the metaphysical construction of concrete, individual substances. Here is Abelard's description of the theory, which he attributes to his own former teacher, William of Champeaux:

> Some people take "universal thing" in such a way that they set up essentially the same substance in things diverse from one another through forms. This substance is the "material essence" of the singulars it is in. It is one in itself, and diverse only through the forms of its inferiors. [...] For example in single, numerically distinct humans there is the same substance *human*, which becomes Plato here through these accidents and Socrates there through those accidents. [...] Likewise, they also posit one and essentially the same substance *animal* in single animals that differ in species. They draw this substance into diverse species by taking on diverse differences [i.e. substantial differentiating forms]. For example, if out of this wax I make on the one hand a statue of a human and on the other a statue of an ox, by adapting diverse forms to entirely the same essence that remains the same throughout.
> (Abelard, *Glosses on Porphyry's "Isagoge"*; translation from Spade 1994, 29–30, with minor changes)

On this way of seeing things, the definition is a recipe for how to construct an individual substance. If you want to create an individual ox, take the form *substance* and first add the form *animate* to make it *animal* (for the definition of animal is animate substance), then add *irrational* to make it *irrational animal*, and finally add the other differentiating forms that together yield *ox*. Once there, all you have to do is individuate using either accidental forms or matter, or perhaps both. To make Daniel, start with *substance*; add *animate* and *rational* to make *rational animal*, which is what a human is. Then individuate accordingly.

Abelard famously found fault with William's material essence realism, but he did not do so because it countenanced a plurality of forms. Indeed, in his discussion of creation, Abelard suggests that God creates substances by adding successive substantial forms (King 2004, 75–6). Thus, a nominalist could and did also maintain the layer-cake account of the composition of a thing. But with the arrival of Aristotle's *Metaphysics*, Latin philosophers were confronted with another face of Aristotle and many of them perceived in this work especially, an iron-clad rule about substances: No actual substance can consist of actual substances. Many medieval readers saw this rule in both Aristotle's treatment of the problem of the unity of a definition, in *Metaphysics* 7.12, and in his discussion of the composition of a substance in chapter 17 of the same book. Aquinas, in particular, sees Aristotle's arguments in 7.12 as lending support to the thesis that a substance can only have one substantial form (see Galluzzo 2013, vol. 1, 298–9). The inclusion of "actual" is important, since following Aristotle, nearly everyone believes that material things at least are composed of matter and substantial form, and these two parts must be substances (see Aristotle, *On the Soul* 2.1, and *Metaphysics* 7.3). Matter and form could be exempted, since they were thought to be "incomplete" substances; they strive to be together, matter underlying form, form inhering in matter. This is quite plain if we hold that matter is always potential in some very real sense – perhaps even merely potential and possessing no actuality when separated from form. But even substantial forms are thought to be in need of their mate. In fact, this is one reason why many medieval thinkers will go on to argue that a soul, strictly speaking, is not a form (see Chapter 4, Section 4.1).

But why would Aristotle maintain this rule? Here is one good reason: If form and matter are intrinsically incomplete and in need of their mates in order to actually be, then their actual combination would seem to form the tightest of unities. Perhaps an image will help here. Take two white shapes and press them together. If you can still see the line between them, then there is a sense in which we still have two shapes that are merely adjacent to one another. Of course, the two contiguous but discrete shapes form one bigger shape in some sense of "one." Medieval Aristotelians will call this an "accidental unity." But to get a shape that is truly one – one in the strongest sense – we need to somehow erase the boundaries between the two original shapes and fuse the two together into one seamless unit. By analogy substantial form and matter form a continuous, seamless "substantial" unity. But this is only possible because their "edges," so to speak, are not clearly defined. A whole composed of two actual substances cannot form a substantial unity. Or rather, more precisely, two actual substances cannot come together to form a substantial unity if they continue to maintain their clear and definite "edges." Substantial unity, in other words, can only arise if the two actual components cease to be actual and become merely potential.

Now, if you think that this sort of erasure of the boundaries of actual substances requires some sort of special power, you are not alone. In fact, a number of medieval thinkers maintained that substantial transformation is literally an act of creation, and since creation is an act reserved solely for God, only God can literally bring about substantial transformations.

Abelard, for instance, claims that when humans make glass (which as I noted above was considered to be a substance), all they do is gather all the materials and set up the right conditions. It is God who works on the sand in the furnace and transforms the sand into glass (Abelard 1970, 419–20).

But let us get back to the main issue at hand. This thesis about substances and their parts leads a number of philosophers to reject the idea that a concrete individual can have more than one substantial form. While a form might be incomplete in the sense that it needs matter, it is harder to see how form could be in need of another form. Forms, remember, are the actualizers. What they actualize is matter. Hence, to combine two forms into something worthy of being called a substantial unity, at least one of the forms would seem to be more "material" in its nature than the other. Of course, that is precisely what Porphyry's analogy to matter and form suggests. But many philosophers felt that this could be nothing stronger than a metaphor. In reality, forms were aligned with actuality, matter with potentiality and receptivity to form. A form with intrinsic potentiality and receptivity for another form seems to be an oxymoron.

Let us call those who hold that each substance has one and only one substantial form "unitarians." (We do so, since that is often what they are called in the literature.) The trouble with the unitarian position is that it does not seem to accommodate all the facts. This is especially true if we turn to the biological facts about humans. I have already mentioned in passing that many medieval thinkers resist the notion that the soul is a form. But as Aristotle's works become more widely known and assimilated, the dominant view in Western universities becomes Aristotle's thought that the soul is the substantial form of a living thing (*On the Soul* 2.1–2). As substantial form, a soul is responsible for the existence, unity, stability, and activity of the living animal. Different powers that a living thing possesses are attributable to the kind of soul it has. Thus, plants have the powers of maintaining their stable existing by means of incorporating nutrients, metabolizing, and repairing damage to itself. They are also capable of reproduction. Plants then have "nutritive" or "vegetative" souls. Animals have these powers as well as more complex ones, in particular, the powers to move about and to sense. (Indeed, as Aristotle argues, in order to be able to move successfully, an animal must be able to sense its surroundings.) Thus, animals have at least a "sensitive" soul. But some animals have even more powers, specifically, the powers associated with thought. These rational animals are humans. Humans, then, have "rational" souls. So far, the unitarian can accommodate this without too much trouble. Aristotle taught that the higher kinds of souls not only have their special powers, they also possess the powers, of lower kinds of life. Hence, the rational soul is responsible not only for reasoning but also for sensing, movement, metabolism, and reproduction.

80 *The Building Blocks of Reality*

The difficulty arises when we think about gestation in the womb. For it appears that well before a fetus belonging to the species *Homo sapiens* has the capacity to think, it exists, and is alive. While in the womb, not only can it metabolize, but it can also move and perhaps even sense – or at least, it begins to move after some time during its tenure in the womb, up to a certain point, it may be no more complex than a plant. So, what are we to make of this? If it really is true that the fetus is incapable of thinking, then it seems to lack the rational soul. And, before it could move under its own power, the fetus seems to lack even a sensitive soul. But the fetus nevertheless is alive, and hence ensouled. What kind of soul does it have?

One option would be to deny the appearances and assert that the rational soul is already present. It just hasn't had the chance to manifest its powers. Surely the soul needs certain organs or instruments to do all the things it is capable of. So, the fact that we don't see a fetus thinking does not necessarily entail that it lacks that power.

Interestingly, at least some unitarians did not pursue that line of thought. Roland of Cremona (1259), a master of arts at the University at Bologna and, like his fellow Dominican Thomas Aquinas, a unitarian, starts out by rehearsing an argument from embryological development.

> This is the reason why they have claimed that there are three souls in a human. They observe that an embryo grows before either the sensible soul or the rational soul is present. Yet, growth does not occur without a vegetative soul. Thus, the vegetative soul has been infused before the sensible, and the sensible before the rational.
> (Roland of Cremona *Summa,* excerpt quoted by Lottin [1957, 465] from MS Paris Maz. 795, f. 34va; my translation)

Roland concedes that the phenomenon is as it appears: at some point the fetus really is incapable of movement and thinking. But, in his view, the inference to the thesis that a human has three souls does not go through.

> But they will find this way blocked. The embryo does not grow or vegetate[10] without the vegetation of its mother, since before the rational soul is infused in it, the embryo is like some kind of part of the mother, as there is continuity between the uterus and the embryo through the umbilical cord. In a human, the sensible and vegetable are powers of the rational soul.
> (idem)

The fetus grows and is alive because it is a part of its mother and thus is governed by her soul. It does not have its own soul. And thus, when the fetus is finally given its own soul (by God, you should know) and becomes an independently existing human being, the only soul that needs to be acquired is the rational soul.

While this is a clever response, it is not the only one utilized by unitarians. Perhaps the most famous, if not notorious, theory of embryology is the one suggested by Thomas Aquinas. He also maintained that at certain stages of embryological development, the fetus had its own soul, but that soul was not a rational soul. Nevertheless, the fetus does not develop by having higher order souls layered on top of persisting lower souls. The transformations that occur are much more radical. There is literally a series of substantial transformations that occur during gestation in the womb. First, there is effectively a vegetable. This thing is corrupted – that is, eliminated – to make way for a brute animal, as one form is removed and another takes its place. Finally, sometime prior to birth, this brute creature is in turn corrupted and the brutish soul is removed from the matter and replaced by a single, rational soul.[11]

Aquinas's position has perhaps the uncomfortable implication that it posits radical yet imperceptible metaphysical changes. It certainly does not *appear* that one substance is being replaced by another in the womb. The process seems to be much more continuous than that. Similar troubles arise for Aquinas and other unitarians at the end of a human's life. We may refer to this as the scar problem (Pasnau 2014b, 645–6, and Pasnau 2011, 581–2).[12] The problem can be formulated as follows. Captain Hook, let us suppose, has a distinctive scar on his right cheek, which is acquired during one of his many fights. This scar is, of course, an accident inhering in Hook's flesh, and thus, like all accidents, it seems to depend upon the flesh for its continued existence. Indeed, as we have already noted, particular accidents seem to depend so strongly upon the particular substances in which they exist, that they cannot transfer from one particular substance to another. Let us call this the No Transfer Thesis (see also Chapter 4, 4.2). Unitarianism in addition holds that Hook's flesh depends upon only one substantial form, Hook's rational soul. This means that if Hook's soul were to leave his body, Hook's flesh would not be Hook's flesh anymore. Indeed, it would not even be flesh (see Section 3.6). Now, let us suppose that Hook dies. Hook is gone. Because of the unitarian thesis, Hook's flesh is gone. But the scar still seems to be present. How can that be? The scar is a particular accident belonging to Hook. The No Transfer Thesis entails that it cannot survive Hook's disappearance. But there it is, or least, there is something that in every inspectable way is just like Hook's scar.

Aquinas and other unitarians will have to bite the bullet and claim that the scar in the corpse – which again, is not Hook – is a new accident that just so happens to resemble in every respect Hook's accident. This is surely a possibility. There is nothing logically incoherent about the position. Nonetheless, it is a particularly tough bullet to bite for Aristotelians, given that Aristotelianism prides itself on saving as much of the appearances of things as it can.

For many, however, the scar problem and other similar cases suggested that Hook's flesh (or rather something in the vicinity, since Hook's *flesh* is also gone) might in fact have its own substantial form. This would allow one to keep the No Transfer Thesis – a thesis, incidentally, that no prominent scholastic seems to have seriously challenged – but also preserve what seemed to be obvious, namely, that the scar persists even though Hook himself is no more. Indeed, if anything, the plurality of forms position is the more popular one in thirteenth- and fourteenth-century scholasticism. The bigger concern is determining *how many* additional substantial forms are required. Some thought that all we need is an additional "form of the body" to preserve everything that needs preserving. But perhaps more than two are needed.

We will not dive into those debates. But it is worth remarking on one common feature in many versions of the plurality of forms thesis. Recall Porphyry's suggestion that the more general substantial forms were importantly analogous to the matter in a statue, and that the differentiating forms were analogous to the statue's form. This idea was adapted by proponents of the plurality of forms and presented as a theory about the "grades of forms." In brief and broad terms, the idea is this. There is actually only one soul, one complete substantial form, in a human being, but this soul is composed of layers of incomplete formal elements. These formal elements are not full-fledged forms because intrinsically they possess unrealized potentialities. They need mates in the guise of additional formal elements that actualize and make the generic element into a complete form with a definite character. An analogue would be contemporary reflections on the relation between determinable and determinate properties. Think about *color* as such, not any specific color, just color. Try to picture it in your mind. Chances are that you cannot. Rather, when I say "color," if anything arises in your mind, it is a picture of some determinate color, a certain shade of red or green, say. Clearly, this specific shade of red is both red and a color. Redness and colored-ness are part of what makes it what it is. But these generic parts of this specific shade cannot stand alone by themselves. They can only appear concretely or in the mind once they have been completed in one determinate way or another.

Observe, then, that the pluralist has to backtrack to some degree from the thought that a form being *matter-like* is oxymoronic. But the theory only backs away as much as it needs to. This is why the generic and differentiating elements are merely formal elements and not full-fledged forms. In other words, mainstream scholastic pluralism is a compromise position. It attempts to find a middle path between two austere, yet inflexible and thus untenable positions. Such is what often happens in medieval metaphysics and, I would suggest, in metaphysics more generally.

3.4 Universal Hylomorphism

We have already asked whether everything that is actual in any sense of the word has form (Section 3.2). One of form's main jobs is to make the potentialities in things actual. It is responsible for a thing actually being fully defined with respect to the kind to which the thing belongs, with respect to precisely how much space it takes up, with respect to what shade of color it is and what powers and abilities it has, and so forth. But if we follow that idea to its logical conclusion, it would appear that pure matter is pure potency, which is about as close to being nothing at all as it seems something can be. If a purely potential existent is incoherent, as some medieval philosophers concluded, first matter will have to have some sort of actuality and determination that it possesses all on its own, and in this case, actuality will not be the sole preserve of form. The point of rehearsing this line of reasoning again is to remind you that peculiar things can happen at the limits of hylomorphic analysis, and perhaps adjustments and compromises will have to be made. Now, let us turn to form's mate, matter, and let us push that concept to some of its apparently logical conclusions. Again, I will suggest that such an investigation will lead us to strange places, and some of the hard Aristotelian dualities may need to be softened.

As we have seen, from the medieval Aristotelian perspective, concrete, determinate, perceptible objects need not only form, but also matter to be present in the world. They might need matter in order to be an individual thing. Even if individuation is caused by something else, matter is often given credit for many of the material and sensible features of things. So, every material thing is a combination of form with matter. But now here is a question: Is *every* created thing either matter or composed of matter? The addition of the word "created" is crucial, since no one – at least no one in the traditions we are examining – maintains that God has matter. There is also a sense in which the answer is obviously negative, in so far as forms are created by God, and forms are not matter or material. But as we have already noticed, a common thought in medieval hylomorphic theory is that forms properly speaking are "incomplete" beings. They are by their nature in need of their complement, matter. So, here is a refined version of the question, a version that does grab the attention of medieval metaphysicians: Does every complete created being have matter? To see why this is not an absurd question consider Albert the Great's (1280) reconstruction of the reasoning behind a position maintained by the great Andalusian Jewish philosopher and poet, Solomon ibn Gabirol (1057/8). Ibn Gabirol's dialogue the *Fountain of Life*, originally written in Arabic, was translated into Latin and intensively studied by the first generations of scholastic thinkers. Ibn Gabirol is perhaps most famous for his claim that every complete created being is a composite of matter and form. This is the view that scholars now refer to as "Universal Hylomorphism." Here is Albert's reconstruction of the motivation for Universal Hylomorphism.

> For instance, the characteristic features of first matter are to receive, to be the first subject of, and to hold within itself form; also to exist through itself, given that existing through itself is the same as not existing in something else. The characteristic features of form, by contrast, are to be in something else, to make matter actual, to delimit the potential of matter, and to be a part of that which is, or of a composite substance.
>
> (Albert the Great, *De causis et processu universitatis a prima causa* ["Concerning causes and the procession of everything from the first cause"], book 1, tract. 1, ch. 5; Albert the Great 1993, 10, column B, my translation)

Some of the characteristic features of matter that Albert lists were not embraced by everyone. For instance, Albert suggests that matter can exist "through itself," whereas form seems to require the existence of matter. Many scholastics would beg to differ, including Albert's student and friend Thomas Aquinas (see Chapter 4, Section 4.1). But some of the other features mentioned are widely held:

- Matter is that which receives or takes on form, and form is that which inheres in matter.
- Matter is thus the underlying subject or substrate of form. It is often thought to be the thing that guarantees continuity of existence through both accidental and substantial changes.
- Form actualizes and delimits the potentialities that are present in matter. Hence, it is the matter that ultimately provides the range of possibilities that the thing can have.

This last feature is especially important because it helps to explain why Universal Hylomorphism only covers created things, and not God as well. Things with matter have potentialities, some of which are presently unactualized. This, incidentally, is a good thing, since it allows created things to *change*. On the Aristotelian analysis of change, something changes because it loses one form and takes on another, and as these forms come and go, some actualities are reduced to mere potential, and other possibilities are realized. If I stand up from my writing desk, go outside, and get sunburned, all of these changes are ultimately possible because I am material. Now, God is usually defined as a perfectly complete being, which medieval philosophers usually interpret to mean, a being whose attributes are fully actualized. If something were merely potential in God, then God would not be perfect. If having matter is to have at least some potentialities that are not actual, God cannot have matter.

That still leaves a whole host of beings in the standard medieval universe that may or may not have matter. Consider angels. Angels are often said to be purely spiritual beings (or as Aquinas for instance would say, "intellectual" and "immaterial" substances), because their essence and existence is entirely separate from matter (*On Being and Essence* 5; Aquinas 2014, 28–30). In fact, for Aquinas and others who hold this view, this separateness is a sign of their greater degree of actuality and thus explains their relative standing in the hierarchy of beings.

And yet, angels are not God. Indeed, they are thought to possess properties and powers that would seem to require something at least analogous to matter. Aquinas's contemporary St. Bonaventure (1274) is vexed by this thought, and his treatment of the composition of angels is especially astute. Bonaventure points to four characteristics of angels that seem to require a material principle.

- Angels can change. But everything that changes must have a source of potentiality in them. This source of the potentiality for change seems to be matter.
- Angels both act and passively undergo things. But the source of these two cannot be the same. Thus, the angel must be composite. The source of the angel's acts is its form. But the source of its passively undergoing things would seem to be not a form, but matter, since passively undergoing something is to take on a form from the outside. In mundane things, matter is the source of passive undergoing. Hence, it seems that angels too must have matter.
- Third, angels are individuals. But the source of individuation seems to be matter. Hence, individual angels have matter.
- Angels are definable substances. But if something has a definition, then it must be composite, since there is one part of its nature that explains why it can be grouped with other things (specifically, with other rational substances), but there is another part of its nature that sets it apart from other rational substances, such as humans. So, an angel has a composite nature. But a nature cannot be composite yet substantially

one unless its parts are incomplete and designed to fit together to form a substantial unity (see Section 3.3). That is, the angel cannot be one substance unless one of its parts is formal and the other is material. Thus, an angel seems to have not only form but also matter.

It is important to note that these four arguments appear at the beginning of a disputation, and they are the preliminary arguments presented in favor of the position that angels have hylomorphic structure. Bonaventure then lists several arguments against the position. One of the arguments appeals to the authority of Aristotle, who says that there are some things that are pure form. Another argues from possibilities and God's power to enact them. It is possible that there are forms that can exist without matter. And God's power makes everything that is possible actual. Therefore, there are such things, and these are the angels. But perhaps the most compelling argument is effectively that if angels had matter, then they would be corporeal. And yet, it seems that angels are incorporeal.

Bonaventure acknowledges these concerns in his determination of the question. And he begins in the way we would expect. He seems to try to find a bit of truth in both positions and then to carve out a middle way. Yes, he claims, there are several ways in which angels are composite which everyone can agree upon, since they do not imply that angels have a material component. Moreover, he concedes that, even if angels have matter, they don't have a material principle that makes it such that they also have the properties that mundane bodies possess. That is, they don't take up space and thus are not divisible into portions of the space they take up. They don't have arms and legs, heads and torsos. They are not a combination of a body and soul, like humans are. And yet, when it comes to the heart of the issue, Bonaventure takes a striking position.

> But concerning the composition of matter and form, or the material and the formal, about this there is doubt. Some have wanted to say that this sort of composition does not apply to an angel, even though the compositions spoken of above are in him. But as it was shown above, in the case of the angel there is a basis of mutability – not only as it pertains to non-existence, but also in terms of diverse properties. Moreover, there is a basis of undergoing something (*ratio possibilitatis*), and in addition there is a basis of individuation and limitation, and lastly a basis of essential composition in keeping with its proper nature. And given all these, I do not see an explanation or argument by which someone can mount a defense against the view that the substance of an angel—indeed, any essence of a created *per se* being—is composed out of different natures, and if there is composition out of different

natures, these two natures will be disposed towards one another in the manner of an actual thing to a potential one, and thus of form to matter. Accordingly, the position that seems to be closer to the truth is that in an angel there is composition out of matter and form.

(Bonaventure, *Commentary on the "Sentences,"* book 2, dist. 3, part 1, art. 1, ques. 1; Bonaventure 1885, vol. 2, 91, column A; my translation)

There is some caution in his statement toward the end. But the upshot is that our best reasoning leads us to the position that angels have matter. Indeed, as Bonaventure acknowledges, every created substance is a composite of a formal part and a material part, the former answering the part responsible for actuality, the latter responsible for the potentialities in substances.

Notice that Bonaventure's Universal Hylomorphism is restricted in two important ways. First, as to be expected, it only encompasses created things, and thus God does not have a material component. Second, it only encompasses what Bonaventure refers to as "*per se* beings," that is, beings that exist independently and in their own right, that is, substances. Thus, accidents themselves do not have a material component, since they are fundamentally dependent beings.

When making his case for Universal Hylomorphism, Bonaventure argues that even if we balk at the claim that a created substance must have a material component, we cannot deny that all created substances, including angels are composite and that at least one of their components must be the source of the substance's potentialities. Interestingly, Aquinas and others who reject Universal Hylomorphism concede this, and thus their task is to find another kind of metaphysical component that can be the substance's intrinsic source of potentiality. Aquinas, for instance, is often interpreted as proposing that angels have "essence-existence composition" (see *On Being and Essence*, ch. 5, and Wippel 2014, 622–34). The question to ask yourself (if you look into this issue) is whether there is any convincing alternative to matter. You might also want to ask yourself whether refusing to call a principle that is the source of potentiality "matter" is merely a semantic sleight of hand.

But what if we side with Bonaventure? Notice that he still has plenty of work to do. He conceded that the *material* component in angels does not make angels *corporeal*. It seems then that Bonaventure and other advocates of Universal Hylomorphism must maintain that there are at least two kinds of matter, corporeal matter and "spiritual" matter. But what is *spiritual* matter? In what ways is it similar to corporeal matter, and in what ways is it distinct? Can Bonaventure come up with a principled way to distinguish them? In particular, can he identify some differentiating properties that carve up matter into these two substantially distinct kinds? We will not pursue this line of inquiry and survey the sorts of answers that defenders of Universal Hylomorphism gave, but you should know that Bonaventure and others appreciated the fact that they needed to provide answers, and they did their best to offer some.

3.5 Are Forms Extended?

A soul is responsible for making an animal's body a living body. But now consider two parts of an animal's body – say, its head and its foot. The head is spatially distant from the foot. But the same soul is supposed to be at work in both the head and the foot, vivifying both and making the head a head and the foot a foot. How does the *same* soul accomplish this feat in two distinct locations? Here are the options:

- Option 1: The soul is wholly present in one part (say the brain or the heart) and not in the others (for instance, the right hand); yet, somehow it is capable of radiating its influence out into the parts it does not inhabit.
- Option 2: The soul is "holenmerically" present in its parts (see Pasnau 2011, 337–49).
- Option 3: The soul itself is in fact not be simple: One part of the soul occupies one part of the body and another part of the soul occupies another part of the body.

On a first pass, Option 1 seems undesirable. If the soul is not *in* the right hand, then the right hand is not imbued by the animal's substantial form. But as Aristotle famously asserted, a bit of matter that is not imbued by the proper substantial form is only a hand "in name" (*On the Soul* 2.1, 412b20–25). Option 3, at the other extreme, seems to invite a pernicious version of the problem of the unity of the substance that we already considered above in Section 3.3.

Option 2, then, seems to be the right path to take. Here is what the view amounts to: A is *holenmerically* present in B if and only if the entirety of A is present in each of the parts of B. Hence, a whole pie is not holenmerically present to the individuals at a dinner party, even though the pie might be fully consumed by those in attendance once each of the attendees is served a piece. The soul, by contrast, is like those universals that we looked at above in Section 3.2: it is entirely present in each part of the matter that it is present in. Because the whole soul is entirely present in each part, each part of the animal is alive and a part of that kind of animal.

A number of philosophers, including Aquinas, concluded that souls are holenmerically present in their bodies (*Questiones de anima* 10 and *Summa Theologiae* 1.76.8; also Pasnau 2002, 93–5). But not everyone thinks this is true. For some, this will be because the soul is not strictly speaking a form (see Chapter 4, Section 4.1). Others assert that the soul is a form, and yet they think holenmerism is absurd. Albert the Great retreats to the position that we identified as Option 1; specifically, the soul resides in the heart and projects its influence on the body out from this center (*De Anima* book 2, tract. 2, c. 7; Albert the Great 1968, 75.74–76). But for others, remarkably enough, it is precisely *because* the soul is a form that it must be divisible into spatial parts. In particular, we see a commitment to Option 3 in later nominalist thinkers like John Buridan (c. 1358).

> But going over these difficulties quickly, I say to the first that without a doubt the quantitative parts of a horse's soul are distinct from one another and are outside one another with respect to place and with respect to subject. It follows that the part existing in the foot is different from the part existing in the ear, and this part of the soul is destroyed if the ear is cut off while the other persists.
> (*Quaestiones in De Anima* [ultima lectura] 2.7; Buridan 1984, 87; my translation)

This view is a logical extension of a trend in later thirteenth- and fourteenth-century scholastic thought which both attributes an intrinsic quantity to prime matter, and which maintains that the material forms of plants and animals are "educed," that is, "drawn out" from potencies that are inherent in matter. Already in Aquinas, we begin to see a kind of concession: the forms of plants and animals are accidentally extended but intrinsically simple. But Buridan and others who take the direction now being investigated are going beyond this; Buridan is claiming that forms educed from matter are intrinsically extended.

The reasons why Buridan and others make the leap to this more radical claim about the extension of the soul proper are still being uncovered by scholars.[13] But the position about the intrinsic extension of souls is bolstered by empirical evidence. Take certain plants – such as my jade plant – and cut them into parts. Then place those parts in water. If all goes well, each part grows into a full plant. Thus, it appears that each part of the plant had a part of the original soul. Likewise, cut a worm in two. Each part squirms and seems to shrink from a needle if one pricks it.[14] Thus, it appears that each part of the worm has a part of the original soul. In fact, it appears that the soul is both divisible and yet "wholly in" each of the separated plant or worm parts. The "whole" soul is in each worm half, not the whole of it as an individual, but the whole of it in the sense that each part cut from the original soul has all the powers of that original soul. In other words, the empirical evidence suggests that in plants and worms, the soul is divisible into homogenous parts. Buridan reasons that if this is the case in "imperfect" animated creatures like plants and worms, it should also be true for "perfect" ones (*Quaes. in De Anima* 2.7; 1984, 90–1). Thus, Buridan thinks the empirical evidence provided by the division of plants and worms gives us grounds to assert that, for all plant and animal souls, the soul is divisible into parts that are the same in *species* as the whole soul.

In the next chapter we will see that Buridan's commitment to extended forms leads to the view that an animal persists only in a weaker sense of numerical sameness over time and change (see Section 4.2). It also turns out that a commitment to Option 3 will have implications for the identity of material substances even at a single moment of time. For, since each bit of matter is an individual, each bit of matter ensouled by a soul part makes a hylomorphic composite. And since the hylomorphic composite of this part of the animal's matter plus this part of the animal's soul possesses all the powers of the animal's whole soul, each of these hylomorphic composites has all that it takes, "quidditatively speaking," to be an animal (*Quaes. in De Anima* 2.7; 1984, 92–3). Therefore, remarkable as it is to say, there is a sense in which an animal is many animals (idem, 95). Ed the horse has many parts. Each of these parts is informed by a soul part with all the powers of the whole soul. Thus, each part is in substance an animate substance. In fact, Buridan notes that if a foot were provided with an ear, it could hear!

Now, Buridan hastens to add that this is a claim about the essence or substance of each of these hylomorphic portions of the whole animal, and he stresses that there is another sense in which a horse is decidedly *not* a collection of individual horses.

> The second conclusion I propose is that if the names "animal", "horse", "donkey", and others like these are not true substantial names, but are connotative (specifically, connotative of a totality), then not every quantitative part of an animal or horse is animal or horse, nor is a horse's foot horse. This conclusion can easily be asserted. For I understand by "total existing thing" something that is an existing thing that is not a part of another existing thing. And I understand by "total substance" something that is a substance and not a part of another substance. Therefore, if this term "animal" signifies an animate, sensitive substance and connotes that this is total and not a part of another substance, then in the prior example [viz. the case of a divided worm] where we posited that A and B are parts of an animal, it is clear that A is really an animal when it is divided from B. But it is not an animal when it is united to B, because it is not a total substance, but rather a part of a substance.
>
> (*Quaes. In De Anima* 2.7; Buridan 1984, 97–8, my translation)

Ed's parts may be essentially horse, and not fern, dog, or human, but they are nonetheless *parts* of Ed. Thus, we don't have many more horses in the barn than we seem to have. There is only one horse in Ed's stall, not uncountably many horses.

But stop to reflect on precisely how Buridan saves the appearances. In the last quoted passage Buridan seems to be most interested in saving our ordinary linguistic practices. It seems that a series of contingent facts, both about what happens to be a part of what, and about our actual linguistic practices, explain why it is not proper to predicate "horse" of Ed's parts, even though metaphysically Ed's foot has everything it needs to be horse. And it seems to me at least that Buridan is happy to let the metaphysical point stand so long as we can keep things manageable when it comes to the everyday practices of animal husbandry. As I have already noted, Aristotelianism, perhaps more than any other school of philosophy, does its very best to preserve our experiences and commonly held opinions, but even it will have to dispense with *some* of what we take to be commonsense. Aristotle saw this. When presenting a topic, Aristotle often canvassed all the things that people tend to believe about the topic. But he did not stop there, since the listed beliefs could not all be true. The Aristotelian philosopher, like many philosophers today, wants a coherent, consistent set of beliefs. Some of the things that we initially take for granted will need to give way. Buridan seems to think that he can preserve how we talk and make our way through the everyday world even though science reveals a more complex, less "commonsense" reality underneath. This is in marked contrast to other medieval Aristotelians, who want to argue that the commonsense picture of reality is much closer to how things actually are.

3.6 Alternatives to Aristotelian Hylomorphism

At this point you have reached the summit of some very intricate and abstract material. My aim was to give you a preliminary understanding of the motivations, power, and problems of a metaphysical framework that takes as its basic principles form and matter. The medieval version of hylomorphism was inspired by close readings of Aristotle's works and the already compendious interpretative literature that medieval thinkers inherited from the ancient Mediterranean world. This Aristotelian metaphysical framework, from which a plethora of elaborate variations emerged, was one of the dominant frameworks in the Middle Ages. But Aristotelianism was not the only framework utilized in the West, Middle East, and Near East. Perhaps the most noteworthy competitors were versions of atomism and less Aristotelianized Platonism.

"Atomism" is the name for a family of views which posit that the basic building blocks of reality are indivisible elements. In the atomism espoused by the pre-Socratic philosophers Leucippus and Democritus (fifth century BCE), and later revived in the Hellenistic period by Epicurus (270 BCE) and Lucretius (first century BCE), these indivisible elemental building blocks were bodies. Visible things and their properties were the result of the motions and configurations of these building blocks.

A materialistic atomism of the ancient Greek variety takes a radically distinct point of departure from hylomorphism, and its analysis of the objects that we most readily encounter stands in stark contrast with the Aristotelian's. My Arlig chair, for instance, is now no longer analyzed into the wood and the form (or forms) that give the chair's being as a chair. Rather, the chair is a composite of very small, uncuttable bits of body which are conglomerated and configured in a certain way for a certain amount of time.

Now, to be fair, at first it may seem that there is not too great of a difference between the two analyses. Yes, the Aristotelian tends to stop his analysis of the material side of things with what philosophers sometimes call *stuff* – in this case, the pine considered as a continuous homogeneous mass. (And, yes, I am not joking: Present-day professional metaphysicians do talk about "stuff" in a technical sense. They also talk about "gunk." But we shall not digress any further.) The atomist, it might seem, is merely pushing the analysis down into the parts of this stuff, which the Aristotelian concedes are there in some sense. But here appearances are deceiving. The details can be quite complicated, but simply put the Aristotelian and the atomist substantially disagree about the *status* of the items that a continuous mass is divided into. Atomists think that the parts are actual, Aristotelians that the parts are potential. And in this case, as far as medieval Aristotelians are concerned, the "potential" parts of a continuous stuff like pine are not the sorts of things that the metaphysician reaches when she gets to the bottom, basic elements. All the subdivisions of a pine board are themselves pine. (Again, work with the medieval pretense that the wood is a homogenous stuff.) Each of these potential piney parts, no matter how tiny, still admits of deeper metaphysical analysis, namely, into forms and (mostly) formless prime matter.

The reason that the atomist analysis of the Arlig chair might at first appear to be similar to the Aristotelian analysis is that the Arlig chair is an artifact, and as we have already mentioned, for Aristotelians artifacts are not substances. Arlig chairs are not one of the fundamental inhabitants of the universe. Chairs in effect *are* merely configurations of substances. But remember, we have been using our Arlig chair as a heuristic. We have been pretending in many instances that it is a substance, with the aim that by examining an artifact *as if* it were a substance, we might easily see how true substances are constructed. So, return to that pretense; treat the Arlig chair as if it were a substance for an Aristotelian. Once we do that, we can see a stark divide between the atomist and the Aristotelian. For the Aristotelian, if the Arlig chair is a substance, then it is more basic than the elements out of which it is composed. You have already had a glimpse of this idea when we were considering how best to formulate the position known as Universal Hylomorphism. For as you may recall, I made a distinction between complete substances and incomplete substances. Matter and form are incomplete substances, because their internal natures drive them toward one another. Matter needs form. Form needs matter. Speaking colloquially, they "want" to be together. And the result of a successful comingling is a complete substance, the hylomorphic composite. The atomist, by contrast, treats the indivisible elements as the basic inhabitants of the universe. These basic inhabitants then produce derivative beings, configured aggregations, as they bump into one another while moving about in the void. (Incidentally, here is another difference. Aristotelians usually deny that there is any void, or what we name a vacuum. Ancient atomists tend to embrace its existence, since utterly empty space is what allows atoms to move about and interact with one another. Perhaps they need not have done so. In the seventeenth century, for instance, we find physicists who posit tiny bodily bits that move about without void.)

Here then we can see how different views about the elements of things are tied up with decisively disjoint views about what is more basic or fundamental. If you are an atomist, you might even be tempted to dispense altogether with the derivative beings. Some atomists might say that the Arlig chair is a thing, present in the world, albeit a derivative being, that is, a being that entirely depends upon its atoms and their present arrangement for its existence. Yet, an atomist could instead say that *strictly speaking* there is no Arlig chair. True, we have a name "Arlig chair," which we utter when we see some bodies hovering in a certain space in a certain configuration. However, that cloud of atoms arranged in a chair shape is not an *additional* inhabitant of the universe. All that are really there are the atoms. Our evidence of the ancient Greek atomists is fragmentary, so it is difficult to determine whether any of them took this second, "eliminativist" option. But it may have been maintained by some of them. It is also worth noting in passing that Aristotelians also have anti-realism or eliminativism as a conceptual option when it comes to artifacts. But they won't take this view about substances. Here then is a stark point of contrast: The Aristotelians insist that the universe has a different set of inhabitants than the atomist. Indeed, if anything is in danger of being eliminated, it is the products of a divided continuous thing. The majority of medieval Aristotelians deny that there are atoms in the material realm.

To date, no one has discovered an Arabic translation of a Greek atomistic text. But one way or another, from the Greeks and possibly also from India, atomist notions made it into the Arabic-speaking world. Moses Maimonides, for instance, has at least some familiarity with Epicurus and some of his doctrines (*Guide of the Perplexed* 1.75; Maimonides 1963, 195, also lxxvi–lxxvii). It was in this milieu that a distinctive family of atomistic views developed among those who practiced '*ilm al-kalam* (literally "science of the word"). These *Mutakallimun* (often identified as "dialectical theologians" in English translations and studies) developed a form of atomism that posited both indivisible bodies and certain kinds of forms. (You should be aware that these forms are often called "accidents", even though the theologians's concept of an accident seems to diverge in some important ways from what their Aristotelian rivals thought accidents were.) These accidents, including the temporal duration of each atomic body, were themselves atomic, that is, indivisible and momentary.

The inclusion of certain kinds of forms into the list of the basic inhabitants of the universe is not unprecedented. Again, we wish we had more surviving works to verify, but Epicurus seems to have mooted the idea already in the Hellenistic period (see *Letter to Herodotus* 68–71; Epicurus 1926, 43–5). It also makes good conceptual sense. As we saw above, it is hard to give a positive account of individuation without the help of forms. But the way in which these forms work in atomistic systems is decidedly anti-Aristotelian. They work in an aggregative way, by which I mean, we still work our way "up" from small, basic bits to a derivative composite. By contrast, Aristotelianism tends to stress a "top-down" approach. Substantial forms give the substance a special sort of unity, and it is often thought that the form is even responsible for the kinds of parts that are actually present in the thing. This is the famous Aristotelian doctrine of "homonymy," which Aristotle espouses in his *On the Soul*.

> Suppose that a tool, e.g. an axe, were a natural body, then being an axe would have been its essence, and so its soul; if this disappeared from it, it would have ceased to be an axe, except in name.
>
> (2.1, 412b12–15)

Here is incidentally one of those places where Aristotle is using an artifact to illustrate a point about substances. If we suppose an axe – like our Arlig chair – is a substance, then if it were to somehow lose its soul (which Aristotle identifies with a substantial form), then what is left is only an axe in a homonymous, or equivocal, sense. That is, what we have left may look like an axe and so we might use the name "axe." But since an axe is supposed to cut things, if this axe-like thing cannot cut, it is not truly an axe. It is no more an axe than a picture of an axe is really an axe. Aristotle makes the point about things losing their form and what happens to the whole material object that is left behind. But medieval authors took this principle to hold for certain kinds of parts as well. This is why Buridan, for instance, claims that if an animal were to lose its substantial form, not only would there not be an animal, there would not be flesh, eyes, or feet.

> In particular, it appears that [an inference] from the whole to the part ought to be valid negatively, and its opposite affirmatively, because "a foot is" entails "an animal is", and conversely, "an animal is not" entails "a foot is not". I prove the first consequence as follows: If a foot is, I ask whether it is something animated by a sensitive soul or not. If it is animated by a sensitive soul, it follows that this is animal. Therefore, it follows that "an animal is". But if you claim that this [alleged foot] is not animated by a sensitive soul, then it follows that there is no foot, which is the opposite of what has been proposed [by the rule that Buridan is commenting on].
>
> (Buridan, *Summulae*, treatise 6.4.4, my translation)

Applying this point to our pseudo-substance, the Arlig chair, the Arlig chair has legs, but it only has legs so long as the Arlig chair form is in the composite. Were that form to leave, even if the remaining stuff looked like chair legs, they would not be chair legs. They would only be chair legs homonymously, or in name alone.

The doctrine of homonymy is perhaps one of the hardest notions for us to comprehend. But I would submit that part of the oddity is due to the fact that we are children of intellectual movements that pointedly rejected Aristotelianism in favor of systems that look more like ancient and medieval atomism. But notice one of the consequences of the atomist framework. It tends to flatten the universe and it seems to erase hard boundaries between natural kinds. Here, for instance, is how Maimonides puts it in his critique of *kalam* atomism:

> These atoms differ from one another only with regard to accidents and in nothing else. Thus according to them, animality, humanity, sensation, and rationality are all accidents having the same status as whiteness, blackness, bitterness, and sweetness, so that the difference existing between an individual belonging to one species and an individual belonging to another is like the difference between individuals belonging to the same species. In consequence, the body of heaven, even the body of the angels, or the body of [God's] throne, as it is imagined in fantasy, and the body of any insect you like from among the insects

of the earth or of any plant you like, are, according to them, of one substance, differing only with regard to accidents and in nothing else.
(*Guide* 1.75; Maimonides 1963, 205)

Now, of course, this might be exactly right. At bottom, every material thing might be made of the same stuff, just configured in different ways and possessing merely contingent properties. It is not my job in this book to adjudicate between the Aristotelian and the atomist. The thing for us to note here is merely the stark contrast in worldviews that emerge from these two metaphysical frameworks.

It is worth noting very quickly another feature of *kalam* metaphysics that while logically distinct from a commitment to atoms is superadded to their atomistic picture of the universe. There was apparently some disagreement about this point, but the Mutakallimun tended to be *occasionalists*. It is a commonplace among medieval philosophers and theologians working within Abrahamic religious traditions to assert that everything is ultimately due to God. Nothing, save perhaps the decisions of free agents (although even here, things are to put it mildly, complicated), exists or acts unless God wills that it be. Occasionalism maintains a very strong version of this thesis. It maintains that the only thing with causal efficacy is God.

> There is unanimity among them with regard to their belief that a white garment that has been put into a vat full of indigo and has become dyed, has not been blackened by the indigo, blackness being an accident that is inherent in the body that is the indigo and that does not go beyond it so as to affect something else. According to them, there is no body at all endowed with the power of action. On the other hand, the ultimate agent is God; and it is He who, in view of the fact that He has instituted such a habit, has created the blackness in the body that is the garment when the latter was juxtaposed with indigo.
> (*Guide* 1.75; Maimonides, 1963, 202)

The only dispute among the Mutakallimun, as Maimonides reports matters, is over whether occasionalism covers the decisions and actions of humans.

> The doctrine of the majority [...] is that when the pen is put into motion, God creates four accidents, no one of which is a cause of any other – all of them being concomitant in regard to their existence, not otherwise. The first accident is my will to put the pen into motion; the second accident, my power to put it into motion; the third accident, human motion itself – I mean the motion of the hand; the fourth accident, the motion of the pen. For they think that when a man wills a

thing and, as he thinks, does it, his will is created for him, his power to do that which he wills is created for him, and his act is created for him.
(idem, 202–3)

In short, each and every momentary event in the story of the universe is discrete and has no causal impact upon any future event. Maimonides is no fan of this worldview, and not just because it undermines freedom of the will. On his view, individual substances are nonderivative beings with causal powers. They are the focal points of changes that we see in the world. True, these substances only exist and perhaps are only preserved from moment to moment because God wills that they exist and persist – in other words, and this a very common medieval view, God must be a *sustaining* cause – but they are not passive, inert results of a micromanaging divinity.

Again, it should be stressed that occasionalism is conceptually separate from atomism. As Maimonides notes, at least some *kalam* atomists wanted to carve out space for human causal efficacy (at least to some limited degree). One can also be an occasionalist but not an atomist. The emphasis on God's power and unconstrained will invites many theologians to say things that, especially if one is not careful, look like forms of occasionalism. Let me also quickly note that in addition to *kalam* atomism, there were a few individuals working in the Western intellectual milieu who altered Aristotelian metaphysics in ways that are broadly speaking, atomistic. Most notable among these are Nicholas of Autrecourt, who we already encountered in Chapter 2, and John Wyclif (c. 1384). Of the two, Nicholas's position is arguably the more radical, and one might even claim that he has completely broken free from medieval Aristotelianism. In the Suggestions for Further Reading, I will point you to some studies of his surviving work and I will let you decide for yourself just how much of an alternative he presents. He clearly is part of a grander story whereby Aristotelian metaphysics and physics gives way to a new "corpuscularian" paradigm in Western philosophy and science.

Kalam atomism and perhaps also its scholastic parallels thin out the perceptible world of things, it reduces them to tiny bits, and in the case of the theory defended by the Mutakallimun, it strips mundane things of their stability, independence, and causal impact. Something similar seems to occur in the theory of another rival of Aristotelianism: the broadly Platonic form of metaphysics developed by various mystics.

Mysticism has a complicated relationship to Aristotelian philosophy; it has both been one of its strongest critics and also a source of rejuvenation and innovation. Perhaps the most well-known mystical critique of Aristotelianism is al-Ghazali's *Deliverance from Error*. After al-Ghazali is cured of his skeptical malady, which we studied in Section 2.3, he proceeds to examine what he takes to be an exhaustive list of the possible ways to truth: *kalam*, esoteric Imanism, Aristotelian philosophy, and Sufism. *Kalam*, in his view, is properly apologetic; when it attempts to make more speculative claims, its positions are highly questionable. Esoteric Imanism is rejected because it demands that we blindly submit to a singular authority (an Imam). The trouble is, however, that none of the followers of this authority seem to know anything. The philosophers are criticized for taking human reason too far and drawing conclusions that are contrary to the faith. (We will pick up that thread to some extent in later chapters, especially in Chapter 7.) Sufism is treated last, and it is deemed to be the only viable way to the truth.

One of the primary aims of Sufism, and mysticism more broadly, is to achieve a direct, personal relation with God. It has a practical dimension focused on rituals designed to tame and purify the self, and it emphasizes knowledge by acquaintance, which is often called "taste" (*dhawq*), over rational deduction. Nevertheless, there were many mystics who also developed more "rationalistic," theoretical frameworks for discussing the nature of God and God's relation to the self and the world. Perhaps the preeminent "rational" mystics are Muhyi al-Din ibn al-'Arabi (1240), Mulla Sadra, and al-Ghazali.

We cannot give a thorough overview of mystical metaphysics. But perhaps the present sketch will be enough to show how mystical speculation, and its broadly Platonic orientation offers a distinct alternative to the Aristotelian picture of the structure and composition of things. In the works of Ibn al-'Arabi, for instance, only God has true being.[15] Everything radiates out from His essence in a series of "theophanies," that is, divine manifestations. The resonances with the form of Platonism developed by Plotinus (270), Proclus (485), and other late ancient Platonists – a form of Platonism that is often given the label "Neoplatonism" – is plain to see. Using the somewhat more familiar way in these Greek Platonists talk, Ibn al-'Arabi's idea in very broad terms is that all created beings are the effects of the process of "emanation," the downward sharing of this primal, true being. Hence, to the degree that we exist, we are thin reflections of the one true being.

We see something similar developed by al-Ghazali in his mystical masterpiece *The Niche of Lights*, where he develops in the first part of the treatise an elaborate metaphysics and epistemology centered around the notion of light. The true light is God. Everything else, including visible light, is a product of a series of illuminations radiating downward. We are dim reflections of this divine source.

In book 6 of the *Republic*, Plato used the metaphor of the Sun radiating its light down to everything else to illustrate how the Form of the Good makes all the other forms possible. These forms, in turn, are the paradigms for all the imperfect materially realized copies that we encounter in the sensory world. Thus, in Plato's scheme, we and the things around us are at least two steps removed from the ultimate basis of reality, the Form of the Good. Later Platonists keep this basic causal story intact. The only difference is that they tend to multiply the number of steps it takes to move from the first source to the material, sensible world. We need not worry about how many steps there are. The basic point is that, on the Platonic scheme, our existence is quite thin and dependent upon the first source of all things in a much more immediate sense than Aristotle's cosmic scheme would suggest. This is how al-Ghazali describes our thin, dependent status.

> Existence can be classified into the existence that a thing possesses in itself and that which it possesses from another. When a thing has existence from another, its existence is borrowed and has no support in itself. When the thing is viewed in itself and with respect to itself, it is pure nonexistence. It only exists inasmuch as it is ascribed to another. This is not a true existence, just as you came to know in the example of the borrowing of clothing and wealth.
>
> (*Niche*, chapter 1, section 41; al-Ghazali 1998, 16)

An Aristotelian could nod along in agreement to a point. After all, this looks like a distinction between a substance and an accident (in the Aristotelian sense). But in the *Niche*, Ghazali makes it abundantly clear that the only thing that has existence in itself is God. Only He is the "Real Existent," even things that the Aristotelian claims are substances exist only in Ghazali's second, dependent sense of existence.

To be sure, neither Ibn al-'Arabi nor Ghazali is claiming that we fail to exist in any manner or degree. And, as have already mentioned, there is a sense in which mainstream Aristotelian scholastics will concede that all created substances depend on God for their essence and actual existence. In point of fact, medieval forms of Aristotelianism typically have a considerable amount of Platonism mixed into them. This should not be too surprising. Many commentators on Aristotle in late antiquity were Platonists, and thus both Boethius and the Arabic philosophers who utilized these works inherited a Platonized Aristotle. Moreover, Augustine is effectively a Platonist. We even find Thomas Aquinas, often portrayed as the great "Christianizer" of Aristotle, employing the notion of "participation" at key points in his metaphysics and cosmological system (although, to be sure, what he thinks participation is might appear to be idiosyncratic from the perspective of a dyed-in-the-wool Platonist).

Still, it seems to me, that there are significant differences between the mystical Platonists and such Platonized Aristotelians as Maimonides and Aquinas. As with *kalam* atomism, our metaphysical status seems to be much more tenuous and ethereal. But there is also an upshot, and here is a way in which mystical Platonism differs importantly from *kalam* atomism: Our connection to God might be more direct. We are not ourselves gods, but in a very clear sense we are images of Him. This is not mere metaphor, the idea that we are the effect of God's essence and resemble it in important respects is very much literal and woven into the mystic's ontology. Accordingly, our ability to understand at least in some small way God's nature and even to return to Him might involve merely that we turn our attention back on to ourselves in the right way. This will be one of the themes that we turn to in the next chapter.

I offer one parting thought: Some scholars are tempted to read various mystics as "monists" and "pantheists," that is, as proponents of the views, respectively, that (1) there is only one thing or kind of thing, and that (2) everything is God. When it comes to the mystics that we have examined in this section, I do not believe Ibn al-'Arabi actually goes that far. Henry Corbin agrees: "This is neither monism nor pantheism; rather, it can be called theomonism and panentheism" (2014, 294–5). Corbin proceeds to define "theomonism" as "no more than the philosophical expression of the interdependence of Creator and created." Pan*en*theism is the position that God is present *in* everything and everywhere. But there are ways of being present "in" something that don't entail that the container takes on the properties of the contained. I certainly don't believe that Ghazali espouses monism or pantheism. I cannot make the case for this in full, although I believe you will see some of my reasons when we turn to the mystical notions of "union," "absorption," and "annihilation" in Chapters 4, 5, and 6. That said, it is possible that there are true pantheists in the medieval philosophical and theological traditions that I am covering in this Introduction. I don't know of any, but there is so much that I don't know and there is so much that we collectively still don't know about this period. The only way to be sure is to go out and look, to read the texts with care, and especially to be clear when literal language is giving way to more figurative ways of expressing truths.

Study Questions

Pick an ordinary object and then give your preferred answer to the following questions. Try to defend your position against the criticisms of proponents of rival views, either medieval or modern. Remember that for Aristotelians, artifacts are not substances, and for that reason the line between the Aristotelian account of a chair or axe and, say, an atomist one won't be as sharp. Hence, if you are going to answer the following questions as an Aristotelian, you might consider performing the exercise for both an artifact and for at least one substance. Paradigmatic substances for Aristotelians are living objects.

1) Does your object have a substantial form? If your object has at least one substantial form, does it have only one?
2) What explains the fact that your object belongs to a kind of object?
3) What explains the fact that it is a particular instance of a kind of object?
4) How real is your object? For instance, is your object distinct from the divine essence? If you answer "yes," what makes this so? Is your object basic or derivative? Does your object sustain itself, or does it require some outside cause or agent to ensure that it exists at a given time?

Notes

1 If you want to trace it back to the Greeks, start by looking at Plato's analogy of the line at the end of book 6 of the *Republic* (509d ff.), and Aristotle *On the Soul*, book 1.1.
2 Boethius wrote *two* commentaries on Porphyry's *Isagoge*. The first was based on an earlier Latin translation of Porphyry's work by a gentleman named Victorinus. Boethius was so dissatisfied with this earlier translation that he took it upon himself to render it anew into Latin and accompany it with an even more detailed commentary. This little, but extremely influential excursus on universals is only found in the second commentary.
3 For Abelard's treatment of the various forms of realism dominant in his day and then his own anti-realist solution to the problem, see his *Glosses on the Isagoge*, translated in Spade 1994, 26–56. Ockham discusses universals in several places, including his *Ordinatio*, distinction 2, questions 4–8, translated in Spade 1994, 114–231.
4 For effectively the same argument, see Abelard 1919, 13 (translated by Spade 1994, 33). See also King 2004, 72–5.
5 Here you might want to remember Descartes, who famously asserted that the only essential attribute of material substance is its extension. See, for instance, *Meditations on First Philosophy*, Meditation 5, and most explicitly, *Principles of Philosophy* 1, prop. 53.
6 Platonists of this sort tend to maintain that the First and pure matter are both unintelligible, but for distinct reasons. The First, or One, is unintelligible since intelligibility requires plurality; whereas the One is absolutely simple. Matter, on the other hand, is unintelligible because it lacks all forms, and forms are what the intellect grasps.
7 Why not posit place and time-stamp forms? Good question. The answer is complicated. The short version of it is that place and time are derivative forms. They get their being from other forms that then stand in relation to one another. Therefore, we cannot just impose place and time-stamps on matter and then use these parceled-up matters to individuate universals like *dog* and *red*.
8 For that story, see the first part of Pasnau 2011, especially chapters 3 and 4.
9 The word "mereology" is derived from the Greek word for "part," *meros*. Thus, mereology is an account of parts and their correlates, wholes. For an overview of medieval thought about mereology, see Arlig 2019.
10 That is, take in and metabolize nutrients, and so forth.
11 Here I follow Robert Pasnau's interpretation (2002, 120–5), which he presents as part of his study of Aquinas's so-called treatise on human nature, specifically,

questions 75–89 in the first part of his *Summa Theologiae*. You should be aware that this part of Pasnau's book has provoked a strong reaction from scholars who want to reconcile Aquinas with the present official Catholic position, which is that *human* life begins at conception. For another recent discussion of Aquinas's views on embryology, see Amerini 2013.

12 For a summary of other arguments for unitarianism and pluralism, see Pasnau 2011, 574–88 and 591–6, as well as Lagerlund 2012, 472–4.

13 Sander De Boer (2012) suggests that Radulphus Brito (c. 1320), a master of arts at Paris, played a significant role.

14 This observation about low-level animals like worms and annelids is made by Aristotle in his *On the Soul* (1.5, 411b19–30). Elsewhere, in his biological works, Aristotle notes that in the case of worms, the wiggling and sensitivity only lasts for a while, since the worm halves do not possess the necessary organs to maintain life for very long (*On Length of Life* c. 6, 467a18–23; *On Youth*, 468a23–b7).

15 Here I am relying on the summary of Ibn al-'Arabi's ontology in Rizvi 2005, 233–9.

Suggestions for Further Reading

For an overview of some of the core metaphysical issues pertaining to the structure and constituents of reality, see Pasnau and Van Dyke 2014, Part VIII, especially chapters 45–49. Even these articles, however, can be dense and they quickly point the reader to often very specialized studies. In fact, it is hard to find good introductory ways into metaphysics in general, let alone medieval metaphysics. The most accessible and also entertaining way into medieval metaphysics that I have found is Paul Vincent Spade's "Warp and Woof of Metaphysics" (1999), which is still (thankfully) easy to find online. Professor Spade's Medieval Logic and Philosophy website (https://pvspade.com/Logic/), inactive as of March 2007 but still available via a casual search on the internet, has a lot of useful resources, including unpublished lectures and translations.

For an entry into medieval understandings of form and matter, see Pasnau 2014b. For a survey of some of the theories on the metaphysical composition of material particulars circulating in the scholastic milieu, including the atomism of Nicholas of Autrecourt and John Wyclif, see Lagerlund 2012. Eleonore Stump's presentation of Aquinas's metaphysics of material particulars is illuminating (2003, 35–60 and 191–216).

At several points, I warned you that as useful as our Arlig chair is for thinking about hylomorphic composition, viewed through medieval Aristotelian eyes it is not a substance. That is only the beginning of the story when it comes to how medieval philosophers thought about houses, wagons, and other human-made objects and groupings. For thirteenth- and fourteenth-century scholastic analyses of artifacts, look for publications by Kamil Majcherek and Jenny Pelletier. They are doing up-to-date and interesting work on artifacts, artistic production, and social groups. Both have contributed to the online, open-source journal *Philosophies* in a special issue entitled "Art vs Nature: The Ontology of Artifacts in the Long Middle Ages" (2022), which is guest edited by Henrik Lagerlund, Sylvain Roudaut, and Eirk Akerlund (https://www.mdpi.com/journal/philosophies/special_issues/art_nature_middle_ages). In that special issue, you will also find a study of mine on twelfth-century metaphysical theorization about artifacts (Arlig 2022).

On universals start with the primary texts collected in Spade 1994. The texts by Porphyry and Boethius are necessary for understanding anyone you read subsequently. The texts by Peter Abelard, John Duns Scotus, and William of Ockham are exceedingly technical and difficult, but they are classics. For guidance, see the references to secondary literature in the notes to this volume, as well as the articles on individual figures and the problem of universals available online from the *Stanford Encyclopedia of Philosophy*.

For an overview of theories of individuation, start with Gracia 1984, and King 2000.

Given that individuation is the opposite side of the coin from the problem of universals, much of the material included in these works will also help you to understand the texts you read in Spade's volume.

Aquinas's proposal that matter is "pure potentiality" has generated a lot of discussion, especially among those who want to claim that Aquinas's position is intelligible. For two markedly different takes on what prime matter considered as pure potentiality might mean for Aquinas, see Pasnau (2002, 131–40) and Brower (2014, 18–21). See also Hughes 2002.

The Jewish philosopher Solomon ibn Gabirol is often credited with being the inspiration for Western European varieties of Universal Hylomorphism. For selections from Ibn Gabirol's *Fountain of Life* that pertain to matter, see Foltz (2019, 416–26). For more on Ibn Gabirol, see Sarah Pessin's article in the *Stanford Encyclopedia of Philosophy*, as well as her book-length study (2013). There is now also a study of the philosophy of Dominicus Gundissalinus (c. 1190/3), translator of the *Fountain* and creator of a fascinating synthesis of Latin and Arabic metaphysics (Polloni 2020).

On challengers to the Aristotelian framework, see the Lagerlund article referenced above. For a rich and comprehensive overview of how later medieval Aristotelianism gave way to early modern "corpuscular" theories, including atomistic ones, see Pasnau 2011. Along the way, Pasnau leads the reader through a host of complications that arise as scholastics attempt to refine the Aristotelian metaphysical framework. For this reason, it is very much a go-to book for anyone interested in hylomorphism in all its medieval permutations.

On *kalam* atomism, start with the brief overviews by Majid Fakhry 2004, 215–23, Henry Corbin 2014, 220–2, and Van Ess 2006, chapter 3. See also the work of Richard Frank (1978, esp. ch. 2, and 1984) and H. A. Wolfson (1976). As you have seen in the chapter, Maimonides provides an overview of *kalam* atomism from an Aristotelian perspective in chapter 75 of book 1 of his *Guide of the Perplexed*. Because he is an Aristotelian, Maimonides's presentation of the views of the *mutakallimun* and their motives for adopting them should be read critically. Nevertheless, a careful study of it and the secondary literature (starting with the translator's introduction, 1963, cxxiv–cxxxi) will give you some sense of how medieval philosophers engaged with one another when it came to competing metaphysical frameworks.

On the tension between Platonism and Aristotelianism, even within the work of a single philosopher such as al-Farabi, Maimonides, or Aquinas, see Druart 1987, Hyman 1987, and Wieland 1987.

Finally, for mysticism, there is a survey of primarily Christian mysticism in Van Dyke 2014. On Islamic mysticism (Sufism), perhaps start with chapter 8 in Fakhry 2004. Schimmel's study (1975) is a classic. On Ibn al-'Arabi's metaphysics and cosmology, see Chittick 1989 and 1998.

4 What Are We?

4.1　Am I but a Soul?	106
4.2　Persistence in This Life and the Next	112
4.3　Mystical Union and the Alleged "Annihilation" of the Self	121
4.4　Individual Humans, Persons, and Moral Standing	131

Our world seems to be one that is inhabited by individuals. There are individual cats sitting on individual chairs looking at individual birds who are sitting on individual tree branches, and so on and so forth. In the last chapter, we examined some of the ways that Aristotelian medieval philosophers analyzed these individuals. They provided us with accounts of why all cats seem to belong to a kind of thing and hence why they all rightfully get the name "cat." At the same time, we saw various accounts of what it is that makes Felix the cat a different cat from Tibbles the cat, and Felix's favorite chair distinct from Tibble's favorite chair. We have seen them attempt to pinpoint what Felix the cat must have in order to be Felix the cat and to distinguish these features and parts from those which can be acquired or lost without compromising Felix's very existence and status as a cat. We also saw in the final section of the previous chapter how Felix, Tibbles, their favorite chairs, and the birds they are coveting would be analyzed in two non-Aristotelian metaphysical frameworks. The Islamic theologians, or Mutakallimun, with their atomist and occasionalist doctrines, reduce individual things like Felix and his chair to other individuals, specifically, to momentary complexes of indivisible bits and accidents. The Platonists also provide a place for Felix and Tibbles and the objects of their desires, but Felix and Tibbles no longer have the status of primary beings, or primary substances. For both the Mutakallimun and for the Platonists, Felix and Tibbles, and the birds and trees, are deeply dependent individuals. In a sense, their being is "thinner" than it is on the Aristotelian account.

DOI: 10.4324/9780429348020-4

To this point, I have been talking about individual artifacts and individual substances at a highly general level. I have stressed that for Aristotelians there is a deep divide between substances and all other things, including and especially items that in many respects *look* substantial, such as chairs. But in the medieval Aristotelian picture of things, there are also deep divides between kinds of substances. Of special concern is the divide between human substances and other substances. In this chapter, we will focus on medieval analyses of individual human substances.

The starting point for many medieval philosophers is that human substances are a special sort of animal, namely, a rational animal. In many respects, then, the metaphysical analysis of a human being follows the format of the metaphysical analysis of any complex substance. But in other respects, human beings present medieval philosophers with special problems. Thus, in this chapter we will need to begin by returning to the question of how to metaphysically construct a human being (Section 4.1). In particular, we will need to ponder whether a human being necessarily is a soul combined with a body, or whether she is merely a soul that has for a time been linked to a body. A common answer, driven by the popularity of the model of metaphysical composition suggested by Aristotle, is that a human is necessarily a soul + body composite. If we assume that this is correct, we then need to consider what conditions must obtain for this composite to persist through time? (Section 4.2) At first, this too might appear to have an easy answer: After all, isn't the persistence and stability of a substance just one of the roles that substantial forms and souls play? But as we will see, if we assume certain premises about the relation of matter to its form, the stability of things over time begins to get complicated. For it may be that form cannot persist if matter comes and goes. On the other hand, if we think that it can, the Aristotelian still has to account for the fact that at death the human soul is separated from its body for a considerable amount of time. What is the soul's status during this period of separation. Has the human being disappeared? And speaking of humans disappearing, what are we to make of the mystic when she claims that she is "annihilated" when she comes face-to-face with God? (Section 4.3) Finally, we will return to the notion that a human being is necessarily a *rational* animal, and we will ask some tough questions about whether this definition is too restrictive (Section 4.4). In particular, doesn't this entail that lots of creatures belonging to the biological species *Homo sapiens* are not human, or not fully human? At this point, we will be starting to look ahead to the ethical implications of metaphysical analyses. Given that being a human is linked to the idea of being a *person*, and given that persons are often thought to have special moral standing, if it turns out that certain individuals are not persons, this may have pernicious ethical and political consequences, as we shall see in later chapters.

4.1 Am I but a Soul?

What am I? I might answer this question by saying that I am a philosophy professor, a romantic partner, an uncle, an amateur photographer, or a rock-climbing fan. I am also a cis-gendered, heterosexual, male of European descent. I suspect that many of you think that giving such answers to the question "what am I?" is perfectly appropriate. I don't disagree. For most of us at least some of the time and for many of us most of the time, the most significant questions about our identities revolve around our cultural and family backgrounds, our race, sex, and gender, and our vocations and affiliations. Such categories, many of them social, have even become the objects of study for present-day metaphysicians. In fact, at present, social ontology is one of the most exciting subfields of metaphysics. (Start with Epstein 2018.) We have learned, however, that medieval Aristotelians like to distinguish between the substantial and the accidental, and while I suspect that even most medieval people would rate social standing, vocation, and so on as that which was most significant to them, for the medieval Aristotelian metaphysician all of these social properties fall on the side of the accidental. They indicate all the ways in which a substance of a certain sort exists. To a medieval Aristotelian's ear, a question of the form *what is __?* is asking for a "quiddity," which is a fancy word for essence.[1] That is, they want to discover what I must have to be this individual human being. And as we learned, all the available options seem to exclude accidental properties (Section 3.2).

Let us follow their way of interpreting the question "What am I?" What am I *in substance*? What am I essentially? Based on what we discovered in the last chapter, the answer should be simple. Given that I am a human, I am a substance consisting of (at least one) substantial form and matter (of the right sort). For someone like Aquinas (1274), both parts were crucial. I cannot be this individual human being unless I am this human form and this designated matter. But this Aristotelian picture sits uneasily with many medieval philosophers and theologians. Arguably the more natural position for a theist, especially a theist from one of the major Abrahamic traditions, is that what I really am is my soul.

In the seventeenth century, Descartes famously proposed that what I am *in substance* is a thinking thing. A natural way to interpret his claim, especially in light of what he says in the second *Meditation*, is that I am a thinking substance that is somehow intertwined with a body, at least for some time, but not in such a way that this body is part of what I am as a substance. This sort of position is a version of mind–body substance *dualism*.[2]

Strictly speaking, this form of dualism only maintains that mind and body, or soul and body, are two fundamentally different types of substances. It still might be the case that to be a human being is to be a composite of a mind and body. And, in fact, some scholars believe that even Descartes holds this to be true. But the general line that seems to be pushed in his *Meditations on First Philosophy* (first published in 1641) is as we have just said: I am my mind or soul, and my body is merely something that I have some sort of relationship with for some time. The Platonic tradition also has a strong dualistic strain running through it that privileges the soul over the body. For instance, in Plato's *Phaedo*, we find a defense of the position that death is the separation of the soul from the body, and that where I go is wherever my soul goes. The body is merely a vessel – or even "prison" (62b) – that temporarily keeps the soul here in the sensible world. Given that the soul is "form-like," its proper home is in the intelligible realm with the true substances, the "forms" or "ideas."

This Platonic brand of dualism which stresses that a human is effectively, if not essentially, just the soul finds numerous followers in the Middle Ages. We can see it manifested when philosophers start musing about the ultimate goal for a human being and, in particular, what will happen if a human person lives a virtuous life here in the material realm. Here, for instance, is al-Farabi (950):

> Felicity means that the human soul reaches a degree of perfection in [its] existence where it is in no need of matter for its support, since it becomes one of the incorporeal things and of the immaterial substances and remains in that state continuously forever.
> (*On the Perfect State*, IV.13.1; al-Farabi 1985, 205–7)

Ibn Sina's (1037) account is even headier. He claims that a human soul, if it becomes perfected, makes its ascent and escape from the material world and "it transforms into an intelligible world that resembles the being of the whole world," and it discerns and "becomes one with" that "which is absolute excellence and absolute goodness and true beauty" (*Metaphysics of "the Healing"* 9.7; Avicenna 2015, 350). In other words, if perfected through a long life of virtue, the human soul becomes almost Godlike. Note as well the suggestion, especially in the description of immortality offered by Ibn Sina, that a perfected human soul might cease to be individual in the intelligible realm. This notion that a perfected human soul is *unified* with the intelligible universe, and perhaps thereby *annihilated*, is something we will query in Section 4.3.

This Platonized picture of the nature of the human soul and its essential separateness from matter trickles down into the Latin intellectual world.

We see it, for instance, in the writings of some of the first Latin readers of Ibn Sina.

> The human body is returned to its first elements, since the first elements belong to its constitution and their powers and their matter are preserved in the body. But this is not how it goes in the case of the soul, since neither the divine essence nor divine providence is a part of the soul. (If that were true, then soul would be entirely unchanging and in no way could it be deserving of merit.) But there does happen to be a return to God through intuition of the divine essence and the cognition of Him. For from Him the soul proceeded and to Him it will return, unless it has been blocked due to its contempt for Him.
> (John Blund [1248], *Tractatus De anima*, xxiii, §328; 1970, 89, my translation)

When death occurs, both of the main constituents of a human will make a kind of "return," but the sense in which they return must be different. The body "returns" to its elements, in the sense that it becomes once again a conglomeration of elements. This can happen because the elemental natures are present in the body. But things are more complicated in the case of the soul. The human soul does not resolve into the four elements, earth, air, fire, and water, since it is immaterial and hence the four elements are not what it is constructed out of. But here is the problem: The human soul cannot return to that from which it came, in the sense of being returned to what it was constructed out of. The human's rational soul is a simple substance that comes directly from a creative action of God. It does *not* come from material that has the same nature as God's nature. If it did have God's nature, the human soul would not be in a position where it had to decide whether to pursue the good or the bad. It would always remain unchangeably fixated on the good. The way is blocked, then, for the rational soul to return to its original materials. Nonetheless, the human soul does "return" to God in another sense. If a person has been virtuous, she will be freed from the body and exist eternally as a spiritual substance in the presence of her creator.

Blund's argument is compressed and there is surely much more that could be said than what I have offered above. The important point to take away from this passage is Blund's fierce commitment to not only the fundamental immateriality of the human soul but also its essential separateness from matter. I also chose Blund as an exhibit because he is one of the first Latin authors to attempt to absorb the teachings of the two most formative accounts of the nature of the human soul, and consequently the human being, namely, Aristotle's *On the Soul* and Ibn Sina's *Book on the Soul*. Ibn Sina agreed with Aristotle on numerous points, and he took over much of Aristotle's technical terminology. Yet, there were deep tensions, which Blund and those who came after him attempt to negotiate.

In the second book of *On the Soul*, Aristotle defines the soul as a substantial form, and more specifically as a substantial form that "perfects" the body (2.1, 412a20–22). This seems to imply that souls cannot exist separately from bodies, for as you will recall from the last chapter, it is often thought that form and matter are "incomplete" substances. They by their very natures cry out for one another, and it is only when form and matter are combined that they bring into being something that actually exists *per se*, that is, in its own right or through itself. For John Blund, this leads to a problem.

> It is maintained by Aristotle that a soul is a perfection of an organic body possessing life in potency. But there is an objection: Form gives being, and in itself matter is imperfect. Every perfection, accordingly, is from form. Thus, since the perfection of an organic body possessing life in potency is soul, soul is form. But no form is a thing that exists per se once separated from substance. Therefore, since a soul is form, a soul cannot be called a thing existing per se once separated from substance. Therefore, a soul cannot be separated from body; rather, it persists with the body.
>
> (John Blund, *Tract. de Anima*, ii.1, §15; 1970, 5)

The objection rehearsed by Blund has a long history in mostly Platonic reactions to Aristotle's definition of the soul.[3] And it is probably through the mediation of late ancient commentaries on Aristotle that Ibn Sina encountered the problem and developed his proposed answer to it, which in turn influenced Blund and others in the Latin milieu. The key idea in this ancient critique of Aristotle's theory is that if a form is by its nature something that is intertwined with matter, then it cannot be a thing that exists per se. But if it cannot exist per se, then the soul cannot exist once its companion matter has been taken away. Thus, it appears that a soul cannot be the sort of thing that persists after death.

Of course, there were strong doctrinal pressures to believe that the human soul *can* persist without the body, at least for some period of time. The most natural interpretations of the Torah, Bible, and Quran imply this. The solution that Ibn Sina offers, and which inspires scholastics like John Blund, is to suggest that the names that we use to describe a soul must be understood to be picking out what the soul does.

> Therefore, we say that a soul can be called a power when taken in comparison to the affections that emanate from it. In like manner, it can be

110 *What Are We?*

> called a power arising from some intellect when taken in comparison to the sensible and intelligible forms that it receives. Moreover, it can be called a form when taken in comparison to the matter in which it exists and due to the fact that vegetable and animal substances are composed out of both [soul and matter]. It can also be called a perfection by comparing it in this way, namely, in that a genus is completed by this thing and through this a species has being.
>
> (*The Book on the Soul, or the Sixth Book on Natural Things*, part 1, chapter 1; Avicenna 1972, 18,[4] my translation)

There are two ideas at work here. First, the same thing can get several names based on different actions or effects it has. Second, it is important to notice how he is construing what it is to be a *perfection* of X. To be a perfection is to make a something that belongs to a highly general, determinable kind of thing (a "genus") into a determinate kind of thing (a "species"). For instance, rationality is the perfection of humanity, because it makes *animal* into a determinate kind of animal, a human. This means that some "perfections" are not forms.

> After this, we say that every form is a perfection, but not every perfection is a form. The master builder is the perfection of a city, and the woodworker is the perfection of a ship, yet they are not forms of the city or the ship.
>
> (Avicenna 1972, 19)

The final stage in Ibn Sina's argument is to point out that given that some of the effects of some souls are not embodied, any proper account of soul should include some things that are separate from matter (20–1). By implication, a proper account of soul will need to include some things that are not forms in the strict sense.

There is an abundance of nuance in Ibn Sina's discussion that we will have to pass over here. Since we have been primarily tracking how early scholastic philosophers understood Aristotle and Ibn Sina, let's turn to what Blund makes of this argument.

> To this one should say that the name "soul" designates its reality in a combination. For [the name "soul"] signifies a substance under a certain accident in relation to an organic body in so far as this body is animated and vivified by it. And it is on account of this accident that it is said to be the body's perfection, namely because it animates that body.
>
> (*Tract. de Anima*, ii.1, §16; 1970, 5–6)

Blund's conclusion is this: Human souls are separable. They may be like forms in many respects, but since forms are inseparable from the things they perfect, they cannot strictly speaking be forms. The soul, however, is what makes this material thing a living body. If Felix's soul were not present this cat would not be alive, sensing, or moving about. There would be one less complete living thing inhabiting the mundane world. The soul will "perfect," or complete, the animal; however, it will do so in such a way that it will not entangle itself in the body. It will act like a driver of a vehicle. The driver makes her vehicle perform, but she can get out and walk away without any damage to her integral being. For this reason, notice that the soul's connection to the body must be "accidental," or coincidental, it is something that happens to occur on occasion and for a time, but the human soul does not need the body to be a soul of a certain sort.

Blund and others who were inclined to go this way can even point to Aristotle to support their reading.

> From this it is clear that the soul is inseparable from its body, or at any rate that certain parts of it are (if it has parts) – for the actuality of some of them is the actuality of the parts themselves. Yet some may be separable because they are not the actualities of any body at all. Further, we have no light on the problem whether the soul may not be the actuality of its body in the sense in which the sailor is the actuality of the ship.
>
> (Aristotle, *On the Soul*, 2.1, 413a3–9)

If you already had Platonic tendencies, as Ibn Sina, John Blund, and others belonging to an Abrahamic tradition did, then this sort of passage might give you the opening that you need to. Here you have an authoritative text that supports the separability of souls and hints that a soul might not be a form.

However, go back to Aristotle's text and note the hesitant way in which he discusses this issue. Note as well that the overall position that Aristotle develops in *On the Soul* appears to be at odds with the idea that some form of Platonic or Cartesian dualism holds true. Aristotle repeatedly states that the soul is a form and most of the time he does so without any caveats. Also, if we consider the Aristotelian framework in the abstract, it was not clear how a thing could perfect the being of the composite of which it is a part *in a substantial way* without itself being a form. John Blund, as we have just seen, is happy to bite the proverbial bullet and assert that the union between soul and body is accidental. This, however, is too much to swallow for most Aristotelians. Composite animate things – including and especially human beings – in the Aristotelian schema are paradigms of composite substances, and substances cannot be accidental unions of bits and pieces. It should thus come as no surprise that as Aristotle's philosophy was further studied and assimilated, his view that the soul is the substantial form of the body became the most prevalent view in scholastic thought. And with it, the central questions concerning the metaphysical construction of a human being transformed into, for instance, the debate about how many substantial *forms* a human possessed (see Section 3.3), not whether a human had a soul in addition to any substantial forms. With this development, we see a move away from a Platonic dualism and toward the hylomorphic model, which is often seen as an attractive alternative to dualism (see, e.g., Stump 2003, 192–4).

4.2 Persistence in This Life and the Next

As we have now seen, a common answer to the question of what I am is driven by the popularity of the model of metaphysical composition suggested by Aristotle. I am a human being, because I am an individual rational animal. I am rational because of one kind of substantial form, rationality or rational soul. I am an animal because this form, perhaps along with other substantial forms, informs some matter. Thus, I am necessarily a soul–body composite, which is equivalent to stating that I am a form–matter composite. One thing that the Platonic dualist seems to get unproblematically is the notion that I exist so long as my soul exists, since it is me and I am it. The Aristotelian, on the other hand, has two parts to keep track of. For I am a soul and a body, they are me and I am they. How might this complicate our attempts to track our survival and persistence through time?

At first, even the Aristotelian seems to have a reasonably straightforward account of persistence and survival. After all, isn't the persistence and stability of a substance just one of the things that substantial forms do? But if we assume certain premises about the relation of a whole to its parts and the relation of matter to its form, the stability of things over time begins to get complicated.

Let us start with some assumptions about parts in relation to their wholes. Suppose you buy a car new from a car dealership. Over time, you replace the wheels, the carburetor, the battery, parts of the engine, and so forth. Such changes are so routine that we usually do not pause to reflect on them. We worry about the price tag, but we don't stop to wonder whether the change in parts means that we are bringing home a different car. But perhaps we should. Is the car that has undergone such changes the same car or not? You might concede that in some very strict sense it is not the very same car. For this car to be the *very same* car, it ought to have all the original parts. The car with new tires or new spark plugs does not. Of course, there may be a sense in which it is the *same* car, even if it is not the *very same* car. The sense in which the car in my driveway still is the same car seems to be a "looser" sense of the word "same." The additional word "very" indicates that we are getting down to fine-grained features, perhaps also to the deep metaphysical structure of things. Aristotelian metaphysicians and logicians will make similar maneuvers.

It is tempting to think that the existence of the parts is necessary for the existence of the whole, and thus, that even if one part were to be removed, the whole would cease to exist. Here, for instance, is Boethius's (c. 536) pronouncement about the dependence of a whole on its parts.

> Every genus is by nature prior to its proper species whereas a while is posterior to its proper parts. The parts, being what make up the whole, sometimes have only natural priority to the completion of that which they compose, sometimes temporal priority as well. [...] Things are just the reverse in the case of a whole, for if a part of the whole perishes then that of which one part has been destroyed will not be whole, whereas if the whole perishes the parts remain, in separation. For example, if someone removes the roof from a house that is complete he destroys the continuity of the whole that existed before; but even though the whole perishes the walls and foundation will continue to exist.
> (Boethius, *On Division* 879b-c; Boethius 1998, 13–5)

This statement occurs in what is effectively an introductory textbook on a portion of logical theory, namely, collecting items together and dividing them from one another. And, thus, it is quite reasonable to assume that some subtleties have been ignored. Still, Boethius presents the claim as if it were true of all parts and wholes, and he gives no indication that there are complications that the more advanced student will need to learn. Notice as well that the dependence of wholes on parts is *asymmetric*. The whole depends upon its parts. The parts do *not* depend upon their whole.

Suppose we grant that this it is a general rule about the deep metaphysical relations of parts to wholes. What does it really amount to? Boethius notes that this claim is about priority in nature, not necessarily about priority in time. This means that parts do not need to exist at some moment of time before the whole exists. The "before" is logical and perhaps metaphysical. If we take it to be a metaphysical claim, what does it amount to? Does he mean *existential* priority? That is, does the rule mean that my car depends on all its original parts and that if even one of those original parts is removed, my car no longer exists? Or, is the "natural" dependence being spelled out with reference to my car as a car? That is, it might be that the rule operates at a general level and says something like the following: In order to have *a* car, one must have tires, spark plugs, an engine, and so forth. All of these kinds of things must be there to have a car. And hence all of these kinds of things must be present in my car in order for me to have a complete car.

What I have just presented is quite subtle, but I hope you can see why we need to be careful. If we interpret Boethius's claim about part-whole dependence as something operating at a *type* level, so that it is telling us something about the makeup of cars in general, then *my car* need not have the original tires or the original spark plugs for *its* entire lifetime. But if we take Boethius's claim to be about particulars and what needs to be true in order for any particular car to exist as that particular car, then the claim is quite radical. For on what I am calling the existential reading of Boethius's rule, *my car* only exists so long as it has all the original parts.

The existential reading seems to entail a thesis that Abelard (1142) once called "destructivism" (1970, 549 ff.), which is a position that has many affinities with a version of "mereological essentialism" defended in recent times by Roderick Chisholm (1976, 97–104) and James Van Cleve (1986). Destructivism in its most unrestricted form would insist that my car ceases to exist when even one spark plug is changed out. That in itself may seem severe, but destructivism also seems to entail that a human being ceases to be if we were to cut off his hands, or even if we give him a manicure.

Many readers of Boethius – probably most, in fact – thought that *that* cannot be right. It cannot be true that *every* part of a whole is existentially prior to that whole. Here, for instance, is John Buridan (1358/61) commenting on Boethius's priority rule:

> About the first worry we argue that from the whole to the part the inference is not valid constructively. For although a finger or a hand is an integral part of a man, yet this is not valid: "A man is; therefore, a finger (or a hand) is", for a man may still exist even if his hand were cut off. And likewise the inference is not valid from the part to the whole negatively, for the maxim "If the integral part is removed, then the whole is removed" is not true, because the man's hand can be removed while the man remains.
> (*Summulae*, treatise 6.4.4; translation follows Buridan 2001, 430, with some modifications)

For that matter, even if "priority in nature" is taken in the more general sense, which we identified as a *type-level* priority, it does not seem to be true in general of parts. As we noted in the last chapter, Aristotle asserts that a hand removed from a human is a hand only in name, not in nature and account, which as you might recall, is part of what motivated the proposal that forms are intrinsically extended (Chapter 3, Section 3.5). This is because the hand is no longer governed by the substantial form of the human, and it is the substantial form that is responsible for the whole being human and for each of the human's parts to be human parts. In fact, if Aristotle is right – and most later Aristotelians took him to be so – then *existential* priority seems to hold in the opposite direction for many parts: the hand depends upon the existence of the whole body.[5]

Thus, when it comes to substances, Boethius's rule cannot apply to all the parts, since for substances many of their parts depend upon the form for their existence. One might even think that for individual animate substances generally and individual humans in particular, the persistence of the individual is guaranteed solely by the persistence of the soul. This second, stronger claim, however, runs into some complications.

It might come as a surprise, but destructivism, at least in an appropriately restricted form, does have its day among many of the men teaching in European universities in the fourteenth century. Several philosophers, including Ockham (1347) and – despite all that he said above – Buridan, hold that for most mundane objects, including plants and nonhuman animals, any loss or gain of a part entails that the whole is different both in a strict and even a "partial" sense. At best, most animals and plants only remain the same in an "improper" sense, namely, in the same way that we can say that the River Seine is the same over time and change of parts.

> Given this, in order to see how a horse remains the same in number, let us turn back to Seneca's view[6] and let us speak of a horse as we do of a river, with this exception, which Seneca rightly claimed: a river flows and changes more quickly and obviously, and with respect to bigger parts all at once, whereas a horse does so more slowly and with respect to smaller parts, and thus, it does so in a more hidden manner, indeed imperceptibly so. [...] I, for one, believe that this numerical identity is maintained with respect to a continuous succession of parts that are newly arriving as the previous parts leave, and thus, if I say "The Seine has lasted for a thousand years", I mean that for a thousand years there has been a continuous succession of some parts following after other parts. And this is also how it goes for both a horse and a dog provided that in this kind of succession they remain the same or similar in figure. And even if there is here no identity without restriction, nevertheless given that this arrival and departure of parts, especially in living things, is not apparent to the senses, everyday folk speak without restriction and without any additional qualification that the animal remains the same.
> (*Questions on Aristotle's "On Generation and Corruption,"* 1.13, Buridan 2010, 114–5, my translation)

On reflection this everyday, "improper" way of talking is not all that strange. It does not seem to strain commonsense to acknowledge that when it comes to rivers and even artifacts, we don't strictly speaking have the same object when parts are changed in and out. The car in my garage is the "same" car as the car that I drove off the sales lot several years ago, but this is because I can give a causal story of how the present mass of metal, plastic, and rubber that has the form of a car is related to that earlier mass of car-formed metal, plastic, and rubber.

It is perhaps harder for us to go along with the notion that an animal or a human being is the same only in an imprecise sense of "same," and it is especially hard to concede at first pass that cats and horses are not different in kind from rivers and cars. To bring us around to conceding this, Buridan will have to bring in a theory. How does he proceed?

Recall the concerns that we raised in Chapter 3 about the way in which a form inhabits matter (Section 3.5). It would seem that the form must be present at every place where the matter is present, otherwise, the parts of the matter in this or that region will not be actualized by the form. But now, either the form is present holenmerically in each part of the matter, or the form must be spread out just as the matter is spread out. The rejection of holenmeric presence forces upon us the notion that the form itself has spatial parts, and which in turn might imply that bits of the form can be chipped off when corresponding bits of matter are. Add to this two premises about the nature of matter, premises which Ockham, Buridan, and many others hold, the first being that prime matter has some low-level intrinsic actuality, the second that matter is divisible and, thus, in some sense it is enumerable and individuated with respect to its parts. Finally, blend in the notion (again, quite common among thirteenth- and fourteenth-century scholastic Aristotelians) that a unique "natural" substantial form is a form that has been "educed," or drawn out, from a unique bundle of matter. (After all, form is what makes something potential actual, and where would this potential reside other than in the matter?) Since this natural form is educed from a bundle of prime material, this natural form is stuck with this specific bundle. *It* cannot migrate from one defined aggregate of prime matter to another one. In sum, these premises and principles have led us to the No Transfer Thesis first mentioned in Section 3.2.

Once we have the No Transfer Thesis in play, identity becomes precarious. For instance, what happens if we cause a defined sum of matter, X, with a substantial form that has been educed from it to increase? Increase is brought about by adding some more matter, Y, to the defined sum of prime matter that we started with. But surely X is not the same in a strict sense as X + Y. They are different aggregations of matter. Now if we employ the No

Transfer Thesis, which I have italicized in what follows, we get an additional and more radical result.

> That which increases is not the same with respect to matter, since as Aristotle claims the material parts arrive and depart, and they do not remain the same. Therefore, this [increased thing] is not the same [as what we started with] with respect to form. This is because there must be a different form in different matter, since *a form cannot move from matter to matter*, but to the contrary, it is drawn out from the potency of its matter. The conclusion, then, is simply that this [i.e. the increased thing] is not the same [as the original], since substantially this [increased thing] is its matter and form taken together.
> (*Questions on Aristotle's "On Generation and Corruption,"* 1.13; Buridan 2010, 111)

This statement appears as the third argument in a set of opening objections in a disputation, and thus, as I advised you above in Chapter 1 (Section 1.3), you should not immediately conclude that Buridan is endorsing the argument. However, as the investigation progresses, it becomes clear that the general thrust of the argument is in fact endorsed by Buridan. He only disputes the conclusion that the initial object is not the same *in any sense* as the remaining object. Even Buridan's poor horse and dog, slow moving rivers as they are, are the "same" over time and change in that aforementioned "improper" sense of remaining the same. But it is still a remarkable concession to destructivism.

What about humans? Buridan's position is that human animals persist in a stronger sense than cars, plants, and brute animals do.

> The third conclusion is that a human from the beginning of life all the way to the end remains the same partially, namely, with respect to the noblest and most principal part, that is, with respect to the intellective soul, as this remains the same always.
> (idem, 113)

Here he means that the human's intellective soul remains the same in the strict sense. This is because he claims that human souls are not only different from the forms of artifacts, like my car's form, they are also different from the souls of plants and horses. Human souls are not "natural" because they are not educed from matter. If they are not educed from a particular bundle of matter, nothing prohibits them from migrating from one particular aggregate of matter to another without ceasing to be.

But what justifies Buridan's claim that human souls are not natural? Here, alas, you may feel some disappointment. No rational explanation or justification can be given.

> And as a matter of fact, I respond that this is miraculous, because the human soul inheres in the human body in a miraculous and supernatural mode, not as something extended or drawn out from the potency of the subject in which it inheres.
> (*Questions pertaining to Aristotle's "On the Soul"* [final lecture], 2.9; Buridan 1984, 138, my translation)

Is this a disingenuous, last-minute attempt to avoid accusations of heresy? Buridan is after all teaching in Paris after the notorious Condemnation of 1277, which listed over 200 propositions that professors were prohibited from teaching at the university. And one of the prohibited propositions is that "by eating a man can become numerically and individually different" (prop. 148 [114]; Piché 1999, 124). Yet, perhaps Buridan honestly does believe that this is a truth about the nature of the human soul, albeit one of those truths that the unaided human intellect is not capable of discerning clearly. I must confess that I am undecided about how to read Buridan here, although at present I lean more toward the latter assessment, especially in light of what he says about certainty (Section 2.4).

But if you think that things are murky when it comes to the relation of a soul to its body in this life, just wait until we turn to what happens after the soul has been stripped of its body.

For philosophers who followed Aristotle in believing not only that a soul is a substantial form but that a human being is essentially a composite of a soul and body (form and matter), the moment of death is especially vexing. For it appears that when the soul is separated from the body, the human being ceases to be. This might be tolerable, since it is an article of faith, both for medieval Christians and for medieval Muslims, that *ultimately* humans will be resurrected as soul–body complexes. (For medieval Jews, the issue is a bit more complicated. See Chapter 5, Section 5.4.)

Does this mean that I will cease to be when my soul is separated from its matter for some period of time and then come to be again when the Final Judgment occurs? Perhaps, but to take this thesis on board it seems that I must contravene some compelling notions, including the principle that once a thing ceases to be it cannot be again. Call this the "No Gappy Existence" principle. The No Gappy Existence principle is quite appealing. Think of it this way. Suppose that some extremely powerful agent completely erases me from existence. No material bits, no vestiges of a soul, nothing that was part of me is present. (Or, if you like, keep the material bits. But of course, they are now probably parts of some other actual creature, perhaps even another human.) Now, at some arbitrary point in time after that (and I think you will see upon reflection that the amount of time makes no difference), suppose that this powerful being creates from absolutely nothing a thing that looks like me, thinks like me, and so on and so forth. Am I this new thing? Or is this new thing merely an exact facsimile, or doppelganger, of me? One's mileage may vary here, which is why philosophical discussions of personal identity can get so heated, but it strikes me as quite reasonable for someone to insist that this newly created human is merely a facsimile of me and that it is not I. If you are inclined to agree, I suspect that what is undergirding this thought is the No Gappy Existence principle.

The No Gappy Existence principle is very compelling, but I have to concede that it is not necessarily true. Even if it is hard for my mortal human mind to see things any other way, it could be false. This might be one of those places where the world outstrips my comprehension of it. That said, I mention the No Gappy Existence principle because as it so happens, many medieval thinkers embrace either it, or some correlate of it, and yet they believe that there are ways to separate the soul from the body for a period of time without violating the principle. Perhaps human souls are special enough that they can survive separation from matter. In chapter 5 of the third book of *On the Soul*, Aristotle himself suggested that there is either a part or a kind of rational soul, intellect (*nous*), which unlike most forms, is separable from matter. (I should hasten to add that this *might* be what Aristotle is claiming. *On the Soul* 3.5 is notoriously difficult and has perhaps generated the most commentary of any of Aristotle's writings.) It might be the case that while nature really prefers to have humans be souls plus bodies, in exceptional circumstances, like those that occur in the period between death and Final Judgment, a disembodied soul can be considered to be a full-fledged human person, just one whose capacities have been impeded by externalities. Just like a vacuum, as soon as the impediment is removed, nature will fill the void in. In the case of an actual vacuum, material will rush into the empty space. By analogy, as soon as the conditions are right, the soul will gain a body again. For that matter, this separated soul does not necessarily need to be me in full actuality. All it needs to do is act as a placeholder, something that allows me to cling to existence in some kind of dormant, half-way state until it is time for me to actually exist in full at the Final Judgment.[7]

In short, a devoted Aristotelian has options. None are without their costs, but they all seem on the face of it to be viable. Given these costs, one might think that the Platonist has the upper hand here, since their dualist assumption that I am merely my soul would seem to avoid such difficulties. Platonists, however, encounter another set of puzzles. To see them, return to that question about what I am. Metaphysically, I am a substance capable of reasoning. For a Platonist, that means I am a rational soul. But now consider a related question. *Who* am I? That is, how can I distinguish myself from other rational souls? It would seem that I do so by means of contingencies that apply to me and to me alone. I have had certain specific events happen to me. I remember them and the emotions that they elicited. In short, all of my experiences may not make me what I am, if we are thinking about essence, but they surely make me who I am.

Notice that I am now allowing us to consider all those accidental features of human beings. Perhaps I should not have done so, but in my view, by prohibiting accidents from the investigation we only arrive at the difficulties that I am trying to set in place even sooner. So, let us keep accidents in play for the present. Both Platonists and Aristotelians tend to attribute emotions, memory, and other related psychological particularities to our being embodied. Aristotle is quite explicit about this in his psychology. Memory has a material basis. But if memory is rooted in the body, then what happens when I am separated from my brain? Where have all those things that made me who I am gone?

Remarkably, many of the Platonist philosophers whom we have already mentioned seem to be utterly uninterested in this possibility. Indeed, in their picture of the afterlife our existence as disembodied intelligences appears to be utterly devoid of many of the things that make us recognizably human, let alone recognizably individual people. Here, now in full, is Ibn Sina's description of what life will be like for a disembodied soul.

> [In the case of] the rational soul, the perfection proper to it consists in its becoming an intellectual world in which there is impressed the form of the whole; the order in the whole that is intellectually apprehended; and the good that emanates on the whole, beginning with the Principle of the whole [and] proceeding then to the noble, spiritual, absolute substances, then to the spiritual substances – [substances] that in some manner are connected to bodies – then to the exalted bodies with their configurations and powers, and so on until it completes within itself [the realization of] the structure of existence in its entirety. It thus becomes transformed into an intelligible world that parallels the existing world in its entirety, witnessing that which is absolute good, absolute beneficence, [and] true absolute beauty, becoming united with it, imprinted with its example and form, affiliated with it, and becoming of its substance.
>
> (*The Metaphysics of "The Healing"* 9.7.11; Avicenna 2015, 350)

This picture of things to come is, to say the least, mind-bending. To some it may even be enticing. But the point I want to stress is that this would be a life of pure contemplation, where I am thinking about abstract truths, pure beauty, and absolute goodness. There is a sense in which *I* literally become absorbed or subsumed. I become the whole world. I am no longer I, or perhaps more precisely, I am no longer *merely* I. What I am not doing is merely thinking about all the things that pertained to me as an individual, embodied human being, such as my beautiful partner and that time we kissed while walking through the snowy park on Christmas Eve, the laughter of my nephews when I told them a stupid joke, or any of the other small but immeasurably valuable joys that I individually experienced over the course of my mortal life. Either all of these things melt away, or, given that my soul becomes a model of the "universe," that is, the whole of existence in all its forms and features, these thoughts of mine are there but so is absolutely everything else, including perhaps all of *your* thoughts and experiences. Suppose my partner and I both succeed at merging with this so-called Active Intellect. It is not entirely clear that we will recognize one another or enjoy any sort of relationship with each other once we are in this state. Certainly, it is hard to see how we could enjoy an *exclusive* relationship. There would seem to be no she, I, and no one else. For that matter, there seems to be no she and I. All thoughts and experiences would appear to be melded together into one undifferentiated whole. In short, Platonism, with its emphasis on the eternal, immutable intelligible forms, seems to be utterly uninterested in much of what many of us think matters. There may well be an afterlife for human souls, but it is not clear that this life will be recognizably personal. It is not even clear that it is distinctively human at this point, since it appears that what human souls do is effectively the same as what other intelligences do as well.[8]

This impersonal picture of what life in Heaven will be like is amplified by the suggestion of certain mystics that what they experience when in their ecstatic states is but a foretaste of the eternal life to come. But if they are to be believed, it seems that every distinction between self and other is broken down in the life to come.

4.3 Mystical Union and the Alleged "Annihilation" of the Self

It is claimed by all in this period that God is the preeminent being, a being that cannot be compared with anything else. Some even claim that God is "beyond being." In all three Abrahamic traditions, we find individuals who claim to have ascended to such heights that they have had a glimpse of the Divine Essence. Often, they report that their awareness of their own selves disappears at such heights and that they are "unified" with or "absorbed" by God. Some claim that the soul of the mystic is "annihilated" when this union occurs. For example, here is what the Christian mystic Marguerite Porete writes in her remarkable book *The Mirror of Simple Souls*.

> She retains nothing more of herself in nothingness, because He is sufficient of Himself, because He is and she is not. Thus, she is stripped of all things because she is without existence, where she was before she was. Thus she has from God what He has, and she is what God is through the transformation of love, in that point in which she was, before she flowed from the Goodness of God.
>
> (ch. 135; Porete 1991, 218)

But can such claims be taken literally? Is a person's soul really absorbed back into the Divine Essence? Does the individual seeker cease to exist? Or are there reasons why such mystical reports can only be considered to be a figurative way of speaking?

The notion of "absorption" or "extinction" is common in all three Abrahamic mystical traditions. And in all three traditions, the claims of these mystics have troubled some. Marguerite's *Mirror* was determined to be heretical by the church authorities. Marguerite refused to recant and, in what was actually a rare event in the Middle Ages, she was executed for her heresy in the center of Paris in 1310. As it happens, in Marguerite's particular case, it appears that the perceived heresy did not stem from her thesis that the soul is annihilated when it returns to God; rather, what seems to have vexed the authorities most was her suggestion that the mystic did not need to cultivate the virtues or submit to the authority of the church (see Chapter 5, Section 5.3). Yet, others specifically find the claim that the soul is annihilated to be extremely unsettling and theologically problematic. To see how this story often plays out, we will focus our attention on some Islamic mystics, or Sufis.

The notion of "extinction" or "annihilation" is a commonplace in Islamic contemplative literature. You can find it discussed in all the Sufi handbooks and lexicons (see, e.g., al-Hujwiri 1959, 58–60 and 242–5; and ibn 'Ajiba 2011, 43–5). Moreover, in accounts of the early Sufi saints, one repeatedly comes across the accusation that at least some of these saints identified themselves with God – that when they reached the apex of the mystical journey back to God, the result was not merely self-annihilation but also absorption and assimilation into the Divine essence. Here, for instance, is a report of what Abu Yazid Bistami, an elusive ninth-century Sufi, allegedly claimed:

> People are saying about Abu Yazid – and I do not know whether it is true or not – that he said: *Once he took me up, placed me before him, and said to me, "O Abu Yazid, my creation would love to seek you."* I said,

> *"Adorn me with your unity, clothe me with your subjectivity, and take me up to your oneness, until when your creation sees me they say 'We have seen you' and you will be that, and I will not be there."*
>
> (Abu Nasr al-Sarraj [988], *The Book of Flashes*, chap. 124, section 1; trans. Sells 1996, 216, modifications to punctuation and formatting)

And there is perhaps the most infamous early Sufi, Al-Husayn ibn Mansur al-Hallaj, who in 922 CE in Baghdad was martyred in a most spectacular and gruesome fashion, allegedly again for the heresy of asserting that he and God are one. These are two poems attributed to him:

> One with Thee make me, O my One, through Oneness
> Faithed in sincerity no path can reach.
> I am the Truth, and Truth, for Truth, is Truth,
> Robed in Its Essence, thus beyond separation.
> Lo, they are manifest, the brightnesses
> That from Thy dawning Presence scintillate,
> Each gleam a brilliance like the lightening flash.
> I am He whom I love, He whom I love is I,
> Two Spirits in one single body dwelling.
> So seest thou me, then seest thou Him.
> And seest thou Him, then seest thou Us.
>
> (*Diwan*; trans. Lings 2004, 28 and 38)

The impression that one gets from these reports and poems is that these individuals truly believed that when they ascended and were present before the Divine essence, they ceased to exist, or if they existed, they did so because they became identical with God.

It very well may be the case that some of these mystics did think that they literally were annihilated or absorbed. These sorts of monistic and pantheistic tendencies are often found in Platonist philosophies (Section 3.6). Yet, as you might have noticed, even in al-Sarraj's report of Bistami's saying, there is already some skepticism among succeeding generations of mystics about whether Bistami and Hallaj really *said* such things or, if they did, whether they really *meant* that they had been *absorbed* into the Divine Essence and thus that they were identical to God. It is a commonplace in Islamic theology, backed by several pronouncements from the Quran, that nothing is equal to God. (There are, of course, parallels in the other two Abrahamic religions.) And surely, no created being can be or could come to be the uncreated being. For the created becoming the creator would appear to be a violation of the order of things.

Even if we put the claim of absorption to one side, the claim of "annihilation" or "extinction" is problematic. For it is unclear that Bistami or Hallaj could have really been *annihilated*. After all, they come back and report these experiences. But once something is gone, how can it come back save by a miraculous act of God? Perhaps the No Gappy Existence principle is false. Perhaps it is metaphysically possible for a thing to return after ceasing to be. But surely no *natural* process seems to allow for it to occur. Moreover, this miracle would have to be twofold, since not only would the mystic have to come back, God would have to create fictitious memories of the experience in a subject who strictly speaking was not there. None of this is impossible, especially for an all-powerful God, and one doesn't achieve mystical union all that often. So, maybe it is true that Bistami and al-Halllaj were annihilated. Miracles can occur. It is strange nonetheless, and it clearly did not sit well with some later mystics, especially those with a more philosophical bent.

The main protagonists in this story are al-Ghazali (1111), whom we have already encountered on several occasions and Ibn Tufayl (1185), who is the author of the great philosophical novel *Hayy ibn Yaqzan*. In the preface to this remarkable work, Tufayl tells us that he aims to reconcile the mystical theology of al-Ghazali with the Platonic–Aristotelian philosophy (*falsafa*) of Ibn Sina. Both al-Ghazali and Ibn Tufayl want to walk back the exuberant, ecstatic pronouncements of their forebearers.

In his mystical masterpiece *The Niche of Lights*, Al-Ghazali suggests that al-Hallaj and Bistami are exuberantly and poetically pointing to a basic ontological truth. They are right when they see that strictly speaking there is only one independent substance.

> Each thing has two faces: a face toward itself, and a face toward its Lord. Viewed in terms of the face of itself, it is nonexistent; but viewed in terms of the face of God, it exists. Hence, nothing exists but God and His face: "Everything is perishing except His face" (Qur'an 28:88) from eternity without beginning to eternity without end. [...] They do not understand the saying "God is most great!" to mean that He is greater than other things. God forbid! After all, there is nothing in existence along with Him that He could be greater than. Or rather, nothing other than He possesses the level of "with-ness"; everything possesses the level of following: Indeed, everything other than God exists only with respect to the face adjacent to Him. The only existent thing is His Face.
> (*Niche of Lights*, chap. 1, sections 43–4; al-Ghazali 1998, 17)

This fact is something that some grasp intellectually, whereas others seem to have hit upon this truth by an unmediated, irreducibly first-personal experience, or "tasting." The problem is that the latter mystics proceed to confuse the phenomenology of their tasting experience for a truth about how things really are. They infer from the fact that they could not see themselves in the experience that they did not really exist.

> Plurality is totally banished from them, and they become immersed in sheer singularity. Their rational faculties become so satiated that in this state they are, as it were, stunned. No room remains in them for the remembrance of any other than God, nor the remembrance of themselves. Nothing is with them but God. They become intoxicated with such an intoxication that the ruling authority of their rational faculty is overthrown. Hence, one of them [al-Hallaj] says, "I am the Real!" another [Bistami], "Glory be to me, how great is my station!" and still another, "There is nothing in my robe but God!" [also attributed to Bistami].
> (*Niche*, chap. 1, section 45; 1998, 17–18)

What al-Hallaj and Bistami have failed to do is to measure their experiences against what "sober" reason tells us must be the case.

> When this intoxication subsides, the ruling authority of the rational faculty – which is God's balance in His earth – is given back to them. They come to know that what they experienced was not the reality of unification but that it was similar to unification. It was like the words of the lover during a state of extreme passionate love: "I am He whom I love, and He whom I love is I!"
> (*Niche*, chap. 1, section 46; 1998, 18)

That Bistami and al-Hallaj fail to listen to reason is extremely problematic. Furthermore, by saying out loud what they feel while reason is overwhelmed, these "intoxicated lovers" actually can undermine proper religious understanding. In his *Faysal al-Tafriqa* ("The Decisive Criterion"), al-Ghazali suggests that if mystics persist in saying outrageous and dangerously misleading things, the authorities may suppress them in order to maintain the common people's faith in the true religion (see Chapter 7, Section 7.4). The fact that this judgment occurs in a work that in its general thrust is quite tolerant of theological disagreement only goes to show how seriously misleading and damaging al-Ghazali thinks the statements of certain mystics can be.

For al-Ghazali, this talk of "annihilation" and "absorption" cannot be literally true. The statements that describe mystical states in these terms are figurative.

> When this state gets the upper hand, it is called "extinction" in relation to the one who possesses it. Or, rather, it is called "extinction from extinction," since the possessor of the state is extinct from himself and from his own extinction. For he is conscious neither of himself in that state, nor of his own unconsciousness of himself. If he were conscious of his own unconsciousness, then he would be conscious of himself. In relation to the one immersed in it, this state is called "unification," according to the language of metaphor, or is called "declaring God's unity," according to the language of reality.
>
> (*Niche*, chap. 1, section 48; 1998, 18)

In short, al-Ghazali does not deny that this is how things *seem* to the mystic who is in the ecstatic state, but how things seem cannot be how they actually are. Thus, this talk about "absorption" and "annihilation" is merely a figurative way of describing what it is like to be in the presence of God.

Al-Ghazali has suggested that once the mystic "sobers up," his own reason will see that this is how things must be. But as you might recall, al-Ghazali has a somewhat jaundiced view of human reason and its capacity to grasp reality by itself (Chapter 2, Section 2.3). Didn't we learn, for instance, that we can only be absolutely certain of such primal axioms of reason as the law of noncontradiction and "the whole is greater than the part" because God has directly intervened and guaranteed these principles? Also, didn't al-Ghazali allude to the perplexing states of the mystics precisely to undermine human reason's confidence? Why then does al-Ghazali now think that human reason is capable of judging the veracity of direct experiences with the highest being?

Ibn Tufayl appreciates this worry, and he has an interesting answer. Ibn Tufayl's allegorical novel tells a tale about a man, Hayy ibn Yaqzan ("Alive son of Awake"), who grows up on an island, isolated completely from all other humans and thus from human civilization. Hayy, nevertheless, is able to teach himself everything about physics and metaphysics. At some point along the way, he catches a glimpse of a higher reality, and he endeavors to explore that in more detail. After training his body and soul in ways that look remarkably like Sufi ascetic exercises, Hayy succeeds at ascending to the highest levels of intelligible reality. At its pinnacle, he experiences what al-Ghazali refers to as "cognitive gnosis" and then "extinction."

> He disciplined himself and practiced endurance until sometimes days could pass without his moving or eating. And sometimes, in the midst of his struggles, all thoughts and memories would vanish – except self-consciousness. [...] This tormented Hayy, for he knew that it was a blot on the purity of the experience, division of his attention as if with some

other God. Hayy made a concerted effort to purge his self-awareness-of-the-truth, die to himself. At last it came. From memory and mind all disappeared, "heaven and earth and all that is between them," all forms of the spirit and powers of the body, even the disembodied powers that know the Truly Existent. And with the rest vanished the identity that was himself. Everything melted away, dissolved, "scattered into fine dust." All that remained was the One, the True Being, Whose experience is eternal, Who uttered the words identical with himself: "Whose is the kingdom on this day? God's alone, One and Triumphant!"

(*Hayy ibn Yaqzan*; Ibn Tufayl 2009, 148–49 [G. 120][9])

Even the result of this rational, or cognitive ascent is described as a state of intoxication.

Hayy had "died" to himself, and to every other self. He had witnessed his vision and seen nothing in existence but the everliving ONE. Recovered now from his seemingly intoxicated ecstasy, he saw other things once more, and the notion came into his head that his identity was none other than that of the Truth. His true self was the Truth. What he had once supposed to be himself, as distinct from the Truth, was really nothing in itself, but was in reality in no way discrete from the Truth.

(idem, 2009, 150 [G. 122-3])

Notice that after "sobering up," and contrary to what al-Ghazali insists the mystic should do, Hayy persists in thinking that he is God. In other words, Hayy's sober reasoning does not rescue him from error, God must intervene.

This specious reasoning might well have taken root in his soul, had not God in His mercy caught hold of him and guided him back to the truth.

(idem, 150 [G. 124])

Ibn Tufayl immediately proceeds to provide a more rationalistic account of why this appearance of annihilation and complete absorption occurs. It is because our conceptions of one and many, identity and difference, and so forth are drawn from our experience of material reality. The soul is confused when it tries to apply these material categories to immaterial realities.

There is a lot that is of interest in Ibn Tufayl's discussion about unity and difference in the intelligible realm, especially in light of the questions we raised about individuation in Chapter 3 (Section 3.2), but for our purposes at present, the salient point again is that Hayy is *not* able to step back and realize that he had made a mistake until God came to his aid.

We, thus, find in Ibn Tufayl's tale a philosophical account of why it is that at the final stage of a complete *rational* ascent to the Divine, the mystic becomes a babbling fool. We also see that this cognitive "gnosis," at its final stage, is indistinguishable from an irreducibly subjective experience. For this reason, Ibn Tufayl thinks that it is impossible to convey it in rational, literal language.

> The ambition to put this into words is reaching for the impossible – like wanting to taste colors, expecting black as such to taste either sweet or sour. Still I shall not leave you without some hint as to the wonders Hayy saw from this height, not by pounding on the gates of truth, but by coining symbols, for there is no way of finding out what truly occurs at this plateau of experience besides reaching it.
> (*Hayy ibn Yaqzan*; 2009, 149 [G. 122])

You can only know what it really is like to be in the presence of God by experiencing it for yourself. But this state is so disorienting that the language of rational, scientific discourse is unable to capture it. It is hard to tell whether this and that are the same or different. You even lose sight of yourself. Yet, perhaps like Ibn Tufayl, you wish to give others a sense of what it is like. Just urging them to "try it" is not enough to motivate them to make the ascent. Even the sober philosopher, therefore, must cast about for language that will give others "hints" and "symbols." But you also need to warn them about the disorienting and dazzling qualities of the experience. You, therefore, might look for analogous mundane experiences that are similarly disorienting and ecstatic. I think it is no accident that mystics across the various traditions make comparisons to those who are intoxicated and those who are head over heels in love.

To sum up, it could be that the exuberant utterances that Bistami and Hallaj use to report their mystical experiences are accurate reflections of reality. That is, it really could be that some radical form of monism or panentheism is true. But as a matter of historical fact, later medieval interpreters of Bistami and Hallaj felt that they had to rescue their forebears from the heresy of identification with God – either that, or chastise them and suppress their works. For these later interpreters, nothing else can be or come to be God. The gap between God and creation is utterly unbridgeable. For some, including al-Ghazali, these earlier mystics did have some insight into the truth. Nothing is really a substance, in the sense of being a stand-alone entity, save God. The mystic "sees" or experiences this either as the result of a rational ascent to the intelligible realm or perhaps as a gift from God. This vision, when experienced to the fullest extent, suppresses the awareness of one's self and the subject's reason is befuddled.

But the befuddled mystic wants to say something and so she resorts to poetic language to give some sort of indication of what is ultimately superrational and hence ineffable.

Those who return understand now that nothing else can compare to God. They wish, like Tufayl's character Hayy, to push away anything that will detract from the purity of the experience, including that last created impurity, their selves. I suspect that when Ibn Tufayl was composing *Hayy ibn Yaqzan,* he had not only al-Ghazali and Ibn Sina but also the anguished lover al-Hallaj in mind.

> Is it you or I? That would be two gods in me;
> far, far be it from you to assert duality!
> The "he-ness" that is yours is in my nothingness forever;
> my "all" added to your "all" would be a double disguise.
> But where is your essence, from my vantage point when I see you,
> since my essence has become plain in the place where I am not?
> And where is your face? It is the object of my gaze,
> whether in my inmost heart or in the glance of my eye.
> Between you and me there is an "I am" that battles me,
> so take away, by your grace, this "I am" from in between.
> (*Diwan*; al-Hallaj 2018, 167)

Here, al-Hallaj is pleading for a pure vision of God and God alone, to be so present to what he loves that nothing else – not even he – is in view. (On this last point, see Chapter 5, Section 5.3.)

This idea that mystical union is not a literal annihilation of the ascending lover, but rather that it is like the union of two lovers – two distinct people, bound together as though they were one – is a trope that we also find in many Christian mystical works, especially in works by the "affective" mystics (Van Dyke 2014). Here, for instance, is a remarkable description of union-with-distinction by Hadewijch, a thirteenth-century Beguine from some place in the Lowlands, possibly Brabant (now in Belgium):[10]

> Where the abyss of his wisdom is, he will teach you what he is, and with what wondrous sweetness the loved one and the Beloved dwell one in the other, and how they penetrate each other in such a way that neither of the two distinguishes himself from the other. But they abide in one another in fruition, mouth in mouth, heart in heart, body in body, and soul in soul, while one sweet *divine Nature* flows through them both (3 Pet. 1:4), and they are both one thing through each other, but at the same time remain two different selves – yes, and remain so forever.
> (Letter 9; Hadewijch 1980, 66)

For some Christian mystics this romantic model of our encounter with the Divine not only helps us to avoid a commitment to literal annihilation and absorption, it also suggests that we do not need to make an ascent to God by leaving this world behind.

> When my Son was lifted up on the wood of the most holy cross, he did not cut off his divinity from the lowly earth of your humanity. Thus, though he was raised so high, he was not raised off the earth. In fact, his divinity is kneaded into the clay of your humanity like one bread.
> (Catherine of Siena, *Dialogue* 26; 1980, 65)

When God became flesh in Jesus Christ, subsequently died as Christ, and then was raised to heaven, it did not follow that God thereby left the world after taking a brief tour within. God is still here; he is "kneaded" into the fabric of this world, and thus, he is available to us now. We do not need to leave the world behind or to wait for death in order to be in "union" with God. This is something we may want to keep in mind when we return to the idea that achieving perfect happiness requires that we "empty" ourselves in Chapter 5 (Section 5.3).

Poetic descriptions of a direct encounter with God which cast our union with Him in terms of an intense loving bond also give us a different picture of what life might be like in Heaven. Our final "return" won't entail our annihilation. Instead, it could be that we stand eternally in an intense loving relation with God.

There are, however, still some peculiar features in this picture, ones that mimic some of the potential downsides to the Platonic after life. Our love for God, according to al-Hallaj and other "love mystics," is so single-minded that everything else is ignored. "Annihilation" may merely mean that we forget ourselves, not that we cease to exist. But forgetting ourselves is still pretty extreme; for this seems to mean that we will put aside our desires and wishes, replacing them with God's. Can I trust that God will want my spouse or my nephews to flourish? How will I know whether they are flourishing? For if I turn my gaze away from God to my spouse, doesn't this amount to my loving something lesser when there is something greater to love? If God's will is that I love *Him*, will I be *disobeying* God if I also love my family? If the mystical state is a foretaste of our state in the afterlife, will we not only forget ourselves there, will we forget all of our ties to other people? We will come back to many of these questions in Chapters 5 and 6. For now, let this suffice: As in the Platonist picture, Heaven seems to exclude reunions with our loved ones. They might be there, since neither they nor I will be annihilated, but both they and I will be fixated solely upon God.

4.4 Individual Humans, Persons, and Moral Standing

At first, I asked you to go along with the Aristotelian and the Platonist and to put aside the accidental features that accrue around each of us. But when we do this, we seem to lose sight of many of the things that we commonly take to be important. The accidental may not make us what we are, but surely it seems to make us *who* we are. One way to think about this is to think of individual humans as having a certain kind of standing, that of a person. As we think of things nowadays, persons are the focal points for a whole host of features that seem to matter quite a bit. In particular, it is persons – and not necessarily human beings considered as biological entities – who are the locus of various rights, privileges, and protections. This notion of personhood is a modern notion, one that developed over time and due to a host of causes. We will not be able to trace all of those, but I propose that we make an initial foray into medieval notions of the person. As we will see, they have a term "persona" and even some of the makings of our modern notion in play, but in other respects, they may not be tracking the same cluster of notions that we are when they talk about "persons."

One thing to note straightaway and before we venture into our survey of some of the metaphysical issues and their ethical ramifications is this: Even though medieval Latin speakers had a word that seems to map on to our notion of person to some extent, any full account of medieval views on persons, their nature, their identity, their rights and privileges, and so forth, will need to track all of the ways in which medieval intellectuals discussed human beings and self-reflexivity. For instance, the Arabic word *nafs*, which is often translated as "the self" – especially, when it appears in Sufi texts – is in its basic sense merely a reflexive pronoun. Thus, in many contexts it just means "itself." Latin, Greek, and Hebrew similarly have reflexive pronouns. There is currently a lot of interest in medieval views about self-knowledge. These too would need to be factored into any full study of personhood.

When thinking about individual humans as persons, the first thing perhaps to observe is that while the notion of a person overlaps with humans, it need not coincide with the set consisting of all and only individual instances of *Homo sapiens*. The set including all persons seems to be bigger. Modern Western law, for instance, often recognizes some entities as persons that are decidedly not human beings. Corporations such as Apple, British Petroleum, or Trader Joe's are treated as "legal persons." For most medieval thinkers, the class of persons included a host of nonhuman substances, namely, angels, demons, and even God. In addition, we might wonder whether there are nonhuman corporeal animals that also count as persons. For instance, what about great apes, dolphins, and whales? Here, however, there does not seem to be a clear medieval analogue. While Aristotle was impressed by the social nature of bees and certain other animals and he was even on some occasions tempted to attribute a certain analogue of practical reasoning to some higher forms of animals, he never went so far as to attribute a rational soul to anything lower than human animals. Medieval philosophers and theologians tend to follow Aristotle's lead. We will explore some of the ethical ramifications of this in Chapter 6.

Nonhuman animals are not the only kinds of things that are excluded from the set of persons. Medieval thought is embedded within broader historical trends. And as is well known, human history is littered with cases where some humans are not granted the status of personhood as we now tend to conceive of it. Since medieval thinking about persons is an outgrowth of ancient law and culture, and Western medieval thinking an outgrowth in particular of Roman law and culture, it is perhaps useful to quickly peruse some of the characteristics of the Greco-Roman notion of a "person."

The Latin word "persona" can be traced back to Hellenistic thought, if not earlier (Brouwer 2019, 29–34). The Greek Stoics, for instance, began to reflect on this idea starting as early as the third century BCE. These Greek discussions were carried over into the Latin tradition by Cicero and Seneca, both of whom were widely read by medieval Latin readers. The Stoics themselves drew upon earlier uses of the word "prosopon." Both the Greek and Latin terms often signified a "role" that someone takes on in a play (Brouwer 2019, 20–9). Thus, we find someone like Seneca distinguishing between the unified agent embodied by the Stoic sage and the majority of humans, who are constantly changing the roles that they take on, or the masks that they wear.

> I believe that it is the greatest thing for a human to act as one. Yet apart from the sage no one acts as one, the rest of us we act in variable ways. At one time we will appear to you as frugal and serious, at another profligate and vain. We constantly change *persona*, putting on one that is contrary to the one we took off.
> (Seneca, *Letter* 120, section 22, my translation)

This constant change of masks leads Seneca to conclude his letter by exclaiming, "Concerning the one whom you presently see, so great is the change that it can rightfully be asked, 'Who is he?'"

The notion of a *persona* as a role is taken up in Roman law, which as early as the second century BCE divided legislation into laws pertaining to persons, laws pertaining to things (*res*), and laws relating to actions.[11] All three divisions concerned individual humans and their actions. The laws pertaining to persons concern an individual's status or standing relative to others. For instance, it covers the rights and obligations of individuals in so far as they are free persons or slaves, citizens or foreigners, heads of households or subordinate family members. By contrast, the laws pertaining to things, as one commentator puts it, treat individuals as "equals." This does not mean that all individuals actually are on equal footing. Laws pertaining to things often involve property, but not all persons can own property and thus engage in transactions involving goods and services. For instance, in Rome, slaves could not own property. Thus, in order to be governed by laws pertaining to transactions of property, an individual already must have a certain kind of status.[12]

The point of this digression into Roman law is merely to see that the Greco-Roman notion of a *persona* does not neatly line up with our rough and ready characterization of the modern notion. In some sense, it is more compendious, since it includes individuals who are not free. For that very reason, under Roman law being considered a person does not automatically entail that said person has a certain set of rights and privileges. One's rights and privileges stemmed from the specific *persona*, that is, role that one is currently playing.

To be sure, the notion of a person being a role that an individual human can take on, and thus perhaps in some cases take off, suggests all sorts of interesting possibilities for developing ethics and political philosophy. It also holds out a number of intriguing possibilities for thinking about one of the central mysteries of Christianity, namely, the Trinity. It is thus a curious fact that one of the key players in developing the framework that scholastic theologians used for discussing the Trinity decisively shifts the notion of a person *away* from the idea of it being a mask or role to that of an individual substance that has a specific property.

In a treatise on the nature of the Incarnation, which is intrinsically tied up with Trinitarian theology, Boethius starts off by reminding his readers that the word "persona" is borrowed from the masks that represent individual humans in comedies and tragedies. But he immediately proceeds to link these "masks" to individual human substances.

> But since, as we have said it was by the *personae* they put on that actors represented the individual humans concerned in a tragedy or a comedy – that is, Hecuba or Medea or Simon or Chremes, and thus, all other humans who could be clearly recognized by their appearance – the Latins used the name *persona*, the Greeks *prosopa*. But the Greeks far more clearly called the individual subsistence of a rational nature by the name *hupostasis*, while we through want of appropriate words have kept the name handed down to us, calling that a person which they call a *hupostasis*.
> (*A Treatise against Eutyches and Nestorius,* 3; Boethius 1973, 87, modified)

Thus, while Boethius acknowledges the original sense of the term "persona," he quickly adopts it to stand in for a term used by the Greek theologians, who have a "richer vocabulary," in order to talk about the metaphysical status of the Father, the Son, and the Holy Spirit, as well as the status of the two natures in Christ.

Boethius's maneuver has a decisive impact on how persons are discussed in a great deal of subsequent scholastic philosophical theology. But rather than attempting to do justice to the tangled and highly technical history of that debate, let us instead turn to one particular feature of Boethius's understanding of a person, namely, his thought that persons are essentially rational. For it is here that we might wonder whether Boethius and those who follow him are constricting the class of true persons in potentially pernicious ways.

In the previous quotation from Boethius we can see his preferred understanding of the proper theological notion of "person": A person is "an individual substance of a rational nature" (1973, 85). Boethius arrives at this by thinking about what sort of thing a person must be. It cannot be an accident, since as he puts it, no one would say that any instance of whiteness, blackness, or size is a person. Thus, a person must be a kind of substance. But what kind or kinds of substances can be persons? Clearly, Boethius thinks, a person cannot be a universal substance. And only some sorts of individual substances seem to fit the bill.

> Now from all this it is clear that "person" cannot be predicated of bodies which have no life (for no one ever says that any stone is a person), nor yet of living things which lack sense (for neither is any tree a person), nor finally of that which is bereft of mind and reason (for person is not attributable to horse or ox or any other of the animals, which dumb and without reasons live a life of sense alone). But we do say there is a person attributable to human, we say it of God, and we say it of angel.
> (*Against Eutyches* 2; Boethius 1973, 85, modified)

Thus, persons can be incorporeal or corporeal, mutable or immutable. But what is essential to personhood are individuality and rationality.

Now, as Christina Van Dyke has observed, medieval intellectuals often insist that "rationality" covers a wide range of abilities, including not only the ability to understand and reason but also the abilities to remember, to will, and to love (2019, 142). This more generous understanding of what the rational soul is capable of might help to mitigate our unease to some measure. We don't have to be good at syllogistic logic, for instance, in order to count as persons. But even with this generous notion of rationality in place, we might still worry that this Boethian notion of personhood is too restrictive, and not merely because it rules out the possibility that dolphins and chimpanzees are persons. We might, for instance, worry that this definition is unnecessarily ableist (Williams 2019b). Are infants persons? What about individual humans with serious cognitive impediments? These worries can become especially pointed, if we combine the ideas that persons are rational with the notion that persons are *foci* for rights, privileges, and obligations.

One of the fascinating possibilities is that rationality may not be all that important after all. As Scott Williams has observed, in the scholastic debates that followed Boethius, the notion of rationality in actual fact played little to no role. The focus was rather on how to best understand, on the one hand, the relationship between Christ and his two natures, and on the other, the relations between the three subsisting manifestations of the Father, Son, and Holy Spirit and the unique Divine essence. To accomplish that, all we need is the notion of a *suppositum*, that is, an individual, complete, independent, incommunicable being (Williams 2019a, 83).

Perhaps Boethius was wrong to link rationality to personhood. But, surely, persons are distinct in *some* ways from a host of other created beings. Are rocks persons? In addition to Boethius's discussion of *persona*, Latin-speaking medieval thinkers could draw upon theoretical discussions of the grammatical notion of *persona* in Priscian (fl 500s) and other late Roman grammarians (Brouwer 2019, 37–8). I wager that it is the grammatical notion of *persona* that is work, for instance, in Peter Abelard's claim that every real thing (*res*) is "personally discrete." For in these contexts, which happen to be on the question of the status of universals (see Chapter 3, Section 3.2), Abelard means that everything is brutely particular. Since every pebble is personally discrete, does it follow that every pebble is a person? I don't think that even Abelard would go so far as to say that, at least, not if we first could explain to him, even if only in some rough sense, what we had in mind. But since we are already imagining a scenario where we could travel in time and talk to Abelard, what *would* he say is the mark of a person? It is not too far-fetched to imagine that he would fall back on rationality being the mark of personhood. If so, we are back to where we started.

Of course, to a great extent, we are being unfair to Boethius, Abelard, and other medieval thinkers if we insist that they use *our* notion of personhood. Historians of philosophy are constantly on their guard against inappropriate anachronisms. Here may be one of those cases where we are trying too hard to find something of ours in their way of thinking. Doing so makes it harder for us to listen to what they are saying. In fact, one of the salutary features of historical work is that it affords us the chance to step back and reappraise our understandings of how the world is and what we ought to think about it. By venturing tentatively into medieval metaphysical speculations about *personae*, we can perhaps see where we came up with some of our ideas. But perhaps we can also see possibilities that we did not take.

Study Questions

1) Which proposal do you find more compelling? Are you essentially a composite of soul and body, or are you merely a soul (or merely a body)? What arguments can you marshal in defense of your preferred view?
2) I suggested that it is not too far-fetched to think that rivers and cars are only improperly the same, but the idea that animals are no different from rivers does strain credulity. Am I right about that? Would you want to resist the claim that cars are only loosely the same over time and changes in parts? If so, what sorts of metaphysical constituents must something like a car have in order to persist as this car? Was Buridan right about rivers, cars, and horses, but wrong about humans?
3) I have suggested that mystical "annihilation" cannot literally be true because it would violate the No Gappy Existence postulate. But ask yourself, is this postulate as obvious as I have proposed that it is? Can you reconstruct the reasons why many medieval philosophers agree that a thing cannot have a "gappy" existence? Are their arguments sound?
4) What sort of thing do you think a person is? Is it a substance? Is it a role? Is it something else altogether? If you think it is a substance, what kind or kinds of substances can be persons? Do you agree with Boethius's account of personhood? Is it too restrictive or too inclusive?

Notes

1 The Latin word *quid* means "what." A quiddity, then, is a "whatness." *Quale* is the word for "in what manner," which is the root of the Latin word *qualitas* and our "quality." Thus, if you were to say that you are a student of philosophy, a medieval metaphysician would point out that you are giving an answer to the *quale* question, not the *quid* question.
2 We need to add "substance" to the label because, in present debates, there are forms of mind–body dualism which do not posit that the mind is a distinct substance, even though the mind is not reducible to mere material stuff. This form of dualism is sometimes referred to in the literature as *property dualism*.
3 See, for instance, the arguments leveled against Aristotle's definition of the soul by Plotinus (270) in his *Ennead* IV.7.8[5]. John Blund and others might also have come across these ancient criticisms in Calcidius's fourth-century *Commentary on Plato's "Timaeus,"* which was written in Latin and widely read, especially in the twelfth century. See *Commentary*, §225 (Calcidius 2016, 475–7).

4 In general, I have tried to use Ibn Sina's Arabic works when presenting his views. However, the use here of the Latin translation of Ibn Sina's work seems to be warranted, given that presently we are examining how Ibn Sina's thought influenced Latin scholastic thinking about the soul and its relation to the body.

5 Even if we restrict our attention to non-substances, like Boethius's house and my car, numerous medieval philosophers argued that the existential reading is too strong. Many suggested that Boethius only intended to be talking about "principal parts," which are the parts that are necessary for the thing to exist. Things like the head and heart of an animal would be principal parts, whereas the fingers or hair would be "non-principal," or "secondary," parts. Likewise, while my car doesn't need this spark plug to persist, it does need its engine. The notion of a principal part does not appear in Boethius's *On Division* or his other treatments of parts and whole. But Boethius does make a distinction between *parts* and *parts of parts* (*On Division*, 888b). And, thus, the formula that a whole "consists of parts" might be taken to be an implicit restriction to those parts that immediately produce or constitute the whole. On this and other interpretations of Boethius's priority claim, see Arlig 2019.

6 Seneca's view is this: "Not one of us in old age is the same as he who was young. Not one of us in the morning is the same as he who was yesterday. Our bodies flow rapidly in the manner of a river. Whatever you see runs away with time; nothing of that which we see persists. Even as I say that those things are changing, I myself have changed. It is as Heraclitus says, 'we descend and we do not descend twice into the same river' [cf. DK frag. 49a]. For while the river's name remains the same, the water has passed on. This is more apparent in a stream than in a human, but we too no less sail by on a quick course. Hence, I am amazed by our madness: we love so much the most fleeting thing, the body, and we dread the fact that at some time we will die, even though at every moment a death of what was before has already occurred" (Seneca *Letters to Lucilius,* 58, 22–3; my translation).

7 Where a particular medieval Aristotelian falls on this map sometimes is a matter of controversy. Of particular note is the robust debate about Aquinas's position. See, e.g., Stump 2003, 206–12, Brower 2014, 250–4.

8 Incidentally, this is not just an oddity of Platonist accounts of the afterlife. Aquinas, for instance, also seems to paint a picture where we persist eternally as embodied cognizers of eternal truths. See Van Dyke 2015 and Brower (2014, 279–310).

9 The designation "G." indicates the pagination to the Arabic edition of Gauthier, which Goodman provides in the margins of his translation.

10 For discussion of the evidence that we have of this remarkable person, see the introduction (esp. 2–5) of Hadewijch 1980.

11 See, e.g., Gaius (fl. 2nd cent. CE), *Institutes*, section 8 (ed. Poste, 39); also, Brouwer 2019, 38–40.

12 See the commentary by Edward Poste, in *Gaius, Institutionum iuris civilis*, 39–44, esp. 44.

Suggestions for Further Reading

When it comes to the composition of human beings, in addition to the resources already identified in Chapter 3, I recommend King 2012 and Klima 2002. On identity over time, as well as a quick survey of some of the ways in which medieval thinkers thought about identity and sameness more generally, see Arlig 2021.

In the previous chapter, I mentioned some general reading for those interested in mysticism, including Van Dyke 2014. On the fascinating story – or perhaps better, legend – of al-Hallaj, see the monumental four-volume study by Massignon 1982. This has been abridged and published as a one-volume paperback (Massignon 1994).

For an overview of medieval notions of persons that places special emphasis on speculation that took place outside of the Western European universities, and thus, removed from much of the debate over the metaphysics of the Incarnation and the Trinity, see Van Dyke 2019 and 2022, chapter 5. Scholars are starting to take an interest in what medieval philosophers have to say about physical and cognitive disabilities. Scott M. Williams has recently edited a collection of articles (2020) on medieval Christian thought about disability.

5 Happiness and the Meaning of Life

> 5.1 The Greek Background: Eudaimonism and the Emphasis on Virtue 141
> 5.2 From Aristotelian *Eudaimonia* to Heavenly Bliss 155
> 5.3 Humility, Emptying Oneself, and Going beyond Virtue 162
> 5.4 Resurrection and the Afterlife: Philosophy Encounters Scripture 171

At the beginning of every term, I ask my students to write a short email where they introduce themselves to me. I ask them to tell me who they are, why they are taking my class, and what they hope to learn by the end of the term. I also routinely ask them about their preconceptions of what philosophy is. Unsurprisingly, many of my students reply to this last question with effectively this answer: Philosophy is supposed to help us pinpoint what the meaning of human life is.

There are several things that we might have in mind when we are interested in "meaning," but often I take it that when we look for the "meaning of life," what we are most keen to discover are our true aims and goals. Certainly, we want food, safety from harm, and pleasure. But we also want more than those. Cows can have all those kinds of things. We are *human* animals. We want a life where we have lived up to our *human* potential, where we flourish as human beings, where we have accomplished the things that we ought to have done given that we are the specific kind of creature that we are. We want to write books and make art. We want to be the fastest runner in the 800-meter dash. We want a partner and kids, and good friends.

Often we say that someone has lived a "meaningful life" when they have left their mark on the world. The "significant" people in our history books often are there merely because of their impact on the course of human history: so-and-so started this war, so-and-so created this vaccine, and so on. But we also record the stories of people who lived life well, who exhibit human excellence. These are people we hold up as role models. We want to

DOI: 10.4324/9780429348020-5

be like them. So, once again, we see that at least part of what most matters to us is what our ultimate goals should be.

In the last chapter, we observed how some medieval philosophers thought about what it is to be a human animal and a human person. For many of them, the distinctive feature of humans – what marks humans off from other animals – is that they have reason (Section 4.4). In this chapter, we will see how the rational aspect of our nature is used to develop an account of what it is to flourish as a human being and what sorts of things human beings should aim for. As we will see in the first part of this chapter (Section 5.1), flourishing, or as it is often translated into English, "happiness," is the central focus of the Aristotelian approach to the question of how we ought to live. In tandem with this is an emphasis on developing certain kinds of habits and dispositions, which they usually call "virtues," and which include many of the things that we nowadays might identify as character traits. But of course, finding accounts of happiness, virtue, and character are only some of the ways in which we would could go about answering the question of how we ought to live in the world. "How should I live?" is an ethical question, and it is generally thought that ethics also deals with the sorts of actions that I should undertake, and specifically what actions I should do or avoid in relation to others. One might even insist that these latter inquiries are the central ones for any ethicist. While we will focus in this chapter on the Aristotelian way of reflecting on the kind of life that humans ought to live and the character traits that they should possess, it would be a mistake to conclude that medieval Aristotelian philosophers have nothing to say about those other questions. In Chapter 6, we will examine one particularly medieval way of thinking about how we ought to treat others, namely, by reflecting on what it means to love one's neighbor, to love God, and to love one's self.

In the previous chapter, we noted how it is not clear whether Aristotle thought that the human soul will survive separation from the body. Even if part of me does survive, it is far from clear whether this intellectual aspect or part of me will survive as an individual personality (Section 4.2). Hence, it is not surprising that *Aristotle*'s account of human flourishing seems to be focused on the life well lived in this mundane period of our existence. We should strive to live like gods to the degree that we can, but there is no indication that this godlike existence will continue after we leave off from this mortal coil. Medieval philosophers, by contrast, embedded their account of human flourishing within the larger fabric of prophetic religion. The scriptures of Judaism, Christianity, and Islam all seem to assume that the individual will persist after death – if not immediately, then at least at some future date – and either flourish or suffer in an afterlife. Accordingly, medieval philosophers not only had to determine how one ought to live here and

Happiness and the Meaning of Life 141

now, they had to say something about how to prepare for the life to come so that they will flourish there and then (Section 5.2).

This, of course, means that we will have to revisit the question that we raised for the philosophers as to what it is precisely that will persist and inhabit this life to come. In the previous chapter we observed that certain Platonic and mystical currents in medieval thought maintain that the individual is "annihilated" or "absorbed" into the divine, intelligible realm (Section 4.3). In this chapter, we will return to this theme and explore some ways in which this notion of union and bliss might come into conflict with establishment notions of ethical behavior and authority (Section 5.3). There is also the question of whether we will be embodied in the afterlife (Section 5.4), for as some argued a complete human nature is a composite of form *and matter*. According to some, Scripture implies that we will be resurrected as an embodied human animal. For others, however, matter and the body are sources of decay, corruption, and sin. It would thus seem to follow that the human individual will only really flourish once they have been released from their bodies and fashioned as something fully immaterial.

5.1 The Greek Background: Eudaimonism and the Emphasis on Virtue

To understand medieval conceptions of the good and flourishing life it is crucial that you have some background in ancient Greek ethics, and especially the ethical framework developed by Aristotle. This does not mean that Aristotelian ethics is the only source utilized by medieval philosophers and theologians. Stoic and Epicurean ethics also had a palpable impact on both Christian and Arabic moral thought. In the Christian world, this is due to the influence of the early Church Fathers as well as the extant writings of Seneca and Cicero, which were often read in one's initial liberal arts education, such as when one was studying grammar and rhetoric. In the Islamic principalities, the sources are not always so easy to trace, but clearly al-Kindi's (ninth-century) ethics, which focuses on modifying one's desires in order to eliminate sorrow and achieve tranquility, has intriguing affinities with Hellenistic philosophy and in particular classical Stoicism. (See his *How to Dispel Sorrows*, in al-Kindi 2012, 249 ff.; also Butterworth 2005, 267–71.) And then there are the ethical traditions of Judaism, Zoroastrianism, and at least in the case for some Muslim thinkers, other Eastern philosophies and religions.[1] Nonetheless, Aristotle's framework and technical terminology is central to how many medieval philosophers carve up the conceptual terrain, especially in many of the works that you are most likely to come across in your reading and your courses. In this section, then, we will take a quick tour of medieval Aristotelian ethics, which, as I have already pointed out, tends to emphasize human flourishing and the cultivation of habits and character, and to downplay the need to develop an elaborate rubric for determining what particular action one should take at this moment of time and in these particular circumstances.

The Aristotelian's ethical theory is a version of eudaimonistic virtue ethics. It will serve our purposes if we elaborate upon the two technical notions that constitute the genus under which Aristotle's theory falls.

Since we have already indicated that the Aristotelian is more interested in virtue than in determining which particular acts are virtuous given a highly specified set of circumstances, let us start with the fact that the Aristotelian theory is a version of *virtue* ethics.

Metaphysically, virtues are a kind of disposition or habit, which in turn is a kind of quality. According to the scheme Aristotle lays out in his *Categories*, this means that virtues are accidental properties of persons. If you head off from here to read more medieval treatises on the virtues, it will be helpful to appreciate this, as the fact that virtues are kinds of accidents informs some of the subtler scholastic inquiries that arise in works that take the *Nicomachean Ethics* as their starting point. For our purposes, we can sidestep such issues.

Aristotle's notion of virtue stems from the basic idea that things have functions. An axe's function is cutting wood. That is why it is made of the kinds of materials axes are made of and why it is shaped in the way that it is. An excellent or "virtuous" axe is an axe that cuts wood well. Of course, my axe often is sitting idly in my shed. But so long as it *can* cut wood well when I use it, it can be said to have its virtue. This is why virtues are said to be dispositions or, as medieval thinkers often will put it, "habits." A virtuous thing need not always be actually performing its function; it merely needs to have the potential to immediately perform its function well when called upon to do so.

Just as artifacts like axes have functions and virtues, so too do living things. Some horses have a constitution that, if developed, would make them fit for racing; other horses are built in such a way that, if this potential were developed, they would be capable of hauling heavy burdens. A horse belonging to the first class is a virtuous horse if it has developed the capacity to run swiftly; the latter kind of horse is virtuous if it is strong. Notice again that the racehorse does not always have to be racing in order to be virtuous. Aristotelians describe the act of racing as a "second act." A disposition to race well is a "first act," and thus it is also a potential. By saying that a racehorse has achieved or acquired a first act, Aristotle means that a latent capacity has been developed to the point that the horse can be immediately taken out of the stall to race. The infant horse, for instance, fails to have this first act, even though it has the potential to race well if put through a rigorous course of training.

You can perhaps see where this is going, just as with axes and horses, we might think that humans have functions, and thus, like axes and horses, we can either perform these functions well or poorly. We are virtuous in so far as we are capable of performing our functions well. We are vicious in so far as we are incapable of performing our functions well.

Human capacities and functions are associated with different "parts" of the human soul. Accordingly, there are two broad classes of virtues. Some correspond to the part of the soul that is capable of reasoning, others to the part of the soul responsible for sensing and desiring.

> As for the virtues, there are two kinds: moral virtues and rational virtues. Opposed to them are two kinds of vices. The rational virtues are found in the rational part [which include the ability to reason from causes to effects, the ability to cognize intelligible objects, and the capacity to grasp things quickly] [...] The moral virtues are found only in the appetitive part, and the sentient part is in this case a servant of the appetitive part. The virtues of this part are very numerous; for example, moderation, liberality, justice, gentleness, humility, contentment, courage, and others. The vices of this part consist in being deficient or excessive with regard to these.
> (Maimonides, *The Eight Chapters*, ch. 2; Maimonides 1975, 65)

However, not all human capacities and functions are associated with virtues. In particular, the lowest part of the soul, the nutritive part, does not have virtues or vices.

> Neither virtue nor vice is ascribed to the nutritive and imaginative parts. Rather, one says that they flow properly or improperly, just as one says that a given man's digestion is excellent, has stopped, or is impaired, or that his imagination is impaired or flows properly. There is neither virtue nor vice in any of these things.
> (idem)

It is worth pointing out that Maimonides (1204) adds our capacity to develop and to store representations of external objects in our souls to the list of capacities that can neither be virtuous nor vicious. It merely functions or fails to function well. Thus, if I have a poor memory, this is not a vice, it is merely an impairment. The same is true of dreams. But the most important point again is that strictly speaking it is improper to say that some aspects of humans and their bodies can be virtuous or vicious.

Those axes and at least some of the capacities of horses must therefore be revisited and seen for what they are. Like my Arlig chair in Chapter 3,

I use these cases as heuristics. Nevertheless, many of the things that I indicate when talking about "virtuous" tools and horses still hold. In particular, Aristotelians insist that the sorts of dispositions which can count as virtues are not present in their actualized form when we are born. It takes training and practice to develop both the moral and the rational virtues. For the lower-level virtues, especially, this requires a long process of habituation.

> Know that these moral virtues and vices are acquired and firmly established in the soul by frequently repeating the actions pertaining to a particular moral habit over a long period of time and by our becoming accustomed to them.
> (*Eight Chapters*, ch. 4; Maimonides 1975, 68)

Clearly, what Maimonides has in mind is the kind of training that every parent of small children is familiar with. Small children don't have fully developed capacities to reason. But surely it is not wise to wait for reason to develop before we try to instill good habits in our kids. Our moral education and the cultivation of some of our virtues begins early on with a combination of rewards and punishments. Notice, then, that our moral development (and also our intellectual one) depends not just on nature but also on nurture. Kids who grow up in bad environments are in danger of being corrupted, as the vices are also something that are instilled only by repetition and habituation.

> Since by nature man does not possess either virtue or vice at the beginning of his life (as we shall explain in the eighth chapter), he undoubtedly is habituated from childhood to actions in accordance with his family's ways of life and that of the people in his town. These actions may be in the mean, excessive, or defective – as we have indicated.
> (idem)

This is a thought that was probably in al-Ghazali's (1111) mind when he noted that he cannot trust those beliefs that were instilled in him by his parents and neighbors (Chapter 2, Section 2.3). This observation about our upbringing and the company we keep will be something we return to in Chapter 6, where we will see it at work in Augustine's explanation of why he stole some pears as a youth. The rational virtues, such as practical know-how or the ability to grasp and reason with abstract concepts, are clearly not inborn. They too require acquisition through rigorous and continuous practice. And thus, as we will see in Chapter 7, the philosophers will argue that we must create a political structure that promotes and sustains the life of the mind.

Some medieval philosophers, especially many in the Western scholastic tradition, maintain that, while many virtues require training and habituation, there are some that a person needs but which she cannot acquire on her own.

> Besides the virtues we acquire by our acts, we must acknowledge that human beings have further virtues infused by God, as I have already remarked [art. 9].
> (Aquinas *Disputed Questions on Virtue*, On the Virtues in General, article 10; Aquinas 2014, 549)

Aquinas (1274) starts to make his case by observing that human goods are diverse, and hence, the human virtues are diverse.

> We must next recognize that there are two goods for human beings. The first corresponds to our nature. The second, however, surpasses the capacity of our nature, for the following reason. Passive subjects must attain the perfections they receive from their corresponding agents in diverse ways, in line with the diversity among those agents' active powers. That is why we see that the perfections and forms caused by a natural agent's action do not surpass the receiver's natural capacity; after all, a natural active power corresponds to a natural passive power.
> (idem)

Aquinas resorts to a lot of technical vocabulary here and he is making full use of the metaphysical framework of act and potency, which we lightly touched upon in our survey of metaphysical issues in Chapter 3. However, I think we can readily see the basic idea if we help ourselves to a simple analogy. Consider a cube of lead. Even when it is at room temperature, we know that it could be heated up considerably without losing is cubic shape and certainly without it being changed into something else. This is the lead cube's "passive natural power." Of course, if we apply too much heat the lead will melt, and if we apply even more heat (or as we would now describe it, energy), we can even transform the lead into some other element. Thus, if we (the agent in this case) want to heat up the lead without compromising it or its shape, we will need to calibrate our action so that it lines up with the lead's capacity to absorb heat. By analogy, we can think about how this might apply to forging good human dispositions. If we are good teachers, we try to calibrate the difficulty of our lessons and training regimes so as to meet our trainee where they presently are. We don't expect infants to run 400-meter intervals or to work through quadratic equations.

There is something else at work in Aquinas's argument that will be important for what comes next. Aquinas notes that there are also limitations of the power of the agent. We can melt lead using technologies that we have to hand. But perhaps there are substances that we cannot melt, no matter how much heat we produce. If we take on board the common medieval ontology, there are in fact substances that are utterly impervious to material manipulation. These are those immaterial, intelligible substances. If something or someone had an intelligible, immaterial aspect or part in them, it might be well beyond anything in our power to cause any kind of change in this part.

> However, the perfections and forms that come from a supernatural agent of infinite power – God – surpasses the capability of the receiver's nature. That is why the rational soul, which God causes directly, surpasses the capacity of its matter, so that the bodily matter cannot entirely contain and confine it. Instead, it retains a power and operation that the matter does not take part in.
>
> (idem)

We have seen glimpses of the underlying metaphysical dispute that Aquinas is entering into here. Recall that, for Aristotelian natural philosophers and metaphysicians, most "natural" forms are "educed" from their matter (Sections 3.5 and 4.2). That is, the matter has certain ways it can be that are, so to speak, latently present in it. What a natural agent does is to activate these latent potentials in the matter. But when it comes to the capacity for thinking about forms in an abstract way, that is, so that the forms are "present" without any matter, this capacity is beyond the capacity of matter. Hence, God has to create the rational part of us and insert it into the human animal. Hopefully, you can begin to glimpse the implication. If only God can make it, it might be that only God can manipulate it.

Here, however, we need to tread carefully. For it seems that we humans can manipulate some immaterial objects, especially since even the capacities that we are targeting in moral training, such a developing temperance and gentleness, are in a sense immaterial. This is even more true when it comes to training in say mathematics and metaphysics. It is hard for me to presently make a quick, clean argument for it; so let it suffice for now that according to Aquinas and many others, even these intellectual activities seem to require the use of material instruments and the "phantasms" that these material processes create.[2] Thus, the activities of human teachers and trainers, even of the intellect, is geared toward working with these material instruments. There is, however, on Aquinas's view an aspect of us that is beyond the reach of human teachers and trainers.

Our human aim in Aquinas's view – and note that here he is in broad agreement with the more Platonist philosophers we are examining – is to know God and to be present with Him. This desire, Aquinas notes, is "natural."

> This is clear from the fact that human beings' natural desire can come to rest in nothing but God alone: It is natural for us, when we encounter effects, to be moved to desire to investigate their causes, and this desire will remain restless until we arrive at the first cause, God.
> (*Disputed Questions*, On the Virtues in General, art. 10; Aquinas 2014, 549)

God creates in a human animal a rational capacity. Thus, it is natural for us to want to reason about the things that we experience. But every time we find an explanation or a cause of something, we see that cause or explanatory principle too is an effect of something else. This chain, then, will never stop until we reach the cause of everything.

The trouble, as Aquinas sees things, is that the last stages in this process of intellectual ascent or return cannot be reached on our own. Nor can they be reached with the aid of any other human being. God must not only provide the "final perfection" of human souls, the "happiness of eternal life"; God has to make certain changes to our rational soul so that it can take those final steps.

> Now, the natural principles of our operations are the soul's essence and its powers, specifically the intellect and will, which are the principles for the operations of a human being as such. The intellect and will could not play this role unless the intellect had a grasp of principles to direct it in further cognition and unless the will had a natural inclination to the good corresponding to its nature, as I have noted in a prior question [art. 8]. Therefore, of performing actions directed to the end of eternal life, human beings are divinely infused, first of all, with grace, which gives the soul a kind of spiritual being, and then with faith, hope, and charity, so that faith might illuminate the intellect regarding certain supernatural objects of cognition [...] In addition, through hope and charity the will acquires an inclination to the supernatural good, which the human will's natural inclination was inadequate to direct us to.
> (*Disputed Questions*, On the Virtues in General, art. 10; Aquinas 2014, 550)

I have said that the technical notion of an "infused" virtue is something that we see most clearly in Western scholasticism. But notice the affinities between Aquinas's reasoning here and al-Ghazali's account of how we are able to escape from skepticism and move forward with certainty (Section 2.3). Both of them argue that at some point, if left on our own, we will get stuck. We won't have the confidence and conviction to embrace the starting points of an intellectual investigation, and as Aquinas notes here, we won't have the motivation to persist on the path of righteousness. God needs to swoop in and tinker with our souls, so that the dim becomes clear and the indifferent or even undesirable becomes the only thing to aim at.

Here I can only gesture at a huge debate that develops in scholasticism between the so-called intellectualists and the so-called voluntarists. (These labels, incidentally, are given by contemporary scholars who study these debates. I know of no scholastic who used these labels.) Aquinas seems to be claiming that God makes it so that my will sees that the only rational way forward is to aim at God and God alone. This comes very close to entailing that reason *forces* or *compels* the will to choose the path toward God. (Compare this to what we said about certainty in Chapter 2, especially in Section 2.2.) Other scholastics thought that this was tantamount to God undermining our free will. John Duns Scotus (1308) and others stressed the importance of the freedom of the will. The will is so free, they thought, that it could even make the obviously irrational choice.[3]

Let that suffice for a brief tour of medieval Aristotelian thinking about the virtues. We can already see how the Aristotelian focus on virtues as the development of potentialities that we have due to what and how we are, helps these philosophers distinguish those aspects of human beings that are distinctive of humans from those aspects that we share with other creatures. Like all plants and animals, we take in water and nutrients, we metabolize them, and we perpetuate the species through the act of reproduction. Like other animals, we move about, which requires that we have sense organs. Some higher-order animals even seem to have memory, which allows them to solve practical problems and to be trained. According to Aristotle, what sets us apart from all other embodied animate creatures is our capacity to reason, and in particular, to reason theoretically. As we will see below, the capacities that make us distinctive as human beings, will give us crucial information when it comes to identifying the way of life that will be most meaningful for us.

But before we turn to that, let me make a couple of brief observations about how Aristotelian virtue ethics differs from many of the dominant contemporary ways of thinking about ethics.

Many philosophers nowadays, following an argument associated most famously with the British philosopher G. E. Moore (1873–1958), think that you cannot derive ethical insights from natures. To do so would be to commit the "naturalistic fallacy." Medieval philosophers of all stripes, but especially Aristotelians, have no qualms about grounding normativity in the nature of things. The natures of things are ultimately determined by God's act of creation. God is all-wise and all-powerful. A common assumption is that these divine attributes entail that God does nothing in vain. Hence, if God makes us with a specific nature, we have this nature for a reason. Our job is to figure out what that purpose is and fulfill it.

The second point of contrast is one that I have already mentioned in the introduction to this chapter. Many of the dominant contemporary ethical theories focus on particular situations and their principal concern is to determine what course of action should be taken in those highly specified situations. Consequentialists ask us to consider the predicted effects of the possible responses that we could have to a particular morally weighted situation, such as how to distribute a limited supply of medicine among a population of sick people given all the other morally relevant details about the situation at hand. Deontologists like Kant ask us to think about the rights that people have and then to determine how best to honor those rights as we attempt to negotiate specific situations that we find ourselves in.

Don't be mistaken: Aristotelians are interested in actions. Given that many medieval Aristotelians are embedded in Judaism and Islam, which have elaborately detailed specifications about what to do when, it would be especially surprising if they ignored this aspect of ethical thought altogether. However, it is interesting to note how medieval philosophers who are impressed by Aristotle's way of thinking tend to view these highly articulated legalistic rules as instruments in service of our ultimate aim, which as Aquinas has nicely articulated for here, is the return to God. On their view, we don't develop the virtues solely in order to be better actors and thereby please God by what we do. We do good actions in order to change who and perhaps even what we are. In effect, the order is reversed: Actions are done in order to develop and sustain a quality or character of our souls. Our good works make us the kind of thing that is worthy of living in the presence of God. This does not mean that having a virtue is our ultimate end. The virtuous life is a life of action. But for many medieval thinkers, both Aristotelians and Platonists, the emphasis is on a specific kind of action, contemplation, which is directed to a unique object, God's essence. All the other virtues and actions that stem from them are conceived as means to achieving that end. For that reason, we will see that some of them even will argue that at some point, we can *dispense* with some or all of the virtues (Section 5.3). This picture seems to be quite different from the contemporary fixation on whether to direct a trolley car one way as opposed to another or whether it is appropriate to lie on a given occasion.

Aristotle and those who follow him distinguish between virtuous persons and virtuous actions. The virtuous person usually does the virtuous thing, but someone can do the right or virtuous thing without being virtuous. The person who is presently training to be virtuous is precisely such a person. Some contemporary commentators are, to say the least, incredulous. And to be fair, if we are not careful, Aristotle's position can be described in ways that suggest that some form of vicious circularity is at work. Aristotle seems to be saying that to know what the virtuous actions are, one must look at the actions of the virtuous person. But how do I find such a person if I don't know what virtue is? (This is precisely the worry expressed by Socrates in Plato's *Meno* [80d–e].) Virtue ethicists have risen to the challenge and provided some interesting replies to this and other criticisms.

I, however, do not want to adjudicate between virtue ethicists and their critics. Instead, I think we should turn to consider some ways in which medieval philosophers build upon Aristotle's framework, which centers on not only the character traits and dispositions we might form but also, more holistically, on the ways of life that are possible for humans to adopt. It is this focus on ways of life and *eudaimonia* that will be especially important for those who hold the Abrahamic tenet that the nature of our afterlife will depend in part not only on what we do, but on the kind of person we are.

The Greek word "eudaimonia" does not have a straightforward English equivalent. The word is composed of a prefix derived from an adverb that means "well" (*eu*) and the word for a kind of spiritual creature, a *daimon*. If you have read Plato's *Apology of Socrates*, you have seen Socrates refer to his guardian *daimon*. This thing, Socrates tells us, has always kept him from going astray, and he takes his *daimon*'s silence during the trial to be a sign that he is doing precisely what the gods wish him to do (40a–c). Thus, a very literal translation of "eudaimonia" would be something like "being well accompanied by a guardian spirit."

By Aristotle's time, the word has been extended to encompass more broadly the notion of living well or flourishing. Very often the Greek term and its Latin and Arabic correlates are translated as "happiness," and so at times we also will use "happiness" to denote this Aristotelian notion. But you should always bear in mind that "happiness" as Aristotle and medieval thinkers conceive of it is not what we often call to mind when we hear the word. In particular, "happiness" nowadays often connotes a *feeling* of a certain sort, such as contentment. Medieval authors are well aware of feelings, or as they often put it, "affections" or "passions," but these feelings are not at the core of what they are interested in when they are theorizing about *eudaimonia* in the sense of flourishing. The feelings that accompany flourishing are perhaps signs that things are going well or poorly, but they should not be confused with actual flourishing. To flourish one must achieve excellence or virtue, and virtue is not the feeling that accompanies the actions done virtuously.

Aristotle thinks that if we ask what is "the highest of all goods achievable by action," everyone will agree that it is happiness. However, he quickly observes that this is merely a case of verbal agreement. As soon as we delve deeper, we will notice that there are a variety of competing conceptions of what it is to live well, and thus, what way of life is choice-worthy (*Nicomachean Ethics,* 1.4, 1095a20–27). It is fruitless, he thinks, to examine every idiosyncratic conception of the good life. But when considered at an abstract, generic level, some patterns begin to emerge. Hence, Aristotle proceeds by listing and then examining the most plausible families of candidates for the flourishing human life. Aristotle lists these as the general ways of life that have been suggested as ways to flourish as a human being.

1   The life devoted to acquiring pleasure and avoiding pain.
2   The life devoted to the acquisition of wealth.
3   The life devoted to acquiring public honors or fame.
4   The life devoted to the cultivation of the virtues.
5   The life devoted to the exercise of human reason.

We will quickly survey what Aristotelians have to say about each of these candidates.

In the course of Aristotle's evaluation of the five candidates, a list of criteria develops. For our purposes, we can list these first and then work backward to see how they are employed to rule out specific candidates. Aristotle reminds us that we are not only looking for the best life lived as a whole, but we are looking for a life that is properly human. In addition to this, as Aristotle observes, we don't think that someone who sleeps for their entire existence is flourishing. If possible, the best life should be active, yet also something that we can sustain. We would also prefer to find a life that many of us can succeed at actually living for more than a single moment as well as one that didn't require a lot of luck or things falling into place for it to be possible. Moreover, Aristotelians insist that we need to distinguish between *means* and *ends*. The best life should center around a good chosen for its own sake, and not for something that is merely a means for acquiring something else. After all, if we chose X merely in order to acquire Y, then Y is really the good that we are after. Indeed, this emphasis on *final* goals over both mere means and intermediate goals implies that the best life will involve leisure: "And happiness is thought to depend on leisure; for we are busy that we may have leisure, and make war that we may live in peace" (*Nicomachean Ethics* 10.7, 1177b4–5). Finally, Aristotle acknowledges that the best life should be one that is pleasurable. The philosophers are not complete and utter killjoys. Plato, Aristotle, and their medieval followers have a lot of interesting things to say about the various kinds of pleasures that humans can enjoy.[4] They do, however, tend to stress that some pleasures are better than others. Some are more refined and more long lasting. Some arise merely by eliminating a disturbance in the body, such as hunger, thirst, or an ache. In the end, the philosophical analysis of pleasure leads to the perhaps unsurprising claim that the pleasures that come from the life of the mind are superior to the pleasures that come from food, drink, and sex. Even friendship, though counted as a good, is usually evaluated in terms of what pleasures and other goods (including and especially, virtues) the friendship cultivates and encourages. Some friends are better for you than others (see Section 6.4).

Here is a list summarizing the criteria that Aristotelians identify.

A. The best life is a life that is properly human.
B. The best life is a life of activity.
C. The best life is a life that is as complete and sustainable as humanly possible.
D. The best life should center around a good chosen for its own sake, and not for something that is merely a means for acquiring something else.
E. The best life is pleasurable.

With these criteria in place, we can easily see why some candidates don't pass muster. The life devoted to pleasure, by which Aristotle means a life devoted to the enjoyment of bodily pleasures associated with food, drink, sex, and so forth, is a life "suitable to beasts" (1.5, 1095b20). We are looking for something that is distinctively human. The life devoted to wealth acquisition is dismissed because it is "undertaken under compulsion" and wealth is desirable merely because it is a means for acquiring other things (1096a5–11). The life of honor is at least on the right track in that it picks something chosen for its own sake. But as Aristotle sees it, the life of honor is too contingent upon the will and whim of others (1095b22–30). Someone can do all the right things and be a good person, and yet the public may fail to appropriately honor her for it.

The life devoted to virtue and the life devoted to contemplation are thus the only two lives left standing. Here things get more complicated, and indeed, there is a considerable amount of scholarly discussion about whether Aristotle really settles on only one kind of life as choice-worthy. Certainly, by the end of the first book of the *Nicomachean Ethics*, the matter does not seem to have been settled. Medieval readers, however, tend to read Aristotle as ultimately favoring the life of contemplation over all others. For one thing, while contemporary scholars have good philological reasons to treat the arrangement of *Nicomachean Ethics* as an artifact of later compilers and editors, medieval readers tend to read Aristotle's books as if they had been intentionally arranged in their present form by him. Thus, they will be inclined to treat the discussion in the tenth book of the *Nicomachean Ethics*, where Aristotle returns to the question of which way of life is best, as the resolution of the question. In the tenth book, Aristotle makes a clear and forceful case that the life of contemplation is the best human life.

> For, firstly, this activity is the best (since not only is reason the best thing in us, but the objects of reason are the best of knowable objects); and secondly, it is the most continuous, since we can contemplate truth more continuously than we can do anything. And we think happiness has pleasure mingled with it, but the activity of philosophic wisdom is admittedly the pleasantest of virtuous activities; at all events the pursuit of it is thought to offer pleasures marvelous for their purity and their enduringness, and it is to be expected that those who know will pass their time more pleasantly than those who inquire. And the self-sufficiency that is spoken of must belong most to the contemplative activity. For while a philosopher, as well as a just man or one possessing any other virtue, needs the necessaries of life, when they are sufficiently equipped with things of that sort the just man needs people towards whom and with whom he shall act justly, and the temperate man, the brave man, and each of the others is in the same case, but the philosopher, even when by himself, can contemplate truth, and the better the wiser he is; he can perhaps do so better if he has fellow-workers, but still he is the most self-sufficient. And this activity alone would seem to be loved for its own sake; for nothing arises from it apart from the contemplating, while from practical activities we gain more or less apart from the action. And happiness is thought to depend on leisure; for we are busy that we may have leisure, and make war that we may live in peace. Now the activity of the practical virtues is exhibited in political or military affairs, but the actions concerned with these seem to be unleisurely.
>
> (*Nicomachean Ethics* 10.7, 1177a20–1177b9)

The life of contemplation is the life that best meets the criteria A–E set out above.

When building his case for the contemplative life, we also can see how Aristotle starts to contrast it with the life devoted to cultivating the other virtues. That life, he observes, is not as complete or easy to sustain. To be just or brave, for instance, we need to be in the presence of others and presented with opportunities for exhibiting the virtues. Contemplation can be done on one's own. The contemplative life is also the life of the gods, and hence, in so far as we can also perform this activity, we are acting as gods act.

> If reason is divine, then, in comparison with man, the life according to it is divine in comparison with human life. But we must not follow those who advise us, being men, to think of human things, and, being mortal, of mortal things, but must, so far as we can, make ourselves immortal, and strain every nerve to live in accordance with the best thing in us; for even if it be small in bulk, much more does it in power and worth surpass everything.
>
> (idem, 1177b30–1178a1)

As we will see shortly, remarks like this will leave a profound imprint on medieval philosophers.

But we can also see in Book 10 of the *Ethics* a legitimate concern. We are animals. We have bodies, and thus bodily needs. We cannot live like gods do. We cannot think well when our stomachs are empty or we are scared or angry. We cannot study when we are deprived of sleep or fear for our safety. We have bodies, at least for some time, and while embodied, these bodily processes, passions, and needs must be managed. Therefore, the cultivation of the other virtues is still important. It is perhaps because the barrier between God and human is so high that Aristotle concedes that there is a sense in which a life devoted to these virtues is also a flourishing life.

> But in a secondary degree the life in accordance with the other kind of virtue is happy; for the activities in accordance with this befit our human estate. [...] Practical wisdom, too, is linked to virtue of character, and this to practical wisdom, since the principles of practical wisdom are in accordance with the moral virtues and rightness in morals is in accordance with practical wisdom. Being connected with the passions also, the moral virtues must belong to our composite nature; and the virtues of our composite nature are human; so, therefore, are the life and the happiness which correspond to these.
>
> (10.8, 1178a9–22)

Thinking about abstract theoretical stuff requires temperance and the other moral virtues. Medieval philosophers will take this point to heart. Theoretical contemplation may be the highest act that we can perform, but we need all the other virtues in place in order to accomplish it. For some medieval thinkers, however, there will be no second-place medals: If we fail to achieve intellectual virtue, this will have dire consequences in the life to come. In fact, our very survival as any sort of soul might depend upon it (see Section 5.2).

Here in outline is the framework that many medieval philosophers will adopt from Aristotle about the good life. It is a theory of human morality that is focused on *eudaimonia*, a whole flourishing existence. Moreover, Aristotle has provided some substance to what this flourishing amounts to. It is one where we must cultivate those capacities in us that are distinctively human. One of these capacities, theoretical contemplation, is a capacity that we share with divine beings. Thus, our aim should be to live as much as possible like gods. Everything else, nourishment and shelter, work, and even friends are to be utilized to contemplate as much as we can.

5.2 From Aristotelian *Eudaimonia* to Heavenly Bliss

Aristotle tells us that the best part of us is something akin to the divine. But this does not mean that *he* thinks our soul is immortal or that we as individual persons will survive the separation of our souls from our bodies. As we have already seen, Aristotle identifies our soul with the substantial form of the body. This would imply that the form is *not* something separable from the body that it actualizes and enlivens. At least, this is how some late ancient and medieval interpreters understood Aristotle's notion of what form is and how it can exist (4.1). It is for this reason that they insist that while the human soul might be something like a form, strictly speaking it cannot be a form. Not all interpreters of Aristotle thought that this had to be the case. Aquinas, for instance, famously defended *both* the claim that the human soul is the substantial form of a human being *and* the claim that the human soul is separable from the body (at least for a time).[5]

Again, as we have already noted (Section 4.2), no matter where one falls on the issue of what kind of thing the human soul is, there is still the question of whether anything like personal identity is preserved upon separation from the body. Here is a place where Aristotle is especially, indeed notoriously, obscure. In chapter 5 of the third book of *On the Soul*, Aristotle notes that some kind of soul, or perhaps some aspect or part of soul, might be separable from matter. This he identifies as a kind of "intellect" (*nous*), namely, something that he calls the "active intellect." But a host of questions are left unanswered. Is there only one active intellect? Is this active intellect a part of human beings, or is it not just separable but actually separate from all material beings? If part of me, my intellect, survives, will it remain individuated? And finally, as we have already observed in Chapter 4, since much of our personality is a function of lower, materially based functions or parts of the soul, will my personality persist when the intellect is separated from my body?

It is well known among scholars of medieval philosophy that some did adopt the more radical interpretations of Aristotle's *On the Soul* 3.5, especially in the Arabic milieu but also among the so-called Latin Averroists (so named because of their assimilation of Ibn Rushd's (1198) interpretation of

156 *Happiness and the Meaning of Life*

Aristotle).[6] However, I think it is safe to say that the mainstream position among medieval philosophers is that the soul, or a part of it, will survive the dissolution of the body. Here they could appeal to arguments inspired by the ancient Greeks, as well as scriptural authority. This leaves plenty of questions to be answered, including the very pressing issue of whether the soul will inhabit a body again at some point in the life to come (see Section 5.4). But for now, let us return to what follows in general about what our ultimate aim and purpose should be, if it is assumed that at least a part of us survives separation from the body.

Aristotle's ethics and political philosophy primarily focuses on how to live in this embodied existence, which is precisely what we would expect given his ambivalence about whether there is anything like human existence after the soul is separated from the body. But once we assume that the best part of us will persist and continue to "live" in some sense,[7] the center of emphasis naturally shifts to the life that comes after this embodied existence, especially since there were compelling arguments in support of the view that this mode of existence will be much more permanent, possibly everlasting. The reason that things wear down, fall apart, and cease to exist is because of their matter. Hence, something that is essentially immaterial can at least in principle persist forever. (I add the "in principle" because, for theists, God not only has the power to bring immaterial beings into existence – as He actually does in the act of creation and, specifically, when He makes and imbues that human embryo with a rational soul – but also the power to make them cease to exist, if He were to will it.)

Here it is especially important to note the influx of Platonic notions into the general framework that medieval authors possess. Aristotle's own views about the nature of forms are the source of much ancient and modern commentary, especially since in the central books of his *Metaphysics*, Aristotle can be read as defending the markedly anti-Platonic claim that it is not the forms themselves but the individual composites of matter and form which are the "primary substances" – that is, the fundamental beings around which the rest of reality is built. Medieval philosophers will sometimes voice agreement with Aristotle's anti-Platonism (often, as it happens, because they have a distorted understanding of what Plato's views in fact were[8]), but they nevertheless hold that there are immaterial substances. Some even will add that these immaterial substances are more real than material beings.

Putting all these elements together, we can see how they will lead medieval thought away from a focus on this life and toward the life to come. Humans are a composite of body and soul, but the soul is the better part of us. It is the part that can survive the separation from the body because it is immaterial and hence not subject to the same principles that govern the composition, maintenance, and dissolution of material things. Some medieval thinkers, inspired by certain remarks in Aristotle's *On the Soul*, even think that they can prove that the soul is immaterial by pointing to the fact that the soul can think (see, e.g., Aquinas *Questions on the Soul*, q. 14). Thinking about some material object X is in effect a process by which the soul has the form of X "in" it. But the soul could not have X's form in it if the soul had its own distinctive, actual form. (As a heuristic, think about a cup of water and two "forms," hot and cold. If the water is actually hot, the water cannot have the form of the cold in it at the same time. If actual coldness were present, the water would be cold, not hot – or perhaps, in actual fact, lukewarm, but hopefully you get the basic idea. You cannot have two actual forms "in" the same subject at the same time.) All material things, however, have a distinctive, actual form. Therefore, the soul cannot be a material thing. Of course, subtleties abound here, including perhaps most noticeably that small but important little word "in." After all, if I am thinking about a horse, my soul does not become a horse! Here, however, allow me to point you to some excellent reconstructions of Aquinas's thinking about the mechanics and metaphysics of thinking, including Eleonore Stump's account of cognition as "assimilation" (2003, 273–5) and the work of Therese Scarpelli Cory (especially, Cory 2013).

Given that the soul is immaterial and imperishable, it behooves us to focus on the soul's intrinsic capacities and virtues, that is, the activity that it performs on its own and not those activities that it does when it is in charge of the body. This activity is none other than thinking, and thinking of a distinctive sort, namely, theoretical reflection. Theoretical reflection is thinking about things at a highly general and abstract level, with an aim to understanding them just because you want to understand them. In other words, it is not the kind of thinking that you are performing when you are trying to solve a practical problem, such as how to quickly get to the store and back. It is more like "pure" mathematics, where one is merely trying to understand the nature of numbers and why they have the properties that they do. Aristotle claimed that the best sort of human life is the life of the rational soul at its most theoretical. The separability and persistence of the soul after death only reinforces the fact that this should be our aim. Indeed, it now makes it all the more imperative that we cultivate our rational faculties, as this will be the part of us that will survive.

You might have already encountered Plato's *Phaedo* in your philosophy courses. If so, you will recall Socrates's startling proclamation that philosophers spend their days here on earth eagerly preparing for and awaiting death (61c ff.). This is because the philosopher loves theory, and theory is impeded in this life by the body. Separation from the body will allow her to get at what she desires most of all. By the time we reach the end of the tenth book of the *Nicomachean Ethics*, Aristotle seems to be more or less on the same page. He might not think that human souls will survive separation from the body, but in as much as we can do so, we need to find ways to theorize as much as we can. Medieval thinkers often subscribe to this Platonic attitude toward the body. Some will go so far as to claim that matter is the source of *all* deformity, decay, and most significantly sin.

> Thus in the case of man, for instance, it is clear that the deformity of his form, the fact that his limbs do not conform to their nature, and also the weakness, the cessation, or the troubling of all his functions – no matter whether all this be inherent in his natural constitution from his beginning or be only a supervening accident – that all this is consequent upon his corrupt matter and not upon his form. Similarly, every living being dies and becomes ill solely because of its matter and not because of its form. All man's acts of disobedience and sins are consequent upon his matter and not upon his form, whereas all his virtues are consequent upon his form.
> (Maimonides *Guide of the Perplexed* III.8; Maimonides 1963, 431)

These philosophers read Aristotle's subordination of the life of virtue to the life of contemplation as a signal that he too sees the cultivation of temperance, justice, bravery, and prudence as important, even necessary, but only necessary because of what it consequently frees us up to accomplish.

> A man should be in control of all these impulses [for food, drink, sex, and so forth], restrict his efforts in relation to them, and admit only what is indispensable. He should take as his end that which is the end of man qua man: namely, solely the mental representation of the intelligibles, the most certain and the noblest of which being the apprehension, in as far as possible, of the deity, of the angels, and of His other works. These individuals are those who are permanently with God.
> (idem; Maimonides 1963, 432–3)

In other words, in the Middle Ages we often see a *Platonized* adaptation of Aristotle's ethics. (I say this because it is unclear whether Aristotle would go so far as to suggest that we ought to reduce our bodily desires to some ascetic, bare minimum.) The cultivation of virtue allows us to tame the body and keep it out of the way as much as is possible while we are embodied.

There is another aspect of Socrates's discussion in the *Phaedo* of the body and its tendency to impede the soul that gets picked up by many medieval philosophers. While talking about the philosopher eagerly awaiting death, Socrates relates a little story about what happens to souls of people who fixate on bodily pleasures at the expense of intellectual goods. These souls, upon separation from the body are pained. Socrates even suggests that a certain degree of corporeality clings to their nature which causes them to linger close to this realm and not to venture forth to the realm of the pure intelligibles. When people claim to see a ghost, Socrates suggests that what they are seeing is one of these "body-like" souls (81c–d). This idea that souls, which are intrinsically immaterial and intelligible, can be in some manner polluted – even corporealized! – by their contact with the body gets picked up, for instance, by Abu Nasr al-Farabi (950). Al-Farabi suggests that human souls that cling too much to bodily pleasures in this life will compromise their very capacity to survive the separation of the soul from the body.

> The souls of the people of the ignorant cities remain in a state of imperfection and necessarily require matter for their preservation, since no trace of truth whatsoever except the first intelligibles has been imprinted on them. Once the material substratum to which they owed their preservation perishes, those faculties of theirs, which needed what has perished for their preservation, perish as well.
> (*On the Perfect State* V, 16, sec. 7; al-Farabi 1985, 271)

In fact, al-Farabi proceeds to describe how this dissolution into "nothingness" occurs in a step-by-step fashion as the body dissolves and loses its ability to sustain complicated operations. The soul changes too. It becomes the "form" for whatever kind of thing it inhabits, until finally it becomes "the form of the elements." At this point, it seems that the human person is gone and gone for good! As we will see below, this is the fate that many medieval philosophers believe is the fate of animal souls (Section 6.5).

Al-Farabi does not believe that every human soul that fails to achieve its proscribed final end will disappear. In particular, there are also those souls that had some acquaintance with intellectual endeavors, but which did not pursue it with all their might and will. In some sense, such souls will have it worse than those souls that merely cease to be, since they will persist and they will be aware that they are missing out on something better.

> And as long as an ill person who feels pain is kept busy by certain things, the distress caused by the pain of his illness is either less, or he is totally unaware of it, but when he is isolated from the things which kept him busy, he becomes aware of the pain, or the pain comes back to him. The same applies to the rational part; as long as it does not cease being kept busy by the things brought to it by the senses, it is unaware of the distress produced in it by the bad dispositions linked to

it; but when it is completely isolated from the senses, it feels or becomes aware of the distress produced by these dispositions, so that it remains in great distress through all eternity.

(*On the Perfect State* V, 16, sec. 8; al-Farabi 1985, 273–5)

We are not born reasoning well. It takes lots of practice. Because these people did not train their rational faculties adequately in this life, even their separated souls have trouble grasping intelligible things. These souls will have trouble seeing the best sorts of intelligible things, the angels and God Himself. Therefore, the souls of lazy learners will be dimly aware that they are eternally missing out on something great and wonderous, and this will cause them immense torment.

Those who come after al-Farabi, like Ibn Sina (1037) or Maimonides, do not say things which suggest that the soul itself changes into a different kind of form. (In fact, Maimonides is quite adamant that the form is permanent and stable [*Guide of the Perplexed* III.8].) Nor will they go so far as to claim that human souls can lose their capacity to survive death. Instead, they emphasize al-Farabi's depiction of the lazy rational soul, a picture incidentally that can be traced back to the *Phaedo*. Such souls will not perish. They will linger, but they will be forever pained by the fact that they can no longer indulge in the things that once gave them such pleasure, for those pleasures require that they have bodily instruments.[9]

Notice how the general outlines of a picture of Heaven and Hell are beginning to take shape. Heaven becomes an event where the human soul is permanently thinking God and thinking about God in a very direct manner – a manner that is sometimes described as "intuitive" cognition – as opposed to a process whereby the mind moves from one idea to another, as it does for instance, in a mathematical proof. This intellectual state is often described as being present with God, and with it comes a certain kind of pleasure. Hell is a psychological torment that is caused by an absence from this intellectual presence with God. The aim, then, for humans is to attain this state of beatitude or blessedness. This is the true shape of *eudaimonia*. Aristotle's happy life in the here and now is subordinated to and serves as a preparation for our true aim and end.

Aristotle claims that theoretical contemplation is what the gods are engaged in (Section 5.1). Thus, there is a sense in which we are like the divine. This idea is expanded upon by later Platonist thinkers, especially Plotinus (270), who sees everything as the product of a series of "emanations" from the "One" source of everything, including intellect and being itself. We are like the source and the higher products of emanation precisely because we are imperfect, delimited copies of the One. Getting a handle on Platonic theories of emanation and "participation" can be difficult.

Perhaps this analogy will help: A computer-generated image (CGI) of a human is like a flesh and blood human in many respects – it has to be in order to help us suspend disbelief and get involved in the fiction that the film is trying to create. But there are many aspects of a real human that a CGI'd human does not have. The CGI'd human is thus an imperfect, limited copy of a human. It is a copy whose source is ultimately a real flesh-and-blood human, a thing made by humans in the image of humans. For this reason, we can also give a causal account of the CGI'd image. It is in a sense an emanation from a human mind, which belongs to a real human. In so far as there is this chain of causation, we can also say that the CGI'd human participates in humanity.

For Plotinus and other later Platonists, the philosopher's quest is an attempt to "return" to one's source, a process that is accomplished by exercising that part of us that is most akin to that source, our intellects. This trope of returning to God is one that numerous medieval philosophers and mystics subsequently pick up and develop. For some medieval thinkers, there is a ceiling to this path back to our source and that ceiling is several steps below God itself. We mentioned that according to Aristotle there is a separable intellect known as the Active Intellect. In Islamic philosophy especially, this Active Intellect is identified with a separate intelligible substance that is several steps removed from God. The Active Intellect is the intelligible substance that is responsible for the maintenance of the mundane realm. It is also the thing to which we are capable of returning. We don't reach God. At best, on this picture, we reach and perhaps "conjoin" with the Active Intellect (Stroumsa 1998, 56).

I should stress that we have here only a general picture of a certain Platonic conception of the final end of human existence. As you can perhaps imagine, there are numerous choices to make when it comes to filling in the details. Does conjunction occur? If so, what would that look like? Do our souls literally melt away and become absorbed by the Active Intellect or God, or do we retain some semblance of individual identity? There is also, as we will see in the final section of this chapter, the question about the body and whether we will have one in the afterlife. After all, either the holy scriptures or at least the received traditional wisdom of Judaism, Christianity, and Islam seem to refer to a time when we will once again have bodies. (I add this caveat about received traditions, since as Maimonides argues, the Hebrew Bible does not say anything definitive about what the afterlife will look like.) Some passages, in particular, suggest that Heaven and Hell will involve not only psychological or spiritual pleasures and torments but also physical ones. But before we turn to that issue and how certain philosophers responded, let us continue to explore what individuals must do in this present life if they wish to enjoy the blessed state of the next one. For even here, we will see that certain philosophical and mystical understandings of the soul's true nature and our proper end might come into conflict with mainstream notions about the proper way to live.

5.3 Humility, Emptying Oneself, and Going beyond Virtue

In medieval Christian thought there are the four "cardinal" virtues (temperance, bravery, justice, and prudence), on top which there are the three "theological" virtues of faith, hope, and charity. But for some there are other virtues that play a pivotal role. Humility, in particular, needs to be singled out.

For some theologians, humility is technically not a virtue. Rather, it is designated as a "fruit" of the virtues.[10] Aquinas, for instance, holds such a view. Others, however, are happy enough to count humility as a virtue. For instance, you might have noticed that humility makes it on to Maimonides's list of the moral virtues (*Eight Chapters*, ch. 2; quoted in 5.1). The distinction between virtues and good effects that spring from them rests on some subtle arguments. For our purposes, I don't think it matters too much about the metaphysical standing of humility, since it is clear that even for Aquinas, the cultivation of proper humility is a vital step in our spiritual progress.

On two occasions in his *Disputed Questions on the Virtues*, Aquinas entertains the objection that humility ought to be counted as one of the fundamental or cardinal virtues.

> Other virtues appear to be more fundamental than these. There is, for instance, magnanimity, which does what is great in the case of all the virtues, as *Ethics* IV says, and also humility, which is the defender of the virtues. [...] Therefore, these [i.e., the standard four] are not the cardinal virtues, but others are instead.
> (On the Virtues in General, article 12, obj. 26; Aquinas 2014, 564)

> The virtue that serves as the foundation for the others is the one that appears above all to be a cardinal virtue. Humility is just such a virtue, for Gregory says that someone who piles up the other virtues without humility is like a person who carries straw against the wind. We should, then, categorize humility as a cardinal virtue.
> (On the Cardinal Virtues, article 1, obj. 13; Aquinas 2014, 593)

Aquinas's replies are subtle, and for our purposes it is not clear that we need to elucidate them fully. The important thing for us is that while Aquinas takes great pains to define the cardinal virtues in such a way that only the standard set makes the cut, he nevertheless does concede much of what is claimed by the objector. Here, for instance, is his reply to the second of the two objections:

> Humility bolsters all the virtues indirectly, by removing what lies in wait to destroy our good works of virtue. In contrast, the cardinal virtues bolster the other virtues directly.
>
> (ad. 13, 598)

Humility is vital, since it is what clears the ground so that the virtues may flourish. Aquinas mentions Gregory the Great (604), and Pope Gregory's insistence on the importance of humility profoundly shaped medieval spiritual life, both inside and outside the academy. We can see this most distinctively in the contemplative, or mystical traditions of Europe, where humility, which is the product of rigorous self-examination, is seen to be "essential for opening oneself up to union with God" (Van Dyke 2017, 135).

In Aristotelian thought, a virtue generally lies at the mean on a continuum whose end points are defined by two vices.[11] Bravery or courage, for instance, is the sweet spot between two sorts of error: The first occurs when one flees too quickly from something scary or distressing. The second occurs when one fails to flee in a truly dangerous situation, where the wiser course of action would be to retreat, recover, and live to fight another day. (As I like to remind my students, true bravery is often *not* on display in blockbuster action films.) Thus, we might expect that humility – especially if it is a virtue, perhaps even if it is merely a concomitant of the virtues – is the sweet spot between two errors. The first is pride. The second doesn't have a standard name, but we might call it excessive self-effacement.

Something like this analysis might at first glance seem to be on display in this remarkable passage by Catherine of Siena (1380), where she imagines Satan expressing frustration as his attempts to undermine Catherine continue to fail.

> Then the devil, unable to bear your humility of spirit and your trust in my goodness, said to you, "Damnable woman! There is no getting at you! If I throw you down in confusion, you lift yourself up to mercy. If I exalt you, you throw yourself down. You come even to hell in your humility, and even in hell you hound me. So I will not come back to you again, because you beat me with the cudgel of charity!"
>
> (*Dialogue* 66; Catherine of Siena 1980, 125)

In fact, Catherine's position is much more complicated. It is true that, whenever she is tempted to think that she is "perfect and pleasing to God" and hence that she no longer needs to "torture" herself or "weep" over her sins, she counters Satan's temptation by replying that she is wretched and that she has only just begun to acknowledge and pay for her sins. But when Satan encourages her to wallow in her misery and confusion, Catherine does not say, "Hey, enough is enough! I am worth something." Instead, she confesses that "her life has been spent wholly in darkness" and she proclaims that she will take shelter in God's love and forgiveness. Strictly speaking, then, *she* does not stand up for herself; God is the one who gives her strength and "consumes" her wickedness.

In Catherine's reckoning, humility is less of a mean between too much self-regard and too little self-esteem. It is something much more radical. For many in her tradition, humility is vital because it helps to destroy the self, or more accurately the self's own will. Some will even go so far as to say that humility is needed not to lay the groundwork for the other virtues to flourish; rather humility makes it possible for the lover of God to go "beyond" the need for virtue.

The idea that the mystic may at some point transcend the need for cultivating the virtues is a distinctive element in the philosophy of Marguerite Porete (1310) and Meister Eckhart (1327). Both individuals faced intense scrutiny and criticism by the church establishment. Porete was spectacularly executed in the center of Paris because she refused to recant. Eckhart was also put under examination for heresy and a set of his doctrines were condemned. However, he died before any violence might have been done to him (*if* violence ever was on the table – contrary to popular conceptions, the execution of heretics was quite rare in the thirteenth and fourteenth centuries, which is why Porete's case is so striking). We have some evidence which suggests he was to the very end "unyielding" in his beliefs (Meister Eckhart 1981, Introduction, 12–5).

Both Porete and Eckhart are part of what Christina Van Dyke calls the "apophatic" tradition of Christian mysticism (2014, 722 f.). This is the tradition that gets the most attention, perhaps precisely because of its seemingly paradoxical pronouncements. In this tradition, God is conceived as a being that is absolutely one and metaphysically simple. This simplicity entails that God's essence cannot be put into words. Every predicate of every possible human language depends upon metaphysical complexity and difference. The only way to know this being is to be in the immediate presence of it. But when this happens, as we have seen in Chapter 4 (Section 4.3), the self at the very least ceases to *see* itself. We did, however, acknowledge that some mystics might maintain something more radical. Here, for instance, is a selection from a remarkable document from the German mystical milieu.

> And consolation comes back to her and she enjoys God. But the moment does not last very long. She goes back to the door and

fetches her confessor and she says: "Father, rejoice with me, I have become God!"
(The "Sister Catherine" Treatise V; in Meister Eckhart 1986, 358)

This author seems to be suggesting that the "annihilation" of the self is literal, metaphysical annihilation. Porete and Eckhart also say things from time to time which suggest this radical metaphysical transformation (see, for instance, the quotation from Porete's *Mirror*, ch. 135, in Section 4.3). It is not clear how the human mind could establish whether this perception of annihilation corresponds to a metaphysical annihilation. If we took these claims by Porete, Eckhart, and others in the apophatic tradition to be assertions about their metaphysical status, they would be overturning a number of firmly held doctrines about the divide between God and creation and about the principles that govern the continuity of objects through time and change (such as the No Gappy Existence principle, mentioned in Section 4.3).

We do not need to linger over these issues again. The important point for the present is that this "annihilation" involves at the very least the suppression or elimination of our *will* and its replacement by the Divine will.

> This Soul, says Love, is no longer with herself, which is why she must be excused from everything. And the One in whom she is does His work through her, for the sake of which she is entirely freed by the witness of God Himself, says Love, who is the worker of this work to the profit of this Soul who no longer has within her any work.
> (Porete, *Mirror* ch. 41; 1991, 121; see also Van Dyke 2014, 726–7)

Notice that it is now God who is the agent and mover within the soul of the mystic. The soul itself no longer has any "work" to do.

This elimination of the soul's will leads to some startling conclusions. The mystic's soul has neither desires, nor any fears.

> But the one, says Love, who has died from love neither feels nor understands either Reason or Nature. Such a Soul wills none of the joys of paradise, however many one might place before her to choose, nor does she refuse any torments of hell, even if it would be completely within her will.
> (idem)

It does not matter anymore to the mystic's soul whether she does good actions for herself, for her neighbors, or even for God.

> This Soul, says Love, does not do any work for God's sake, nor for her own, nor for her neighbors' either, as was said above. But God, who is

able to do it, does it, if He wills. And if He does not will, it does not matter to her one way or the other; she is always in one state.

(*Mirror* c. 71; 1991, 145, slightly modified)

This lack of desire and lack of feeling is what Eckhart will later refer to as the virtue of "detachment," which he argues is the highest of the virtues. Detachment is superior even to humility, even though he concedes that humility and detachment tend to come together. In particular, perfect humility is an effect of the annihilation of the self, and annihilation of the self is indistinguishable from perfect detachment.

Lesser forms of humility involve mortification and abasement of the kind that Catherine of Siena alluded to above. Perfect detachment, by contrast,

> has no looking up to, no abasement, not beneath any created thing or above it; it wishes to be neither beneath nor above, it wants to exist by itself, not giving joy or sorrow to anyone, not wanting equality or inequality with any created thing, not wishing for this or that.
>
> ("On Detachment"; Meister Eckhart 1981, 286–7)

Compare this to what Catherine of Siena said above. Catherine seemed to invite all the hard feelings of guilt and grief. She told us that she constantly "weeps." These feelings, which come from a brutally honest self-assessment, helped her to remain humble. They do not consume her because she takes refuge in God's mercy. Eckhart and Porete suggest a different route. They propose that the soul can transcend the tough feelings of guilt, want, and obligation as well as the pain that comes from seeing others suffering. It does so by detaching from the world, emptying itself, and seeking to have God take the self's place.

Because the soul that has "died from love" has no desires, no fears, no feelings of her own, and no agency, Porete proposes that this soul is "free." And from this freedom stems her claim that the mystic's soul, once it has died from love, no longer needs to cultivate the traditional virtues. Nor does such a soul need the church!

> This Soul is gently noble in prosperity, and supremely noble in adversity, and excellently noble in all places whatever they might be. This Soul who is such no longer seeks God through penitence, not through any sacrament of Holy Church; not through thoughts, nor through words, nor through works; not through creature here below, nor through creature above; not through justice, nor through mercy, not through glory of glory; not through divine understanding, nor through divine love, nor through divine praise.
>
> (*Mirror* c. 85; 1991, 160)

Porete clearly and unapologetically is challenging the establishment. The church maintains that it is through it that humans can build and maintain a relationship with God. Porete is claiming that for the mystic who has died in love, the church and all its rituals are no longer necessary. Porete's espousal of this antinomian position probably played a part in her condemnation by the church and its secular enforcers. This antinomian tendency made even some mystics uncomfortable. In the Islamic mystical tradition, we also find claims that the rituals mandated by holy law are not binding for those who have achieved union with God. As we will see in Chapter 7 (Section 7.4), al-Ghazali is so concerned about this that he sanctions the violent suppression of anyone making pronouncements that might lead people to think that they need not follow religiously proscribed laws.

Notice one important thing: Even though Porete claims that the person who has achieved union with God is no longer bound by the rules of this world, this does not mean that the mystic will act indifferently or do harm. Recall the quotation from chapter 71 of the *Mirror*: "But God, who is able to do it, does it, if He wills." God is in the driver's seat. If He wills that something will be done, it will be done. If He chooses not to act, that is His will. The mystic's soul has no say in the matter, nor is she glad or perturbed by what God does through her. She "neither feels nor understands either Reason or Nature" (c. 41). However, God has reason; God is good. We can, therefore, expect that God will do good works through the mystic. If, on some occasion, God does not provide aid to a sick person, the only reason we can point to is that God did not will that it be so. We may not understand why God did not come to a person's aid in specific instances, but that is because humans cannot fathom the fullness of divine wisdom. But what *is* true is that if the mystic has "died from love," if her soul is driven by God's will and not her own, then the mystic is not to be blamed or praised for any action that we see her performing.

Porete and Eckhart insist that the detached or annihilated soul is the happiest soul. But there is something unsettling about this picture of happiness. As one of my students once said after reading Porete, it seems like the happy mystic is effectively God's puppet. My student did not want to be God's puppet, even if it meant that she would not achieve ultimate happiness. I am sympathetic to this reaction, for it seems that Porete and Eckhart indeed are urging us to depart from our humanity.

> I also praise detachment above all mercifulness, because mercifulness is nothing else than man's going out of himself to the shortcomings of his fellow men, and through this his heart becomes troubled. But detachment remains free of this, and remains in itself, and allows nothing to trouble it, for nothing can ever trouble a man unless things are not well with him.
> ("On Detachment"; Eckhart 1981, 287–8)

This passage echoes the ideal of Hellenistic philosophers and especially the Stoics, where happiness was not the primary aim. Rather it was "unperturbedness" (*ataraxia*). But there is something rather unsettling about the idea that it would be good if we were indifferent to the suffering of others. As we noted above, we might have good reasons to believe that God is in charge and that He will show his love and mercy to those in need. But does that really excuse us from having to sympathize with our fellow humans? Moreover, there are things Eckhart says that undercut our confidence that God will feel the suffering of those around me even when I do not.

> And yet I praise detachment above all love. First, because the best thing about love is that it compels me to love God, yet detachment compels God to love me. Now it is far greater for me to compel God to come to me than to compel myself to come to God; and that is because God is able to conform to himself, far better and with more suppleness, and to unite himself with me than I could unite myself with God. And I prove that detachment compels God to come to me in this way; it is because everything longs to achieve its own natural place. Now God's own natural place is unity and purity, and that comes from detachment.
> ("On Detachment"; Meister Eckhart 1981, 286)

Let us put aside the extremely intriguing suggestion that the mystic can somehow "compel" God to come to her. The real worry at present is the suggestion that God is attracted to the detached mystic because God too is detached. But if our detachment leads us to a state where we are indifferent to the suffering of others, does it not seem to follow that God Himself is also a remote, unfeeling being?

The apophatic mystics like Porete and Eckhart get most of the attention nowadays. But this tradition is decidedly the minority tradition, at least if we look to medieval Christendom. The bulk of Christian mystics are "affective" mystics (Van Dyke 2018, 164). Whereas apophatic mysticism tends to emphasize the Godhead and to downplay the Incarnation, affective mysticism emphasizes the fact that God became a human and suffered as we do, and it tends to see the goal of presence with God not in terms of annihilation or self-abnegation, but rather as something akin to an intimate loving relationship between two individuals. Mystical union on this model "does not remove us from our senses or transcend physical reality in a way that renders its irrelevant; rather, it brings those senses and that physical reality into their fullest form" (Van Dyke 2014, 723). Here, then, would be a model for a spiritual form of flourishing which preserves our humanity. This is quite possibly one reason why affective mysticism is the dominant tradition in Christian Europe in the Middle Ages.

Mystics often suggest that their visions provide them with a foretaste of what the afterlife will be like. If that is right, we can begin to see how there might be two competing models of what life will be like for humans after they die: one where we transform into something quite unlike what we presently are; another where our human nature in all of its particularity is perfected, not transcended. This will be the subject of the final section of this chapter.

But before we do that, let us ponder for a bit longer this mystical notion that the love for God, when pursued properly and diligently, leads to an emptying of one's will and its replacement with the will of God. For it seems that the mystic's single-minded focus on God may in fact be in tension with God's will. To see this, consider the case of Satan.

Scripture and tradition suggest that the fundamental sin of Satan is either pride or something stemming from pride. Here, for instance, is the Quran's account of Iblis's fall and transformation into Satan:

> [Remember] when thy Lord said unto the angels, "Behold! I am creating a human being from clay. When I have proportioned him and breathed into him of My Spirit, fall down before him prostrating." Then the angels prostrated, all of them together. Not so Iblis. He waxed arrogant, and was among the disbelievers. [God] said, "O Iblis! What has prevented thee from prostrating unto that which I created with My two hands? Dost thou wax arrogant, or art thou among the exalted?" He said, "I am better than him. Thou hast created me from fire, while Thou hast created him from clay." [God] said, "Go forth from it! Surely thou art outcast! And surely My curse shall be upon thee till the Day of Judgment."
>
> (Quran 38:71–78, trans. Nasr et al. 2015; see also 2:30–34)

Iblis cannot believe that God wants him to bow to humans. He is superior in nature to Adam. Iblis is made from fire, whereas Adam is formed from clay. Why is God asking him to show submission to such a lowly part of creation? Pride is one of the hardest vices to eliminate since it is so closely linked to our love for ourselves. And isn't self-love a good thing? After all, it is my love for myself that prompts me to carry on existing and to strive to be the best that I can be (see Chapter 6, Section 6.1). As we have seen above, the Aristotelian answer is that pride, like most vices, is an excess of something that is in moderation a good thing. God was not asking Iblis to eliminate completely his sense of self-worth. God was displeased with Iblis because Iblis had an excessive and, therefore, vicious conception of his worth.

There is much more that could be said about this and related passages recounting Iblis's rebellion in the Quran (see, for a start, the commentary in Nasr et al. 2015, 1114–6). But at present, I want to indicate a fascinating minority reading of this famous passage, since it will tie in with our discussion in Chapter 6 (Section 6.2) of what it takes to love God fully and properly. This minority interpretation, which I sometimes jokingly refer to as the "sympathy for the devil" reading, is offered by Al-Husayn ibn Mansur al-Hallaj (922), the notorious mystic who we already encountered in Chapter 4 (Section 4.3). On al-Hallaj's reading, Iblis is a tragic lover of God.

> Among the inhabitants of heaven, there was no affirmer of unity like Iblis. When Iblis was veiled by the *'ayn*, and he fled the glances and gazed into the secret, and worshiped his deity stripped of all else, only to be cursed when he attained individuation and given demands when he demanded more. He was told: "Bow down!" He said, "[to] no other!" He was asked, "Even if you receive my curse?" He said, "It does not matter. I have no way to an other-than-you. I am an abject lover."
>
> (*Tawasin* 6–9; Sells 1996, 274)

We cannot elucidate all the mysteries that appear in this remarkable passage. The basic plot, however, is clear enough. On al-Hallaj's telling, Iblis achieved ecstatic "union" with God. He is then drawn back into himself (he is "individuated" again), at which point he is asked to bow down to a creature that is not identical to God. The fact that *Adam* happens to be the creature to whom Iblis is to bow turns out to be irrelevant. That Iblis should bow down to *any* thing that is not God is unacceptable. Iblis tells God that he will only love and worship Him. "Even if I punish you for refusing?", asks God. "Yes," answers Iblis.

Here is where the tension seems to arise. God is justified in punishing Iblis. If God demands that any of His creatures do something, that creature must do it. No questions asked; no "but"s. But what is the lover to do? Wasn't he supposed to love nothing other than God? Thus, on al-Hallaj's reading of the fall of Iblis, we should feel some sympathy for God's chief rebel. It seems that Iblis's rebellion is not generated by pride; it is the result of love. This is why say that Iblis's fall is tragic.

At one point in the drama related in the al-Hallaj's *Tawasin* Iblis says that he is being "tested" (14; Sells 1996, 275). We might hope for his sake that Iblis is right, and that God will eventually show mercy for His ardent, uncompromising lover. Iblis's tragedy points to a conundrum for any true lover of God: True and complete love for God might require that I give up everything else, perhaps even my own self. Yet, if I succeed in doing that, as al-Hallaj suggests Iblis did, it will be extremely difficult to then shift my attention away from He whom I love most, even if my beloved is the one who demands it.

I have suggested that Iblis does not sin out of pride. But perhaps I am wrong. It might be that, even on al-Hallaj's reading, Iblis can still be said to have sinned because of pride. Iblis has refused to will precisely the same thing that his Beloved wills. Whether this amounts to Iblis having an overweening and hence vicious sense of self-worth will depend upon what one takes humility to be. For many of the mystics we have mentioned, it seems that any lingering notion of self and self-worth entails that the soul has failed to be properly humbled. Iblis in particular has failed to achieve the emptying of the individual will that Porete and Eckart instruct us to strive for, and thus, on their account Iblis did not have perfect humility – he was not fully "detached." For this reason, and despite his love for God, Iblis fell.

5.4 Resurrection and the Afterlife: Philosophy Encounters Scripture

Death is generally defined as the separation of the soul from the body. The Platonist celebrates this separation, since at this point the soul is released from a "prison" (Plato, *Phaedo* 62b). Death gives the soul its chance to be free and to live as truly as it was meant to live. And yet, many thinkers coming from one of the three major Abrahamic faiths have insisted that it is a fundamental, nonnegotiable doctrine of the faith that there will be a day when we are resurrected. This is the Final Judgment, when we will return to our bodies and be judged for what we have done and what we have left undone. There are, of course, nuances in how references to resurrection and the Final Judgment are interpreted by theologians in this period (as well as in our own). In the next chapter, in particular, we will see how Ibn Rushd tries to interpret such references in scripture (Section 7.4). Here in this chapter, we will examine whether reason can show us that references to resurrection in scripture and tradition may be taken literally.

For some, the doctrine of resurrection is in perfect harmony with what reason discerns. A famous instance of this is Thomas Aquinas's position. Aquinas is in many respects a thoroughgoing Aristotelian. As we observed in Section 4.1, some medieval thinkers believed that the soul cannot be a form, since forms are necessarily tied to the matter that they inform. Aquinas followed Aristotle in insisting that souls are forms, and indeed, they are the substantial forms of living bodies. Aquinas also reads Aristotle as maintaining that the essence of a composite substance must include both that substance's substantial form and its matter (Section 3.1). In other words, to be a human being is to be a composite of a substantial human form and the sort of matter that is potentially capable of becoming human. If that is true, then think about what happens to you, the human being, when your soul is separated from your body. Once the body dissolves (because it lacks the form that holds it together), you only partially exist or you exist in an unnatural and, therefore, unsustainable state. The human soul persists. But it cannot be a complete human being, since a human being is a soul *plus* a body. The soul wants nothing more than to be back with its body. Only a complete human being can enjoy complete happiness. Resurrection, then, is a good thing because it restores the human soul to its proper place; it makes the individual whole once again. An omnibenevolent God would not deprive things of what they truly need.

This is not to say that philosophers like Aquinas rescue every aspect of popular conceptions of what happens once we are resurrected. One quite common conception of life after resurrection, both now and then, is one where we humans will go back to doing all the things we presently enjoy. The only difference is that there will not be any impediments to our moderate enjoyment of these bodily goods. For instance, Sa'd ibn Mansur ibn Kammuna (c. 1285), a Jewish intellectual who flourished for a time in Baghdad, claims that this is the Islamic conception of the afterlife.

> [Muhammad] announced God would, on the day of resurrection, raise up the dead, call them to account for their beliefs and deeds, and reward them according to merit. [...] and on that day all men will be divided into two factions, one in paradise, the other in the fire called hell. Those who enter paradise will enjoy bliss eternal and unceasing, having whatever their souls may desire and whatever may please the eye, for in paradise there is of bliss what no eye has seen, no ear has heard, and what no human mind has thought of. There they will eat, drink, and marry.
>
> (*Examination of the Three Faiths*, chapter 4; Perlmann 1971, 100–1)

Ibn Kammuna claims that Christians also believe that there is bodily resurrection, but unlike Muslims, the Christian intelligentsia maintain that rewards and punishments will only be spiritual, not corporeal. The virtuous, on that view, "will become angel-like in the Kingdom of Heaven" (chap. 3, 81).

Ibn Kammuna does not know Aquinas's works or those of others in Aquinas's milieu, but his report is not inaccurate when it comes to describing how Aquinas thinks about what human life is like after resurrection. On Aquinas's thinking, the afterlife will be a time when there are no needs or wants. It will also be a time when there is no more generation or corruption, that is, reproduction, growth, or decay. Our bodies, then, will be constructed differently. They will be impervious to injury and decay. They will also not need any replenishment. They will be capable of doing remarkable things as well. Christina Van Dyke offers a particularly contemporary analogy (2015,

277, n. 20): Our bodies will be like the bodies of the vampires described by Stephanie Meyer in a series of *Twilight* novels that were wildly popular not too long ago. But here is the twist, which Ibn Kammuna alludes to: While our bodies are capable of all sorts of amazing feats and they will be impervious to injury, Aquinas seems to think that we won't actually *use* them much, if at all. This is because the human soul in this paradise on the new earth will be solely fixated on one thing, God's essence. Life after resurrection, therefore, will not be one where we gather for dinner with friends, or where we hike for hours on end, or where we engage in the pleasures of food, drink, and sex. All of these things are lesser goods when compared to contemplation of God's essence. If we were to imagine alien explorers landing on such a perfected earth, it seems that they would encounter a host of shining humanoid creatures standing completely still and in deep meditation.

Aquinas's Aristotelian picture of the afterlife has the advantage of making a place for the body to some extent. But his was not the only strategy for resolving the tension between reason and religious doctrine. Another strategy, one which we will explore in much more detail in later chapters, is to suggest that scriptural references to bodily resurrection must be read allegorically. They are merely symbolic ways of letting the uneducated know about the life after death, and the choice of metaphors and figures of speech is determined by what the uneducated can grasp and be motivated by.

A medieval philosopher of the more Platonic persuasion might find this avenue to be particularly attractive. Consider, again, Maimonides's assertion that matter is the source of all change, decay, deceit, and sin. Matter is a "veil" which prevents us from the apprehension of intelligible objects as they really are (*Guide* III.9; 1963, 436–7). Since, the natural end for human beings is to apprehend as much as possible the divine essence and the other pure intelligibles, we should hope that we are not reattached to a material component, certainly not reattached to a body for the remainder of eternity.

In the philosophical tradition that Maimonides is part of, we even find arguments that purport to demonstrate that resurrection is irrational or incoherent. Ibn Sina in particular devotes a whole treatise to examining various pictures of the fate of the soul, including the resurrection of the soul in a body and metempsychosis (Jaffer 2003, see also Marmura 1992). Many of these arguments are rehearsed in al-Ghazali's critical study of the positions of the "philosophers."

We don't have the space to go into these arguments in close detail, but it is worth pointing out that many of them rely on what we identified as the No Transfer and No Gappy Existence principles (see Sections 4.2 and 4.3, respectively). For instance, according to al-Ghazali, this is what a philosopher like Ibn Sina says to someone who maintains that if the bodily part of a human persists intact, then we have all that we need to preserve the very same human after an alleged case of resurrection.

> [The philosophers] say: At this point it would be correct to say that the earth has returned to becoming animate after life having been severed from it. This, however, would not be a resurrection for the human nor a return [to life] of that identical human being. For the human is a human not by virtue of his matter and the earth that is in him, since all or most of [his] parts are changed for him through nourishment while he remains that very same individual. For he is what he is by virtue of his spirit or soul. If, then, life of spirit ceases to exist, then the return of what ceases to exist is unintelligible. What commences to exist is only that which is similar to it. And whenever God creates human life in earth that derives from the body of a tree, a horse, or a plant, this would be a creation anew of a human. The return to existence of the nonexistent is unintelligible.
> (al-Ghazali *The Incoherence of the Philosophers*, discussion 20; Ghazali 2000, 220)

The response reported by al-Ghazali is twofold. (To make things somewhat less abstract, let's talk about a human who has not yet perished, Bob.) First, the philosophers note, Bob's body is in fact not stable throughout Bob's life before death. Material bits come and go, while Bob persists. Hence, keeping the body intact will not ground a claim that Bob is identical to the human who comes into being some time after Bob dies. Moreover, once Bob's form of life is separated from Bob's body and disappears, any combination of Bob's body with a form of life will only produce a doppelganger of Bob, since this form of life cannot be *Bob's* form of life. It makes no difference how similar this reconstructed human is to Bob. Once Bob has ceased to be, *Bob* does not – cannot – come back into being.

In the larger discussion in which the quoted passage occurs, the primary target is clearly a view where the soul is the kind of form that is inseparable from the body. This is why it disappears when separated from the body (per No Transfer). And once gone, per the No Gappy Existence principle, there is no coming back. Thus, we might think that this argument does not apply to a case where the soul is capable of persisting after separation, which is what the majority of Aristotelians and Platonists maintain. If Bob's soul survives separation from his body and then comes back to a body, it seems that Bob never left, and hence we have no violation of No Gappy Existence. Al-Ghazali makes precisely this claim when he begins to criticize the philosophers' argument. The identity of a human over time is solely determined by a self-subsisting human soul (Ghazali 2000, 223).

Thus, since the philosophers do not object to the notion that Bob persists even as the material parts come and go via natural processes of metabolism, they should not reject the notion that Bob's soul can inhabit an entirely refurbished body that God creates for him and make it be his body.

Ibn Sina was aware of this kind of maneuver and he thought that he could counter it. He argued that in order to have proper *resurrection*, a soul cannot return to just any old body; it has to return to *its* body. But once the soul is separated from its body, the body ceases to be. (Recall that other Aristotelian thesis mentioned in Sections 3.5–6 and 4.2, the one about homonymy.) Even if the parts of Bob's body are all kept in one place, they no longer possess a human substantial form; and hence, they are not a human body. Accordingly, the pile of parts ceases to be Bob's body, since Bob's body must be a human body. Any subsequent reconstitution of a human body will be a new combination of a human substantial form with matter that lacks such a form. The result has to be a new human body. So, at best, this newly constituted human body may be a *replica* of Bob's original body. But if the only thing that God can make is a replica of Bob's body, Bob's soul will have nothing to properly return to: Bob's soul needed Bob's body. On the other hand, if Bob's soul does attach itself to this replica body – it is after all, the only available human body – Ibn Sina argues that we don't have *resurrection*, but rather *transmigration*, and transmigration is a position that Ibn Sina thinks his Muslim opponents are unwilling to embrace.

A careful study of my reconstruction of Ibn Sina's argument may well reveal some leaps of logic. In particular, it seems to me that Ibn Sina sees a crucial difference between gradual changes in material makeup and wholesale material change. Gradual change was fine, but if there is ever a time when no matter is informed by Bob's soul, *then* we have a case where Bob's body no longer is. Ibn Sina needs something like this premise to be in a position to subsequently employ No Gappy Existence. But Ibn Sina's premise may not be warranted. It is at least something to ponder at greater length.

Interestingly, al-Ghazali does not take the path that I just outlined. Rather, he seems to think that he can take the sting out of Ibn Sina's argument by suggesting that a true Muslim *can* embrace transmigration, if the word turns out to be the label we apply to what has happened to Bob's soul when it attaches to a replica of Bob's original body. "There is no need to squabble over terms," he says, "What the religious law has conveyed must be believed. Let it be 'transmigration.' We only deny transmigration in this world" (224).

It is important to keep in view the fact that al-Ghazali concedes that there are cases where reason shows us that the Quran must be read in a *nonliteral* way (see also Section 7.4). If a literal interpretation leads to something irrational, the pronouncement of scripture is what needs to bend. Al-Ghazali is therefore in broad agreement with those who maintain that natural reason has a place in theological explorations. In his discussion of resurrection, he maintains that the philosophers' arguments do not hold up to *rational* examination. In other words, their arguments are faulty because they made the kind of missteps that finite reasoners sometimes make and which can be caught by other finite reasoners. What the Quran says about resurrection "must be believed." But this is because, in al-Ghazali's view, there are no reasons to deny that the Quran's depiction of an afterlife in which we have bodies and in which we enjoy bodily pleasures and pains.

But one could instead maintain that if reason and scripture conflict, *reason* is what has to give in. While this is a *strong* view, from a medieval perspective, it is not a *radical* position. As we have noted on several occasions, medieval philosophers and theologians acknowledge quite often that human reason is finite and fallible. Reason might suggest that paradise and God's rewards and punishments are merely spiritual. From a rational perspective, it might even be absurd to assert that humans will be embodied again, that they will be back again as embodied creatures (see Section 2.3). But if scripture says that the afterlife will be both spiritual and corporeal, then perhaps it will be. No living human can know with certainty since at most an elect minority of individuals have ever been given a glimpse of what reality is really like once the "veil" has been lifted. Resurrection then might be a proposition that one must take merely on faith.

All of this should be born in mind when we turn to what Maimonides says in his *Essay on Resurrection*, which he composed around 1191. Maimonides claims that the Torah does not mention resurrection "in any way, certainly not plainly, nor even by a hint" (Halkin and Hartman 1985, 226; see also Stroumsa 1998, 67). Nevertheless, he stresses that the belief in resurrection is a fundamental tenet of the faith. Indeed, to deny the Resurrection is tantamount to denying miracles. But if one denies miracles, then one is effectively denying God and His law (221). Maimonides is thus gravely concerned when he learns that some people are citing his authority when they deny resurrection. Maimonides tries to set the record straight, but in doing so we get an interesting twist. The belief in resurrection is a fundamental teaching of the Torah of Moses, yet it is "not the ultimate goal." The ultimate goal is "the life in the world-to-come," which is a life that comes *after* resurrection (213 and 217). Resurrection is part of the period in history when the Messiah comes and reigns over the earth. But that era, like all others, will ultimately give way to the final life of human souls, the world-to-come. In that world, Maimonides asserts, there will be no desires, and thus, no food, no drink, no sex.

Here we see Platonic elements coming to the fore. The body, Maimonides insists, is "only the carrier of the soul." The soul is incorporeal, and as the "learned" know, the incorporeal is both more permanent and more real than anything bodily (215). Hence, it stands to reason that the eternal life of the world-to-come will be a life inhabited by separated souls. Maimonides even offers an argument for why people in the world-to-come will not have bodies.

> It is my view a valid assumption with every intelligent person, that the world-to-come is made up of souls without bodies, like the angels. The reason for it is that the body is an aggregate of limbs and organs solely for the actions of the soul, as has been definitively established. [...] It thus becomes clear that the existence of the entire body is needed for certain ends, nourishment for its maintenance and reproduction of the like for its continued presence. Now, since these ends are discarded and unneeded in the world-to-come – the reason being, as the sages have all made clear, that there is no eating in it, nor drinking, nor intercourse – it is obvious there is no body. God creates absolutely nothing in vain, makes things only for things.
>
> (Halkin and Hartman 1985, 220)

Here we might imagine Maimonides challenging Aquinas's picture of the embodied afterlife. (Although, you should remember that Maimonides lived before Aquinas.) In the world-to-come, the soul will not need any of the tools that the body provides. The body then will be superfluous. But God neither makes nor sustains anything that is superfluous. Hence, it is absurd to think that people will have bodies in the world-to-come. Why would God put us back into bodies that we don't need and don't use?

Maimonides also picks up on elements from one of the other strategies that we listed, namely, the allegorical approach to reconciling reason with scripture. The uneducated masses "do not recognize true existence other than in a body" (215). Only the learned can comprehend that there are things that are incorporeal and indeed even more real than the bodily. Thus, Maimonides concludes that "there is no harm" if someone believes that angels and "separated beings" are corporeal, so long as they deny that God Himself is in any way a body (Halkin and Hartman 1985, 215; cf. *Guide for the Perplexed* 1:49). This is Maimonides only demand: One may read the Torah flat-footedly and literally, provided that they do not interpret the anthropomorphic language attributed to God in a straightforward, literal sense. He won't quarrel with those who insist on understanding the world-to-come in bodily terms. All he is concerned to rebut is the suggestion that he is denying resurrection. This, he reiterates, is a fundamental tenet and it is not to be "explained away" (219). Anyone who attempts to deny that has strayed from the true faith.

Maimonides's *Essay* has raised some eyebrows. It is a little strange to defend resurrection only to then point out that it really is not the final stage in the afterlife. It has also been observed that while Maimonides talks in several places and at some length about the final end in spiritual terms in his *Guide of the Perplexed*, it is hard to find any explicit mention of resurrection in that more philosophical work (Kellner 1982). Why then does Maimonides insist that belief in resurrection is one of the thirteen *fundamental* tenants of the faith in his commentary on the *Mishnah*?

Some scholars think that when it comes to questions where reason seems to conflict with scripture, Maimonides often deliberately obfuscates. The most prominent and influential interpreter of Maimonides who reads him in this way is Leo Strauss.

> Maimonides teaches the truth not plainly, but secretly; i.e., he reveals the truth to those learned men who are able to understand by themselves and at the same time he hides it from the vulgar. There is probably no better way of hiding the truth than to contradict it. Consequently, Maimonides makes contradictory statements about all important subjects: he reveals the truth by stating it, and hides it by contradicting it.
> (Strauss 1952, 73–4)

To see that this interpretation has some basis, recall that Maimonides himself reports that he wrote the *Essay on Resurrection* because some people were using his writings to teach that the soul in the afterlife will not be returned to a body. Given what he says in the *Guide* about the body being the source of corruption and sin, it would seem that the afterlife ought to be one where the blessed are released from bodies. Why then are these people who use Maimonides's writings wrong? When Maimonides merely states that resurrection is a fundamental tenant of the faith, but offers no elaborate arguments in defense of the position, is this an indication that he is merely trying to head off accusations of heresy but that he really doesn't believe what he is saying?

As we will see in more detail in Chapter 7, Maimonides and his contemporaries lived in times and places where there was political pressure to conform to specific doctrinal positions. This would make it potentially dangerous to say, let alone write down, something that could be taken in the wrong way. At the same time, writers like Maimonides and Ibn Rushd wanted to communicate with like-minded individuals. Thus, they might have developed rhetorical strategies so that their true views could be hiding in plain sight. Maimonides himself claims that the *Guide* is written with different readers in mind, while some will learn a lot, others will glean only a little from its pages, and still others will be repulsed.

> I know that, among men generally, every beginner will derive benefit from some of the chapters of the Treatise, though he lacks even an inkling of what is involved in speculation. A perfect man, on the other hand, devoted to Law and, as I have mentioned, perplexed, will benefit from all its chapters. [...] But those who are confused and whose brains have been polluted by false opinions and misleading ways deemed by them to be true sciences, and who hold themselves to be men of speculation without having any knowledge of anything that can truly be called science, those will flee from many of its chapters.
>
> (Maimonides 1963, 16)

He also advises his readers to read everything with close attention, and that if something at first pass appears to be potentially harmful, to interpret what they have read "even if in a far-fetched way, in order to pass a favorable judgement" (15).

It is not my purpose here to determine whether Strauss is right when he asserts that "the *Guide* contains a public teaching and a secret teaching" (Maimonides 1963, xvii). And even if that is the proper way to interpret the Guide, it is not clear whether we should extend this strategy when attempting to interpret the *Essay on Resurrection*. For it seems that Maimonides is fairly up-front about the fact that the final state of affairs will be one where we live as pure, incorporeal beings.

It is important to bear in mind that authors often write in different genres and for different audiences. If one carefully examines everything that Maimonides says across his philosophical, medical, rabbinical, and popular writings, there may well be discrepancies. Whether what is being expressed in different modes is at bottom one and the same thing can only be determined after careful study and once one has accounted for all the potentially significant factors that dictated the need to write the work at all and the choice of genre and modes of expression that were then employed.

Study Questions

1) Before you head off to study more medieval answers to the meaning of life, pause and write down your own conception of what makes a human life worth living. Are the Aristotelians right that there is only one kind of this-worldly life that all humans should aim for?
2) Now take your model of the flourishing this-worldly life and ask yourself whether this is something that could be reproduced in a life after this one. Would you need a body in this second life, or are the best goods merely spiritual or intellectual in nature? Does this good life require that you retain your individual personality?

3) Is humility a desirable character trait? In particular is the mystical understanding of humility, one that leads to "detachment," a desirable character trait?
4) Think about my former student's worry. Would you give up your own will in order to achieve eternal bliss in the presence of God?
5) When thinking about what it would mean for God's will to be acting through the mystic and the mystic's detachment, we arrived at the precipice of a very deep issue that is of perennial concern to theists, namely, the problem of evil. The mystic will not be perturbed if God does not drive her to alleviate someone's suffering. But shouldn't we be disturbed? God surely sees my neighbor suffering. Why doesn't He always help? (As you begin to wade into these deep waters, you might want to read Stump 2014 and for Aquinas's extremely influential views about God's providence and theodicy, Stump 2003, ch. 16.)

Notes

1 See, for instance, al-Biruni's (c. 1050) translation and commentary on Yogic philosophy (al-Biruni 2020).
2 On this, see Stump 2003, 211–2 and 262–76. For Aquinas's solution to the puzzle of how the soul can think when it is disembodied, see Pasnau 2002, 366–77.
3 For an entry point into this literature, see Pink 2012, Hoffmann 2021, and Celano 2021. On Aquinas's views about the relation of the will to intellect and the will's freedom, see Pasnau 2002, 235–41, and Stump 2003, 277–306 and 389–404.
4 As a start, see Plato's *Philebus* and Aristotle's *Nicomachean Ethics* book 10.1–5. As a framework for medieval discussions of pleasure, which is often thought to be one of the most basic human emotions, see Hirvonen 2021.
5 See, for instance, *Summa Theologiae* 1.76.1; *Questions on the Soul*, esp. qq. 1–2, 8, 14; as well as reconstruction and commentary on his arguments by Stump (2003, 191–216) and Pasnau (2002, 45–72). As both Stump and Pasnau point out, Aquinas's position is quite subtle. The human rational soul is self-subsistent, but as they argue this does not entail that Aquinas is a substance dualist of Platonic or Cartesian sort.
6 On Ibn Rushd's "monopsychism," start with Taylor (2005, 193–4) and Black (2005, 321–2). On the Latin Averroists's challenge to Aquinas's position in particular, see Pasnau (2002, 160 and 339).
7 Al-Farabi argues that God is a mind, and since thinking is a way of living, we are thus entitled to also assert that God is alive (*On the Perfect State* 1.10; al-Farabi 1985, 75–7).
8 This is something you should keep in mind as you read around. In both the Arabic and Latin worlds, fewer complete works of Plato were circulating in translation than Aristotle's. Thus, much of what people knew about Plato came from reports by others, and some of these reports were by individuals who were not necessarily sympathetic to the Platonic program.
9 See, for instance, Ibn Sina, *Metaphysics*, 9.7.24 (Avicenna 2015, 355–6). This also seems to be the implication of Maimonides treatment of matter, form, and the human end in *Guide* III.8. Those who emphasize bodily pleasure are described as having a "veil" drawn between them and God (430 and 433).

10 This might explain why there is little discussion of humility in the overview of Aquinas's moral theory by Rebecca Konyndyk DeYoung, Colleen McCluskey, and Christina Van Dyke (2009).
11 Aristotle *Nicomachean Ethics*, book 2, chapters 6–9. The view is not without difficulties, as many medieval thinkers noted. Justice, for example, might appear to be a virtue that lies at an endpoint, not in the mean. Aquinas also notes that there are special difficulties for the intellectual virtues, and he determines that the three theological virtues (faith, charity, and hope) do not lie in a mean. *Disputed Questions on Virtue*, On the Virtues in General, article 13, resp. (Aquinas 2014, 575–6). Maimonides connects this Aristotelian notion of virtue lying at the middle of continuum to Galenic medicine, which often views illness as the result of some lack of equilibrium in the body. See his *Eight Chapters*, ch. 4 (Maimonides 1975, 68–69). Interestingly, Maimonides advises the virtuous to err slightly on the side of excess asceticism so as to avoid the other more dangerous extreme (69–70).

Suggestions for Further Reading

For a comprehensive presentation of a Christianized version of Aristotle's eudaimonism and virtue ethics, start with the relevant portions of his masterpiece, the *Summa Theologiae*: Part 1 of the Second Part (I–II), questions 1–5 (the so-called "Treatise on Happiness") and I–II, qq. 49–67 (the "Treatise on the Virtues"). There is a recent translation of *The Treatise on Happiness* (Aquinas 2016) which includes an extensive commentary by Christina Van Dyke and Thomas Williams. As a companion to these primary texts, start with the overview of Aquinas's ethical theory provided by Rebecca Konyndyk DeYoung, Colleen McCluskey, and Christina Van Dyke 2009. There is much profit to be gained by studying the essays by some of the leading scholars of Aquinas in Scott MacDonald and Eleonore Stump 1998.

On the role of rigorous self-examination as a crucial stage on the way toward humility and ultimately blessedness, see Van Dyke 2017. On Marguerite Porete's theory about the will and virtue, and an argument that her position was not that far outside of the mainstream in her day and age, see King 2018. On Porete, Eckhart, and others in their milieu, see volumes III and IV in the pathbreaking series *The Prescence of God: A History of Western Christian Mysticism* by Bernard McGinn (McGinn 1998 and 2005).

On conceptions of the afterlife according to the Islamic philosophers and Maimonides, start with Stroumsa 1998. For the translation of Maimonides's *Essay on Resurrection*, as well as a helpful discussion of the essay, see Halkin and Hartman 1985. More generally, you might want to review some of the basic creeds of the three major Abrahamic religious traditions. For medieval versions of these creeds, see "Appendix A: Doctrinal Creeds," in Pasnau and Van Dyke 2014 (vol. 2, 787–92).

For Leo Strauss's reading of Maimonides, see his introduction to what is currently the standard translation of the *Guide* (Maimonides 1963, xi–lvi), as well as his important essays "Persecution and the Art of Writing" and "The Literary Character of the Guide for the Perplexed," both of which are included in Strauss 1952

6 Love Thy Neighbor

6.1 Self-Love	183
6.2 Can We Love God? Can God Love Us?	187
6.3 Loving Your Neighbor and Tough Love	193
6.4 Bad Company	197
6.5 Love for All Creation	203

The Middle Ages are dominated by three major religious faiths, Judaism, Christianity, and Islam. Each of these faiths presents us with vast catalogs of obligations and prohibitions. There is a sense, however, in which all three religiously based ethics boil down to two precepts. The first is love and obey God. The second is to love your neighbor as you love yourself. We have said some things about how to love God in the previous chapter, especially when we turned to the importance of humility. But there are still some lingering issues that we need to resolve. In particular, it is unclear whether it is even possible to love a perfect being or for a perfect being to love us. When scriptures speak of "love," perhaps this is mere metaphor. Our old friend Abu Hamid al-Ghazali will lead the charge and argue that loving God is the truest form of love (Section 6.2). To make his case, however, he will first need to provide us with an analysis of love and its causes. Curiously, al-Ghazali will suggest that love of something else stems from love of one's own self (Section 6.1). This raises the question of whether there is anything like true altruism.

After we finish examining the issue of love, self-love, and the loving relationship between God and humans, we will turn to the second precept (Section 6.3). What must one do to love one's neighbor in all the ways that God commands? As it turns out, to love our neighbor, from time to time we might need to cause them pain. In that regard, we will briefly look at Aquinas on fraternal correction, or what we might think of as tough love. Tough love must strike a balance between support and punishment. As Aquinas

DOI: 10.4324/9780429348020-6

Love Thy Neighbor 183

will argue, there are some rules for when we should practice tough love and how much discomfort and pain to heap on one's friends and neighbors. Friends, after all, should make one another better, not worse. It is this last thought which will lead us to an interesting meditation by Saint Augustine on the reasons why we do bad things (Section 6.4). We will learn that the old saying is true: We really ought to choose our friends wisely.

The precept to love our neighbor acknowledges the fact that humans are social animals. We live in groups. Aristotle maintained that humans are by their very nature social or political animals. Hence, it might be *best* for us if we lived in groups. This idea is repeated by numerous medieval philosophers and it is something that we will explore both in this chapter and the next. In Chapter 7, we will consider mid-sized social unities, the city and the state. In this chapter, we will think about both smaller social groups (family, friends, immediate neighbors, coworkers, and the like) and also wider, more amorphous groups, such as humanity as a whole. In the final section of this chapter, we will look beyond humanity to the ecosystem of which humans are a part (Section 6.5). Is there a sense in which loving one's neighbor extends to animals, plants, and even to the entirety of creation?

6.1 Self-Love

One question that interests moral philosophers is whether a person can love someone else for the beloved's sake and not because of any benefit that the beloved might bring to the lover. Often this is framed in terms of actions. Can one truly ever act selflessly? Al-Ghazali (1111) will say things which suggest on a first pass that we can love selflessly. But matters are not so clear. Consider for instance this passage:

> The third cause lies in loving a thing for its own sake, and not for some advantage arising from it outside its own nature. Rather, its innermost nature is its very advantage. This is a deep and authentic love that grows ever stronger as it continues.
>
> (al-Ghazali 2016, 16)

Notice that there is still a suggestion that the beloved thing provides something advantageous or desirable to the lover. This impression is only reinforced by how al-Ghazali continues.

> This is similar to the love of beauty and comeliness, for every beautiful thing is deemed lovable in the sight of him who apprehends beauty; that is due to the nature of beauty itself. The very quintessence of pleasure

resides in perception of the beautiful. Pleasure is loved for itself, and not for something other than itself.

(idem)

Al-Ghazali is working with the same division that we saw Aristotelians using in the previous chapter (Section 5.1) between things that are desirable solely for what they in turn produce (such as foul-tasting medicine) and things desirable in themselves (such as happiness and pleasure). But this division does not precisely align with the distinction we are presently drawing between things desirable for what they provide to me versus things that are desirable for what they bring to someone else. We might insist that a *pure* form of altruism would involve a desire to do something solely for what it will provide to another person. Thus, this third "cause" that al-Ghazali points to may still be linked to self-love in so far as loving something for its own sake brings with it a kind of pleasure for the lover.

In fact, to establish that a person can love God, al-Ghazali thinks that we must begin by acknowledging how all love boils down to self-love.

> The primary object of love for every living being is its own self. Self-love signifies that there exists within one's very nature a desire to prolong one's being and to avoid non-being and annihilation; furthermore, there is a natural correspondence between him who loves and the object of his love. But what could be more perfectly in harmony with one's own self than prolongation of existence, and what could be more powerfully at variance than non-existence and destruction?
>
> (al-Ghazali 2016, 13)

This observation, incidentally, gives al-Ghazali the tools to reject a position espoused most famously by the ancient Epicureans that "death is nothing to us" (see Diogenes Laertius *Lives of the Eminent Philosophers* 10.124–5 = Epicurus 1926, 85), and a similar idea suggested by Socrates at the end of Plato's *Apology*, where he muses that if death were annihilation, then it should be nothing to fear, since it would be like an eternal, dreamless sleep (40d–e). These Greeks are arguing that it makes no sense to fear a thing if we are not present to experience it. Hence, we can loathe and attempt to avoid a painful death, because we will be experiencing pain. But once we cease to exist, there is *nothing* that will experience any torment of any sort. Many of my students (and many philosophers) are uneasy about this claim – and not without reason. There is something horrible about the mere thought that I won't exist. Al-Ghazali agrees, and he takes this intuitive horror that many (if not most) of us feel as a sign that this aversion to nonexistence is hardwired into our very nature as conscious beings. (According to al-Ghazali, love is something that only a "living sentient being" can possess [2016, 10].)

In addition, al-Ghazali observes that people desire not mere existence but "perfected" existence. This is why people love such things as health and property, as well as friends and relatives. He even proposes that a person's love for their own children is really an instance of this basic sort of self-love.

> Because of his intense love for his own survival, he loves the survival of the child who will supplant him; he himself cannot hope to survive forever but the child is, as it were, a part of him. In fact, were he to be offered a choice between his own death and that of his son, he would – assuming that his nature is well-balanced – prefer his own survival over his son's because though his son's survival resembles his own, it is not after all his own actual survival.
>
> (al-Ghazali 2016, 14)

Al-Ghazali's final thought might seem to be overkill, but even if a parent's choosing to sacrifice themselves for the sake of their children is actually a sign that they have a "well-balanced" nature, al-Ghazali's basic point still has much going for it, especially if we bring in current thinking about biological evolution and, as Richard Dawkins famously put it, "selfish genes" (1976).

This combination of a desire to exist and to flourish is what al-Ghazali identifies as the first of five causes of love. But as we soon see, self-love in a wide sense is at work in many, if not the remainder of the causes that he lists. For instance, the second cause that al-Ghazali lists is benevolence, by which he means love for "those who do us good" and hate for those who do us evil (2016, 15). As al-Ghazali quickly concedes, if "examined properly," this second cause of love can be traced back to the first (15–6). His ruminations on beneficence also reinforce the impression that for al-Ghazali true altruism is not possible for humans. For example, in a subsequent chapter we get this startling pronouncement:

> Goodness to anyone other than himself is inconceivable in man's case; indeed, goodness to any other being on the part of created beings is preposterous. A man does not spend his money for other than his own ends in spending [...] A man does not fling his money into the sea, for there is no purpose in that; in the same way he does not toss it into another man's hand without having some purpose that redounds to him. It is that purpose that he seeks and strives to have, not you; you are not what he is striving for.
>
> (al-Ghazali 2016, 27)

Al-Ghazali seems to leave no room for selfless acts by created beings. Only God might be altruistic, since God is self-sufficient and thus needs nothing from His creation. This thought will be important to keep in mind when in the following section we turn to the question of whether God can love us.

We have already encountered al-Ghazali's third cause of love, the love of something for its own sake, and not for any good that it might allow us to get or achieve. And we have already discussed the sense in which this too seems to require a certain kind of self-regard or self-interest. The examples that al-Ghazali gives of beloved objects of this third kind are pleasure and beauty. It is here that al-Ghazali expands upon the notion of beauty so that it includes not only forms visible to the five senses but also "inner forms." Unsurprisingly, and in keeping with his generally Platonic heritage and inclinations, he also makes the case that the love for inner forms of beauty is superior to the love for external beauty.

Our love of beauty, and especially inner beauty, also explains why it makes sense to love someone we have never met, such as the Prophet, his Companions, or other saintly figures (al-Ghazali 2016, 19). We love them for the beauty that they exhibit in their lives and writings. It is for a similar reason that I can love a person who does beneficial things for someone other than me. When a benefactor does something good for a stranger, we see the beauty in that act and it is that beauty that we love (21).

So far, al-Ghazali has identified four causes of love: (1) my love for my preservation and flourishing, (2) my love for someone who provides a benefit to me and facilitates my ability to persist and flourish, (3) my love for someone who is good to people, even if that person is not doing good for me personally, and (4) my love for everything beautiful in itself. In addition to these, al-Ghazali adds a final cause: (5) "the love for someone with whom there exists a hidden, inner affinity" (22). In this final instance, the love is due to "sheer spiritual affinity." The basic idea is intuitive enough. We observe it happening all the time. People often desire to be around people who are like them. In some cases, this is as basic as people preferring to be with people who look like themselves. In more rarified cases, the affinity is, as al-Ghazali puts it, more intellectual or spiritual. That is, we prefer to be around people who share our interests and values. If you look back, you will in fact see that al-Ghazali already alluded to this cause when he was explicating the first cause, for after all, the thing that is most like me is me. Again, this is a case of self-interest or self-love in a broad sense. As we will see in Section 6.4, being around people and acting collectively brings with it a certain kind of pleasure.

In sum, al-Ghazali believes that only conscious beings can love something or someone. He also seems to believe that, at least for created beings, love ultimately stems from self-love, since even loving something else for that other's sake provides a certain "advantage" to the lover, namely, pleasure. To be sure, there is more to the story. For as we will see, the best form of love is love for God, and this love for God will lead us into that state of mystical absorption or "annihilation," which we have already considered in Chapters 4 and 5. In a sense, then, the truest form of love will require a form of self-effacement. But before we can get to that, we need to first see why al-Ghazali believes that true and proper love is love of God.

6.2 Can We Love God? Can God Love Us?[1]

Al-Ghazali's discussion of the five basic causes of love is part of the case he is making for the claim that love of God really is love, and not just "love" in some metaphorical sense. From our vantage, it might be difficult to understand why al-Ghazali felt the need to do such a thing. First, scripture seems to flatly and unambiguously proclaim that God loves us and that we can love God.

> Say, "If you love God, follow me, and God will love you and forgive you your sins."
> (Quran 3:31; trans. Nasr et al. 2015)

Second, famous Islamic mystics like Rumi (1273) and Hafiz (1390) are associated with highly exuberant depictions of ardent love for God. Some of their verses cause more conservative listeners to cringe because of their highly erotic overtones. Those mystics might have gone overboard a bit. (We have already noted how even some mystics, including al-Ghazali, were unsettled by some of the wilder claims of their colleagues.) But who would deny that we can love God?

It turns out that a number of medieval Islamic theologians did just that. In al-Ghazali's day and age, Abu al-Qasim al-Zamakhshari (1144) claimed that

> Man's love for God lies in obedience to Him, in striving for His approval and in not doing whatever necessarily brings His wrath and punishment. God's love for His servants lies in that He lets them enjoy the finest reward for their obedience.
> (*al-Kashshaf* I.621; quoted by Ormsby in al Ghazali 2016, xxi–xxii; see also, al-Ghazali's Prologue, idem, 2)

Zamakhshari was especially critical of the earlier Sufis. What they did amounted to a certain vicious form of anthropomorphism. Underlying Zamakhshari's complaint is a compelling and, in the Middle Ages, quite commonplace notion: God is unlike anything else. Due to this vast ontological distance, it is unclear whether it makes any sense to think we could enter into a relationship with God that was anything like love properly speaking. When Aristotle was discussing *philia*, which is usually translated as "friendship," but which includes a family of affectionate reciprocal relationships, he observed that equality between the parties is crucial.

> This becomes clear if there is a great interval in respect of excellence or vice or wealth or anything else between parties; for then they are no longer friends, and do not even expect to be so. And this is most manifest in the case of the gods; for they surpass us most decisively in all good things.
> (*Nicomachean Ethics* 8.7, 1158b32–1159a1)

Even if love does not require reciprocity and thus equality, it is still not clear whether it makes sense for us to *love* a being that is utterly unlike anything else that we know. It makes sense to fear what God might do to us if we disobey His commands. But as for affection or even desire for Him, that is hard to grasp.[2] And surely, it seems most unfitting to desire God in the same way that we desire food, drink, or an object of sexual desire.

If it is hard to fathom how we can love God, it is even harder to understand how a perfect being like God could love us. God is complete and self-sufficient. What, then, could God desire from or in His creatures? It is reasoning like this that leads Zamakhshari and other like-minded scholars to conclude that "love," when it occurs in the Quran, is a mere metaphor.

Al-Ghazali's rebuttal is quite straightforward. We love something for one of the five abovementioned reasons. Moreover, our love increases if these reasons are combined into a single thing or person.

> This is like the case of a man whose son is beautifully formed, fine in character, of consummate knowledge, upstanding in disposition, kind to others as well as good to his parents – such a son is loved irresistibly and to the utmost.
> (al-Ghazali 2016, 22)

And our love is increased even more to the degree that the beloved has these lovely qualities. Given all this, it stands to reason that if there is some being that combines all of these causes and possesses them to the highest degree, then this is the worthiest object of our love. Such a being does, indeed, exist. It is God.

But al-Ghazali will go one step further: he argues that "God *alone* merits love" (al-Ghazali 2016, 22, *my emphasis*). Al-Ghazali cleverly defends this stronger claim by employing a claim about transference: If you love X, then you love X's cause. And since causes are superior to their effects and mediators, if you love X, then you love X's cause even more. Let's look quickly at two examples. The first pertains to the first cause of love, namely, our desire to exist and thrive. Al-Ghazali argues that a person's love for himself necessitates the love of God, since everything "comes from God and goes to God and is by God" (24). If you love your existence, then surely you love what makes it so that you can exist. This is why people love food and water and shelter. But all these things are due to God. Hence, we should love God, and we should love Him more because the food is only lovable because it sustains us. It is an instrument through which God sustains us. The same line of reasoning is behind al-Ghazali's observations about our love for the benefactor. We love the person who gives us things because of the benefits that her gifts give us. But now imagine that the person bringing you the gifts is merely an emissary of, say, a prince. Surely, it is more appropriate to love the prince who sent the emissary than to love the emissary (just as we are advised by that adage to "not shoot the messenger"). But now, as al-Ghazali argues, every benefactor other than God is in fact compelled to bring you goods by God, just as our imagined emissary is compelled to send good things on behalf of his prince (27). It stands to reason, then, that God above all is to be loved for being our benefactor.

After showing us that we ought to love God more, because He is the cause of all the things that we love, al-Ghazali then uses the following reasoning to undercut the lesser objects of love. The love of worldly things weakens one's love for God (al-Ghazali 2016, 69). The happiest people are those who detach as much as they can from this world so as to focus on what is most real and most valuable. This notion of a trade-off or, as Eric Ormsby puts it, "equilibrium of gain and loss" (69, note A) is quite common in ancient and medieval philosophies and religions. In philosophy, the idea can be found throughout Plato's works. In his defense speech, for instance, Socrates suggests that his fellow Athenians cannot pay attention to their bodies, the accumulation of wealth, and other such lesser goods and at the same time cultivate the virtues in their souls (29e–30b; 36c–d), and in the *Phaedo*, we find Socrates looking forward to his release from his body so that he can focus on what really matters (64d–69e; compare al-Ghazali 2016, 64 and 110). This Socratic and Platonic thinking both reinforces and is reinforced by scripture, which also often asks the faithful to reorient themselves away from this world and to fixate on the world to come.

This same sort of equilibrium model can be employed to narrow down the field of inner forms and spiritual objects of love. The upshot is that any time we focus on something other than God, we are taking our eye off the supreme being and the supreme good, and in effect, we are pursuing a lesser good at the expense of a greater good. "God alone," then, "is worthy of love in its source and in its perfection" (al-Ghazali 2016, 41).

This does not, however, mean that the lover of God ignores others and does nothing for the good of other creatures. Al-Ghazali and others who follow his line of thinking take pains to stress that the lover of God still follows the outward commandments of the faith, which includes not only such obligations as prayer and ritual acts of purification but also things like charitable contributions to aid the poor and less fortunate. Here, for instance, is a passage from 'A'ishah al-Ba'uniyyah's (1517) *Principles of Sufism*, which draws upon the same Sufi traditions that al-Ghazali does.[3]

> If you understand that, then know that one sign of love is just as one of them said,[4] "One who claims to love God without abstaining from what is forbidden him is an imposter! One who claims to love Paradise without giving charity is an imposter! One who claims to love His Emissary without loving poverty[5] is an imposter!"
>
> ('A'ishah al-Ba'uniyyah 2014, 113)

The sign of a true lover of God in fact is that he or she does not see these obligations as in any way a burden. Moreover, the love of God seems to overflow and transition into a love for everything else.

> Thus, a mark of love of God is the love of mentioning Him, together with a love of the Qur'an which is His word, love of His Prophet, and love of all who are related to him. Whoever loves someone loves even the dog in his neighborhood. When love is strong, it stretches from the beloved to everything that concerns him and that stands linked with his affairs.
>
> (al-Ghazali 2016, 113)

By loving God and God alone, the lover acts like a conduit through which God's love can spread to the rest of creation.

Of course, this naturally leads us to the second question. Even if we can love God, can God love us? We could immediately answer in the affirmative if love required reciprocity. But, as we will soon see, while there is a certain interconnection and virtuous feedback loop between the lover of God and God, the way that al-Ghazali frames the discussion makes it clear that reciprocity in kind is not required. Indeed, our love for God and God's love for us cannot be of the same sort.

Al-Ghazali agrees with al-Zamakhshari on one fundamental point: God is absolutely other. God is the "most manifest of existents" as well as "conceptually the most exalted," but this can only really be understood by analogy (al-Ghazali 2016, 81). No word that is applied to God and to what is not-God can be used univocally, not even, al-Ghazali argues, the word "existence" (100). This is in keeping with an idea that we saw expressed elsewhere that only God is truly and fully real. Everything else exists as a being that is dependent upon God. This is why we see al-Ghazali saying that when it comes to the five causes of love, in God alone are these real, "but in others, their existence is mere fanciful supposition – metaphor pure and simple, devoid of all reality" (23).

But there is also a more specific reason why God cannot love us in the same sense that we love Him.

> In linguistic convention, "love" designates the soul's inclination towards what is fitting and congruent. But this is conceivable only in a deficient soul which lacks whatever is congruent with it. Accordingly, it wishes to perfect itself by attaining that missing thing and delights in attaining it. In God's case, this would be absurd.
>
> (al-Ghazali 2016, 101)

Love, like all inclinations, is a movement toward and desire to attain something that is currently lacking. God, however, is complete in every respect. Hence, He feels no inclination toward anything else whatsoever. God, therefore, cannot long for us and move toward us in the way that we long and move toward Him.[6] The only inclination or love (in so far as it even makes sense to say this) that God possesses is an inclination or love toward Himself. God "only sees His own essence and His own acts exclusively since nothing exists except His essence and His acts" (idem).

This does not mean that God is a narcissistic and remote deity. He cannot be so, given that the Quran says that He loves us, and al-Ghazali is reluctant to read scripture allegorically unless he absolutely must.[7] Nevertheless, as al-Ghazali will concede, His love for us does take on a seemingly paradoxical air.

> For this reason, the master Abu Sa'id al -Mihani said, when God's statement *He loves them and they love Him* [Quran 5:54] was recited to him, "In truth He loves them for He loves only Himself," meaning that God is all and that there is nothing in existence other than God.
>
> (al-Ghazali 2016, 101)

We are dependent beings and effects of God's acts. Thus, to really know ourselves is to know our cause, God; and when God knows Himself, He knows us too. This helps to explain why for al-Ghazali and other Sufis, the love of God ends in the "annihilation" of our selves. The lover, as we will recall, is focused solely on God. Everything else is a distraction. Accordingly, all aspects of our personality are distractions and must be bracketed off and put to one side.

As you will remember from Chapter 4 (Section 4.3), however, this annihilation is not literal (at least not for al-Ghazali). It is not as if we are literally dissolved into or become God. Our ceasing to be is never so complete as that.

> While the utmost perfection belongs to God alone, nearness to God stands in proportion to one's perfection. The pupil may come close to his teacher, may equal or even surpass him, but that is impossible with respect to God Whose perfection is endless. Man's progress along the degrees of perfection is finite and terminates only at a prescribed limit; he has no craving for equality with God.
>
> (al-Ghazali 2016, 104)

In so far as we can purify ourselves, we can get closer to perfection. But there will always be a gap between us and Him.

This, however, has led us back into thinking about our love for God. We are back to thinking about *our* striving toward God, *our* attempt to become as perfect as we humanly can. But is there any more content to the idea that *God* loves us? Al-Ghazali adds this:

> So then, God's love for man lies in His drawing him near, and out of himself, by warding off distractions and sins and in purifying his inmost nature from the spots of this world and in lifting the veil from his heart until he eyes Him as though he saw Him with his very heart.
>
> (idem)

Notice who the agent is in this passage. The actions described are ones involving the human aspirant, but the *instigator* of the actions is God, not the human. God's love is to move an effect of His toward Himself. Al-Ghazali admits that this picture is hard for the human mind to grasp. There really is no way to adequately convey how things really are. This is why at this point in his discussion al-Ghazali feels compelled to resort to parables (see 103–4).

As we have seen time and time again, when thinking about the perfect being, our concepts and distinctions tend to collapse in on themselves, just as matter collapses to the size of a point in things that present-day astrophysicists call "singularities." There is at least this to say: Al-Ghazali's way of describing how God loves His creation is consistent with his position about causation, one that he shares with many Islamic theologians. Only

God is truly an agent and cause (see Section 3.6). In so far as we can lift up the hood and discern how reality works, it should not, therefore, be surprising that God's love for His creation is a kind, if not indeed the most radical kind, of self-love that we can conceive.

6.3 Loving Your Neighbor and Tough Love

One of the chief commandments in Judaism, Christianity, and Islam is to love one's neighbor. One of the things that this commandment means is that we should lend a helping hand when it is needed. Feed the hungry. Give shelter to the cold. Heal the sick. Some argued that lending a hand when needed not only applies to offering aid and comfort, it also entails that we have a duty to admonish and even punish those who stray from the virtuous and righteous path. In the middle of a series of often highly theoretical and abstract questions about the virtues, Aquinas (1274) pauses to ask whether we have a duty to correct others who go astray.

The first question concerns whether there is in fact a precept about brotherly correction. The investigation proceeds in the manner of a standard scholastic investigation (see Chapter 1, Section 1.3). After canvassing arguments for and against, Aquinas gives his own view of the matter before finally turning to address some of the minutiae in the initial arguments. Aquinas concludes that there is an obligation to correct those who go astray, and he argues that this precept falls out of the fundamental commandment to love one's neighbor (*Disputed Questions on the Virtues*, On Brotherly Correction, Article 1; trans. Aquinas 2005, 199). To love a person is to want what is good for that person. If a person is lacking a good, the precept to love our neighbor also requires that we want to eliminate that lack. At this point in his reply, Aquinas adds that it is not enough to *want* to provide a good or eliminate a lack. You only honor the precept to love one's neighbor if you act on that want, that is, that you try – to the best of your ability – to provide the good or eliminate the lack. If correction is part of what it takes to love one's neighbor, then this means that one must actually engage in correction. You cannot just harbor the wish that someone will improve morally, you must do something to put your neighbor back on the correct path.

Aquinas proceeds to pinpoint precisely where correction falls among the acts that one is obliged to perform (199–200). First, he notes that there are three kinds of goods: (1) the "external" or "temporal" goods, like food and shelter; (2) the "goods of the body," by which Aquinas means the preservation of life and limb; and (3) the goods that pertain to virtue. "Love your neighbor" entails obligations on all three fronts. If your neighbors lose their garden or flock, you are obligated to provide food so that they won't starve. If your neighbors are threatened with violence, you are obligated to assist and protect them. And finally, we are obligated to help one another to develop and maintain virtue and to avoid evil. Indeed, since the third sorts of goods are higher in rank than the first two, we have an even stronger obligation to assist with cultivating and protecting virtue in others.

There is still the question of *when* correction is appropriate. Here Aquinas returns to the notion of a precept or commandment. Some are "positive" precepts, others are "negative." Sins are bad in and of themselves no matter when they occur or how they occur. Therefore, according to Aquinas, sins are prohibited by a negative precept ("thou shalt not..."): "they must not be done at any time nor in any way" (200).

Positive precepts, however, are different. They do not need to be followed at every time and in every way. They are commanded only when the situation calls for them. Aquinas uses the example of a precept from the Ten Commandments.

> For example, "Honour your parents" does not need to be put into practice at every time and place and in every way, but where the appropriate circumstances are present.
> (*Disputed Questions*, On Brotherly Correction, Article 1; Aquinas 2005, 201)

In other words, you do not need to drop everything and constantly attend to your parents in order to obey the precept. You only need to obey and fulfill it when it is right to do so. The same holds for brotherly correction: "it takes effect in appropriate circumstances."

Okay, we might say, but when does the obligation to correct our friends and neighbors take effect? Here Aquinas demurs.

> It is not possible to provide a discourse that defines these circumstances, because judging them must take place in individual cases. This is the job of practical wisdom, whether acquired by experience and over time, or, better still, infused: as I John 2:27 puts it, "Anointing will teach you concerning everything."
>
> (idem)

Here incidentally is a case where critics of virtue ethics express frustration, and understandably so (see Chapter 5, Section 5.1). We would like some hard, fast rules, or at least some guidelines for how to act in concrete situations. But it is precisely in such cases that the virtue ethicist often claims that things are complicated and that the right path is only arrived at by practice and the patient accrual of experience. In Aquinas's case, there is another avenue toward something closer to certainty: one can pray that God will give them insight and prudence. But for those of us whose prayers have not yet been heard, we are left with the directive to seek out those who have learned through experience.

That said, I don't want to leave you with the impression that virtue ethics is obviously wrongheaded. Think about it for a moment. Is there really a succinct, handy set of guidelines which tell you when and precisely how to, for instance, honor your parents in every situation that might arise? Do you always need to lend a hand if you parents call? How many times a week do you need to call them? Should you always hold your tongue when your father says something that you deem to be bigoted or ignorant? Should you always call him out for being rude, insensitive, or the like?[8] On reflection, I think you might see that it is not clear whether any simple rule of thumb can capture all the nuances and contributing factors. Each situation is unique. Your parents and my parents differ when it comes to what they need, what they will heed, and so forth. Thus, the virtue ethicist might be right. The best that we can say is that the right course of action for dealing with your parents will come from trial and error over a lifetime of living with them.

Similarly, knowing when to correct one's neighbor requires practical wisdom, which is something that most of us will acquire only through experience. But Aquinas does have some general practical advice as to how we should proceed to correct our friends and neighbors, once we decide that action must be taken. In the next part of the investigation, Aquinas considers whether we should admonish our neighbors publicly or in private. The Bible seems to offer conflicting advice here. At one point, we are told to "reprove the sinner in the presence of everyone" (I Timothy 5:20). But elsewhere, we are advised to "accuse him between the two of you alone" (Matthew 18:15).

Here Aquinas displays a keen understanding of human psychology. First, he notes that sin presents a danger both to a person's "conscience" and to their reputation (*Disputed Questions on the Virtues*, On Brotherly Correction, Article 2, Aquinas 2005, 209–10). Conscience is something witnessed only by the person and God, and it is something that a person only needs for their own sake. Reputation, on the other hand, involves other humans and it matters both for what it brings to the person and for what it does for others. Conscience, therefore, is of higher importance. And, thus, it is advised that one begin by attempting to appeal to the sinner's conscience, which can be done with a private warning. One should only move to a public act of censure if the appeal to conscience does not work.

There is another reason to start by pulling one's friend aside for a private chat about their behavior. Public admonishment will surely damage the sinner's reputation. But damage to one's reputation can have severe consequences, and hence, a person's good name and standing in the community should not be taken away unless it is absolutely necessary. According to Aquinas, a person's reputation is the most important of the external goods. It makes it possible for that person to carry out their roles and duties in society. Think about our own societies. Employers are often reluctant to hire former criminals. Someone who is thought to be a liar will not be taken seriously in court. Someone who has a reputation for being irresponsible will not be asked to look after the kids. Of course, if someone is a pathological liar, we have good reason to not put them in positions where truth-telling is essential. But what about the person who lies once but gets caught? Is it not an extreme punishment to make it *impossible* for that person to take on various jobs or be entrusted with responsibilities?

The loss of reputation can also cause people to become worse as opposed to becoming better.

> Therefore, if it is a sin to deprive a neighbour of his wealth where that is not necessary, it is far more of a sin to deprive him of his reputation where that is not necessary, by making his sin public where that is not necessary; because frequently people refrain from sinning in order to keep their reputation. Consequently, those who see that they have already lost their reputation may think nothing of sinning, in accordance with Jeremiah 3:3, "Your face has become like a prostitute's, and you have forgotten how to blush."
> (*Disputed Questions*, On Brotherly Correction, Article 2; Aquinas 2005, 210)

If a person is already ostracized because of things that they have done in the past, they have nothing to lose. Admonishment and punishment, as Aquinas reminds us, is always done with the aim of reforming the sinner. The cure should be tailored to the individual and their crime so that it does not make matters worse. Hence, we are once again advised to start by pulling our friend aside and having a frank conversation in private.

Aquinas notes that a public rebuke of a sinner can have two other potentially damaging consequences. First, once the sinner has been exposed, the public might begin to distrust the innocent as well. Aquinas quotes Augustine (430) at this point:

> When it is rumoured falsely or revealed truly that someone who has a reputation for holiness has committed a crime, immediately people busy themselves in trying to believe the same of everyone.
> (Letter 78.6, quoted in Aquinas, *Disputed Questions*, Article 2; Aquinas 2005, 210)

Augustine and Aquinas are pointing to the well-known phenomenon of guilt by association. Someone in a certain group, say, a church or a corporation or an identifiable ethnic group, acts badly. This quickly casts suspicion on others who are members of the same group. Of course, in some cases, suspicion is warranted. The "few bad apples" rhetoric sometimes is used to obfuscate and cover up broader systemic problems in an organization. But often enough, blanket suspicion is not justified, and as we know, this can have terrible consequences for innocent people.

The second worry is that if a famous person is exposed as a sinner, this will encourage others to sin as well. After all, if this person thinks it is okay, then surely it must be. This is the reasoning behind the worry that many of us have about what our children (and our adult friends!) consume on social media. Sometimes the people they follow are not ideal role models. (I will let you think about your own candidates for illustrating this claim. I don't want to outdate this book immediately.)

Aquinas knows that sometimes a person must be publicly exposed and publicly humiliated. But this is the extreme option, and because of all the possible knock-on effects of a public admonishment, it should be utilized only when all else fails. Admonishment, as we must remember, is supposed to reform the individual, to make them a better person. Thus, we must determine what it will take to set our friend back on the straight path without making the situation worse. Perhaps all it will take is a private one-on-one conversation. If that does not work, Aquinas advises us to approach our wayward neighbor with "two or three witnesses" (211). As with many a disease, it is best to start with the least invasive procedure, and then only gradually implement more and more invasive and aggressive treatments. With hope we can set our neighbors back on the right path. The commandment to love our neighbor demands that we intervene when they make a serious mistake, but it also demands that we treat our neighbors with respect and gentleness and to protect what is most valuable of theirs.

6.4 Bad Company

Perhaps you have heard the saying that you ought to choose your friends wisely. This is because the people around us can have real effects on how we think about things and how we act. Our classmates, neighbors, and friends can make us better people – sometimes through tough love. They also can encourage the worst in us. We have not said much to this point about why people do *bad* things, that is, why we sometimes fail to love one another. In this section, I propose that we treat these two issues together. It seems that rebellion is often at the root of bad behavior. Should this merely be explained as a pathology, a quirk of our fallen human nature? Arguably not. For it seems that many of us end up doing the bad, rebellious thing because we are egged on by those around us. Accordingly, if peer pressure can be avoided, we might be able to reduce – reduce, not eradicate – bad actions done out of rebellion.

The Socratic analysis, which is effectively picked up by Aristotle, is that when we do something bad or wrong, we are picking what *appears* to be best for us. For, as Socrates famously posited, no one would willingly choose something that they know is harmful for them (see, e.g., Plato *Protagoras* 345c–e, *Gorgias* 467a–b; Segvic 2000). Often, we are not wrong about the fact that the thing we choose is good or even choice-worthy. The error or sin stems from the fact that we chose a *lesser* good over a *greater* good. But why did we choose a lesser good, when a better good was available? The Socratic answer is that we chose the lesser good because the lesser good *appeared* to us to be the greater good. In sum, the Socratic philosopher maintains that moral error stems from an epistemic error.

This Socratic assumption gains a lot of traction in various quarters of medieval thought about error and sin. But the thesis is not left unchallenged. Perhaps the most intriguing instance of this might be on display in a meditation on evildoing in Augustine's masterpiece *The Confessions*. (I say that it "might" be present because elsewhere, Augustine seems to endorse the notion that sin does stem from ignorance.) In the second book of this complex work – a mixture of autobiography, philosophical investigation, scriptural exegesis, and prayer – Augustine relates a story from when he was a teenager. At the age of sixteen, Augustine left school for a time and moved back in with his parents. He begins to hang around with a rough and rowdy crowd of boys and he begins to get into all sorts of mischief. One evening, he and his buddies come upon a pear tree. Even though the pears are "not enticing in either appearance or taste," he and his friends decide to steal a number of the pears and then toss them to the pigs (2.4.9; Augustine 2019, 23). Recalling this story prompts Augustine to pause and meditate on what really caused him to commit this crime against the farmer and against God. In doing so, Augustine lands upon some startling and subtle insights about why we do bad things.

At first Augustine seems to pay lip service to the Socratic idea that this had to be a case of picking a lesser good for a greater one (2.5.10). And to drive the point home that he is interested not just in his situation but also in human psychology more generally, Augustine adds this rhetorical setup to the Socratic position.

> When a question arises about why some criminal act was done, people do not typically accept any explanation until it appears that there was a desire to attain, or a fear of losing, one of those good that we have

called the lower goods. These are beautiful and becoming, though they are abject and contemptible in comparison with the higher goods that bring true happiness. Someone has committed murder. Why did he do it? He loved his victim's wife or estate, or he wanted to steal enough to live on, or he was afraid of losing something to his victim, or he was burning to revenge himself on someone who had injured him. Surely no one has ever committed murder simply because he delighted in murder itself! Who would believe such a thing?

(*Confessions*, 2.5.11; trans. Augustine 2019, 24)

Here Augustine is showing us how intuitive the Socratic analysis is. This intuition is still operative and has a powerful appeal on us. Many of us find pure evil – evil done merely for the sake of doing evil – fascinating and unintelligible. Yet, as Augustine proceeds to show, this might in fact be the reason, at least on some occasions, for why people do horrible things. Given that on Augustine's analysis evil is merely a privation or lack of a good (*Confessions* 3.7.12, 7.12.18), if someone does something bad merely because it is a bad or evil thing, in a sense this person did it *for nothing*.

Before we proceed, we should draw a few distinctions. If we ask why someone did what they did, we might be looking for the *end* of their action. That is, we might be trying to identify the object that they desired to obtain (say, the fruit or pleasure) or a state of affairs that they hoped their action would bring about (such as causing harm to the farmer, which is what one does for instance when one is stealing in order to exact revenge). But another thing we could be asking for when we want to make sense of why someone did what they did is the *motive*. Here the answer to our query takes the form of something like this: "I wanted to steal the pears and cause the farmer harm because I wanted to exact revenge." Or: "I lied to you about how much money is in the bank account out of fear and shame." I stated that when we exact revenge, for instance, it seems that part of what we want is to cause our victim harm. But this does not fully explain the reason why I harmed, say, the farmer. If I harmed the farmer because I was afraid of him, that is a different explanation of the fact that I stole the pears than one where I stole because I wanted to exact revenge. The loss of the pears occurs in both cases, but we treat these as distinct motives. We often think that it is important to track motives in addition to effects when evaluating the agent's moral culpability and when we go about determining how we will fix the problem.

Augustine considers his own crime as a teen. Perhaps, he stole the pears because he was attracted to their beauty. He curtly rules that out. Of course, the pears were beautiful; everything that God creates is beautiful. But the beauty of the pears was not what his "wretched soul lusted after." Perhaps he desired them because he was hungry or because he merely wanted the pleasure of their sweet taste. No, it was not that either.

> The pears that I had plucked I threw away. The only thing I tasted from them was iniquity; enjoying that was what made me happy. For even if something from those pears did enter my mouth, it was the crime that gave it savor.
>
> (2.6.12; Augustine 2019, 25)

In short, Augustine claims that he cannot identify any end to which his theft was directed. Augustine also states that he and his friends did not steal them in order to exact revenge on the tree's owner (2.9.17). We can also infer that Augustine and his friends did not do it in order to make money or for fear of losing anything. In other words, upon examination, Augustine claims that he cannot identify any clear motive for the theft. This leaves Augustine to wonder why he stole the pears. He does admit that he loved the theft "and nothing else," but since "the theft was nothing" this makes his act (and him) "all the more wretched" (2.8.16, 27). Did Augustine steal the pears for no reason at all?

Now, Augustine could be wrong. After all, he is not strictly speaking *introspecting* when he is querying his reasons for stealing the pears. He is reconstructing events that happened long ago, and as we know humans can make all sorts of errors when they attempt to remember both what they did and why they did it. But I think we can sidestep these worries, for I think that even if Augustine is wrong about why *he* stole, he nevertheless has his finger on something profound. I can tell you what I discover when I introspect. On many occasions, even now as an adult, it sure *seems* that sometimes I do things merely to rebel. When Augustine asks,

> Did it please me to act against your law, at least by deceit – since I could not do so by force – and thus mimic the curtailed freedom of a prisoner by getting away with doing what was not permitted, in a shadowy likeness of omnipotence?
>
> (2.6.14, 26)

I want to agree. That is precisely how it sometimes seems to be.

Here we need to be careful. Does this mean that Augustine and I sometimes do things for no reason at all? It certainly does seem to be the case that if I did an action because it was rebellious, I did not act for an *end*. Arguably, "because the action was rebellious" also fails to count as a *motive*. If we think that the reasons why we do the things we do must boil down to either ends or motives, then it appears sometimes evil is irrational, that it cannot be explained. But this may be taking things a step too far.[9] If Augustine steals the pears because stealing is rebellious, it seems that we have found a *reason*, and even a reason for acting as he did. If that is right, then Augustine's action is not utterly inexplicable or resistant to explanation.

There is something odd and unsettling about doing something *because it is rebellious*. This is what I think is in large part behind Augustine's puzzlement and horror about the fact that he did something for no end and for no motive, or as he puts, for nothing. It makes good sense to us that we act because we want something or because some affection of the soul (fear, lust, anger, etc.) moved us to do it. Rebellion, when decoupled from ends and motives, seems a bit more nebulous. I think this goes some way toward explaining why I hastened to note that Augustine's reconstruction of his past psychology could be wrong. Sometimes ends and motives are not entirely clear, even to ourselves. But this does not mean they are not there.

On the other hand, just because something is unsettling or hard to grasp with clarity, it does not mean that it is not real. And, as I have already said, it sure seems to me that doing something *because it is rebellious* is a reason why I act on occasion. It is also worth pointing out that Augustine's discussion of the pear incident does not mean that he rejects ends and motives as explanations of our actions on many occasions. I think the best way to read this admittedly difficult passage in the *Confessions* is that Augustine is revising our picture of desire, motivation, and action by adding to, not replacing, our arsenal of explanations for why we do the things that we do.

I think that there is much more going on this passage than that. For instance, it seems that Augustine is trying to reduce all rebellion to rebellion against God. It may also be the case that Augustine wants us to see that every case where we choose a lesser good over a greater good – that is, cases where we can identify ends or motives – boils down to a case of rebellion against God. There are also issues with whether and to what degree his analysis of the theft of the pears is relying on his famous metaphysical analysis of evil, namely, that it is a privation and thus nothing.[10] For that matter, as latter medieval commentators note, it is not entirely clear what the claim that "evil is nothing" amounts to.

But for the remainder of this discussion, let us take it as having been established that one possible reason to act badly is that the action is rebellious. It may be true that some actions are due to a mixture of reasons. It may be the case that on some occasions we act both for the goods that they bring and out of, say, fear. Likewise, it may be that in many cases of rebellion, the full explanation of our action is that there was a mix of ends and motives, which was accompanied by the fact that the action is also rebellious. Perhaps this is just muddy thinking on my part. Perhaps I am conflating different acts that need explanation or I am failing to distinguish the real *reason* from accompanying *factors*. For my purposes, I don't think it matters.

What does matter is that even if an act is done merely because it is a rebellious act, it appears to be true that the *prevalence* of such actions is influenced by the fact that others are present and also acting in the same way. Augustine may be able to explain why *he* stole. But, for all Augustine knows, one of his friends did steal because he desired the pears or because he hated the farmer. That is not the issue. What is important is that Augustine sees that there is something about being in a group that enhances and reinforces the bad choices that he makes. Acting as part of a group may even be the reason why we act upon a bad reason. Augustine tells us that he is not sure he would have *actually* stolen the pears if his friends had not been present and sinning with him. Indeed, he is more emphatic about that than he is perhaps warranted: He "certainly" would not have done it.

> But I would not have done it by myself. I would certainly not have done it by myself. Behold before you, my God, this living recollection in my soul. If I had been by myself, I would not have done that theft in which what pleased me was not what I stole, but that I stole; it would not have pleased me to do it alone, and I would not have done it. O you too unfriendly friendship, unsearchable seduction of the mind! Out of playing and joking came a passion to do harm and a desire to damage someone else without any gain for myself., without any lust for revenged! But when someone says, "Let's go, let's do it," we are ashamed not to be shameless.
>
> (2.9.17; Augustine 2019, 27)

In addition, there was a lesser good that arose from the fact that he acted in conjunction with the group. There was a kind of pleasure that came from the crime itself and was "created" by this "companionship with fellow sinners" (2.8.16).

Once again, Augustine has hit upon something that seems to be right. I will be the first to admit that being in a group encouraged me to *actually* go ahead with some very silly, and sometimes dangerous and wrong things. Again, we should be clear-eyed. Sometimes we refer to "peer pressure" as an explanation for why someone did a bad thing. But peer pressure can involve any number of ends and motives, such as gaining admission to a group (as "hazing" rituals purport to promise) or fear of being an outcast or "weird" (which is probably also at work in hazing rituals). If we grant that Augustine is right about what was going on in his head at the moment, none of those goods or motives were in play. When his companions urged him on, it was not by promising some gain or threating some penalty for not going along with the group. It was rather that by seeing them rebel, he wanted to do it too, and in turn when they saw him rebelling, their commitment to the rebellious action was strengthened. The vigor with which they went about stealing the pears was bolstered by the fact that they were doing it together. Acting in a crowd can indeed be "infectious" in this way, and we often find that when we are "swept up" in the energy of the crowd, we end up doing things that we might otherwise not have done.

Augustine is not claiming that people who do bad actions *necessarily* do these things because they are in a group and thus receive pleasure from being in a community of sinners. Indeed, if experience is any guide, some people do not need this sort of community to commit awful acts of rebellion. Nonetheless, I suspect that young Augustine was like many of us at that age: He was in general a "good kid," but when surrounded by the wrong crowd, the worst in him blossomed.

Of course, being in a group can work in the opposite direction as well. We are more likely to step up to the mike, sing karaoke, and even enjoy it, when we are among friends. It might be the case that we sing because we are motivated by pleasure and fear. But not necessarily. Here is another instance: We are more likely to stand up to injustice when we are in a like-minded group. Again, specific instances of standing up to injustices might have different explanations. But it is conceivable that the explanation for at least some of them is one that is analogous to Augustine's explanation of the theft.

The main point is that Augustine knows that the character of your companions matters. In the *Confessions*, he tells us that he cut ties with many of his old relationships (and indeed, much of his family), and that he subsequently surrounded himself with a small group of like-minded individuals so that he could pursue the true and straight spiritual path. Bad friends and neighbors can encourage you to act on your worst impulses. Good friends and neighbors can be a bulwark against moral error. In Late Antiquity and the Middle Ages, when individuals retreated from society at large, they tended to cluster together in enclaves, monasteries, and the like. The hermetic sage was the exceptional case, even for spiritual masters and saints. The notion that the communities we live in can make us better or worse will be something we pursue vigorously in Chapter 7.

6.5 Love for All Creation

You might have encountered the great German philosopher Immanuel Kant (1724–1804) in your introductory course in philosophy. His ethical philosophy, which has had a profound impact on subsequent thinking about the subject, is sometimes simplified and boiled down to two basic maxims. The first is a refinement of the so-called Golden Rule. (Think about what his "categorical imperative" implies: "Act only in accordance with that maxim through which you can at the same time will that it become a universal law." (*Groundwork of the Metaphysics of Morals*; Kant 1998, 31)) The second is that we should always treat persons as ends in themselves, never as means to something else. In other words, no person's value stems from their usefulness. In contrast, it is often thought that plants, certain animals, and the environment more generally are valuable precisely because of what they provide for us. In this section, we will examine this assumption from a medieval perspective. For it might turn out that we are fundamentally wrong about this.

In Chapter 4 (Section 4.4), we raised the issue of whether persons are essentially rational. And while we observed that there is conceptual space for thinking of nonrational things as persons in some contexts, when it comes to thinking of persons as the focal points for *ethical* considerations, there is a strong prejudice in the Middle Ages toward rationality. This fixation on rationality as the hallmark of humanity is all but universally coupled with what is decidedly an anthropocentric approach to value and ethical obligation. This fixation on humans and what *their* aims and purposes should be is understandable. All three Abrahamic scriptural traditions focus almost exclusively on humanity. The book of Genesis, for instance, starts with an origin story of the cosmos as a whole, but it very quickly narrows down, with the creation of Adam, to the history of humankind, so that the rest of the Old and New Testaments focus upon the subsequent travails of Adam's and Eve's descendants and God's demands and promises to *them*.

Scripture is also often interpreted as sanctioning the view that the remainder of creation is merely an instrument for the eventual salvation of humankind. Many medieval philosophers, following a certain interpretation of Aristotle's biology, maintained that plants and animals did not have the kind of soul capable of surviving the dissolution of the body (see Section 4.2). There would therefore be no afterlife, let alone Final Judgment for plants and animals. By itself, this notion does not entail that plants and animals, or the environment more generally, are not valuable for their own sakes. But it is easy to see how the stronger view which maintains that such things have no intrinsic value could take hold. The notion that all of material creation is created for the use of humans as they make their spiritual progression toward God is sometimes even employed as a reason why plants and animals will not enjoy an afterlife. Here, for instance, is William of Auvergne (1249).

> Animals, vegetables, and also metals and other things that humans make use of in this habitat are only necessary in so far as they are for

humans. Thus, once humans are moved to their place of permanent habitation, the utility of these other things will cease, and then necessarily generation and corruption of these things will cease. [...] Wherefore, as a consequence, if animals of this sort have been created or are to be created only for use, and in particular the utility of humans, then they neither ought to be nor can they exist once this use and utility has ceased.
(*De universo* 1.2.39, 741B and 742B; my translation, cf. Wei 2020, 47)

If William is right about this, then as sad as it is to say, your favorite houseplant or pet will not be present in the afterlife with you.

If we think that plants and animals will not enjoy an afterlife and we think that the whole purpose of creation is so that it can rejoice in its creator, then it would seem to follow that everything should be geared to that species or set of species that have the capability to know God and rejoice in Him. Furthermore, both Genesis and the Quran suggest that humans have been given dominion over the rest of material creation.

As you might suspect, this anthropocentric view can lead to some potentially unsettling conclusions. William and many other thirteenth-century theologians, for instance, thought that it was morally permissible to enslave, beat, and kill animals. Yes, they conceded, the Bible does stipulate penalties for someone who kills another person's animal. But these penalties, they argued, were grounded in the fact that the killer has done something to the property of another person. The penalties were not grounded in the fact that something with intrinsic worth has been destroyed.

From our vantage, it is not hard to see how this prejudice in favor of the human, which is grounded in rationality, could easily be harnessed to dehumanize certain individuals who were deemed to not be capable of reason. A particularly troubling occurrence of this can be found in Aristotle's account of the "pygmy," a humanoid creature alleged to exist in Egypt. Many medieval philosophers, including Albert the Great (1280), devoted considerable attention to the case of the pygmy in their biological works.[11] The mythical pygmy as well as other real cases of apparent animal intelligence did not prompt Albert and others to rethink their criterion of rationality. Instead, it prompted them to define rationally narrowly. Humans are really and truly rational because they are capable of particular kinds of mental activity, namely, the abilities to grasp universals and to reason with them syllogistically. These might seem to you, as they do to me, to be very specific modes of cognition. And it does not take too much reflection to see how this very rigid notion of "reason" could subsequently be weaponized in order to dehumanize individuals who did not seem to be capable of this specific, highly refined mode of reasoning.

Thus, there is a strong current in medieval thought which holds that things incapable of reasoning are somehow less valuable and perhaps even completely lacking in intrinsic worth. But medieval thinking is not uniform about this. You may have heard some of the stories about Saint Francis (1226), and specifically, about how he preached to the birds and seemed to care for all of nature. Just how much of this is legend and how much is true is a subject of recent scholarly debate (Harris 2020, 88–9). But Francis is far from alone in having "pro-animal" values. Such attitudes can already be seen, for instance, in the writings of the third-century ascetic Desert Fathers. There are also two particularly intriguing discussions of animals in the Islamic philosophical tradition. For the remainder of this section, we will devote our attention to them.

The first of the two texts that we will examine is an entertaining tale that is included in series of epitomes of philosophy by the Brethren of Purity (*Ikhwan al-Safa*). There is much that we don't know about the Brethren, including definitive information about any of the individuals who belonged to this society of scholars centered around Baghdad and Basra in the tenth century. Based on the content of these epitomes, collectively referred to as their *Epistles*, the group had a decidedly Platonic and neo-Pythagorean inclination. In Late Antiquity, many Platonists and the neo-Pythagoreans had pro-animal tendencies.[12] The original Pythagoreans, we are told, often advocated vegetarianism. Hence, it is not too surprising that the Brethren might turn to the issue of animals and their value, as they in fact do, in the twenty-second *Epistle*, *The Case of the Animals versus Man Before the King of the Jinn* (Goodman and McGregor 2009).

The story begins when a human ship lands in the kingdom of the Jinn. The animals aboard the ship make an appeal to the king, seeking protection from the abuse and exploitation of the humans. What ensues is an elaborate trial where the humans attempt to justify their claim that they have dominion over all other animals and thus that they are entitled to exploit, beat, and even kill animals. The humans try several tactics, including appeals to their greater perfection and powers of discernment. The animals' rebuttals are extremely interesting. The human litigants, for instance, claim that human bodies are superior to animal bodies. The animals retort that this is not true. In many respects, animal bodies are superior to human bodies. Moreover, each kind of thing is given the tools that it needs. It is then suggested that humans are capable of reasoning, whereas other animals are not. To this, the animals reply by pointing out that many animals have powers of discernment and many animals are skilled artisans. Discernment and skill at making things suggest a certain kind of intelligence or rationality.

The animals patiently bolster their claim that they are not merely slaves to be exploited. Yes, they are useful to others, but this is because they – and everything – is part of a greater system. Animals have their own aims and purposes and they are intrinsically good. Humans may not legitimately inflict pain on animals. When harm cannot be avoided, it must be minimized. It is admitted by the animals that they cannot sin. However, as the animals like to point out, this could be construed as an advantage. At one point, for instance, they note that prophets are only sent to ignorant creatures. Animals "are clear of" sin: "We submit to our Lord, acknowledge Him and humbly believe in Him, proclaiming His oneness without cavil or doubt" (ch. 30; Goodman and McGregor 2009, 256).

Thus, it looks like the animals will win their case. But then a curious thing happens. The humans argue that they are the most noble species of animal; they are the completion and perfection of the animal kingdom. They further add that they alone among all living things have a special purpose. As one of the delegates from the human party puts it, "we of all living beings will be resurrected and raised up, brought forth from our graves and dealt our reckoning on the Day of Judgement, admitted by the Straight Path and entered into Paradise, the Lovely Garden, the Eternal Garden, the Garden of Eden" (ch. 42, 311). This is what justifies humanity's claim to be masters and animals servants. The animal delegation concedes, although they hasten to add:

> Yes, as you say, O human. But bear in mind the rest of the promise, O humans – chastisement in the grave, the interrogation of Nakir and Munkar, the terrors of Judgement Day, the strict reckoning, the threat of the flames and torments of hell [...] All this is for you, not for us. We are exempt. We have no promised reward, but we face no threat of retribution. We accept our Lord's judgement, neither for nor against us. He withheld the blessing of His promise but spared us the dread of his threat.
>
> (Goodman and McGregor 2009, 311–2)

Curiously, this is where the original version of the story ends. And so, it might appear that animals are in fact doomed to serve humans. But this conclusion is perhaps too hasty. Humans might be set apart from other animals by being singled out for judgment and an individual afterlife. But this does not necessarily erase the conclusions of the previous arguments. Humans are special, but it does not follow that they have permission to exploit and mistreat the rest of creation. All created beings have intrinsic worth in the Platonic picture developed by the Brethren, and things with intrinsic worth demand certain obligations and duties. Much of this, however, is merely left to the reader of the *Epistle* to work out. A more explicit statement of these duties can be found in Ibn Tufayl's (1185) remarkable philosophical novel *Hayy ibn Yaqzan*.

We already encountered Ibn Tufayl's character Hayy ("Alive") in Chapter 4 (Section 4.3). There we quickly skipped to the end of Hayy's intellectual ascent to the divine. But now let us back up and examine some of the aspects of Hayy's earlier development. Hayy is a Robinson Crusoe-like character. There are two origin stories that Tufayl relates to us. On one telling, Hayy is the product of spontaneous generation, which is brought about by the ideal mixture of natural forces at work on the island where he is born and grows up. But "others" found this idea too incredible. In their telling, Hayy is born from a human mother and father, but like Moses, his birth must be concealed. Hence, he is placed in a vessel and put out to sea, whence he arrives on an island devoid of any other humans. No matter which story you prefer, says Tufayl, the upshot is the same: Hayy grows up without any contact with other humans. Instead, he is raised by a doe and the remainder of the herd.

Hayy spends the first years of his life imitating the animals around him. But soon he notices that he is different from them. In particular, he lacks fur and natural means of defending himself. The death of his surrogate mother sets him on an elaborate study of animal natures and the natural world more generally. This is also around the time that Hayy discovers and masters fire (Ibn Tufayl 2009, 115–6, G. 47–9). It is during this period that Hayy develops many of the skills that we associate with civilization (118 f., G. 53 f.). He learns how to fashion tools and clothes. He domesticates horses and hunts animals for food and skins. He even practices vivisection in order to learn everything that he can about animal physiology (117, G. 51). In short, he is what Souleymane Bachir Diagne describes as an embodiment of humanity driven by the *libido sciendi* (i.e., the drive to know), and it is this drive that leads to violence against creation (2018, 50).

Things radically change, however, once Hayy begins to grasp that there must be a first, non-corporeal cause of all that he perceives with his senses. By the age of thirty-five, we are told, this thought of the first cause is so "deeply rooted" in him that he ceases to be interested in the study of nature for its own sake. Everywhere he looks, he sees "signs" and "intimations" of the Creator (135, G. 90). And from this point on he devotes all his energies to learning more about this being.

Along the way, Hayy learns that while he is like other animals in many respects, there is something about him that is distinctive. Everything had an immaterial aspect to them, a form, but not all forms were capable of being aware of and desiring to be present with God.

> Apparently, none of them [i.e., other animals or plants] was aware of this Being, desired Him, or had any notion of Him. All of them would turn to nothing, or next to nothing.
>
> (Ibn Tufayl 2009, 138; G. 98)

Thus, as with the Brethren and with medieval thinking more generally, animals and plants will not enjoy an afterlife. At most, they will enjoy long-lasting continuity by persisting as a species. Hayy was different. Since he knew of God, he would have one of two fates (compare to Section 5.2): Either he would turn away from God and toward lower things, and thus, in the afterlife, he would suffer tremendous psychological torment. Or, he can stay turned toward God, and in this case, he would "live on in infinite joy, bliss and delight, happiness unbroken" (138, G. 96).

With respect to this capacity to know and rejoice in the Creator, Hayy discerns that he is like the heavenly beings. In fact, he reasons, he is like all three grades of beings: nonrational animals, celestial beings, and God Himself. Due to these three resemblances, Hayy has three sets of obligations (142, G. 105–7). While his body is determined to be something other than his "true self" and a hindrance to attaining a vision of the divine, Hayy concludes that he cannot neglect it completely. At the same time, he sees that he cannot indulge the body. Instead, his obligation is to "keep the vital spirit on the brink of survival," but nothing more (143, G. 109). Moreover, he reasons, killing and eating plants and animals are acts "in opposition to the work of the Creator." Still, since he cannot starve himself, he concludes that he must choose the lesser of two evils, a "slighter form of opposition to His work" (144–5, G. 111–3). It is worth noting that this does not mean that Hayy must be a strict vegetarian. At certain points of the year, fruits and other plants may not be available. In such cases, it is permissible to eat meat or eggs.[13] But in every case, it was important that Hayy consume only as much as his body needed for minimal survival and he was to choose "only from the most abundant and not root out a whole species." In short, Hayy has discovered what we might call an ethic of sustainability and stewardship: take only what you need and take special care to ensure the perpetuation of every species.

This ethic of environmental stewardship is reinforced when Hayy reasons about the obligations that come from his likeness to celestial beings. One of the things that the celestial beings are responsible for is the perpetuation of organic cycles in the mundane realm, where the cycles of generation and corruption occur. Hayy discerns in this an obligation to imitate the celestial beings in this respect. As a rule, he never will allow himself "to see any plant or animal hurt, sick, encumbered, or in need without helping it if he could" (Ibn Tufayl 2009, 146, G. 114–5). Upon concluding this, Hayy stops to free animals who are trapped or to mend branches that are broken. He even detangles flowers from weeds in such a way that, as best as he can, he does no harm to *either* plant.

Ibn Tufayl's ethics is still anthropocentric in several respects. Humans are essentially different from other animals and they are destined for something higher than any other mundane living beings,[14] whose lives consist merely of survival and the perpetuation of the species (141, G. 104). The philosopher's ethic is, therefore, also – for lack of a better word – patronizing. Humanity, in Tufayl's system, still has dominion. It is the dominion of the caretaker, not of the master, but it is dominion nonetheless. And yet, there is much to recommend in Tufayl's picture, especially its emphasis on the value of all of creation and the obligation that we have to be thoughtful, caring stewards of God's works.

One final thing to ponder is what Tufayl's tale tells us about the permissibility of civilization. As we will see in Section 7.5, Tufayl's own view seems to be that the best human life – that is, a human life which has realized its fullest potential, which is to be a knower and lover of God – is achievable only to the degree that one can detach oneself from society and civilization. It is also worth remembering that many of the hallmarks of Hayy's "civilized" or "technological" period involved exploitation of, if not outright cruelty to, plants and animals. Is Tufayl, then, suggesting that civilization cannot develop in a morally permissible way? I don't have a definitive answer. But pursuing the question with further close readings of Tufayl's text as well as others from the Platonic tradition, broadly construed, is certainly encouraged.[15]

Study Questions

1) What sorts of love are there? What are the hallmarks for these kinds of love? Based on your characterization of the kinds of love, do you think that a human can in any proper sense "love" something that is not human? What about something utterly unlike us, namely, God?
2) Al-Ghazali seems to think that all love is at root self-love. Is he right about this?
3) Think about Augustine's analysis of his theft of the pears. Did he miss something crucial in his analysis?
4) Aquinas and Augustine seem to think that we need friends – the right ones – to flourish. In the next chapter, we will follow more of the adventures of Ibn Tufayl's protagonist and we will see suggestions that he might reject Augustine's and Aquinas's proposal (Section 7.5). In preparation for Chapter 7, think about whether we need to be in a social setting to flourish. If so, why? What do friends and community give us? What might make it difficult to live alone as Hayy does?
5) Reflect on the Brethren of Purity's and Ibn Tufayl's theories about environmentalism and animal rights. Did they go too far? Did they not go far enough? In particular, think about the position of dominion that these thinkers still grant to humanity. Are they right about this?

Notes

1. This section relies heavily on the wonderful introduction by Eric Ormsby to his translation of *Love, Longing, Intimacy* (al-Ghazali 2016). In general, I urge you to not skip over introductions to the translations that you use as you discover more medieval philosophy. They usually provide valuable historical and contextual detail as well as a guide into the treatise.
2. See also the discussion of the meaning of "love" in Nasr et al. 2015, 71–2, which is a commentary on verse 2:165 of the Quran.
3. 'A'ishah is a remarkable sixteenth-century *female* Muslim mystic, which hopefully will undermine a common misconception that Islam forbade women from undertaking scholarly endeavors. For more on her life, thought, and intellectual background, see Homerin 2019. Homerin has also translated some of 'A'ishah's mystical poetry (Homerin 2011).
4. The translator indicates that he was unable to trace an exact reference. But there are parallels in the traditions that 'A'ishah is drawing upon. We should remember that a lot of medieval intellectual transmission is oral, and so it makes sense that we often find only close parallels and not verbatim reports in the static written records of these traditions.
5. So that there is no misunderstanding, this Sufi authority is not saying that we should celebrate the fact that others lack food, clothing, and shelter and thus are in need. What the authority means is that the Sufi should love her own poverty, that is, her own lack of material possessions. Giving up material possessions is a way of detaching oneself from this world.
6. Compare this to what Meister Eckhart suggested when he claimed that the detached mystic can in some sense compel God to come down to him (1981, 286; quoted in Section 5.3).
7. On al-Ghazali's reluctance to read scripture allegorically, see his discussion of the "vision" that believers will have in the afterlife (2016, 66). We look at al-Ghazali's attitude toward religious tolerance in more detail in Chapter 7.
8. For the record, I would like to say that *my* father is rather enlightened and not a bigot. I still think he is wrong on occasion. But then I too am wrong about a lot of things. I love you, Dad.
9. Here I must thank Jeffrey Hause for helping me to appreciate this point.
10. In fact, the more I reflect on the episode, the more I am inclined to think that the claim that evil is nothing is a red herring.
11. For Albert's treatment of the pygmy and the monkey, the two closest animals to humans in the hierarchy of the animal kingdom, see Wei 2020, 159–165. Harris calls Albert's discussion of the pygmy "confused and confusing" (2020, 34).
12. See, for instance, Porphyry's *On Abstinence from Killing Animals* (2000).
13. Ibn Tufayl's contemporary, Moses Maimonides argues that meat is a necessary part of the human diet. Plants are not sufficient. See *Guide of the Perplexed* III.48 (1963, 599).
14. It is important to remember that like many medieval philosophers, Tufayl thinks that heavenly beings are also aware of God (139, G. 99). If awareness and intelligence require being ensouled, then in one sense of the word, celestial creatures are also "animals."
15. When thinking about sustainability and what is needed for humans to flourish, I encourage you to read *Hayy ibn Yaqzan* in tandem with Plato's *Republic*, book 2, 369b ff., where Socrates begins to lay out the fundamental reasons why human societies form and what is needed to allow humans to survive and to be healthy and happy.

Suggestions for Further Reading

For a selection of Sufi poems and aphorisms on love that draws from both early and later sources, look for Omid Safi's collection *Radical Love* (2018). The most famous proponent of mystical love is Jalal al-Din Rumi (1207–73). There are numerous popular editions of Rumi's poetry on bookstore shelves, but as Safi notes, many of these are by "translators" who know little if any of the original Persian. Instead, they work off earlier, more literal translations by such scholars as A. J. Arberry and R. E. Nicholson. Arberry and Nicholson, however, were distinguished, pioneering scholars, and their work while perhaps lacking in poetic finesse, is still worth consulting. There is also a new multi-volume translation of Rumi's magnum opus *The Masnavi* by Jawid Mojaddedi in the Oxford World's Classics series (Oxford University Press). For a slimmer disquisition on the Sufi understanding of love, try the *Sawanih* (1986), a little treatise by al-Ghazali's younger brother Ahmad Ghazzali (1126).

For more on Aquinas on fraternal correction, start with Stump 2003 and Hause 2018.

For discussion of Augustine's famous pear tree incident, see Matthews 2005, chapter 13, and MacDonald 2003. For Augustine's explanation of how sin first appeared, see MacDonald 1999.

Philosophical interest in animals and the environment has grown substantially in the last few years. Thus, it is no surprise that there has been a recent burst in scholarly activity on medieval views on animals. For a helpful conspectus of thirteenth-century Western medieval views on animals, both in theology and philosophy, and also in literature and chivalric culture, see Nigel Harris's study (2020). Ian Wei's survey (2020) of several important thirteenth-century theologians on animals is so close to the text that it is often effectively a translation of the primary sources.

For the inspiration to look to Ibn Tufayl for an environmentalist philosophy, I owe much gratitude to *Open to Reason* (2018), a wonderful little book of essays on both classical and modern Islamic philosophy by Souleymane Bachir Diagne. For more on Ibn Tufayl, start with Taneli Kukkonen's overview of his life and thought (2014). There is also a book on the Brethren of Purity in the same series by Godefroid de Callatay (2005).

7 The Philosopher in Society

7.1 Al-Farabi on the Perfect State	215
7.2 The Critique of Democracy	224
7.3 You Can't Handle the Truth: How the State Talks to Its Citizens	229
7.4 The Freedom to Be Wrong	233
7.5 The Philosopher as Stranger in the World	253

We have now seen how medieval thinkers have taken on and adapted Greek notions about the good and flourishing life, one which centers around *eudaimonia* and the virtues. But how can we give humans their best chance to cultivate the virtues and to achieve *eudaimonia* and blessedness? Is this a task that we can perform individually and in solitude, or does our best chance to flourish involve banding together and forming a community?

No human is self-sufficient. Each of us has talents but also weaknesses. I have certain kinds of intellectual aptitudes, but I lack a certain kind of quickness and ability to think on the fly and in the heat of the moment. I am pretty strong and I have decent spatial reasoning, but I am terrible at tasks that require a lot of hand-eye coordination. And so on, and so forth. I am sure that if you do your own personal inventory, you will come up with similar kinds of lists. Plato made a similar observation in his *Republic*, a book which you might have already encountered. (If not, I encourage you to read it, especially if you are interested in medieval political philosophy.) He reasoned more or less as follows (cf. book 2, 369b ff.): I could try to do every task myself that I need to survive. But that would be woefully inefficient. Not only would it take me a lot of time to learn how, for example, to make a shelter and clothes, to farm, or to hunt; even if I did manage to learn to do these things to some extent, I wouldn't necessarily be very good at it. I might catch a fish every fifth time, whereas a skilled fisher might succeed at double that rate (or more, I don't know how to fish; I am making these numbers up). My shelter might stand for a while, but it will be

DOI: 10.4324/9780429348020-7

wobbly and the roof eventually will leak. Moreover, after exerting myself from dusk until dawn each day to eke out an existence, I would have little time or energy to devote to intellectual pursuits. Thus, assuming that the ancients and medieval sages are right about what my end as a human being is, if I strike out on my own, there seems to be very little chance that I will come anywhere close to achieving it. If there is any chance for happiness in this life, or the next, it seems that I need the help of others.

Plato's observations were based on our human nature, and in particular the fact that by nature we seem to be born with different capacities and talents. Aristotle crystallized this thought when he claimed that humans are "political" animals (*Politics* 1.2, 1253a3–6). A good number of medieval philosophers followed Plato and Aristotle in this regard, especially in the Arabic-speaking tradition.

> It has been explained with utmost clarity that man is political by nature and that it is his nature to live in society. He is not like the other animals for which society is not a necessity. Because of the manifold composition of this species – for as you know, it is the last one to have been composed – there are many differences between the individuals belonging to it, so that you can hardly find two individuals who are in any accord with respect to one of the species of moral habits, except in a way similar to that in which their visible forms may be in accord with one another.
>
> (*The Guide of the Perplexed* II.40; Maimonides 1963, 381)

If this is right – and our own experience seems to conform with that of Maimonides (1204) and others in this tradition – the next project after determining what we are and what our end is (as we have done in Chapters 4 and 5), is to embark upon an investigation into what the ideal society or political community is.

> Now as the nature of the human species requires that there be those differences among the individuals belonging to it and as in addition society is a necessity for this nature, it is by no means possible that his society should be perfected except – and this is necessarily so – through a ruler who gauges the actions of the individuals, perfecting that which is deficient and reducing that which is excessive, and who prescribes actions and moral habits that all of them must always practice in the same way, so that the natural diversity is hidden through the multiple points of conventional accord and so that the community becomes well ordered.
>
> (idem, Maimonides 1963, 382)

As Maimonides observes, the point of community is to make up for, to "hide," the deficiencies that each of us possess due to our material make-up and upbringing.[1] We need to identify those social organizations that will allow all of us to achieve virtue and happiness in this life, and since we are human, blessedness in the life after this.

To get a sense of how medieval philosophers thought about the ideal society, we will examine in some detail the views of al-Farabi (950), whom one commentator has described as the "architect" of subsequent political philosophy in the Arabic-speaking philosophical tradition to which Maimonides also belongs (Marmura 1979, 417) (Section 7.1). Al-Farabi's theory of the perfect state includes a highly articulated theory of the nature of religion and religious language. Religion is a symbolic portrayal of the fundamental points of true philosophy. It is portrayed in symbolic form because this is the format in which such truths can be appreciated by those who are ruled. In fact, philosophers in the Farabian tradition will insist that the masses *must* be spoken to in symbolic language. Speaking in a plain, literal manner about the nature of God, the cosmos, and the fate of humanity is beyond the common person's capacity to understand.

From our modern-day vantage, Farabian political theory will have some potentially troubling implications: First, Farabians are fundamentally opposed to democracy (Section 7.2). Their theocratic state is rigidly hierarchical. Second, the state seems to be given license to practice propaganda and to restrict access to education and the pursuit of the unvarnished truth (Section 7.3). Finally, there is a worry about the state's use of political violence (Section 7.4). It would seem that the state not only *de facto* has power to coerce individuals with threats and sanctions, but at least in some political communities the state's use of force is morally legitimate. We will need to examine what Farabi and others say about "weeds," that is, individuals who are unable to assimilate and integrate into the community (Section 7.5). This question will become all the more pressing once we reflect on the situation of iconoclasts in actual human societies, that is, societies that Farabians would consider to be corrupted states.

7.1 Al-Farabi on the Perfect State

Al-Farabi's theory of metaphysics, ethics, and society is very Platonic. The universe arises from a series of emanations from the First Cause. Humans have a distinctive place in this metaphysical hierarchy. We sit at the juncture between the intelligible realms and the material realm, and we have a share in each. But in order for us to achieve our naturally determined end, we need to cultivate the intellect. Human souls that have purified themselves of the body and perfected their intellects will enjoy an afterlife as a beatified intellectual substance. Human souls that do not will cease to be when the human body dies and dissipates (see Chapter 5, 5.2).

Al-Farabi takes it as axiomatic that humans are essentially social beings. We belong to "the species that cannot complete its necessary affairs nor gain its most excellent state except by coming together as many associations in a single dwelling-place" (*Political Regime*, II.64; trans. Parens 2011, 37). Indeed, al-Farabi suggests that there is something pathological about anti-social humans.

> Then there are the people who are bestial by nature. Now those who are bestial by nature are not citizens, nor do they have any civic associations at all. Rather some of them are like domesticated beasts and some are like wild beasts. And some of the latter are like predatory animals. [...] These are found at the extremities of the inhabited dwelling-places either at the northern or southern tips. And they ought to be treated as beasts. Now any of them who is domestic and useful in some way to the cities is to be spared, enslaved, and used as beasts are used. What is done to the rest of the harmful animals is to be done to any of them who is not useful or is harmful.
> (*Political Regime*, II.92; al-Farabi 2011, 46)

In Chapters 4 and 6, we ruminated on the idea that rationality might be sufficient to gain social standing. Notice here that al-Farabi is picking out another property, sociability, as a sign that an individual human being has intrinsic moral worth. Now, in light of what al-Farabi says elsewhere, this lack of sociability is probably on his view due to a deficiency of reason. Certainly, in later historical developments there has been a tendency to slip back and forth between the two notions, especially when those in power have tried to morally justify the enslavement or extermination of other humans. Especially worthy of note is al-Farabi's claim about *where* one finds these "bestial" humans, as they happen to live in those parts of the inhabitable world that would in later centuries be colonized by European powers. And for that matter, we also get the suggestion that the state should practice eugenics, as al-Farabi goes on to say that we ought to enslave or kill "any children of the inhabitants of the cities who happen to be bestial" (idem).

In addition to these unsettling implications of al-Farabi's theory of human nature, we are also beginning to see how the state will be granted the moral authority to subjugate and coerce individuals who refuse to submit to the state and its rules. Thus, we may begin to worry that something has gone amiss. The state is there for individuals to flourish, but it is beginning to seem that the individual's happiness may be subordinate to the flourishing of the state. At the very least, al-Farabi and others in his tradition will have to make the case that individuals only flourish when the state flourishes. This, however, may be hard to do, since there will be many cases where philosophical individuals are trapped in states that do not promote human flourishing (see Section 7.5). Does it follow that they cannot flourish either?

As we have already noted, al-Farabi and those in his tradition maintain that individual humans are born with different capacities and talents. The cognitive capacities of some humans are so dim that they are unable to form proper practical judgments. If they are to flourish to any degree, such humans must subordinate themselves to others who can look after them and direct them toward the good.

> It is not within the power of every human being to guide someone else. Nor is it within the power of every human being to prompt someone else to do these things. One having no ability at all to arouse someone else to do one of the things nor to use him in it, having instead only the ability to do always what he is guided to, is in no way a ruler – not with respect to anything. Rather, he is always ruled in everything.
> (*Political Regime*, II.78, Al-Farabi 2011, 41)

The majority of us are not in a position where we are merely ruled, and never rulers. Most of us are both rulers and one of those who are ruled.

> One who has the power to guide someone else to a particular thing, to prompt him to do it, or to use him in it, is – with respect to that thing – a ruler over the one who is not able to do that thing by himself, but is able to when guided toward it and instructed in doing it. Then, one having the ability to arouse someone else toward that thing he was instructed in and guided toward and use him in it is a ruler over one human being and ruled by another human being.
> (*Political Regime*, II.78, Al-Farabi 2011, 41–2)

Most of us have the capacity to learn and know some things, to make proper judgments about what course of action to take, and to guide others about the course of action to take within a specific domain. In those domains, we are rulers. But when it comes to other aspects of our lives, we will need to take our cue from others. In those domains we are the ruled. I may be good at discerning how mechanical parts are put together, and thus, in the mechanic's shop, I am a ruler. But it may be that I am terrible at deciphering tax documents and balancing the books. Here, I follow the lead of my accountant. It also might be the case that I know how to put together a car engine and to guide other workers to help in the manufacture of car engines. But if I don't know how an engine fits into the car as a whole, I may be a floor manager of a team that makes car engines, but I should be willing to follow the guidance of the managers and engineers who know how to make the car whole.

Thus, al-Farabi assumes that humans fall into a hierarchy. Following a prejudice that we already see in Plato and Aristotle, al-Farabi favors theory over technical know-how. Some of us are better at discerning the theoretical, and in al-Farabi's view such persons are higher up in the pecking order than individuals who only have experience about particular, concrete things. Among those with a knack for theory, some are better at discerning the superior theoretical objects, namely, the metaphysical structure of things. Al-Farabi believes that the human intellect is capable of reading norms from nature. Hence, the person who has a perfect human intellect and thus knows the most about the natures of things will also be able to know what the good is.

One important matter to pause over is whether these hierarchies are fixed solely by our inborn natures. Al-Farabi's presentation of human nature and the things he chooses to emphasize might suggest that this is indeed how things are, that our biology determines where we will fall in the hierarchy (*Political Regime*, II.73–77). But as a matter of fact, al-Farabi seems to be resistant to the idea that nature entirely determines who we will grow up to be (see esp. II.75). This point is made much more explicitly by Maimonides.

> Still, it is possible to be naturally disposed toward a virtue or a vice, so that it is easier to perform the actions that accord with a [particular virtue] or a [particular vice]. For example, if his temperament is more inclined toward dryness and the substance of his brain is pure and has less moisture, memorization and understanding meanings are easier for him than a phlegmatic individual who has much moisture in his brain. However, if the individual disposed by temperament toward this virtue is left without any instruction and none of his powers is given direction, he will undoubtedly remain ignorant. Similarly, if a natural dolt with much moisture is instructed and made to understand, then he will attain knowledge and understand, but with difficulty and hard work.
> (*Eight Chapters*, ch. 8; Maimonides 1975, 84)

Maimonides goes on to point out that we are similarly not determined by our biology to be courageous or cowards. Thus, it seems to me that Maimonides is *logically* committed to the notion that while our material constitution is potentially one of several causal factors, it does not by itself determine whether we are criminals or upstanding citizens, production line workers or managers. The fact that our material make-up is only part of the causal story and that our upbringing is also important gives the Farabians the logical space to allow for upward mobility and something resembling what we would now call a meritocracy. It also gives the Farabian the opportunity to stress the importance of education and the conceptual space to rule out hasty assessments of someone's ability, which as we will see shortly will determine one's standing in the state. Whether al-Farabi, Maimonides, or any particular philosopher in this tradition will take these resources in hand and utilize them to mitigate some of our growing concerns about the shape of the state that is emerging is another matter.

Unsurprisingly, the philosopher stands at the top of the heap – or at least some philosophers do, since al-Farabi concedes that some philosophers don't have the knack for ruling others. To rule others, you must be able to persuade them that your proposed course of action is for their good. But for most people, persuasion does not come in the form of a philosophical deduction. Subtler, rhetorical arts are required to motivate most humans. Al-Farabi interprets Plato along these lines.

> Here [Plato] delineated once again Socrates' method for realizing his aim of making his own people understand through scientific investigation the ignorance that they were in. He explained Thrasymachus' method and made it known that Thrasymachus was more able than Socrates to form the character of the youth and instruct the multitude; Socrates possessed only the ability to conduct a scientific investigation of justice and the virtues, and a power of love, but did not possess the ability to form the character of the youth and the multitude; and the philosopher, the prince, and the legislator ought to be able to use both methods: the Socratic method with the elect, and Thrasymachus' method with the youth and the multitude.
>
> (*Philosophy of Plato* X.36; al-Farabi 1969, 66–7)

Thrasymachus, as some of you might know, is the orator who famously taunts and challenges Socrates in the first book of Plato's *Republic*. In al-Farabi's quote, Socrates stands for a paradigm of someone who has perfect theoretical understanding, but who is unable to speak in a way that the masses will understand and get behind. It is the master of rhetoric, someone like Thrasymachus, who will succeed at motivating people to act in the right way. (Al-Farabi seems to be oblivious to the fact that the Thrasymachus who appears in Plato's *Republic* forcefully defends an anti-realist theory of ethics: Justice is merely what the powerful say is just, and hence, it is always a coded way for the powerful to acquire what they desire.)

The perfect ruler, then, is complete both with respect to theory and with respect to the art of motivating and regulating others.

> The first ruler without qualification is the one who does not need – not in anything at all – to be ruled by another human being. Rather, he has already attained the sciences and cognitions in actuality and has no need of a human being to guide him in anything. He has the ability for excellent apprehension of each one of the particular things that ought to be done and the faculty for excellently guiding everyone other than himself to all that he has instructed them in; the ability to use everyone as a means to do a particular thing pertaining to that action he is intent upon; and the ability to determine, define, and direct the activities toward happiness.
> (*Political Regime*, II.79, al-Farabi 2011, 42)

This perfected individual is not merely a complete philosopher and complete rhetorician, this person is also a prophet.

> This human being is the king in truth according to the ancients, and he is one of whom it ought to be sad that he receives revelation. For a human being receives revelation only when he obtains this rank, and that is when there remains no intermediary between him and the active intellect.
> (*Political Regime*, II.80; al-Farabi 2011, 42)

Here in particular is where we see al-Farabi's innovation: He has adapted Platonic political theory to accommodate prophetic, monotheistic religion. The supreme ruler is also the lawgiver in both a secular and a religious sense. Indeed, as it is often asserted in Islam, there is no difference at the end of the day between the worldly and the spiritual, the secular and the religious.

Al-Farabi does not explicitly mention Islam as he is outlining the formation and constitution of the perfect state, but surely he is thinking of the model of the Prophet Muhammad (Marmura 1983, 397–8). One traditional reading of Islamic history is that after God revealed His will to Muhammad, the Prophet then created a concrete political organization, first at Madina and later at Mecca, guided by the principles that God gave him. To this day, many (but of course not all) Muslims often see the society that was established at Madina as the paradigm of an Islamic state. In fact, it is for this reason that 'Ali 'Abd al-Raziq caused a scandal when he proposed in his essay "Islam and the Bases of Power" (1924) that Muhammad's mission on earth was merely spiritual and "that he established no kingdom in the political sense of the word nor anything synonymous with it, that he was a prophet only, like his brother prophets who preceded him, and that he was neither a king nor a founder of a state, nor did he make any appeal for a temporal empire" (2007, 24).

One of the proofs that al-Raziq adduced in favor of his position is that the Prophet did not name a political successor before he died (2007, 29). This is, of course, a controversial point. The Shi'i maintain that Muhammad appointed 'Ali as his successor. Others have sometimes asserted that Muhammad gave clear signs that Abu Bakr, the de facto successor to Muhammad and the first caliph, was to take charge of the religious and political community. Having noted this dispute, we will not wade any further into it. The only reason to bring it up is that al-Farabi would have been aware of the problem of political succession, and more fundamentally, the problem of how to sustain the perfect state once it has been founded by the philosopher-lawgiver.

Al-Farabi's solution is that rulership should ideally pass from the founder to another philosopher, since truth is stable and it is impossible for there to be disagreement between two individuals who both have perfectly grasped the truth (*On the Perfect State*, ch. 17 sections 2–3; 1985, 279–81). But as have already seen, al-Farabi has conceded that philosophers are not always capable of ruling: Some have theoretical skill but lack the capacity to motivate and manage others. For this reason, al-Farabi claims that the virtuous state does not need to have the structure of an absolute monarchy. If a single individual possessing the right qualities cannot be found, then rule can fall to a group of elites. The key is not the number of rulers per se, but that they think as one, both at a time and over the course of life of the state.

> If there happens to be an association of these kings at a single moment in a single city, a single nation, or many nations, then their whole association is like a single king due to the agreement in their endeavors, purposes, opinions, and ways of life. If they succeed one another in time, their souls will be as a single soul. The second will proceed according to the way of life of the first, and the one now present according to the way of life of the one who has passed away. Just as it is permissible for one of them to change a law he legislated at one moment if he is of the opinion that it is more fitting to change it at another moment, so may the one now present who succeeds the one who has passed away change what the one who has passed away has already legislated. For the one who has passed away would change [it] himself, were he to observe the [new] condition.
>
> (*Political Regime*, II.82; al-Farabi 2011, 43)

Notice that a premium is placed on stasis and preservation. This is justified on the grounds that the truth is fixed and that all true rulers will be bound to this truth. As you can see, this does not mean that the philosophical rulers cannot change their minds. New situations might arise that demand that the ruler revisits a precedent. But if the present ruler makes a revision, he can be confident that his revision is precisely what his predecessors would have done if they had been aware of the new circumstances.

Precedent, however, is not subject to revision if the state happens to currently lack someone who is a philosopher. If it were to come to pass that there are no philosophers in a position to rule, al-Farabi suggests that leadership can transfer to a group of people who are not philosophers, so long as these caretakers do not stray from the original, fundamental principles of the philosopher-prophet.

> When there does not happen to be a human being of this condition, the laws that the former [kings] prescribed or ordained are to be adopted, then written down and preserved, and the city is to be governed by means of them.
> (*Political Regime*, II.82; al-Farabi 2011, 43)

As one commentator observes, this would result in "a static, traditional society," but a state guided by competent, conservative caretakers could still be virtuous if "it is governed by legal rulers in accordance with the revealed law, the replica of theoretical knowledge" (Marmura 1979, 415).

The cultivation of virtue is the primary reason why al-Farabi is so obsessed with succession and the stability of the law.

> When each of the inhabitants of the city does what is such as to be entrusted to him – having either learned that on his own or the ruler having guided and prompted him to it – those actions of his earn him good traits of the soul. [...] Similarly, the actions that are determined and directed toward happiness empower the part of the soul disposed by innate character toward happiness and make it become actual and perfect. So, from the power attained in becoming perfect, it manages to dispense with matter and gets to be free from it. Yet it does not perish when matter perishes, since in its constitution and its existence it has come not to need matter. Then it attains happiness.
> (*Political Regime*, II.83; al-Farabi 2011, 43)

Here is the answer to one of our burning questions. The reason why we should subordinate ourselves to the philosopher rulers, or their legal proxies, is because the state institutions and laws laid down by such individuals work to our individual advantage. Living in a state organized and run by philosophers is the best way, perhaps even the only way, to flourish as human beings.

You will have noticed that al-Farabi is helping himself to what we have previously observed is a very rarified Platonic notion of true flourishing or happiness, which is to be an immaterial substance, free of matter and thinking, perhaps even "uniting with" intelligible objects (Sections 4.2–3 and 5.2). However, this does not mean that we have to forgo all benefits in this lifetime. We are told that by obeying the instructions of the rulers, we will enjoy greater pleasure and delight. Ibn Bajja (1139), an Andalusian philosopher belonging to this Farabian tradition, points to other material advantages that stem from living in a state run by philosophical rulers.

> The virtuous city is characterized by the absence of the art of medicine and of the art of judication. For friendship binds all its citizens, and they do not quarrel with among themselves at all. Therefore it is only when a part of the city is bereft of friendship and quarrelsomeness breaks out that recourse must be had to the laying down of justice and the need arises for someone, who is judge, to dispense it. Moreover, since all actions of the virtuous city are right – this being the distinguishing characteristic that adheres to it – its citizens do not eat harmful foods. [...] When the citizens forgo exercise, this too, gives rise to numerous diseases; but it is evident that the virtuous city is not subject to such diseases.
> (*The Governance of the Solitary*, 1.3; trans. in Parens and Macfarland 2011, 100)

Now, before you protest, you should know that Ibn Bajja immediately goes on to address other issues for which we might need doctors, such as broken bones and the like. He claims that the virtuous city will need treatments "for dislocation and the like, and in general, for such diseases whose specific causes are external and that the healthy body cannot ward off by its own effort." Thus, it looks like his claim that the virtuous city will not need *any* doctors is hyperbolic. We will need artisans who can help us with broken bones, dislocated shoulders, and infectious diseases. Nonetheless, his main point still stands. In a well-regulated state, where citizens either know the good themselves or listen to those who do, a host of this-worldly problems evaporate, and with them perhaps also the lawyers, mediators, nutritionists, and life coaches who thrive on the existence of these problems.

7.2 The Critique of Democracy

I suspect that some of you are still leery of the Farabian state, and not just because we should worry about some of the eugenicist and dehumanizing elements that we have already noticed in al-Farabi's particular portrait of the perfect state. In many instances, it seems that we are asked to be merely means to some further end, and for those at the bottom, there is the patronizing suggestion that their best chance at flourishing is to always be a mere instrument in the projects devised and run by the ruling classes.

> Thus the parts of the city are then tied to one another, in concord with one another, and ranked with some having precedence and others being subordinate. It comes to resemble the natural beings, and its rankings also resemble the rankings of the beings that begin at the first and terminate at primary matter and the elements. The way it is tied together and its concord are similar to the way the different beings are tied to one another and to their concord. And the governor of that city is similar to the first cause through which is the existence of the rest of the beings. Then, the rankings of the being go on descending little by little, each of them coming to be ruler and ruled, until they terminate at the possible beings that have no rulership at all but only serve and exist for the sake of something else – namely primary matter and the elements.
> (*Political Regime*, II.87; al-Farabi 2011, 44)

Now, to be fair to al-Farabi, the part of the perfect city that is analogous to prime matter and the elements might not be human beings. Instead, he could be referring to the material possessions of the city. But given that he has explicitly licensed the subjugation of certain humans on the grounds that they are no different in status from beasts of burden, we cannot rule out the possibility that in this perfect state some individual human beings, indeed many of them, might be serving and existing for the sake of others.

In addition to the worry about the class stratification that is inherently baked into the system is the idea that the state will as a matter of fact be autocratic, or at best oligarchic. The reason that Farabians adduce to justify this undemocratic political structure is that those who know the truth and the good happen to be few in number. Thus, the Farabian is not going to be at all sympathetic to the complaint that there is something wrong with their picture merely because the political structure is such that the ruled will be many and the rulers will be few.

Here we need to add some nuance. Given that says there could be many "kings" living at the same time, it would seem that a Farabian political philosopher would have to concede that *if* the many were enlightened, then the many ought to be rulers. In principle (if not in fact) there could be a Farabian philosophical democracy. We will, therefore, need to tread carefully as we explore the case for and against democracy. Otherwise, our insistence that we should be living in a democracy might reduce to a case of stubborn, baseless resistance to something that really is good for us.

It seems that for similar reasons the Farabian must concede that there could be a democratic second-best state, that is, a state ruled by those who are able to make good inferences from the founder's laws and the precedents that these set to arrive at answers to novel cases. Again, at least in theory, the many could be qualified to interpret the language of the lawgivers' rules once they are written down and thereby fixed in some very important sense.

For the Platonist, the trouble with political organizations is that they tend to erode over time, especially when philosopher rulers are not securely at the helm. So, instead of asking whether al-Farabi would view a democratic state as the second-best option, as he clearly would not (given his views about the actual way the world is), perhaps we can pose this question to him: Of all the states that a virtuous state might degrade into, which of *these* is the most choice-worthy? After all, we live in the real world, not the ideal world where either the first choice or even the second choice for a political organization is available.

In book 9 of his *Republic*, Plato presents a story of the gradual decline of the perfect state into various forms of corrupted political organizations. Al-Farabi does not describe the decline of the state in exactly this manner, but his itemization of the various imperfect political organizations broadly conforms to Plato's final list. Here is al-Farabi's itemization in the *Political Regime* (II.93 ff.).[2]

- Cities that provide basic needs (the "necessary" cities)
- Cities that provide opportunities to gain wealth and property (the "depraved" cities)
- Cities that provide opportunities for sensual pleasure (the "vile" cities)
- Cities that provide opportunities to be honored in speech and deed (the "timocratic" cities)
- The "city of domination": a city where everyone does what they do for the sake of the tyrant, who is himself driven by a false conception of the good
- The "democratic city" and "city of the free"

In most instances, al-Farabi's reasons for describing these cities as imperfect political organizations are easy to discern. Surely, no one should want to live in a city run by a tyrant, not even the tyrant himself if we are thinking about human flourishing and not merely the satisfaction of whim and desire. The same holds for the necessary city and the base city. Such organizations may, at best, keep us alive. But our end is to transcend our brute animal nature. Such cities provide no opportunity for cultivating virtue and the intellect.[3] The depraved city likewise is focused on the wrong sorts of things.

> The depraved city or association of depraved inhabitants is the one in which they assist one another in gaining prosperity and wealth, being excessive in acquiring the necessities and what take their place with respect to dirhams and dinars, and accumulating them beyond the extent they are needed. [This is] for nothing other than love of, and greed for, wealth, while spending of it only what is necessary to constitute bodies.
> (*Political Regime*, II.95; al-Farabi 2011, 47)

The timocratic city appears on paper to be moving in the right direction. But we should remember that honor is not identical to virtue. Moreover, a city that centers only on practice and ignores the higher pursuits of the intellect is still a city that fails to encourage individuals to be the best versions of themselves.

This leaves us with the democratic city. Many of the things that al-Farabi says about democratic states seem to be quite appealing.

> The democratic city is the city in which every one of its inhabitants is unrestrained and left to himself to do what he likes. Its inhabitants are equal to one another, and their traditional law is that no human being is superior to one another in anything at all. One [inhabitant] has authority over another or over someone else only insofar as he does what removes that person's freedom. Thus there arises among them many moral habits, many endeavors, many desires, and taking pleasure in countless things.
> (*Political Regime*, II.113; al-Farabi 2011, 51)

This kind of city is one where the multitude "have the upper hand." The rulers rule according to will of the people whom they rule. Moreover, this sort of city is the most exciting city to live in.

> All the endeavors and purposes of the ignorant [cities] are present in this city in the most perfect manner, and more. Of [all] their cities, this is the admirable and happy city. On the surface it is like an embroidered garment replete with colored figures and dyes. Everyone loves it and loves to dwell in it, because every human who has a passion or desire

for anything is able to gain it in this city. The nations repair to it and dwell in it, so it becomes great beyond measure. People of every tribe are procreated in it by every sort of pairing off and sexual intercourse. The children generated in it are of very different innate characters and of very different education and upbringing.
(*Political Regime*, II.114–15; al-Farabi 2011, 52)

I teach in New York City, and every time I read this particular passage, pictures of my home, the "city that never sleeps," pop into my head. The democratic city as al-Farabi portrays it is a huge melting pot. It is the place that everyone goes to because they know, no matter who they are and what they like, they will find others like them there.

Note as well that this sort of city alone among the imperfect cities seems to provide opportunities for the philosopher and thus for virtue to flourish.

All kinds of the passions and ways of life come together in it. Therefore, it is not impossible as time draws on that virtuous people emerge in it. There may chance to exist in it wise men, rhetoricians, and poets concerned with every type of object. It is possible to glean from it parts of the virtuous city, and this is the best that emerges in this city.
(*Political Regime*, II.115; al-Farabi 2011, 52)

Al-Farabi appreciates the fact that virtuous people can emerge in the democratic city, and that once a virtuous class takes root, this virtuous class will grow as the city grows in size. But he immediately adds that the democratic city "has both the most good and the most evil," and just as the size of the city determines the quantity of good in it, the size of the city also increases the quantity of *evil* present in it. Notice as well that while al-Farabi concedes that philosophers might exist in such a city, this is a contingent, even "chance" state of affairs. Nothing about the democratic city guarantees that philosophy (or rhetoric, or poetry) will arise in it or flourish. In large part, this is because what the city promotes depends on what the multitude currently values. If the multitude is convinced that philosophy, and education more generally, is important, then the city will promote philosophy and education. But if the whims of the majority change – and think about how often the political winds change in modern-day democracies – support for philosophy and education can swiftly vanish.

In fact, given al-Farabi's reliance on Plato for the backbone of his political theory, it should come as no surprise that his view about the philosopher's fate in a democracy is pessimistic. The core principle of democracy is that a person is made a ruler by the multitude because she promises to give the multitude what they *think* they want.

> According to them, the virtuous ruler is the one who is excellent at deliberation and fine at using stratagems to gain them their different and variegated desires and passions, preserving them from their enemies, and not depriving [them] of any of their money but restricting himself only to what is necessary for his power.
> (*Political Regime*, II.117; al-Farabi 2011, 52)

For one thing, notice that in al-Farabi's view, democracies tend to default to what we nowadays often refer to as a "libertarian" position: Don't tax us too much, defend our property, and otherwise stay out of our way. Yet, that is not the essence of al-Farabi's concern (although, I think a Farabian critique of libertarianism would make use of what comes next). As he sees matters, the problem with electing someone who gives us what we think we want is that it usually undercuts the ability of the state to do what is actually choice-worthy.

What, then, happens when a philosopher comes along and tells the multitude that they are desiring the wrong sorts of things?

> The one who is virtuous in truth – namely, the one who, when he rules them, determines their actions and directs them toward happiness – is not made a ruler by them. If he chances to rule them, he is soon deposed or killed, or his rulership is disturbed and challenged.
> (idem)

In short, al-Farabi is forcing us to acknowledge the unpredictability and instability of governance in democratic associations. (And, here you might want to think about the dynamics of democratic associations of all sizes.) A program that is doing actual tangible good can lose its momentum or have its funding withdrawn when a new group comes to power and key people leave the group. If the majority has mistaken views, members of minority groups can suffer, sometimes in terrible ways. And actions that require all of us to make sacrifices for the long-term good of all, including future generations, can all too often be overridden by our desires for short-term advantages. Given that acquiring virtue takes hard work and asks us to give up things that we find extremely pleasurable, the deck seems to be heavily stacked against those who are competent guides toward the good. We can, therefore, imagine al-Farabi asking us this question: Do you want to put your chances for flourishing as a human being, truly flourishing, in the hands of the fickle majority? For that matter, do you want to put the group's fortunes in the hands of the majority?

I can imagine that many of you might answer, "Yes, I see all that, but I will take my chances; for the alternatives are worse." We observe political associations in the real world, both those presently existing and those in our history textbooks, that resemble many of al-Farabi's ignorant cities, whereas there are no clear concrete instances of anything like the virtuous city. And it does in fact appear to be the case that if forced to choose between all the imperfect states, even al-Farabi would choose the democratic one.

Furthermore, if you are like me, you might be quite worried about even the virtuous city. As we have seen, for the virtuous city to operate sustainably, each citizen must play their own rigidly specified part. As we noted above, there were indications that it is not merely our inborn natural which will determine our standing in this city. There may really be a meritocratic element in the sense that hard work, and not just raw talent, can get you places in the Farabian state. That said, it is hard to avoid the impression that al-Farabi is asking many of us – in fact, most of us – to give up our liberty. The benefit of sacrificing our autonomy is guaranteed virtue and happiness. But many of us have been raised to believe that liberty is inalienable. We might even think that liberty is so fundamental that we have the right to be wrong and unhappy, at least to the degree that this does not directly harm others. We will turn to the issue of whether we have the right to be wrong later in this chapter. But before we do so, let us explore another paternalistic dimension of al-Farabi's perfect state.

7.3 You Can't Handle the Truth: How the State Talks to Its Citizens

Another thing that disturbs many readers of Platonic political theory is the paternalistic nature of the state. There is no doubt about it: The Platonic state does talk down to its citizens, and it takes many decisions out of their hands. The justification that al-Farabi and his followers give for this paternalism stems from their view about human nature, thought, and language. It is also intimately tied to their thinking about religion and religion's relationship to philosophy.

Farabian political theorists maintain that there are objective truths. The world really is this way, and not that. They also maintain that some individuals, either through their own innate powers or with the help of God, can gain a clear view of at least some of these objective truths. As we have already mentioned, following in the footsteps of Plato and Aristotle, Farabians believe that we can read morals from nature as well. Hence, the truly enlightened person knows both the nature of reality and the proper end for human beings. Such people, however, are rare. Most individuals must be given only a glimpse of the truth and even at that, the truth cannot be presented to them in direct, philosophically accurate language. Instead, the prophets and philosophers must use symbols, stories, analogies, and allegories in order to convey the essentials to the masses. Religion, in their view, is the corpus of symbols and stories used to educate the majority of humans. It is an imitation of philosophy.

There are two salient features of this theory about the nature of religion and the nature of law. The first is that some information is omitted when the enlightened rulers talk to the masses. Here is Ibn Sina (1037), who is also part of the Farabian tradition we are considering.

> [The prophet-philosopher] ought not to involve [the masses] with anything pertaining to the knowledge of God, exalted be He, beyond the knowledge that He is One, the Truth, and has nothing similar to Him. To go beyond this and obligate them to believe in His existence as being not referred to in place, as being not subject to verbal classifications, as being neither inside nor outside the world, nor anything of this kind [is to ask too much]. He will render their task too great, confuse the religion they have, and cause them to fall into something from which deliverance is only for one who is [divinely] helped and led to success.
>
> (*Metaphysics of the "Healing"*, book 10, chapter 2, section 5; Avicenna 2005, 365–6)

Ibn Sina goes on to suggest that such metaphysical speculations, when done by those who cannot handle the requisite rigor, could even lead the masses to "adopt views contrary to the city's welfare." Thus, it is vital to withhold some of the truth from the masses.

But it is worse than that, and this is the second point that we need to emphasize. It is not only vital to withhold some of the truth from the masses, the rulers must in addition withhold the fact that they are withholding the truth:

> Nor is it proper for any human to reveal that he possesses knowledge he is hiding from the commonality. Indeed, he must never permit any reference to this.
>
> (*Metaphysics*, 10.2, section 6; Avicenna 2005, 366)

Al-Ghazali (1111), whom you have met already, is often highly critical of philosophers like al-Farabi and Ibn Sina. But on this issue, he agrees with them. Philosophical speculation should be discouraged in those who are not capable of doing it well. He even gives us a nice image for thinking about the damage that can occur if a philosopher ruler were even to suggest to a common person that what he has been taught is not the whole story (*Deliverance from Error*; 1980, 58–9; Watt 1994, 27). This person would be like a jar that has been shattered. Once the jar is shattered, the pieces cannot be put back together and hold water reliably. Rather, such a person must hope that their jar is forged anew. Since the jar in question is the common person's worldview, which was forged when they were young and impressionable, the task of reforging the jar after it has been shattered as an adult is something that no human can do. (Or, if we could, it could only be done using highly questionable methods like memory erasure and psychological reprogramming; in short, the sorts of things we see in dystopian science fiction movies or worry are being practiced in some "dark" spy facility somewhere in the world.)

Since it will be important in later discussions, let us quickly examine some of the specific points of doctrine where the common person is only told part of the truth. We have already seen Ibn Sina claim that the common person should be told that God exists and that He is unlike anything else in the universe. But the common person should not be exposed to all the niceties that this position involves. This person should not be told that God, for instance, is in no place or that no predicate in our human languages is attributable to Him. Such subtleties are only likely to confuse such a person. Instead, philosopher prophets and the other elites tell the masses that God is "up" in heaven and that He has a "hand" and "sits" on a throne. Ibn Rushd (1198), who also subscribes to al-Farabi's political thinking and views about religious language, gives a nice example of how to help the common, unphilosophical person understand that God is unlike any other being by appealing to concepts that the latter is familiar with. The common person has only had experience of corporeal beings. Hence, it is not good to say that God is an incorporeal being. That is tantamount to saying that God is nothing at all. So, instead, Ibn Rushd advises the elite to tell the masses that God is like the most ethereal and subtle of substances, namely, light (Averroes 2001b, 61–2 and 76).

Another significant point where the philosophers present a deliberately distorted picture of reality is when they talk about the afterlife to the masses.

> Similarly, he [viz. the prophet] must instill in them the belief in the resurrection in a manner that they can conceive and in which their souls find rest. He must tell them about [eternal] bliss and misery in parables derived from what they can comprehend and conceive.
> (Ibn Sina, *Metaphysics* 10.2, section 6; Avicenna 2005, 366)

The Farabians believe that the common person is incapable of comprehending that in the afterlife the virtuous human soul will become a purely intellectual substance and stand in eternal union with the pure intelligible beings (see Sections 4.2 and 5.2). Depending upon how we interpret the claims of the philosophers, they may even be "absorbed" into an intelligible substance called the Active Intellect. What this means in practice is that much of what we take to be *who* we are, our memories, our personality traces, and so on, will be stripped away. The "bliss" and "happiness" experienced by the disembodied immaterial soul will be unlike anything we have experienced while embodied. The punishment for humans who did not practice the philosophical life is equally rarified. Those souls that paid no attention to spiritual and intellectual matters at all will either disappear altogether when separated from the body, or if they persist, they will be eternally tormented by the fact that they are disembodied and cannot thereby enjoy the very bodily pleasures to which they are so attracted. For those who have had some inkling of God but who strayed from the virtuous path, their torment consists in being aware of the fact that they are prohibited from intellectual union with God. Such abstractions, admittedly, are hard for even a trained intellectual like me to picture, let alone feel as a motivating force.

Al-Farabi and Ibn Sina appreciate this, and they claim that the prophets also saw this fact about human nature. Thus, the founders and lawmakers of the virtuous city recast the afterlife in more materialistic terms. The philosopher rulers tell the masses that they will be reborn into their bodies, and it is with their bodies that they will experience either eternal bliss or eternal torments. Notice, then, that al-Farabi's and Ibn Sina's response to the issue raised in Chapter 5 (Section 5.4) about how to interpret references to resurrection is that these passages in scripture are in effect telling a noble lie. This will be important to keep in mind when in the next section we turn to al-Ghazali's views about freedom of thought and expression.

Much more could be said about the philosopher's understanding of God's nature and the afterlife. But what is pertinent for the present is to emphasize the ways in which the truth is either recast or withheld from most of the followers of a religion and most of the citizens of the state. Several of the philosophers in the Farabian tradition will insist that we should convey the ways things really are to everyday folk, just in a form that they can easily understand. But I invite you to reflect on whether this really is the case. Are the common people getting an appropriately processed version of the truth, or are they getting what is in effect a noble lie? As we will see in the following section, at least some readers of Farabian philosophy thought that their position devolved into the latter, and they found the suggestion that the prophets tell lies deeply problematic.

Here is another question prompted by the Farabian philosopher's suggestion that philosophical discourse might undermine the faith of the common people and compromise societal cohesion. Given that the state's aim is to preserve social cohesion and to keep people on "the straight path" (cf. Quran 1:6), should the state get involved in policing speech in general and philosophical speech in particular?

7.4 The Freedom to Be Wrong

For those of us who have been raised in modern-day liberal democracies, the notion that individuals have the right to speak freely, especially about matters of grave political, ethical, or religious importance, is often taken to be too obvious to need any justification. As I write this book, the world has seen how misguided dissent (say, about the legitimacy of an election or the health benefits of masks and vaccines) can lead to serious harm to the community. And yet, there are many who still would defend tooth and nail the right of all individuals not only to believe anything they wish but to *utter* and *write* what they sincerely believe, even if what they say is all but certainly wrong. (It is important to stress that while we often talk about freedom of thought, what we usually mean is freedom of expression. Thoughts are hard to police. Words are not.) In short, to borrow a phrase from Cary Nederman (2014), many take the "right to be wrong" to be fundamental and inalienable.

There are some very common and very compelling arguments in favor of such freedoms. One of the strongest justifications stems from the insights of the skeptics (see Chapter 2). Human perception and human reason are far from perfect, and thus, even many of our most sincere and most unshakeable beliefs could be wrong. The twelfth-century philosopher John of Salisbury (1180) was impressed by the lessons of the Academic skeptics, which he mostly learned about through Cicero and Seneca. (On this ancient sect of skeptics, see Section 2.1.) His study of "the ancients" led to one of the most striking defenses of freedom of speech in the Christian West. All of us are looking for happiness, but humans are not perfect.

> Nevertheless, because not everyone can do everything, and the Holy Spirit resides wherever it wishes, and it is frequently the case that those things which are discovered by the learned are understood in diverse ways by the multitude, many schools emanate from the words of Socrates and Plato, yet all are rushing towards one goal but by various paths. For in fact there is no one who does not wish to be happy; but those who desire this do not all advance along a single path. A single route is laid for all but it branches into many paths like the king's highway.
>
> (*Policraticus* VII.8; John of Salisbury 1990, 156–7)

234 *The Philosopher in Society*

This highway, John goes on to tell us, is virtue. But here, even the philosophers have diverged from one another. One has no choice but to engage in free and open inquiry: "one is free to doubt and inquire up to the point when truth shines forth from the comparison of positions as a result of the collision of doctrines" (160).

John does not advocate democracy. His theory of government is very hierarchical, with the chief secular authority resting in the office of "the prince." Nonetheless, John makes the case that freedom of expression is part of a healthy, functioning principality. Thus, he argues that everyone, but especially the authorities should cultivate the virtue of "patience." "Liberty," John says, "judges in accordance with the free will of the individual, and it is not afraid to censure that which seems to oppose sound moral character" (*Policraticus* VII.25, 175). Indeed, virtue and liberty are so intertwined that philosophers have been and should be willing to lay down their life for virtue. Such was the fate of Socrates. But if those in charge are wise, the outspoken philosopher will not need to forfeit his life.

> The best and wisest man is moderate with the reins of liberty and patiently takes note of whatever is said to him. And he does not oppose himself to the works of liberty, so long as damage to virtue does not occur. For when virtue shines everywhere from its own source, the reputation of patience becomes evident with more glorious renown.
> (VII.25; 1990, 177)

John devotes much of the remainder of the chapter to examples from history where wise rulers patiently endured criticisms of their rule.

John does set some limits on speech. He admonishes us to avoid taunting and other forms of incivility. And just as I have the right to speak my mind, my listeners have the right to admonish me if they think that I say something false. Still, it is noteworthy that John ends the chapter by returning to the issue of speaking truth to power.

> Therefore, man is to be free and it is always permitted to a free man to speak to persons about restraining their vices. Thus, there is even a legal right according to which it is permitted to express the truth in speech, and this December liberty indulges even slave in opposition to their lords so long as they speak the truth.
> (idem, 180)

Here, we see that it is not just something that is morally permissible, this freedom to speak what one sincerely believes to be the truth is given the status of a right (*ius*) (which, you will note, is formalized as a liberty that one can especially practice at a specific time of year). Accordingly, the authorities are not just good when they tolerate sincere dissent, they are obligated to do so.

Note two things. First, as mentioned, a line has been drawn between sanctioned dissent and taunts. For this reason, John allows the authorities to admonish anyone whom they take to be speaking abusively. Second, notice that, strictly speaking, John says nothing in the passages that I have quoted about the internal state of mind of the dissenter. That is, John is not interested in intent or even whether the person who expresses a thought actually believes it. The test for separating legitimate dissent from incivility seems to be completely *external*. We measure a person based on their position relative to objective truth, not with respect to any subjective aspect. John is not alone in conceiving of matters in this way, and it is understandable why he does so. It is extremely difficult to determine from our third-person standpoint whether someone really believes what they are saying. John's belief that there is an objective measure by which we can measure people's statements in relation to how things really are, while very much a commonplace in his time, is something that we nowadays often give up. It is quite common nowadays to assume that for certain domains of inquiry, especially those involving values, that there is no "fact of the matter" about whether something is good, beautiful, pleasure, and so forth. Once objectivity is given up, the default is a certain kind of quietism: You believe what you believe, I will believe what I believe, and we will just agree to disagree. But as I said, medieval thinkers generally do not take this route, especially when it comes to what is perhaps the most charged forum of debate, that of religious doctrine.

Perhaps many of you are shocked to learn that someone like John of Salisbury lived and even thrived in the Middle Ages. After all, there is a cartoon version of the Middle Ages out there which depicts medieval life as anything but free. Individuals were subject to not only the crown but also the crushing authority of establishment religion. The Middle Ages, we imagine, are times of excommunications, inquisitions, burnings at the stake, and forced conversions. Sadly, there is some truth to this picture, but perhaps not as much as you might think. Remember our heroine Marguerite Porete (Sections 4.3, 5.3): She was burned publicly at the stake in the center of Paris in 1310 for refusing to renounce her *Mirror of Simple Souls*. But her execution was exceptional, not typical.[4] Nor is such violence restricted to the Middle Ages, as you probably know all too well. Yes, accusations of heresy were tossed around, and these accusations often had severe this-worldly consequences, but it would be false to think that there was no pushback to any of this. And as we will see, sometimes this pushback came from surprising corners.

Most thoughtful medieval individuals maintained that it is impossible for the human mind to fully comprehend God and the Divine plan. For that matter, scripture sometimes even seems to advertise this.

> He it is Who sent down the Book upon thee; therein are signs determined; they are the Mother of the Book, and others symbolic. As for those whose hearts are given to swerving, they follow that of which is symbolic, seeking temptation and seeking its interpretation. And none know its interpretation save God and those firmly rooted in knowledge. They say, "We believe in it; all is from our Lord." And none remember, save those who possess intellect.
> (Quran 3:7, trans. Nasr et. al. 2015)

There are many ways that this famous verse could be interpreted, and indeed, some of those interpretations even hinge on punctuation (Nasr et al. 2015, 129–32). For example, an alternative rendering of one key portion of this verse would be "And none know its interpretation save God. And those rooted in knowledge say, 'We believe in it; all is from our Lord.' "

What 3:7 indisputably does is divide the "signs," or verses, of the Quran into those that are "determined" and those that are "symbolic" or "underdetermined" (the word can also be translated in some contexts as "unknown"). Many interpreters take this to be an indication that everyone is in the same boat: Not every verse in the Quran has a clear and obvious meaning. In fact, some verses may be so obscure that God alone knows what they really say. Both Al-Ghazali and Ibn Rushd take it to mean something else: First, only some individuals are qualified to interpret some of the symbolic verses. But second, *every* qualified reader of the Quran must engage in acts of interpretation that sometimes go beyond the literal. In other words, the question is not *whether* there are verses that require allegorical interpretation, but rather the question becomes *when* the move from the literal to the allegorical is required.

Ghazali's animus toward "philosophy" is well known. But we should be absolutely clear about who in particular al-Ghazali has in mind when he is targeting the "philosophers" and their positions. What he means is the philosophy of the Greeks, and most importantly, Plato and Aristotle, as well as their adherents in the Arabic-speaking milieu. Al-Ghazali especially has in mind the systems of al-Farabi and Ibn Sina. In what follows, you should understand all references to "philosophy" and the "philosophers" to be references to this particular group of thinkers and what they taught.

Al-Ghazali wrote a whole book, the *Incoherence of the Philosophers*, devoted to pointing out some of the most serious mistakes of this Greco-Arabic philosophy. In fact, it is easy to get carried away and think that

Ghazali has nothing nice to say about philosophy, or that he is singlehandedly responsible for the demise of philosophy and more generally free inquiry in the Islamic world.[5] The reality is much more complex. For one thing, many scholars detect a considerable amount of Ibn Sina's philosophy in Ghazali's works (see Griffel 2009 and Treiger 2012). Even if we focus on his critique of the philosophers in *Deliverance from Error*, we see that Ghazali is a far cry from a simpleminded, reactionary book burner. Most philosophy, he argues, is perfectly fine and in fact quite useful. The mathematical sciences and logic, for instance, form parts of the philosophical curriculum, and what these books teach is thoroughly correct and useful. The danger that comes from these parts of philosophy is that they can lead the unsophisticated reader into committing one of two fallacies (*Deliverance from Error*; 1980, 63–5; Watt 1994, 33–4). Some will hear the stories about how the philosophers are heretics and unbelievers, but then read their books on astronomy, optics, or logic and wonder what all the fuss is about. "If this is philosophy," they might say, "then philosophy says clear and obviously true things. The defenders of religion, therefore, must be wrong; perhaps the religion is wrong." On the other hand, another sort of incautious reader might believe the stories and commit an ad hominem fallacy. That is, they might say, "The philosophers are heretics; thus, what they say about mathematics and logic must be false." This would be like someone who often needs to cut down trees throwing away a solidly constructed axe merely because the blacksmith who made it cursed a lot and had a reputation for cheating at card games.

Ghazali's recommendation is not to destroy books, even the highly suspect metaphysical ones. Instead, he urges us to restrict access to the books of the philosophers. To illustrate his point, he uses two analogies (1980, 70; Watt 1994, 43–4). One is the story of a professional snake handler. This person is skilled at dealing with dangerous animals. But precisely because these animals are especially deadly to the unskilled, the snake handler should not practice his art in front of his kids or anyone else who might be tempted to imitate him. The second is the example of the expert money handler. He can reach into the trickster's bag and find the true gold pieces, while rejecting the counterfeit coins. The philosopher's books are like those bags of coins: They contain both true gold and counterfeit coins. The experts will be able to sort through the books and glean what is useful while avoiding the elements that are contrary to the faith.

While much of what the philosophers write is true and useful, al-Ghazali maintains that their natural philosophy and metaphysics are problematic and may potentially lead to damaging "innovation" in the faith. He tells us in his *Deliverance* that there are seventeen instances where the philosophers' teachings amount to innovation, and three that amount to "unbelief." He reserves the innovative doctrines for a detailed critique in his *Incoherence*. But while innovation is something to be avoided by the faithful, this sin pales in comparison to unbelief. And it is here that we get to the heart of the matter.

Ghazali thinks that three doctrines professed by the philosophers are "opposed to the belief of all Muslims" (*Deliverance*; 1980, 66; Watt 1994, 38):

1. The philosophers claim that the afterlife will be fully spiritual in nature. The body will be dissolved, while the soul persists alone to enjoy either eternal union with God or eternal torment through absence.
2. The philosophers maintain that God is only capable of knowing universals and not particulars. Thus, God knows humanity, but not me (an individual instance of humanity).
3. The philosophers maintain the universe is eternal. It had no beginning, and it will have no end.

These three teachings, in Ghazali's view, are incompatible with Islam. One cannot hold them and be a true Muslim. The first proposition is incompatible with Islam because Ghazali maintains that bodily resurrection is unambiguously supported by scripture. In the afterlife, people will be resurrected and that they will enjoy eternal *physical* as well as mental pleasures, or they will suffer eternal *physical* as well as psychological torment. The second proposition is hard to square with scripture's many references to how God knows everything and that he will punish and reward individuals for what they have done. Even God, however, cannot punish Usman and reward Amina if He cannot know their individual deeds and their individual intentions. In a particularly flamboyant version of this accusation Judah Halevi (1141), a Jewish thinker who is heavily influenced by al-Ghazali, goes so far as to suggest in a rhetorical flourish that the philosophers' position could lead to immoral behavior in this life.

> In fact [the philosophers] are not concerned about receiving a reward for that God-fearing behavior [they display], nor do they think that if they were to steal forbidden property or to commit murder that they would be punished [hereafter] for it.
> (*Kuzari* 4:19; trans. Parens and Macfarland 2011, 176)

Halevi, we should note, immediately backs away from accusing any specific philosophers of acting in such a manner: "they have commanded what is good and forbidden what is reprehensible in the most appropriate way, and to imitate the Creator." But if we were standing in al-Ghazali's or Halevi's shoes, we could see why they might be worried about what unphilosophical readers would make of the philosophers' claim that God does not know what we are doing at any given moment. The third proposition also seems to run up against unambiguous references in scripture to God's act of creation ex nihilo. It is also hard to square the philosophers' proclamation that the universe is eternal with the numerous references in scripture to the Last Day. Although, here Ghazali acknowledges that there can be legitimate disagreement. This is why he specifically targets the philosophers' claim that the universe had no beginning, that it is "*pre*-eternal."

Ghazali could be wrong about what the philosophers in fact say. And this is precisely Ibn Rushd's rebuttal to the second charge of unbelief (*Decisive Treatise* §17; Averroes 2001a, 13–4). Ibn Rushd denies that the philosophers – or at least, the true ones – ever maintained that God knows only universals (such as *human, chopping, fig tree,* and *axe*) and not particulars (such as *Usman chopped down Amina's fig tree with this axe*). God's knowledge in fact transcends both universality and particularity. Universality and particularity are properties of the ways in which created minds like ours grasp, think, and know about the effects of God's creative will. God, however, knows all things in the way that a cause knows its effects. Since God causes everything that actually exists, God thereby also knows them.

Here is an analogy. Suppose that Isabelle writes, produces, and directs a film. Before the film is ever made, Isabelle knows a lot about what happens to the various characters that she has created. She knows what each of them will do and when they will do it in the fictional world that she crafts. Of course, the analogy is not a perfect match, since by making the film, Isabelle brings into being a material representation of her fictional world and when this happens various unforeseen contingencies can enter into and either mar or enhance the actual film. God's creative act does not lead to contingencies outside of His control or knowledge. God sees everything and nothing happens that He did not will.

Ibn Rushd's solution also explains how God can know everything about me without being subject to change. When Amina stands, I have a thought in my head *Amina is standing*. When Amina sits down, that thought goes away and another one comes to be, namely, *Amina is sitting*. That is, my thoughts change as the world changes. But God is absolutely incapable of changing. Therefore, either He cannot know any change, or He must know about the particular facts *Amina is sitting (at t2)* and *Amina is standing (at t1)* in a different way than I can. If we grasp the first horn, this would lead to the thought that God only knows universals and not what happens to any material realizations of these universals. But in Ibn Rushd's view, we would only be forced to think that God cannot know any changes, if we persisted in thinking of His knowing as operating like ours, such that it changes along with the changing things. We cannot hold *Amina is standing now* and *Amina is sitting now* in our minds at the same time, since our thoughts are reacting to and conforming to reality. *Amina is standing now* and *Amina is sitting now* cannot both be present in our minds *and* be accurately representing the effect that is currently "out there" in extra mental reality unless it is the case that Amina is now "out there" both sitting and not sitting. While that cannot be true, think about Isabelle and her characters. Suppose that Amina is one of her protagonists. In a sense, once Isabelle has the script settled and before she ever makes the film, she knows at the same time that *Amina is standing (at t1)* and *Amina is sitting (at t2)*. Again, the analogy cannot be pushed too far, but Ibn Rushd thinks that something along these lines is what is happening when God as cause knows all at once that *Amina is standing (at t1)* and *Amina is sitting (at t2)*. Since He is the timeless, unchanging cause of both *Amina is standing (at t1)* and *Amina is sitting (at t2)*, He is capable of knowing both facts in an unchanging, timeless way.

Incidentally, we have just touched upon a problem of considerable interest to both medieval theologians and contemporary philosophers of religion, namely, the problem of how a metaphysically simple and unchanging God can know a complex and changing universe. Connected to this are specific worries about God's *fore*knowledge. Suppose that (1) the future is indeterminate and hence God does not know how things will go in the future. This seems to undercut entailments that stem from reflections on perfection and scripture. Reason tells us that a perfect being has complete knowledge. Scripture constantly reminds us that nothing escapes God's notice. A truly open future, therefore, seems to undercut God's omniscience. Thus, it seems that (2) God's knowledge must extend even to all future events. Yet, this would appear to entail that the future is already fixed. Right now, I am making what I hope will be the final revisions to this book. Even if it does come into print – and I hope it does – I would like to think that it really was up to me whether I finished it or not. If right now, God knows that I do finish the book in a few days, doesn't this entail that I was destined to finish the book? But if I were destined to do it, then in some sense it really was not "up to me" whether I did it or not. Philosophers refer to events in the future that do not need to happen but might happen as "future contingent" events. God's foreknowledge of what will happen seems to remove the *contingency* from such events.

I have been deliberating portraying the reasoning behind (1), (2), and their alleged entailments in a way that *should* invite closer scrutiny. Medieval philosophers have come up with any number of ingenious solutions to these riddles. But I fear we have already digressed down this path for far too long. We now need to return to our main line of inquiry and see how Ibn Rushd will address the other two charges.

When it comes to the other two charges, Ghazali has correctly understood the philosophers' position. Al-Farabi and Ibn Sina assert that the afterlife will be entirely spiritual and that the universe is pre-eternal. With regard to the proposition regarding the pre-eternity of the universe, you will have to take my word for it; with regard to the proposition about the nature of the afterlife, go back and review the exhibits from al-Farabi's and Ibn Sina's writings in Chapters 4 and 5. Thus, Ibn Rushd will not be able to resort to the same strategy that he employs to rebut the charge about God's knowledge. The question is whether a correct reading of scripture really is at odds with the philosophers' conclusions that the afterlife will be entirely spiritual and that the world may, for all we know, be pre-eternal.[6]

Ghazali argued that the position of the philosophers is contrary to any correct understanding of Islam. On several occasions, Ibn Rushd took it upon himself to rebut Ghazali. In the mode of the philosopher, he wrote the *Tahafut al-Tahafut* (*The Incoherence of the "Incoherence"*, trans. Averroes 1954), a point-by-point rebuttal of Ghazali's treatise. But mindful of the audience that would take Ghazali's charges against the philosophers most seriously, Ibn Rushd also composed a reply that played on Ghazali's own turf, so to speak. Notice, in particular, both the title and the introduction of *The Book of the Decisive Treatise Determining the Connection between the Law and Wisdom*.

> The jurist, imam, judge, and uniquely learned Abu al-Walid Muhammad ibn Ahmad ibn Rushd (may God be pleased with him) said: Praise be to God with all praises, and a prayer for Muhammad, His chosen servant and messenger. Now, the goal of this statement is for us to investigate, from the perspective of the Law-based reflection, whether reflection upon philosophy and the sciences of logic is permitted, prohibited, or commanded – and this as a recommendation or as an obligation – by the Law.
>
> (§1; Averroes 2001a, 1)

The opening statement explicitly mentions both "philosophy" and logic, but as the title suggests, he is also interested in "wisdom." Now, as it will turn out, "wisdom" is later identified with the "art of arts" (§8, 6), which for an Aristotelian like Ibn Rushd will be identical to metaphysics, or theology. But it is not hard to think that this choice of term was also due to the simple fact that it would connote things less objectionable to a devout readership. The list of titles that Ibn Rushd gives to himself is also no accident. Ibn Rushd is reminding his readers that he is qualified in *fiqh*, that is, the interpretation of Islamic law (*sharia*). And he proceeds to frame the question in the terms of those familiar with *sharia*. In Islamic law, things and actions are placed into one of these basic categories: the obligatory, the recommended (but not obligatory), the permissible, what is not recommended (but not prohibited), what is not permissible. In short, then, notice that what Ibn Rushd is presenting in this book is a *fatwa*, or legal opinion.

Ibn Rushd doesn't play things safe. Before he proceeds to give a point-by-point rebuttal to Ghazali's three big charges, Ibn Rushd argues, using the materials familiar to those used in making legal decisions (i.e., the Quran and the Sunna), that philosophy is not merely permissible, it is in fact *obligatory* for some. The argument in outline is this (§2, 1):

1 Philosophy is nothing more than reflection by the intellect upon existing things and a consideration of them in so far as they are indications of "the artisan" (i.e., God).
2 Statements in the Quran and Sunna (or what Ibn Rushd refers to as "the Law") clearly indicate that we have an obligation to reflect upon existing things and to consider them in so far as they are indications of the artisan.
Therefore,
3 Philosophy is obligatory.

True to the mode of a religious legal opinion, Ibn Rushd's supporting argument for premise (2) is a series of texts from the Quran (§2, 2).[7] Now, (3) does not imply that everyone has this obligation. In Islamic law, there are obligations that need only be discharged collectively and there are obligations that must be discharged by each and every one of us. For instance, we might think that there is an obligation to care for the sick. This does not mean that all of us should try to be doctors. It only means that we as a collective should ensure that some people become doctors. By comparison, there is also an obligation to tell the truth. This is something that we cannot discharge in the same manner as we discharged the obligation to care for the sick. That is, we cannot designate a truth-teller and then continue to lie ourselves. On Ibn Rushd's way of thinking, the obligation to practice philosophy is like the obligation to care for the sick. We need not do philosophy ourselves; we only need to play our part in the community to ensure that some people can practice this science.

Ibn Rushd believes that philosophy is not merely a way of reflecting upon the works of the creator, he argues that it is the best way that a human can do such a thing (*Decisive Treatise* §3–8; Averroes 2001a, 2–6). This is because philosophy, when done properly, employs the best mode of reasoning, something which he calls "demonstrative reasoning" and which we nowadays often refer to as deductive reasoning. The hallmark of a perfect demonstration is that, first, it has the best kind of truth-preserving structure (if the premises are true, the conclusion must be true) and, second, its premises are not only true but necessarily true. Hence, the result of a demonstration, when done correctly, should be necessarily true.

Incidentally, one of Ghazali's complaints is that the philosophers set this high standard for reasoning, but then they cut corners (*Deliverance*; 1980, 66; Watt 1994, 37). This, in Ghazali's view, explains why the philosophers in fact differ so much when it comes to metaphysical speculation. Ghazali has a point. As al-Farabi notes, there should not be any disagreement when it comes to conclusions established by demonstrations; disputes about matters – especially religious matters – should only arise when it comes to symbolic discourse (*On the Perfect State* 17.3; 1985, 281). Hence, if we find disagreement among philosophers, someone must have made a mistake somewhere.

Ibn Rushd is not blind to this. He knows that mistakes are made. But Ibn Rushd takes a page from Ghazali here. Don't blame philosophy for the error, blame the individual who made the mistake. He even provides an analogy to illustrate his point.

> Indeed, we say that anyone who prevents someone suited to reflect upon the books of wisdom from doing so on the grounds that it is supposed some vicious people became perplexed due to reflecting upon them is like one who prevents thirsty people from drinking cool, fresh water until they die of thirst because some people choked on it and died.
>
> (*Decisive Treatise* §10; Averroes 2001a, 7)

It is important to see here that, like Ghazali, Ibn Rushd makes a distinction between those who have the requisite skills and aptitude for philosophy and those who do not. Just as the obligation only falls on those who have what it takes (and secondarily on the rest of us only in the sense of providing material support), Ibn Rushd also thinks that a harm has been done to one of the elites by denying them access to the books of the philosophers. In fact, as we will soon see, Ibn Rushd will turn the tables on Ghazali by suggesting that he has been providing the public access to material that should be reserved only for the eyes of the elite. But before we get to that, let us briefly look at Ibn Rushd's direct replies to the big three accusations against the philosophers.

We have already seen how Ibn Rushd attempts to deal with one of the three charges leveled against philosophers, namely, the accusation that their theory of divine cognition makes it impossible for God to know us as individuals and to pinpoint our unique virtues and vices. In that case, Ibn Rushd thinks that Ghazali misunderstood the philosophers. For the other two, Ibn Rushd has to employ a different strategy, one which employs an additional Islamic legal principle. By Ibn Rushd's time, it was a well-established legal principle that if "consensus" had been reached on some particular question, then that matter has been settled once and for all. In other words, after consensus has been reached, if someone attempted to reopen the case, that person could be legitimately charged with the sin of "innovation." It takes only a moment of reflection to see that a host of thorny issues pertain to consensus: Who gets to participate in the formation of a consensus? Can a consensus really be something binding for all of time? For that matter, could any serious religious question ever be settled by consensus? As we will see, Ibn Rushd will exploit many of these difficulties in order to demonstrate that not only has no consensus been reached, but perhaps it is not even *possible* to reach a consensus on the metaphysical questions that Ghazali assumes have been settled and which thus mark the boundary between belief and unbelief.

To begin with, Ibn Rushd claims that there is a consensus about the need for constrained interpretation.

> Muslims have formed a consensus that it is not obligatory for all the utterances of the Law to be taken in their apparent sense, nor for all of them to be drawn out from their apparent sense by means of interpretation.
>
> (*Decisive Treatise* §14; Averroes 2001a, 10)

The only disagreement is over which verses should be interpreted and which should not. He points out that Ghazali agrees with this. Ibn Rushd then proceeds to argue that in theoretical cases the bar is very high for achieving consensus.

> What may indicate to you that consensus is not to be determined with certainty about theoretical matters [...] is that it is not possible for consensus to be determined about a particular question at a particular epoch unless: that epoch is delimited by us; all the learned men existing in that epoch are known to us, I mean, known as individuals and in their total number; the doctrine of each one of them on the question is transmitted to us by means of an uninterrupted transmission; and, in addition to all this, it has been certified to us that the learned men existing at that time agreed that there is not an apparent and an inner sense to the Law, that it is obligatory that knowledge of every question

be concealed from no one, and that there is only one method for people to know the Law.

(*Decisive Treatise* §15; Averroes 2001a, 11)

Armed with these stringent criteria for consensus, Ibn Rushd turns to the charges leveled by Ghazali and he argues that "it is not possible for consensus to be determined with respect to questions like these because of what is related about many of the first followers" of Islam "as well as others" (§16, 12). This is the main argument that Ibn Rushd uses to blunt the charges. Ibn Rushd's point about Ghazali's failure to understand the philosopher's views about God's knowledge appears as an additional consideration, as does Ibn Rushd's highly interesting suggestion that the disagreement between all the parties over the question of the eternity of the world seems to be "a disagreement about naming" (§18, 14). In Ibn Rushd's view, they agree about the meaning of the names "generated" and "eternal," but they disagree about which predicate applies to the universe taken as a whole, which is "an existent thing that has not come into existence from something and that time does not precede, but that does come into existence by something – I mean, by an agent" (§18, 15).

Another part of Ibn Rushd's strategy is to point out Ghazali's hypocrisy. Ghazali is worried about the integrity of the faith of the common folk, and especially how it could be undermined if the public learns of nonliteral interpretations of the Quran. But it is Ghazali, not the philosophers, who sow confusion. The true philosophers keep their doctrine secret and don't circulate their books among the uninitiated. Ghazali on the other hand presents allegorical interpretations of scripture in works written for those who are not philosophers (*Decisive Treatise* §35, 21–2).

Finally, Ibn Rushd points to Ghazali's *Decisive Criterion* (on which, see below), where the latter argued that scholars should be very careful about tossing around accusations of heresy and infidelity (§16, 12). Ibn Rushd agrees, and he argues that if an individual makes an honest effort to interpret the meaning of a difficult verse, they should not be accused on heresy or unbelief. He even cites a saying attributed to Muhammad: "If the judge hits the mark after exerting himself, he will be rewarded twofold; and if he errs, he will have a single reward" (§23, 17).

Of course, the "judge" is someone qualified to endeavor to answer difficult questions of interpretation. Ibn Rushd reinforces the point by likening the philosopher to a doctor who sometimes makes an honest error (§25, 18). In both cases, the error is forgivable so long as the person has the required expertise and aptitude. What is not excusable is if someone attempts to do something that they are not trained to do. I, for instance, would *not* be forgiven if my scalpel slipped. I should never have been handed a scalpel, I am not that kind of doctor. Moreover, there are some errors that no one, neophyte and expert alike, may be forgiven for. If one denies any of the "roots of the Law," they are an unbeliever. In the *Decisive Treatise*, Ibn Rushd begins to gesture at what some of these roots are.

> Such, for example, is affirmation of [the existence of] God (may he be blessed and exalted); of the prophetic missions; and of happiness in the hereafter and misery in the hereafter.
>
> (§26, 18)

In the sequel to the *Decisive Treatise*, *The Exposition of the Methods of Proof* (trans. Averroes 2001b), Ibn Rushd devotes considerably more attention to what the fundamentals of the faith are and what every person, both the learned and the common person, should know about them.

So far Ghazali has been portrayed as the bad guy, but as Ibn Rushd has pointed out, elsewhere in his vast corpus Ghazali makes an impassioned case for some degree of toleration. Let us now turn to that facet of Ghazali's thinking.

When we first met Ghazali in Chapter 2 (Section 2.3), I noted that he lived in a very tumultuous time. Some of this upheaval was due to invasions from the Asian steppes. But much of the tumult was due to the rivalries between various sects from within the Islamic fold. Some of the rivalries were exacerbated by the political intrigues of the Shi'ite Fatamid dynasty based in Egypt, which was posing both a serious political and also ideological threat to the crumbling Abbasid caliphate and the "Sunni" form of Islam. On top of this, Ghazali notes that there were numerous scholars and theologians driven seemingly more by pride than piety, who were all too easily and casually flinging accusations of heresy and unbelief at anyone who disagreed with their particular take on religious matters. In his *The Decisive Criterion for Distinguishing Islam from Heresy* (*al-Zandaqa*) (trans. Jackson 2002), Ghazali attempts to tone down the rhetoric and to provide a set of guidelines for when, if ever, it is permissible to accuse someone of unbelief or illegitimate freethinking.

Ghazali is, in fact, part of a wider tendency toward tolerance in Islam, one that has its roots in the Quran itself. For instance, in Surah 4, verses 92–94, God warns his listeners that to kill a believer is an egregious sin. Hence, when fighting on God's behalf, believers must take great care to not kill someone who greets them in peace. The suggestion is (in part) that if there is any doubt about the sincerity of the greeter's belief, it is best to err on the side of caution. Elsewhere, God seems to indicate that He wants there to be a plurality of viewpoints: "If your Lord had pleased, He would have made all people a single community, but they continue to have their differences" (11:118).

The Sunni tradition developed in the aftermath of several key moments of strife. Violence broke out between the partisans of the third and fourth of the Rightly Guided caliphs, Uthman and 'Ali. Unresolved tensions from that flashpoint led to the civil war between 'Ali and Mu'awiya, founder of the first Islamic dynasty (the Umayyad dynasty). These two struggles in turn led to the eventual split between the Sunnis and the Shi'ites. And then there was the *mihna* ("inquisition") carried out by the Abbasid caliph 'Abd Allah al-Ma'mun (r. 813–33). Al-Ma'mun attempted to coerce all scholars to adopt a set of state-sanctioned answers to certain theological questions. So, in sum, in the Sunni world at least there was a tendency to tolerate a certain amount of diversity of doctrine for the sake of social cohesion.

In keeping with this general attitude of tolerance, Ghazali offers his readers some advice and a maxim. The advice echoes Quran 4:92–4:

> As for the Advice, it is that you restrain your tongue, to the best of your ability, from indicting the people who face Mecca as long as they say, "There is no god but God, and Muhammad is the messenger of God," without categorically contradicting this. And for them to contradict this categorically is for them to affirm the possibility that the Prophet (peace be upon him), with or without excuse, delivered lies.
> (*Decisive Criterion*; Jackson 2002, 112)

The maxim, interestingly, echoes Ibn Rushd's claim about what is most fundamental about the faith.

> As for the Maxim, it is that you know that speculative matters are of two types. One is connected with the fundamental principles of the creed, the other with secondary issues. The fundamental principles are acknowledging the existence of God, the prophethood of his Prophet, and the reality of the Last Day. Everything else is secondary. Know that there should be no branding any person an Unbeliever over any secondary issue whatsoever, as a matter of principle, with one exception: that such a person rejects a religious tenet that was learned from the Prophet (pbuh) and passed down via diffusely congruent channels.
> (idem)

The exception added at the end of the maxim allows Ghazali to charge someone with unbelief, if they say, for instance, that it is permissible to drink alcohol. While this prohibition is not a fundamental principle, it is a doctrine mentioned in the Quran and reinforced in multiple, authenticated sayings of Muhammad.

It is crucial to note a principle that undergirds both unbelief with respect to the fundamentals and unbelief with respect to secondary matters. In both cases, the unbelief stems from the fact that the unbeliever is claiming that the Prophet has lied. It does not matter *why* the Prophet lies. Even so-called white or noble lies – that is, lies told in order to promote the greater good – are still lies, and Ghazali will not countenance the possibility that Muhammad would ever do that.

As we have already seen in our exposition of the theocratic state and its propaganda machine (Section 7.3), al-Farabi and Ibn Rushd thought that there are ways to reach people of all levels of cognitive power without telling something that is essentially an untruth. Specifically, one can employ figurative language to convey difficult concepts in simple ways. Ghazali agrees that everyone is in fact stuck with the problem of interpretation (101–3). He even cites verse 3:7 of the Quran in support of this claim. The problem, as Ghazali sees it, is not how to prevent allegorical interpretations of scripture; rather, it is how to prevent unnecessary allegorical interpretations.

Here is where the trickier concept of "heresy" (*zandaqa*) comes into play. Ghazali used this term in the *Deliverance from Error* to indicate places where someone stays on the right side of the belief/unbelief line but flirts with dangerous ideas about the faith. Ghazali counts only three beliefs of the philosophers that amount to outright unbelief (*kufr*), but there are also seventeen propositions that are "heretical" (1980, 66; Watt 1994, 38). In the *Decisive Criterion*, the notion of *zandaqa* seems to cleave closer to unbelief, which is why Jackson translates the term as "masked infidelity" (see 2002, 7–8, 55–9). The basic idea seems to be this: A *zandiq* is someone who outwardly espouses Islam, but whose interpretations of key texts and doctrines is unwarrantedly and dangerously free.[8]

To distinguish legitimate from illegitimate interpretations of scripture, Ghazali develops an elaborate hierarchy of levels of meaning, starting with the literal (or as he calls it, the "ontological") and ending with the "analogous" (Jackson 2002, 94). Ghazali then gives us rules for determining when it is legitimate to move from one level to the next one up. Someone is entitled to move up if maintaining a reading at the lower level leads to an impossibility or absurdity (104). For instance, a reference to God sitting on a throne cannot be taken literally because it conflicts with the established truth that God does not have a body. Thus, we are entitled to move from the "ontological" level to the next one up, the "sensory," where we test this reading to see if it leads to contradictions. In Ghazali's view, so long as interpreters make a good faith effort to work systematically up from the ontological level to the first level where no contradiction occurs, and so long as their reading corresponds to one of the five levels that he lists, their interpretation of scripture cannot be considered unbelief. Unbelief only occurs if one denies that a verse of the Quran corresponds to any of the levels. This is tantamount to claiming that Muhammad lied and that his "aim in delivering [a verse] was simply to deceive people or to promote the common good" (101).

Even with these rules in place, Ghazali concedes that there is room for reasonable and legitimate disagreement about whether one has reached an absurdity and thus is entitled to read scripture allegorically. Many religious matters cannot be settled once and for all with certainty. Indeed, in the spirit of the Quranic verse 3:7, Ghazali concedes that some verses may be impossible to interpret. For this reason, it is best in many cases to mind our own business and let God be the judge. This relatively tolerant attitude and call for forbearance is perhaps best encapsulated by Ghazali's discussion of a famous saying of Muhammad. In one telling, the Prophet reportedly claimed, "My community will divide into over seventy sects; only one of them will be saved." Ghazali acknowledges that this is the more popular version, but he claims that there is an alternate version of the saying, which goes as follows: "My community will divide into over seventy sects; all of them will enter Paradise except the *zanadiqa*" (Jackson 2002, 111 and 125). Ghazali tells us that he prefers the minority report, but even if the more popular version were true, this does not necessarily mean that those who made erroneous interpretations of scripture will be damned to Hell for all eternity. After all, God is merciful, and thus we have good reason to hope that He will intercede after some amount of time and save even those who are not Muslims but who believe in God from eternal torment (126–9).

We have now seen that far from being a narrow-minded authoritarian, quick to tamp down on free thought, Ghazali can be somewhat lenient when it comes to religious disagreement. So long as someone has made an honest effort, we should not accuse them of heresy or unbelief. This allows him to offer a generous truce to opposing theological schools and even to the Shiites (113). That said, even in the *Decisive Criterion*, "most of" the philosophers are singled out for chastisement and banished as unbelievers. When it comes to the fundamentals of the faith, such as the resurrection of the body, "anyone who alters the apparent meaning of a text without a definitive logical proof must be branded an Unbeliever" (Jackson 2002, 109). But there is no proof that can demonstrate that bodily resurrection is logically impossible (see Section 5.4). Hence, in Ghazali's view, if the philosophers persist in reading texts referring to bodily resurrection figuratively, they effectively have ceased to practice legitimate interpretation. Moreover, Ghazali claims, the philosophers admit that they are not offering even an allegorical interpretation. Rather, the philosophers's position is that Muhammad told a lie to the masses. He did so for a noble reason: common people need to fear the afterlife, but they have no capacity for conceiving of it as something merely spiritual (110).[9] But, for Ghazali, a noble lie is still a lie. And the Prophet does not tell lies.

As for the mystics, Ghazali is willing to let them bend his rules quite a bit when it comes to matters that are not central to the faith (109), but he takes a hard line when it comes to certain elements of Islam.

> Included among such matters would be the claims of some who style themselves Sufis to the effect that they have reached a state between themselves and God wherein they are no longer obligated to pray, and that drinking wine, devouring state funds, and other forms of disobedience are rendered licit to them. Such people, without doubt, must be executed, even if there remains some question as to whether they will abide in the Hellfire forever. Indeed, executing one of these people is better than killing a hundred Unbelievers, because the harm they bring to religion is greater, and because they open doors of libertinism that can never be closed.
>
> (Jackson 2002, 115)

In short, even Ghazali's tolerance has its limits, and these limits seem to be much more restrictive than we in our age might prefer.

It is also abundantly clear that al-Ghazali's toleration does not extend to atheism. If someone hears about the Prophet Muhammad and his ministry but "turns away from it, refuses to ponder it, and takes no initiative to confirm it," this person is a "cynical self-deceiver" and an unbeliever (128). Such a person betrays an attachment to this world and a lack of "fear" of the next one. Individuals who have not heard of Islam, such as those living in Byzantium or in the East beyond the reaches of the Islamic empire (or as he refers to them, "the Turks") will be forgiven by God so long as they possess faith in God and in the Last Day. But even in their case, if any of these Turks or Christians were to come across a Muslim mission, Ghazali is confident that those who truly have faith in God and the Last Day "cannot betray this motivation" to investigate the claims of Muhammad and his followers (idem). In short, while Ghazali is willing to extend tolerance in some measure even to those outside of the fold of Islam, his attitude is uncompromisingly harsh to those who have heard but reject the word of God and his prophet outright. Atheism, then, is not a protected intellectual position.

Ghazali is not alone in this regard. Consider once more the "humanism" of John of Salisbury. Even such a strong advocate of the freedom to be wrong seems to hedge and hem at the boundaries. Freedom to disagree and to dispute seems to be restricted to matters that have been left unsettled. It is easy to imagine that by this John means matters that involve tricky points of church doctrine, not basic questions such as whether a providential God exists. So, for instance, while he says that we are "permitted to imitate the uncertainties of the Academics" to a degree, John is not shy about pointing out when the ancients went astray. For instance, most of them "believed in the mortality of the soul" and hence, they "had not yet received instruction about the eternal life which is to be after this one" (*Policraticus* VII.8; 1990, 160). Nor, for that matter, is it clear whether John would be happy to extend his principles of toleration to include the non-Christian theist.

Here, then, is a question: Does anyone in the Middle Ages go so far as to defend the atheist or the agnostic? My suspicion is that none would put anything of the sort in writing, even if they thought such a position had any merit. Some, including William of Ockham (1347), were so bold as to suggest that even if someone expressed clearly wrongheaded views, the authorities do not necessarily have the right to violently coerce or punish such a person. Ockham maintains that there are strict conditions under which clerical and secular authorities may punish a person for holding heretical views, and this is true not only because all humans are fallible in religious matters. Authorities may only coerce or punish an individual if that person explicitly admits that their position is erroneous *and* they still refuse to surrender it (Nederman 2014, 563). Thus, if a heretic refuses to concede that they are wrong, neither the church nor the state is entitled to coerce them with threats or punish them for their views. But did Ockham himself think that such a hard position extended to the agnostic and the atheist, let alone to the non-Christian? That is unclear, but my suspicion is that he would not be willing to extend the boundaries of toleration quite that far. At best, in writings of Ockham and others of his spirit, we are beginning to see some small steps toward a truly liberal notion of freedom of speech and religion. But I think it would be naïve for us to assume that any medieval author is willing to defend the kind of freethinking that many of us now believe is a fundamental human right.

While we are in the business of comparing medieval views to our contemporary sensibilities, it is worth noting one other way in which even the more "liberal" medieval positions do not line up with our present-day notions of freedom. Consider Ibn Rushd once more. Ibn Rushd is sometimes portrayed as a defender of free thought in the face of conservative religious opposition. We have now seen how such a caricature fails to do justice to, say, Ghazali's worries about philosophy. But there is another distortion in this cartoon version of the history of philosophy: It fails to appreciate Ibn Rushd's strident elitism. Some people, on his view, are entitled to the freedom to pursue philosophical understanding. But this freedom to think, and perhaps even to be wrong is reserved only for the select few. We have already seen Ghazali advise us to keep the books of the philosophers out of reach of those who cannot understand them properly. Despite his many differences from Ghazali, Ibn Rushd shares this sentiment.

> For anyone not adept in science, it is obligatory to take them [viz. the descriptions of the next life portrayed in scripture] in their apparent sense; for him, it is unbelief to interpret them because it leads to unbelief.
> (*Decisive Treatise* §34; Averroes 2001a, 21)

All the major figures subscribe to this elitist position, including al-Farabi, Ibn Sina, and Ibn Tufayl. Indeed, I can think of no one in the medieval Arabic-speaking philosophical tradition who does not openly maintain this posture. And while it is often harder to discern this elitism in Western Christian circles, I suspect that even our champions John of Salisbury and William of Ockham are not thinking about the common person when they are defending freedom of thought and speech. They too seem to have specific, highly educated audiences in mind.

Nowadays the suggestion that only some people have the right to read certain books or to undertake a course in philosophy would immediately evoke shock and condemnation. Here again, however, we should pay attention to the precise contours of this medieval elitism. There are currently movements in the academy and the broader culture to remove barriers to access to education in general and to fields like philosophy and the sciences in particular. Our medieval authors, I suspect, would not be too troubled about making education more inclusive in some of these respects. Historical evidence confirms that the universities and *studia* of medieval Europe were relatively welcoming to men from a variety of ethnic, racial, and socio-economic backgrounds. Women, of course, were another matter. They were barred from the universities (but not necessarily from education). The elitism of the Farabians stems from a different source, which we might call an ableist principle: Philosophy should be reserved for those who have the cognitive capacity for it. Don't get me wrong, I am not raising this issue in order to argue that removing access to education on ableist grounds is morally defensible. I am only advising that we take care to see precisely where medieval views agree and disagree with our current sensibilities and principles. We can and should be critical of the Farabian's positions, but we need to make sure that we understand what it is that he is saying before we evaluate and assess.

7.5 The Philosopher as Stranger in the World

The Farabian virtuous state is an *ideal*. In actual fact the philosopher is surrounded by people, both everyday folk and elites, who have very different values. They perhaps even find themselves in societies that are acutely suspicious or inimical to philosophy. In theory philosophers might have the right to be wrong, but it is far from clear that they should demand that others honor this right, especially when those in power are concerned more about social cohesion than they are on the open-ended pursuit of truth. What should the philosophical person do in such cases? Should they act like Socrates as he is portrayed in Plato's *Apology* and nobly confront their neighbors, even if it costs them their lives? Or should philosophers follow the suggestion that the character Socrates makes in Plato's *Republic*? There Socrates asserts that if the philosopher finds that he is in a city that is hostile toward the life of the mind, the philosopher should try to emigrate or, if that is not an option, he should lie low and pursue his philosophical pursuits in private (book 6, 496b–e). In other words, in the *Republic* we find the recommendation that the philosopher in some situations should retreat from society. But given that Farabians maintain that humans are by their very nature political animals, is retreat even a viable option for flourishing as a human being?

After establishing the framework of the virtuous city, al-Farabi notes that in addition to the various corrupted forms of the state, there are the "weeds" in the virtuous city, whose position is like "that of dranel in wheat, the thorns of plants within the crop, or the rest of the grasses that are useless or even harmful to the crop or seedlings" (*Political Regime*, II.92; al-Farabi 2011, 46). Elsewhere, these weeds are described as "opportunists," "distorters," and other things (II.122–6, 53–5). In general, al-Farabi discusses the weeds that arise in a virtuous city. Given their disruptive and corrosive actions, the philosophical rulers of the state will have to deal harshly with such individuals.

This, however, is how things should be when the philosophers are in charge and the state is constituted in such a way as to make most of the citizens happy. But suppose we turn the tables and consider the philosophers who live in, for instance, the democratic city. Remember that there the philosophers are usually on the defensive, and indeed, if they ever are in charge, this will be in effect a lucky break and their rule will not last for long. The Andalusian philosopher Ibn Bajja, whom we introduced in Section 7.1, appreciated this. To get at the predicament of the philosopher in a nonideal state, he repurposed al-Farabi's notion of the "weed" so that it named any individual who had difficulty integrating into a society. According to this use of the term, in many societies the philosopher is the solitary weed.

In his *Governance of the Solitary*, Ibn Bajja concedes that weeds can be "the cause that leads to the rise of the perfect city," but the fact that there are weeds in the city is an indication that "the city is already diseased and disintegrating and has ceased to be perfect" (*Governance* 1.3; Parens and Macfarland 2011, 101). Happiness is, therefore, something that in all likelihood one can only achieve on an individual basis.

> We leave it to those who devote themselves to the investigation of the ways of life that exist in this time to supply the details. We merely remark that the three types of men – the Weeds, the judges, and the doctors – exist or can exist in these ways of life. The happy, were it possible for them to exist in these cities, will possess only the happiness of an isolated individual; and the only right governance is the governance of an isolated individual, regardless of whether there is one isolated individual or more than one, so long as a nation or a city has not adopted their opinion.
> (*Governance* 1.3; Parens and Macfarland 2011, 101)

Ibn Bajja concedes that this state of affairs is "unnatural" and that his advice to the solitary philosophical weed does not contradict the philosophers' position that humans are by nature political animals and that in the abstract isolation is a deprivation and evil.

> But it is only evil as such; accidentally it may be good, which happens with reference to many things pertaining to nature. For instance, bread and meat are by nature beneficial and nourishing, while opium and colocynth are mortal poisons. But the body may possess certain unnatural states in which the latter two are beneficial and must be employed, and the natural nourishment is harmful and must be avoided. However, such states are necessarily diseases and deviations from the natural order.
> (*Governance* 17.2; 104)

Ibn Bajja argues that the solitary philosopher finds himself in an analogous predicament to someone who needs to forgo food or take a painkiller that is otherwise detrimental to one's health.

Ibn Bajja offers a physician's advice to the philosopher. In many cases, you must live like a "stranger" in your own land. Like a sick person who must deny himself food in order to heal, the philosophical weed must withdraw as much as possible from the corrosive society in which he lives.

> It is clear from the situation of the solitary that he must not associate with those whose end is corporeal nor with those whose end is the

spirituality that is adulterated with corporeality. Rather, he must associate with those who pursue the sciences. Now since those who pursue the sciences are few in some ways of life and many in others – there even being ways of life in which they do not exist at all – it follows that in some of the ways of life the solitary must keep away from men completely so far as he can, and not deal with them except in indispensable matters and to the extent that it is indispensable for him to do so; or to emigrate to the ways of life in which the sciences are pursued – if such are to be found.
(*Governance* 17.2; Parens and Macfarland 2011, 104)

He must avoid entanglements with most people, because their ways of life are in fact "unnatural." The only natural way of life is the one directed at achieving the Platonic philosopher's idiosyncratic conception of happiness, to contemplate "simple essential intellects" and then "become one of these intellects" (13.2, 104).

What seems to emerge from all this is a somewhat deflated and pessimistic portrayal of the philosopher in a corrupt society. If he keeps his head down and quietly focuses on his intellectual endeavors, the philosopher may achieve individual happiness, but society as a whole it seems has very little chance of redemption (Montada 2005, 164–5). Certainly, there is nothing in Ibn Bajja's treatise which would suggest that the philosopher ought to try to make a difference for the greater good.

Ibn Bajja's fellow Andalusian, Ibn Tufayl (1185) also seems to come to the same conclusion. As we have already seen, the main plot in Tufayl's philosophical tale is the gradual ascent of his hero Hayy to knowledge of God. This plot reaches its resolution with Hayy's mystical experience of "union" with the divine (*Hayy ibn Yaqzan*; 2009, 149–54; G. 120–32; see Chapter 4, Section 4.3).

But the tale does not end at that point. Instead, a new plot develops. On an island not too far from Hayy's, there is a sophisticated civilization. The people on this civilized island follow a religion that was founded by a true prophet. But following Farabi's analysis of religion, there is an external literal aspect to the religion and then there is a deeper meaning of the texts and legal principles, one that is discernible only to the more philosophical individuals. Tufayl introduces us to two friends Salaman and Absal. Both are said to be pious, but they differ in their attitudes toward the religion of the island. Salaman "was more anxious to preserve the literal and less prone to seek subtle meanings [behind the literal]"; whereas Absal "was the more deeply concerned with getting to the heart of things, the more eager to discover spiritual values, and the more ready to attempt a more or less allegorical interpretation" (156, G. 136–7). The scripture followed by Salaman and Absal contained some passages which seem to recommend a life of seclusion and individual spiritual practice. But other passages seemed to recommend living in community and participation in society. Absal favored the passages recommending solitary contemplation, Salaman preferred the passages recommending sociality. "In staying with the group he saw some means of fending off demonic promptings, dispelling distracting thoughts, and in general guarding against the goadings of the devil" (157, G. 137).

It is worth pausing to quickly note that Salaman has a point. As many contemplatives in the Islamic, Jewish, and Christian traditions know, being alone with one's thoughts comes with risks. Even if no demons are lurking about to send us down the wrong path, we are still prone to error. We are finite beings with finite intellects. Even the best of us make mental errors. One way to mitigate and minimize this risk is to have someone else check our work. As it happens, this is how academics work nowadays. We might compose our papers in the solitude of our studies and offices, but we are constantly submitting it to "peer review." We present our findings in lectures, and our papers and book manuscripts are submitted to external review. Every paper that you encounter in an academic journal, every book published by an established academic press is the product of a communal effort to some extent. This same general principle is at work in medieval approaches to theology and the faith. There is a constant worry that errors will enter the system. One way to guard against these unwarranted and potentially dangerous "innovations" is to submit theology and religious practice to rigorous peer review.

Tufayl does not tell us whether Absal thought about this, but I think it is safe to say that he was aware of these arguments. After all, Absal and Salaman are said to be friends – friends who strongly disagree about some very important things – but *friends*, nonetheless. Absal does not leave the civilized island because he fears for his life. But we are told that Absal's disagreement with Salaman over whether one should live in a community was the cause of their parting (157, G. 138). Absal sells all his possessions, gives away his wealth to the poor, and then he travels to an isolated island that he has heard about. This isolated place turns out to be the island where Hayy is living. The story of their meeting is amusing, but I will leave that for you to read for yourselves. What transpires after they meet and learn to communicate with one another (remember: Hayy has never met another human being before) is what is most important at present. Hayy tells Absal what he has discovered in his mystical contemplation. Absal sees that this is the true heart of his religion, the one which he has been so ardently seeking for all these years. Absal in turn tells Hayy about the formal religion on the civilized island.

> Hayy understood all this and found none of it in contradiction with what he had seen for himself from his supernal vantage point. He

recognized that whoever had offered this description had given a faithful picture and spoken truly. This man must have been a "messenger sent by his Lord".

(161, G. 145)

Hayy, however, is puzzled about three things. First, the founder of this religion used symbols that allowed people to anthropomorphize God and to think of Him as being embodied. Second, this prophet described the rewards and punishments of the afterlife in ways that might suggest that they have a corporeal element (see Section 7.3, and also Chapter 5, Section 5.4). Finally,

> why did [this founder of the religion] confine himself to these particular rituals and duties and allow the amassing of wealth and overindulgence in eating, leaving men idle to busy themselves with inane pastimes and neglect the Truth [i.e. God]?

(161, G. 146)

Hayy, by contrast, had determined that all bodily functions needed to be minimized. They were distractions from his true and essential aim, which is to contemplate and imitate God and the other immaterial substances.

Absal convinces Hayy to journey with him back to the civilized island to teach Absal's circle of scholarly friends about the truth. They soon manage to do so. But things do not go well.

> Hayy ibn Yaqzan began to teach this group and explain some of his profound wisdom to them. But the moment he rose the slightest bit above the literal or began to portray things against which they were prejudiced, they recoiled in horror from his ideas and closed their minds.

(163, G. 150)

Absal's friends were polite toward Hayy, but Hayy could discern that they were resistant to his teachings and he began to despair of helping them.

> He saw that most men are no better than unreasoning animals, and realized that all wisdom and guidance, all that could possibly help them was contained already in the words of the prophets and religious traditions.

(164, G. 153)

Teaching such people "publicly and openly," that is, in the rigorous language of philosophy, was impossible. For most people, the best to be hoped for is that the religious laws would allow them "to live decent lives without others encroaching on what belonged to them" (idem, G. 152). Only the few, however, would ever achieve the true happiness that comes with the contemplative life.

Once Hayy reached this pessimistic appraisal of the human condition, he publicly recanted his teachings and advised Absal's friends to continue to follow their religion as they understood it. He and Absal then made discreet arrangements to leave the civilized island and to return to the isolated island on which Hayy grew up. There Hayy and Absal stayed and practiced the solitary contemplative life. We are even told that after much practice, Absal was eventually able to reach the "same heights, or nearly so" (165, G. 154). Thus, things end happily for Hayy and Absal but not necessarily for the remainder of humanity.

Ibn Tufayl seems to be following Ibn Bajja's lead in maintaining that actual human civilizations – even ones organized around religions founded by a true prophet – are impediments to true human happiness and that if one really wants to flourish as a human being, they need to extricate themselves from society at large and live either the life of a solitary hermit or perhaps, acknowledging the risks of being completely alone, in a small community of like-minded individuals. This is a place where we can see a connection to the Christian West. In the Christian setting we see in the Middle Ages not only a separation of religious from secular authority, but also on many occasions a tension between those who advocate withdrawal from the world and those who thought that the church should do more to alleviate suffering and provide spiritual guidance to the masses (see Casuto 2014).

It is worth noting that not everyone reads Ibn Tufayl in this manner. Michael Marmura, for instance, argues that on a closer reading of the tale, we can see that Tufayl is not intent on demolishing the principle that humans are by nature social animals. Nor is Tufayl advocating a complete withdrawal from society. On Marmura's view, Hayy's individual path to enlightenment is meant to emphasize the Sufi dictum that the contemplative needs isolation. But this does not contradict what Marmura calls the "Farabian political framework," one which sees the philosophers as playing an essential role in the formation and maintenance of society. "For philosophers, whether or not engaged in political activity, require isolation" (1979, 422). As for Hayy's disastrous attempt to teach Absal's friends, Marmura thinks that this allows Tufayl to make "the hero in a dramatic way discover for himself" one of the cardinal principles of Farabi's political philosophy, namely, that the philosophers should not speak to the unphilosophical (including Absal's friends) in a philosophical manner. Hayy "is no Thrasymachus, or at least when he attempts to be one, he fails" (423).

Marmura acknowledges that the next event that takes place is that Hayy and Absal retreat back to the island, but he does not think that this forces us to conclude that Ibn Tufayl is advocating a withdrawal from all societies, even ones that are resistant to esoteric interpretations of scripture and religious tradition.

Yet, there still is the question as to what the philosopher should do if they are living in an irredeemably corrupt society, not in Salaman's and Absal's city. That is, what if we are in a place where it is difficult to engage, even in private, the intellectual and spiritual life? Returning to a theme we explored in Chapter 6 (Section 6.4), what if the only company that we could keep would be the wrong sort of company? If we return to the Platonic source of the notion that the philosopher should retreat from society, that is, to that passage in the *Republic*, we will see that the kind of city that is described is a terrible place to be. It is not merely a society where philosophers are not in charge and the truth is not valued, it is an actively violent and corrosive society. It is the kind of place where living virtuously is nearly impossible and the souls of virtuous people are in danger of being ruined over time. Farabi acknowledges that such conditions may obtain. Ibn Bajja writes as if he might be actually living in such a place. And in these cases, their advice is that the philosopher should live as a stranger or foreigner. If another city is more virtuous, the philosopher should emigrate to that city and be a foreigner in a literal sense. If no such city is available, they should live in their home city as if they were a foreigner: Follow the laws of the land, don't rock the boat, keep one's head down.

Perhaps a foreigner can mostly get by in the city he lives in by keeping his mouth shut. On some occasions, however, he might be compelled to publicly espouse something that he knows to be false. That can not only be psychologically distressing; in some cases, it is a sin. What should this person do in such cases? When is it acceptable to dissimulate in order to preserve one's livelihood, if not life and limb? When must one speak up, even if it will put them in danger? Moses Maimonides was clearly familiar with the philosophy of al-Farabi and Ibn Bajja, and he lived for a time in the same part of the world as Ibn Bajja. He has some interesting things to say about what we should do when society makes it hard to be virtuous.

At the time when Maimonides was born, Andalusia, the Islamic portion of the Iberian Peninsula, and Morocco were parts of an empire that was both religiously diverse and culturally vibrant. But when the Almohads crossed over from Northern Africa, displaced the Almoravid dynasty, and seized power in Andalusia, they swiftly instituted a policy of forced conversion. Jews in particular were given the choice between publicly professing Islam or being executed. Maimonides and his family fled, eventually landing in Egypt. But many of his coreligionists stayed behind. Some chose martyrdom, others decided it was better to publicly profess Islam while continuing to practice Judaism in private. At some point, a letter began to circulate in which a rabbi pronounced that those who publicly professed Islam but continued to practice Judaism in private had committed a terrible and irredeemable sin, a sin that warranted their exclusion from the Jewish community. Maimonides was outraged and around 1165, he wrote the *Epistle on Martyrdom* as a response.

Maimonides's position in the *Epistle* is nuanced. On the one hand, he affirms that it is a sin to publicly profess Islam, and thus, "desecrate God's name." In a sense, then, religious law demands that the observant Jew stand up to his oppressor and refuse to profess Islam. On the other hand, Maimonides is to some extent compassionate toward those who fail to do this. As one commentator observes, the law is asking people to do something "heroic" (Halkin and Hartman 1985, 46 ff.). Most of us fall short of heroism. What do we say to such people? What do we say to ourselves in such instances?

For much of the *Epistle*, Maimonides takes pains to reassure forced converts that what they have done has not put them irredeemably outside the fold. The Torah gives many instances of God rebuking someone for judging others to be beyond redemption. Moreover, Maimonides reminds his audience that there is a morally significant difference between someone acting willfully and someone who acts under duress. He also asserts that the sin of publicly confessing Islam gets thrown into one's account with all one's other sins and virtuous deeds.

> None can claim that he was guilty of a more serious sin. This principle is applicable only in man-made laws in this world. God inflicts punishment for grievous sins and for minor ones, and He rewards people for everything they do. Hence it is important to bear in mind that one is punished for every sin committed and is rewarded for every precept fulfilled.
>
> (Halkin and Hartman, 1985, 31)

Publicly professing Islam is in fact a grievous sin, in Maimonides's view, but it is not so grievous that it annuls any other acts that an observant Jew subsequently does. Nor, he argues, is it grounds for punishing the forced convert by any of the "seven means of punishment."

> He is not dubbed a transgressor, nor a wicked man, nor is he disqualified from giving testimony, unless he committed a sin that disqualifies him from serving as a witness. He simply did not fulfill the commandment of sanctifying God's name, but he can under no circumstance be named a deliberate profaner of God's name. Therefore, anyone who

claims or thinks that a person who transgressed is to be condemned to death, because the sages established the principle that one must surrender himself to death and not transgress, is absolutely wrong.

(idem, 29)

Finally, Maimonides notes a distinction between speech and action. The Almohads merely asked Jews to say certain words in public. But they did not ask Jews to perform actions that are forbidden for them to do. Maimonides argues that it is only in the latter case that religious law unequivocally demands that a Jew refuse and forfeit his life.

Maimonides's letter displays much sympathy and compassion for the plight of his coreligionists living under extreme duress. But his *Epistle* does contain some hard edges and he does ask his readers to perform some difficult and potentially painful self-examinations of their motivations. Both in his *Epistle on Martyrdom* and in his *Epistle to Yemen* (1172), Maimonides urges his coreligionists to emigrate to a place where they can openly practice their faith.

> What I counsel myself, and what I should like to suggest to all my friends and everyone who consults me, is to leave these places and go to where he can practice religion and fulfill the Law without compulsion or fear. Let him leave his family and his home and all he has, because the divine Law that He bequeathed to us is more valuable than the ephemeral, worthless incidentals that the intellectuals scorn; they are transient, whereas the fear of God is eternal.
>
> (Halkin and Hartman 1985, 31; cf. *Epistle to Yemen*, idem, 106)

He adds that if there are two cities where Jews openly practice, but one practices the law more faithfully than the other, then it is incumbent on all to move to the better Jewish city.

The important thing to see here is that Maimonides is asking a lot of his coreligionists. He is asking them to give up their jobs, their homes, perhaps even their close friends and family. All such things are less important than fearing and honoring God. Thus, while he attempts to console those Jews who stayed behind in Andalusia and the Magreb, he does force them to take a hard and honest look at what their motives are for staying, and he points out that some of these motives might be sinful.

> Anyone who cannot leave because of his attachments, or because of the dangers of a sea voyage, and stays where he is, must look upon himself as one who profanes God's name, not exactly willingly, but almost so.
>
> (33)

It is unclear what reasons to stay could stand up to such a harsh assessment. What could be a reason that did not amount to one of these worldly attachments? To be sure, after giving this assessment, Maimonides immediately adds what may seem to be some emollient: One who stays and fulfills some of the commands of the religious law will be rewarded doubly, "because he acted so for God only, and not to show off or be accepted as an observant individual." He also notes that God rewards those who are willing to practice their faith when they know that they could be killed if they are discovered. Still, Maimonides ends this paragraph by again urging his friends and coreligionists to exert every effort to emigrate as soon as it is feasible.

Maimonides's recommendation is broadly in line with the Platonic philosophy developed and promulgated by al-Farabi and his followers. The best situation for the virtuous person is to live in a virtuous city. For al-Farabi and Maimonides, the virtuous city will be founded and managed by individuals with philosophical aptitude. In the real world the philosopher, and, more generally, the person interested in virtue and human flourishing will need to evaluate the kind and degree of corruption in the city in which he currently lives. If a better city actually exists, the virtuous person should move to that city. If no such option presents itself, but the imperfect city that one lives in is potentially improvable, then the virtuous person should stay and attempt to make the city better. This will require some skill in rhetoric, which is the mode of discourse appropriate for communicating to those who are not philosophers. There are, however, some cases where the city is irredeemable and potentially even hazardous for the virtuous person. In such cases, the virtuous person is a stranger in their own home, and it might even be advisable for them to leave everything behind and to depart for "the desert or the wilderness" (cf. *Epistle to Yemen*; Halkin and Hartman 1985, 106), just as Abraham, the patriarch of all three great monotheistic religions, did long ago.

Study Questions

1) Al-Farabi assumes several key propositions in his defense of a hierarchical, authoritarian state structure, including these two: (a) Those who do not know the good or how to attain it should submit to the authority of those who do, and (b) the number of those who truly know the good is few, whereas most people do not know the good or how to attain it. Do you think that al-Farabi is right about these two claims?
2) Think about your answer to the question at the end of Chapter 5 about the flourishing human life. Does your answer there have any implications for how we ought to evaluate al-Farabi's critique of democracy?

3) In your view, are people in positions of authority ever permitted to tell a noble lie? If so, in which positions of authority might this be permissible and under what conditions would a noble lie be warranted? How does your answer compare to the philosophers we surveyed in Section 7.3?
4) John of Salisbury suggests that we can draw a line between uncivil (or "taunts") and civil speech, and that tolerance really only applies to the latter. What do you think? Can such a line be drawn in any way that would actually allow us to enforce it?
5) Does the philosopher have an obligation to stay in the city and speak truth to power, even if it could cost him his life?

Notes

1 Maimonides attributes the differences in our dispositions, which are for him accidents, to our material constitution. The fact that our material make-up is only part of the causal story and that our upbringing is also important is something that Maimonides emphasizes his *Eight Chapters* (Maimonides 1975, 84). See Section 5.1.
2 Strictly speaking, what we have here is a division of the "ignorant cities." Al-Farabi also mentions that there are "immoral" and "errant" cities. However, on closer inspection, these two kinds of cities are distinguished from the ignorant cities because of their starting point, not because of the political structures that they subsequently adopt which, like the ignorant cities, are determined by the dominant aims of its citizens (II.120–1).
3 You might want to compare al-Farabi's unfavorable view of this kind of city to Socrates's seemingly more favorable assessment of this regime in *Republic* Bk. 2, 369b–372d.
4 This does not mean that there were not ugly inquisitions and moral panics in the Middle Ages, broadly construed. For an instance of moral panic in the "twilight" years of the Middle Ages, see Philipp Rosemann's discussion of Heinrich Kramer and his book *Malleus Maleficarum* ("Witch Hunter"), which was published in Strasbourg in 1487 (1999, 165–72). But as Rosemann reminds us, witch-hunts did not start before around 1430 and they reached their peak in the sixteenth and seventeenth centuries, that is, "the ages of the Renaissance, humanism, and the Reformation" (165).
5 In older and especially older popular treatments of the history of philosophy, one unfortunately encounters such hyperbolic claims.
6 Ibn Tufayl's protagonist Hayy wrestles with whether the universe is pre-eternal "for some years." But rather than coming to a decision about whether the universe had a beginning or not, he decides that ultimately, it does not matter which position is true. Both positions lead to the same further conclusion that there is a first cause of everything else (*Hayy ibn Yaqzan*; 2009, 131–2, G. 81–5). In other words, Ibn Tufayl is signaling that, *pace* Ghazali, taking one position over another on this question does not determine whether you are a believer or not.
7 I once had a student who examined all of the passages surrounding the texts that Ibn Rushd quotes. He argued that these "proof texts," when read in context, did not unambiguously support Ibn Rushd's premise. I encourage those who are interested in Ibn Rushd's case to do the same and see what they think.

8 See Griffel 2009, 104–5, as well as McCarthy's notes to his translation of the *Deliverance* (1980, 102, n. 20). The word seems to be a loan word from Persian. Sometimes it is used to refer to Manichean dualism. Later and up to the present day, it becomes a term of approbation for any freethinker, heretic, or atheist (see, e.g., Hans Wehr, *Arabisches Woerterbuch*; English version: *Arabic-English Dictionary*, 445).

9 Ghazali is not wrong about this. See Averroes 2001b, 123–4.

Suggestions for Further Reading

You may have noticed that this chapter is the culmination of several themes running throughout this book, including, for instance, the Platonic notion of the afterlife and more generally the philosophers's understanding of human nature and human flourishing. It also has referred you back to issues that came up at the beginning about human knowledge and its limits. Therefore, many of the resources that I have already identified will serve you well if you wish to pursue the themes and topics in this chapter.

For medieval Islamic thinking about the state and the role of the philosopher in various kinds of political organizations, I found several of Michael Marmura's essays to be extremely accessible and lucid. In particular, I recommend starting with this one:

"The Philosopher in Society: Some Medieval Arabic Discussions," *Arabic Studies Quarterly* I, 4 (1979): 309–23.

This essay is reprinted in a marvelous collection of Marmura's pioneering articles entitled *Probing in Islamic Philosophy* (2005). For more on Ibn Bajja, start with Montada's article (2005), which I cited in the chapter. For a useful introduction to Ibn Rushd, his *Decisive Treatise*, and the political and cultural context in which he composed this work, see Hourani's introduction to his translation of the treatise (1961, esp. 1–43).

My focus on the Farabian tradition in this chapter should not lead you to conclude that Christian thinkers were uninterested in political philosophy. For a selection of primary sources and general orientation, see Joshua Parens's and Joseph C. Macfarland's updated sourcebook (2011). In addition, consult Jacobs 2021. Something of particular interest to scholars has been the notion of "natural law," especially as it was developed in the scholastic setting and in canon law. On this see G. R. Evans 2014 and Anthony Lisska's important work (1998 and 2012).

One form of political violence that we have not discussed is war. All three monotheistic faiths have had to wrestle with whether the violence and destruction wrought by warfare is ever moral. Even if God explicitly sanctions it, as He seems to do on occasion in the Old Testament and the Quran, it is nevertheless true that most wars are initiated without any clear mandate from God. Are any of *these* wars moral? For a way into these issues, start with Russell 2014. In the Christian tradition, Saint Augustine is generally thought to be the father of what is now called Just War theory. In a fascinating article (1999), Robert Holmes examines this idea thoroughly. Holmes is keen to determine whether Augustine's views about the morality and legitimacy of war are consistent with his "interiority" and "personal pacifism."

When discussing Ibn Rushd's rebuttals of al-Ghazali's three main charges against the philosophers, I noted that there were some fascinating puzzles involving God's omniscience, simplicity, and immutability. For a classic contemporary statement of the issues, see Norman Kretzmann's "Omniscience and Immutability" (1966). For medieval discussions of some of these puzzles, consult the articles in Rudavsky 1985 as well as Father Wippel's study of Aquinas and Henry of Ghent (1984, 243–70). A famous medieval statement of the problem of divine foreknowledge and future contingents can be found in book 5 of Boethius's *Consolation of Philosophy*. For discussion of that presentation of the puzzle and its solution, see Marenbon 2003 and the shorter discussion in his 2007 (42–6). The solution that Boethius proposed has fascinated both medieval thinkers and contemporary philosophers of religion. William of Ockham's treatment of these issues (1983) is rigorous, thought-provoking, and extremely important, but be prepared and keep your wits about you, as Ockham's writings tend to be the sort of extremely complex version of the scholastic disputation that I warned you about in Chapter 1 (Section 1.3).

One of the central notions that Boethius employs when he is developing his solution to the problem of God's foreknowledge is an influential model of eternity. See Kukkonen 2012 for a discussion of this model as well as other medieval ways of conceiving eternity. When it comes to contemporary speculations on divine eternity that take their inspiration from Boethius, the *locus classicus* is a paper by Eleonore Stump and Norman Kretzmann 1981. Kukkonen's article can also get you started if you are interested in medieval discussions of the eternity of the universe.

8 From Here, Where?

8.1 Why Study the History of Philosophy?	267
8.2 Why Study Medieval Philosophy?	273
8.3 What Now?	274

You have now finished all the items on my tasting menu. I hope that you were delighted by at least some of the things I served, and perhaps you are interested in sampling more medieval philosophy. At the very least, I hope you can now see that many thinkers from these times and places offer interesting proposals. Sometimes they even seem to be speaking to us and our concerns. I selected the items on my menu in the hopes that they might resonate with you. I also picked things that excite me, because I believe that excitement is infectious. I warned you from the beginning that this would be an opinionated introduction to medieval philosophy; it is also a highly personal one.

At this point, however, you might be wondering whether I am trying too hard to make medieval philosophers relevant for us here and now. Isn't this a distortion of what they were up to? I hope you will agree that I in fact tried to let medieval philosophers speak for themselves, and at several points I acknowledged that medieval ways of looking at certain issues are quite different from the ways that we look at them. But then, you might start to wonder why we should be at all interested in these antiquated ways of thinking. I want to end this contemporary introduction by stepping back and addressing these concerns head on. I want to think about the value of the history of philosophy.

I could have addressed these issues in Chapter 1. But upon reflection, I thought it would be best if you first had some interactions with medieval philosophy. I don't think that anything I could have said at the beginning would have actually convinced you to continue to read the book. Moreover, now that you have some familiarity with medieval philosophy, I think

DOI: 10.4324/9780429348020-8

that my arguments about the purposes and value of historical work will be easier to make.

Once I have laid out my case for why I think the study of medieval philosophy is valuable, I want to quickly survey what work still needs to be done in the field of medieval philosophy and what you will need to do if you wish to pursue further study of medieval philosophy. One of the exciting things about the discipline is that there is a lot of very basic scholarship that still needs doing.

8.1 Why Study the History of Philosophy?

There are two questions to which every historian of medieval philosophy ought to have an answer. First and foremost, why study *medieval* philosophy? But secondly, and more generally, why study the history of philosophy at all? Let us begin by tackling the latter question, since it is logically prior. I will offer my answer by situating it among a panorama of possible attitudes one could take to historical philosophy. While I will focus on why, and for that matter, *whether* we should value philosophical works developed by people from the past, I trust that you will see how many of the positions and their supporting arguments can easily be modified in order to consider the questions whether and why we should value philosophical works produced by people from different cultures and intellectual traditions.

There was a time not too long ago when if you were studying in a typical American or British philosophy department, a common justification offered for why one should study historical figures is that they have some usefulness for how we presently philosophize. In many instances, it appears to be the case that historical figures were interested in problems that we still recognize as philosophical problems. Perhaps, then, their answers are still viable solutions. Consider those problems pertaining to universality and individuation that we considered in Chapter 3 (Section 3.2). The problems raised by medieval Aristotelians seem to be the same problems that still inspire and vex us today. We are still interested in whether our universal terms and concepts pick out entities of a certain sort. We are still interested in pinpointing what makes an individual thing an individual instance of a general kind. And the answers that Boethius (sixth century), Abelard (twelfth century), or Ockham (fourteenth century) give seem to have affinities with some of the viable twenty-first-century options that philosophers entertain. Therefore, we might be tempted to think that *this* is why we should read Boethius or Ockham. They might help us to identify the right solution to some perennial problem. Dominik Perler has called this the "Dialogue Model" (2018, 141). We treat historical figures as if they are "colleagues just down the hall."

The problem, as Perler and others have pointed out, is that this model diminishes our understanding and estimation of a historical figure and their milieu. The strange, the unusual, and the seemingly irrelevant features of a historical figure's position are overlooked. In some cases, this means that whole portions of a figure's *oeuvre* are ignored. Indeed, if followed to its logical conclusion, the Dialogue Model seems to entail an even stronger view. If the reason to study a historical author is for their utility for us, then if an author is not presently useful to us, we philosophers have no reason to give their work any heed. In short, it appears that the Dialogue Model reduces to what John Marenbon picturesquely describes as the "plunder approach" to the history of philosophy.

> Past philosophy is envisaged as an abandoned burnt-out city, from which there may be some stray items worth plundering. Their original function does not matter, so long as they can serve a purpose now.
>
> (2013, 203–4)

Both Perler and Marenbon argue that this is an impoverished approach to the history of philosophy. And I agree.

Still there appears to be *something* to the notion that historical philosophy is valuable because of what it can offer to us as we philosophize now. After all, why did you take an introductory course in philosophy? Was it because you thought that it might give you the tools for solving (if not the answers to) some of our most basic and burning questions? Did you want to know how best to live? Did you want to learn how to distinguish truth from falsity? Did you want to know how the world is really structured and what the meaning of it all is? I certainly did when I signed up for my first philosophy class. And one of the reasons why I keep coming back to historical works of philosophy is because I think that they can offer me some insights about the nature and purpose of my existence.

While I have tried to give our thinkers a chance to speak in their own voices, to indicate the ways in which medieval philosophers are embodied and embedded in their cultures and traditions, and to acknowledge when their problems were not precisely the ones that we focus on, I have been operating on the assumption that medieval philosophy is valuable *in part* because of what it can do for us now. Perhaps even this weaker assumption is unfounded. In another essay of his on the value of studying the history of philosophy, John Marenbon offers this challenge to the idea that *philosophy* is instrumentally valuable.

> I do not accept this high assessment of the instrumental value of philosophy, since philosophy has never reached firm, agreed conclusions

on which people could reliably base their manner of life, or a political society its structure; and there is no strong reason to believe that, instrumentally, philosophy has brought about or now brings about more good than harm – the obvious evidence points, indeed, to the opposite conclusion.

(2018, 38)

Think about some of the commonly held assumptions of medieval philosophers. We can see without too much effort how some of these assumptions and the conclusions that medieval thinkers drew from them would eventually mutate into justifications for some horrible actions and policies. The intelligentsia in many cases are the ones *supporting* state violence and other forms of oppression.

Marenbon goes on to argue that even if we grant that philosophy has instrumental value, it is not clear that *historical* philosophy does. Thinking of philosophy as instrumental encourages us to think of philosophy as if it were like one of the hard sciences (say, chemistry or physics). In the sciences, there seems to be progress in our understanding of, say, biological entities and their underlying chemistry or the composition of the celestial bodies that we observe from Earth. Old ideas and theories are overturned by new evidence. No one thinks that Aristotle's biology or meteorology has much to offer us now in terms of utility and the understanding of organisms or weather patterns.

None of that, of course, implies that Aristotle's biological works or Boyle's chemistry are not valuable. To the contrary, Aristotelian and early modern science is still thought to be worth studying in the academy. However, the ones who value it enough to study it are historians – or perhaps better, antiquarians – not practicing scientists, and they justify their study of it by pointing to its intrinsic value.

Sometimes we value things merely because they are old. They are monuments to human ingenuity and creativity, even if they no longer are useful for our daily lives. Even if someone buys an antique tool and *does* use it to produce something new, they and we often value those artisanal products precisely because they are made using an outmoded and inefficient technique. For instance, I know of people who print on old-fashioned printing presses and photographers who make daguerreotypes and ambrotypes with old camera setups and toxic chemicals. Print runs on antique printing presses are usually small in number, and thus the rarity of the printed bulletin or poster adds to its mystique and value. Daguerreotypes and ambrotypes are one-of-a-kind artifacts (and otherworldly in their beauty). Perhaps the same holds, or ought to hold, for historical philosophy. It is a monument to human creativity. In this case, however, it would seem silly for someone to practice philosophy in an outmoded way. Unlike artisanal posters or newly made daguerreotypes, there doesn't seem to be any value in practicing neo-Boethianism or neo-Ockhamism, or at least no *philosopher* should feel compelled to treat such a person as a serious philosophical interlocutor.

Inspired by a metaphor by Kurt Flasch, Perler calls this theory of valuation the "Rug Dealer Model" (2018, 144). On this model, historical texts are treated like fine, antique rugs. A dealer in old rugs can bring out a rug and describe it in all its fine internal detail. He is also expected to know details about its provenance and the processes that went into constructing it. In like manner, the historian of old philosophies pulls a text out of the library and details its contents in all its internal intricacies as well as its immediate historical context. But no attempt need be made to trace connections between this historical object and contemporary ideas and concerns. Indeed, this model appears to stress the radical *discontinuity* between the concerns of a historical author and our present-day concerns.

At certain points in his several meditations on the value of the history of philosophy, Marenbon says things that suggest that this might be an acceptable approach to historical material. He does take pains to add that in order to adequately understand a historical work of philosophy, historians of philosophy need to be "thoroughly at home in the world of philosophical argument"; otherwise, their work will not merely be insufficient as philosophy, it will be bad history (2018, 39). As a point of comparison, a military historian ought to have some sense of how a military functions, what the difference is between a strategy and tactics, and so forth. A historian of science ought to have some basic understanding of the science they are studying. But a military historian does not need to be a general and a historian of science does not need to be a practicing scientist. Likewise, a historian of philosophy does not need to be someone producing her own philosophical systems and arguments with an aim to furthering the discipline as it is now.

Yet, to be fair, I don't think that Marenbon fully endorses the Rug Dealer Model. It seems to me that he is not opposed to the idea that historical figures *might* be fruitfully put into dialogue with contemporary philosophy. His choice to fixate on the intrinsic merits of historical philosophy has a different purpose. He is primarily interested in steering us away from thinking that a historical figure's capacity to "speak to us" is their only value and he is rightfully worried about the possibility that the attempt to translate historical philosophy into languages that we find most comfortable might distort the true positions held by historical authors (see, e.g., Marenbon 2013, 206).

Perler is more emphatic in rejecting a thoroughgoing antiquarian approach to historical texts. And so, at this point, I will let him take the lead. He argues that the Rug Dealer Model's emphasis on discontinuities leaves us "imprisoned by history" (2018, 147). We are unable to determine whether a philosophical position or argument from a historical figure is any good as philosophy, nor does it seem to leave philosophers with any reason to see it as worth their time or effort. At this point, someone might say, "So much the worse for historical philosophy! Thanks, by the way, I never liked reading that stuff." Perler thinks that someone who says this is deeply mistaken. I do too.

For one thing, this sort of attitude seems to ignore the fact that all philosophy is embedded in a time, place, culture, and tradition. Moreover, it fails to appreciate that history is continuous. Even apparently radical leaps in our understanding of the world and ourselves, what have sometimes been referred to as "paradigm shifts," don't come out of nothing at all. These shifts are in addition quite rare, even rarer than often it is alleged. For instance, if we uncritically accept the rhetoric of Descartes and his followers, his philosophy would be one of those radical breaks from the past. But more and more scholars – and not only medievalists but also scholars trained to study seventeenth- and eighteenth-century philosophy – have come to see that whole new vistas for understanding Descartes and other early "modern" philosophers appear once we read their work as the "culmination" of intellectual processes and currents that started in antiquity and the Middle Ages (Marenbon 2007, 350). Culminations, however, can only be *culminations* of traditions and trends if these traditions and trends are continuous. Moreover, as Perler points out, the Rug Dealer Model encourages us to overlook the fact that there are certain problems that *do* arise over and over in different times and places, not necessarily in precisely the same manner, but still in ways that invite comparisons.

Perler's preferred model, which I too endorse, tries to blend the best aspects of the Dialogue and Rug Dealer Models while avoiding their shortcomings. The Dialogue Model appreciates the fact that there seem to be some continuities between the past and the present. It also gives us a clear understanding of why some historical figures are worth study. The Rug Dealer Model helps us to see, however, that despite the similarities and continuities, these historical figures are not our colleagues. We should not pretend that we are entering into a dialogue with contemporaries. There are aspects of historical philosophy that are strange and alien. This strangeness, however, is a virtue.

> The fact that we question our own assumptions leads to a double alienation effect: we distance ourselves not only from a theory elaborated in the 14th century, but also theories from our own time. We no longer subscribe [for example] to the seemingly natural view that every theory

of mental language should be part of a materialist framework, and we no longer uncritically participate in the project of "naturalising the mind". We rather become aware that this project is anchored in a larger metaphysical project, strongly influenced by current science, and we become open to serious alternatives.

(Perler 2018, 151)

You need not linger over the details of Perler's example of fourteenth-century theories of mental language (in particular, he focuses on Ockham's position), which is being contrasted with contemporary theories of Jerry Fodor and others. (However, I encourage you to go and read about it. The thesis, both in its medieval and its modern guises, that there is a language of thought is fascinating.) I think we can readily glean from this passage Perler's general point. It is the interplay of the familiar and the unfamiliar in a historical text which prompts us to recognize some of *our* unspoken assumptions and to cast a critical eye on them.

I don't believe that reading history is the only way that we can get critical distance from our own basic ways of thinking, but it is a particularly useful way to do it. We immediately perceive the distance between historical figures and ourselves. They are long dead. They are from different parts of the world. They write in different languages from the ones we use. It takes work and a healthy dose of sympathy and charitable reconstruction just to get them into a form where we can begin to recognize their affinities with us. When we recognize a little bit of us in them, it comes as a shock. That they then do not think exactly like we do about this or that issue prompts us to ask why they didn't see what we take to be so obvious.

I wholeheartedly agree that history is *also* intrinsically valuable. I like old objects, old art, and old ideas. If I had more money (and my partner's blessing), I would have more dusty leatherbound tomes on my shelves and ambrotypes hanging on my walls. They are indeed monuments to the seemingly limitless creativity of human beings. But I also believe that sometimes historical figures can talk to us. And what they have to say can prompt us to rethink what we take to be true and what we value. When I was deciding what to include and what to omit from this volume, I wanted to find places where you would recognize medieval thinkers and be tempted to engage in a conversation with them. All of this was in turn intended to entice you to enter through the door labeled "medieval philosophy" and perhaps even to take a course in the subject from one of my many friends and colleagues. But don't believe for a second that medieval figures are of interest solely because they can help us to address our concerns.

8.2 Why Study Medieval Philosophy?

As you can see, I have already started to address this question. If you read the Acknowledgments of this book, you will know that I took a long and winding path toward medieval philosophy. I decided to study medieval philosophy because these particular people spoke to me. I recognized a bit of me in them. But I was also fascinated by their otherness. I have been having conversations with them ever since.

What about you? My hope is that you had a similar moment of recognition mixed with alienation as you read this book. If not, that is okay. I encourage you to keep reading around in the history of philosophy. There may be another generation of philosophers who will speak to you.

At the very least, I hope that you now see that the medieval world is much more complicated than the usual stereotypes would suggest. Medieval thought is not something that the modern world had to overcome or replace. Quite the contrary. Many of our "modern" notions about political organization, toleration of diverging opinions, separation of religious and secular authority, animal rights, and punishment as therapy and rehabilitation, have ancient and medieval roots. If you read around in contemporary metaphysics, you might notice that an updated Aristotelianism is making a comeback – or at least it was for a time, like all historical movements, "neo-Aristotelianism" will ebb and flow in popularity.

One thing that I often hear both from non-philosophers and philosophers is that the medieval philosophers were hemmed in by religious authority, whether it be scripture or the church. We already encountered this thought in Chapter 1, and there we already began to consider the ways in which this myth, one propagated most notably by philosophers of the so-called Enlightenment, could distort our understanding of what medieval philosophers were up to. To be sure, the Middle Ages were religious ages. But then again, so were the seventeenth and eighteenth centuries. Moreover, even a casual perusal of "current events," that is, recent *history*, will reveal that our age is also a religious age. Here in particular I suspect – even hope – that many of you had that moment of faint recognition. Medieval developments in speculative theology, religious law, and mystical spiritualism have left deep imprints on our present understanding of our faiths. Historical research might help us to reevaluate what is taken to be obvious. Many of the allegedly "time honored," nonnegotiable elements in modern-day religions are not only conceivably contestable, history shows that they were *in fact* hotly disputed by serious yet devout individuals. Historical research, and especially research in medieval history, allows people of faith to retrace their steps and to reimagine what is possible.

8.3 What Now?

Suppose your interest is piqued. What is next? Start by reading in full the texts that I discuss in this book. In most cases, there is a good translation of the work in English. Make sure you read the translator's introduction. This will provide an orientation for the work in front of you, and it should also give you some indications where you might venture next. The Suggested Readings at the end of each chapter are generally secondary sources, but all of them will give you pointers to more primary texts as well as mountains of interpretative studies.

Suppose after even more reading and more coursework, you fall in love with medieval philosophy. What next? I and many of my fellow philosophers would only advise you to pursue a graduate-level degree in philosophy, or any field in the humanities and social sciences, if you cannot imagine having a flourishing life without knowing all you can about it. Graduate study is a long and sometimes lonely road, and it is certainly not for everyone. Also, as I write this, the academy as a whole is going through a number of changes. The financial models of universities are being disrupted. Curricula are being revisited and revised. The very notion that a college degree is essential for upward mobility is being challenged. One of the immediately tangible results of many of these changes and disruptions is that the traditional career path from untenured but full-time assistant professor to tenured full-time professor is becoming a much rarer thing. Pursue a graduate degree in philosophy (or religion, or history, or so on) because you love it. You might not – indeed, you probably will not – be so lucky as to have a position like the one that I presently have. You might call this pessimism. I call it going in with eyes wide open.

If you don't choose the academic route, there is still plenty that you can do to carry on a conversation with medieval thinkers. More and more medieval works are being translated into modern English. Even if you only had the ones currently available, you have a lifetime's worth of reading in your off hours. Being a "lay reader" can be enormously pleasurable and satisfying. I say this from experience. In my off hours, I read widely in other fields.

One of the exciting things about medieval history in general, and medieval philosophy in particular, is that there is much more that needs to be done before we will have anything close to an adequate understanding of the period and its peoples. There are still libraries full of manuscripts that we have not sorted through or appraised. Even some of the works of major figures have not been published in accordance with the stringent standards for critical editions. Moreover, there are large swathes of philosophical material that have been historically ignored because they were determined to be *un*philosophical. One of the most notorious instances of this is the vast body of contemplative, or mystical, literature, which just so happens to encompass most of the written work by women in the period (see Van Dyke 2018 and 2022).

If you are an undergraduate and think you want to study medieval philosophy as deep as it goes, perhaps even one day become a specialist in the field, my advice is that you start learning some languages. The sooner, the better. A good language to start with is Latin. This will be handy in most cases, and even if you pull up stakes and move to, say, seventeenth- and eighteenth-century European philosophy, competence in Latin will serve you well. A little knowledge of ancient Greek is helpful for serious study of any of the figures or traditions touched upon in this book. Solid competency in Greek will be essential if you want to explore the vast unknown that is Byzantine thought. (And I mean it when I say that Byzantine philosophy is *still* vastly understudied, despite several decade's worth of calls for more study of the period.) Medieval specialists of all stripes realize the importance of philosophy written in Arabic. If you wish to study Islamic mysticism and philosophy, you will need to know Arabic and ideally also medieval Persian dialects. If you want to study medieval Jewish philosophy, you will need Arabic and Hebrew. If you are interested in Christian contemplatives, you will probably need some competence in one or more of the many medieval vernacular languages. I don't mean to overwhelm or discourage you. But the state of things is such that there is no way to get by with English translations. No matter what historical period you work in, serious scholars are generally expected to be competent in the languages in which their authors write. So, if you want to do a deep dive into Kant, Nietzsche, or Wittgenstein, you need German. If you decide that serious study of Sartre or Simone de Beauvoir is the only thing that will give meaning to your existence, start learning your French.

Again, the last few paragraphs have been primarily directed at only a tiny subset of you. Most of you will not pursue medieval philosophy to any great depth. And as I have taken pains to stress, I see nothing wrong with this. I hope you have gotten something of value out of reading this book. I hope your curiosity to pursue new – or in this case, old – and unfamiliar books, art, cultures, and traditions persists and continues to grow. May your path from here take you to interesting, uplifting, challenging, and nourishing places.

Appendix
Timeline of People and Events

In this appendix, I have provided a timeline on which I plot the major protagonists in the story I have told here. I have also added a few other noteworthy figures, as well as some, but by no means all, of the significant historical and cultural transformations that were happening around them. For a recent highly accessible and refreshingly revisionist account of the Middle Ages, see Gabriele and Perry 2021. All dates refer to the Common Era (CE). A single date associated with an author indicates when that individual died. A small "c" (for the Latin word "circa") indicates that there is some uncertainty about dating and that the best scholars can provide is a rough estimate of when an author lived or died.

Protagonists	Major Events
St. Augustine (354–430)	**c. 361:** The West's first known monastic community was established in France by a man named Martin (MacCulloch 2009, 312–13).
Proclus (c. 416–85), an important "neo-Platonist." Portions of his *Elements of Theology* are translated into Arabic as the *Book of Causes* and attributed to Aristotle. The pseudo-Aristotelian *Book of Causes* is subsequently translated into Latin. Aquinas is one of the first to determine that it is not a work by Aristotle.	
Boethius (c. 475–c. 526)	**529:** The Roman Emperor Justinian (r. 527–65) closes the Academy in Athens. It is sometimes claimed that this precipitated an eastward migration of many important philosophers from Greece to the court of the Sassanid king Chosroes I. Recently some scholars have wondered whether Justinian's decree in 529 was as definitive and effective as the legend would suggest. We should be careful in making broad claims, such as that philosophy ceased to be practiced in the Greek-speaking world. Nevertheless, the event is a potent reminder of the antipathy that many powerful Christians felt toward Greek philosophy, and it remains a symbol of the very real and well-documented shift of intellectual energy and innovation to the Eastern Mediterranean and greater Persia.
Pseudo-Dionysius (fifth–sixth centuries), a mysterious author whose writings were sometimes thought to be by the Dionysius who is converted by St. Paul (Acts 17:34). The works draw heavily on Proclus's version of Platonism. The author's exposition of "negative theology" is extremely influential in both the Greek-speaking East and the Latin-speaking West.	
John Philoponus (c. 490–c. 570), an important Christian theologian and commentator on Aristotle's corpus.	

(Continued)

Protagonists	Major Events
John of Damascus (c. 655–c. 750), an important and influential Greek-speaking theologian and philosopher. Several of his writings were translated into Latin, and he was often cited as an authority in Western theological disputations.	**610:** Muhammad receives his first of many revelations while on retreat on Mount Hira. Tradition maintains that the first words Muhammad received were verses 1–5 of Quran, surah 96 (Al-'Alaq, or The Clot).
Abu Yusuf Ya'qub ibn Ishaq **al-Kindi** (c. 866), often credited with being the first Islamic philosopher (see Fakhry 2004, 67–95).	**630:** Mecca capitulates to Muhammad and his followers.
	632: Muhammad dies.
	By 661: The Sassanian empire centered in Persia has crumbled and large chunks of the Byzantine Empire have capitulated to the new regional power, which is now consolidated under the 'Umayyad Caliphate centered in Damascus.
	680: The caliph 'Ali's son and grandson of the Prophet, Hussain, is killed at Karbala (now part of present-day Iraq). This is one of the decisive moments in the gradual split between Sunnis and Shiites.
	750s to 900s: A massive translation effort is undertaken by the 'Abbasid caliphs, especially al-Mansur (r. 754–75) and his son al-Mahdi (r. 775–85). It is sometimes claimed that this activity centered around the "House of Wisdom" (*bayt al-hikma*). However, some recent scholars have questioned whether there was a unique institute that went by this name (Gutas 1998, 53–60).
	750s–800s: Under the patronage of Charlemagne (c. 742–814) and his heirs, there was what some scholars have referred to as a Carolingian Renaissance in the sciences. Identified most prominently with Alcuin (c. 740–804), we begin to see a renewed interest in the acquisition, copying, and study of logical and scientific works in Britain and Continental Europe.

Protagonists	Major Events
Al-Husayn ibn Mansur **al-Hallaj** (922)	
Abu Nasr Muhammad ibn Muhammad **al-Farabi** (950)	
The Brethren of Purity (*Ikhwan al-Safa*), a mysterious collective of intellectuals centered around Baghdad and Basra in the ninth century.	
Sa'adya Gaon (892–942), a Jewish theologian of note. Author of the *Book of Doctrines and Beliefs*.	
Isaac Israeli (855–955), a Jewish Platonist.	
Abu 'Ali al-Husayn ibn 'Abd Allah **ibn Sina** (aka Avicenna, 980–1037)	
Solomon **ibn Gabirol** (1021/2–1057/8)	
St. Anselm of Canterbury (1033–1109)	**1095:** Pope Urban II convinced the secular powers in Western Europe to inaugurate the first of several "crusades" to liberate the Holy Land. The first crusade was relatively successful. Western soldiers captured Jerusalem in 1099 and they were, for a time, able to establish a Latin kingdom there.
Abu Hamid Muhammad ibn Muhammad **al-Ghazali** (c. 1058–1111)	
Ibn Bajja (1139)	
Peter Abelard (1079–1142)	
Jehuda Halevi (c. 1075–c. 1141), Jewish theologian and poet, author of the *Kuzari*.	**Early to mid-1100s:** The so-called Twelfth-century Renaissance in France. During this period, there are numerous advances in the arts and sciences. In philosophy, there is a quantum leap forward in sophistication, especially in the fields of logic and the philosophy of language.
Peter Lombard (c. 1160–64), author of the *Book of Sentences*, which subsequently becomes the standard theology textbook in European universities. Eventually, Aquinas's *Summa Theologiae* supplants Lombard's *Sentences* as the theology students' principal textbook, but this does not begin to happen until the sixteenth century (Marenbon 2007, 245–6).	
	1130–50: James of Venice translates several important works of Aristotle from Greek into Latin.
John of Salisbury (c. 1115–80)	**1150s:** Toledo in Spain becomes a center of translation for Arabic scientific and philosophical into Latin. Famous translators: Gerard of Cremona (d. 1187) worked in Toledo starting from at least 1157. Dominicus Gundissalinus (c. 1190–3) moves to Toledo in 1162 and joins a
Abu Bakr Muhammad **ibn Tufayl** (c. 1110–85)	
Abu Walid ibn Ahmad ibn Muhammad **ibn Rushd** (Averroes, c. 1126–98)	

(Continued)

Protagonists	Major Events
Maimonides (1138–1204)	team of translators, including Abraham ibn Daud and John of Spain. Together, they are responsible for translating Solomon Ibn Gabirol's *Fountain of Life* and Ibn Sina's *Metaphysics* and *On the Soul*. Gundissalinus also wrote his own philosophical treatises where he attempted to meld twelfth-century Latin speculation with the new ideas he found in Ibn Gabirol and Ibn Sina (Polloni 2020).
	1187: Jerusalem is captured by Saladin. Subsequent Christian campaigns in the Holy Land end with less than spectacular results. A campaign in 1204, the Fourth Crusade, which was originally aimed at Egypt, turns instead on Constantinople, thus ruining any chances of a reunion of the Byzantine and Roman Catholic Churches (MacCulloch 2009, 385 and 473–9). The crusades drain the wealth and human power of Western Europe and it sometimes contributes to tensions between secular powers and the papacy.
Muhyi al-Din ibn al 'Arabi (1165–1240), important Spanish Sufi mystic.	**1200:** Charter of Paris University gives all students at the university some of the rights of clerics.
Albert the Great (1280)	**1204:** "Legatine Ordinance" is issued to resolve a dispute about the immunity of students, as clerics, from punishment by the civic authorities. It "marks the real beginning of Oxford's institutional university structure" (Marenbon 2007, 206).
Thomas Aquinas (1124/5–1274)	
St. Bonaventure (c. 1217–74)	
John Blund (1248)	
Hadewijch (thirteenth century)	**1220s on:** The Mongols begin to raid the eastern edges of the 'Abbasid Empire. These raids quickly disrupt the economy in Transoxonia, Iran, and other eastern regions, and it hastens the disintegration of the 'Abbasid caliphate. In 1258, Mongols sack the 'Abbasid capitol Baghdad. By the 1250s, the Mongols convert to Islam and over time many of their *khans* become patrons of art, literature, and science.
Peter of Spain (fl. 1230s–1240s), author of the *Summulae Logicales*, a widely used textbook on logic.	
	1230s–1250s: The mendicant orders, especially the members of the orders founded by St. Francis (1226) and St. Dominic (1221), had a profound influence

Protagonists	Major Events
	on the trajectory of philosophy in the Latin-speaking West. Many of the major figures in scholastic thought are either Dominicans (e.g., Albert the Great, Thomas Aquinas) or Franciscans (Henry of Ghent, John Duns Scotus, William of Ockham). The rise in visibility and influence of the mendicant orders in the burgeoning universities of Western Europe makes some worried. In particular, the "secular" teachers at Paris are concerned that the mendicant teachers destroying their monopoly on the profession. The secular masters go on strike in 1229–30. But this and other maneuvers fail to turn the tide. Roland of Cremona (1259) becomes the first mendicant master of Theology at Paris, soon thereafter Alexander of Hales (1245), who is already in a teaching post as a secular master, joins the Franciscan order in 1231. By 1254, only three out of fifteen chairs of theology are held by secular masters (Marenbon 2007, 210). **1260–1286:** William of Moerbeke, a Dominican, goes through and revises all the existing translations of Aristotle. He then translates for the first time the remainder of the Aristotelian corpus into Latin. His translations become the standard versions for all but the logical works, where Boethius's translations are still used. **1277:** The perceived threat from non-Christian philosophies prompts the authorities at the University of Paris to draw up several lists of condemned propositions. Teachers at the University are prohibited from endorsing these theses. The list of propositions circulated in 1277 is the most prominent of a series of such condemnations that appear around this time. **1290:** Edward I orders the expulsion of the entire Jewish population (estimated to be around 3,000 people) from England.

(Continued)

Protagonists	Major Events
Gersonides (Levi ben Gerson, 1288–1344), an important Jewish philosopher who lived in Provence, which at the time is a lively center of Jewish culture in the Western Christian world.	**c. 1300 (to c. 1700):** The "Little Ice Age" ravages Europe causing crop failures and famine. **1302:** Boniface VIII issues a papal bull in which he claims ultimate political jurisdiction over the entire world.
Marguerite Porete (1310)	**1309:** Pope Clement V moves the seat of papal authority from Rome to Avignon.
Meister Eckhart (1260–1327)	
William of Ockham (c. 1287–1347)	**1320s:** Pope John XXII engages in a controversy with the Franciscans over the issue of poverty. William of Ockham and others deem John a heretic.
John Buridan (1295/1300–1358/61)	
Gregory Palamas (1296–1359), Byzantine theologian, important for understanding developments in Trinitarian thought in the Eastern Church.	**1346–48:** The apex of the global pandemic known as the Black Death. There are subsequent flare-ups of the bubonic plague throughout the remainder of the fourteenth century. It is estimated that roughly one-third of Europe's population perished during the Black Death.
Catherine of Siena (1347–80)	
John Wyclif (c. 1325–84), an important English philosopher and theologian.	
Hasdai Crescas (c. 1340–c. 1410/11), the head of the Jewish community in Aragon in Christian Spain. He was a forceful critic of various aspects of Aristotelian philosophy.	**1377:** Gregory XI moves the seat of papal authority back to Rome; however, the schism in the Church is not fully repaired until 1417, when all factions recognize Martin V as the newly elected pope (MacColloch 2009, 558–60).
Christine de Pizan (c. 1365–c. 1429), author of *The Book of the City of Ladies*, a defense of the intellectual abilities of women.	**1453:** The city of Constantinople, longtime capital of the Eastern Roman Empire, falls to the Ottomans.
Nicholas of Cusa (1401–64)	**1492:** Fall of Granada to the combined forces of the Christian kingdoms of Aragon and Castile. Muslim rule in Spain has now definitively ended. In October of the same year, Christopher Columbus makes landfall in the Americas.
Marsilio Ficino (1433–99), translator of Plato's and Plotinus's works into Latin and author of several important works, including commentaries on Platonic works and his multivolume *Platonic Theology*. Usually considered a Renaissance philosopher, but a close reading of his works shows his deep debt to Aquinas and scholastic philosophy more generally.	

Protagonists	Major Events
'A'ishah al-Ba'uniyyah (1517)	
Martin Luther (1483–1546)	
St. Teresa of Avila (1515–82), a celebrated mystic.	c. 1503–16: Leonardo da Vinci paints the *Mona Lisa*.
Giordano Bruno (1548–1600)	
Francisco Suarez (1548–1617)	
Mulla Sadra (Sadr al-Din al-Shirazi, 1641)	**1632:** Galileo publishes his *Dialogue Concerning Two Chief World Systems*.
René Descartes (1596–1650)	**1687:** The first edition of Isaac Newton's *Principia Mathematica* is published.
Gottfried Wilhelm Leibniz (1646–1716), a prominent and very influential "early modern" philosopher and mathematician. Many scholars nowadays point to the Aristotelian elements in his philosophy.	

Bibliography

Note about format: I have tried to list primary source authors as they typically appear in the bibliographies and indices of resources that you are most likely to go to next. It is the standard practice of medievalists to list medieval Latin authors... but not necessarily non-Latin authors... by their surname. Thus, look for texts by Buridan under "John Buridan" and those by Aquinas under "Thomas Aquinas", but Muhammad al-Ghazali under "Ghazali" and not "Muhammad". One reason for this practice is that in many cases the commonly used "last name" is not in fact a family name, but rather a description of some sort, such as a description of where they came from. For instance, John Duns Scotus is not from the Scotus family, but rather "Scotus" refers to the fact that he is a "Scot". This not universally true. Peter Abelard was born in Le Pallet (c. 1079), on the frontier of Brittany. And for that matter, "ibn Tufayl" and "al-Ghazali" are not technically last names either. The word "ibn" just means "son of" and "al-Ghazali" might either mean "the spinner", i.e., a professional designation, or it could be a place name, such as for Ghazala, which is a village near Tus (Ormsby 2008, 22). This of course has not stopped scholars from using all sorts of shorthand in their writings. I follow the lead of numerous scholars when I talk about Abelard, Scotus, and Ghazali. On top of this, even today scholars of Arabic philosophy will often refer to Arabic authors by their Latinate names, such as Avicenna, instead of Abu 'Ali al-Husyan ibn 'Abd Allah ibn Sina. In short, medieval scholarship and bibliographies can be disorienting to those new to the field. I have tried to signal some cases where you should look elsewhere in this bibliography, but not necessarily for all primary source authors. So, if at first you fail to find a reference, try searching under a different part of the author's name.

Abelard. See Peter Abelard.
Adamson, Peter. 2016. *Philosophy in the Islamic World: A History of Philosophy without Any Gaps,* vol. 3. Oxford/New York: Oxford University Press.
———. 2019. *Medieval Philosophy: A History of Philosophy without Any Gaps,* vol. 4. Oxford/New York: Oxford University Press.

Adamson, Peter, and Richard C. Taylor. eds. 2005. *The Cambridge Companion to Arabic Philosophy*. Cambridge: Cambridge University Press.

'Ajiba, Ahmad ibn. 2011. *The Book of Ascension to the Essential Truths of Sufism: Mi'raj al-tashawwuf ila haqa'iq al tasawwuf, A Lexicon of Sufic Terminology*. Translated by Mohamed Fouad Aresmouk and Michael Abdurrahman Fitzgerald. Louisville, KY: Fons Vitae.

Alan of Lille. 2013. *Literary Works*. Edited and translated by Winthrop Wetherbee. Dumbarton Oaks Medieval Library, vol. 22. Cambridge, MA/London: Harvard University Press.

Albert the Great. 1968. *De anima*. Edited by C. Stroick. Alberti Magni Opera Omnia, vol. 7.1. Münster: Aschendorff.

———. 1993. *De causis et processu universitatis a prima causa*. Edited by W. Fauser. Alberti Magni Opera Omnia, vol. 17.2. Münster: Institutum Alberti Magni Coloniense.

———. 2008. *De homine*. Edited by H. Anzulewicz and J. R. Söder. Alberti Magni Opera Omnia, vol. 27.2. Münster: Aschendorff.

Amerini, Fabrizio. 2013. *Aquinas on the Beginning and End of Human Life*. Translated by Mark Henninger. Cambridge, MA: Harvard University Press.

Angela of Foligno. 1993. *The Complete Works*. Translated by Paul LaChance. New York/Mahwah, NJ: Paulist Press.

Anselm. 1995. *Monologion and Proslogion, with the Replies of Gaunilo and Anselm*. Translate by Thomas Williams. Indianapolis, IN: Hackett.

Aristotle. 1957. *On the Soul, Parva Naturalia, On Breath*. Revised edition. Translated by W. S. Hett. Loeb Classical Library, vol. 288. Cambridge, MA: Harvard University Press.

———. 1984. *The Complete Works of Aristotle: The Revised Oxford Translation*. Edited by Jonathan Barnes. Princeton: Princeton University Press.

Arlig, Andrew. 2009. "The Metaphysics of Individuals in the *Opuscula Sacra*." Pp. 129–54 in *The Cambridge Companion to Boethius*, edited by John Marenbon. Cambridge: Cambridge University Press.

———. 2019. "Medieval Mereology." In *The Stanford Encyclopedia of Philosophy* (Fall 2019 edition), edited by Edward N. Zalta. URL = <https://plato.stanford.edu/archives/fall2019/entries/mereology-medieval/>

———. 2021. "Identity and Sameness." Pp. 126–38 in *The Routledge Companion to Medieval Philosophy*, edited by Richard Cross and JT Paasch. New York/London: Routledge.

———. 2022. "Abelard and Other Twelfth-Century Thinkers on Social Constructions." *Philosophies* 7, no. 4: 84. https://doi.org/10.3390/philosophies7040084

Armstrong, D. M. 2018. *Universals: An Opinionated Introduction*. New York: Routledge [originally published by Westview, 1989].

Augustine. 2019. *The Confessions*. Translated by Thomas Williams. Indianapolis, IN: Hackett.

Averroes. 1954. *Averroes' Tahafut al-Tahafut (The Incoherence of the Incoherence)*. Translated by Simon Van Den Bergh. 2 volumes. London: The Trustees of the "E. J. W. Gibb Memorial".

———. 2001a. *Decisive Treatise and Epistle Dedicatory*. Translated by Charles E. Butterworth. Provo, UT: Brigham Young University Press.

———. 2001b. *Faith and Reason in Islam: Averroes' Exposition of Religious Arguments*. Translated by Ibrahim Najjar. Oxford: Oneworld.
Avicenna. 1972. *Liber de Anima, seu sextus de Naturalibus*. I-II-II. Edited by S. Van Riet. Louvain: E. Peeters/Leiden: Brill.
———. 2005. *The Metaphysics of 'The Healing'*. Translated by Michael E. Marmura. Provo, UT: Brigham Young University Press.
al-Ba'uniyyah, 'A'ishah. 2014. *The Principles of Sufism*. Translated by T. H. Emil Homerin. New York: New York University Press.
al-Biruni, Abu Rayhan. 2020. *The Yoga Sutras of Patanjali*. Translated by Mario Kozah. New York: New York University Press.
Black, Antony. 2014. "Religious Authority and the State." Pp. 539–50 in *The Cambridge History of Medieval Philosophy*, vol. 2, edited by Robert Pasnau with Christina Van Dyke. Revised edition. Cambridge: Cambridge University Press.
Black, Deborah L. 2005. "Psychology: soul and intellect." Pp. 308–26 in *The Cambridge Companion to Arabic Philosophy*, edited by Peter Adamson and Richard C. Taylor. Cambridge: Cambridge University Press.
———. 2006. "Knowledge (*'ilm*) and Certitude (*yaqin*) in al-Farabi's Epistemology," *Arabic Sciences and Philosophy* 16: 11–45.
Boethius. 1906. *In Isagogen Porphyrii Commenta*. Edited by G. Schepss and S. Brandt. Corpus Scriptorum Ecclesiasticorum Latinorum, vol. 48. Vienna/Leipzig: F. Tempsky/G. Freytag.
———. 1973. *The Theological Tractates/The Consolation of Philosophy*. Edited and translated by H. F. Stewart, E. K. Rand, and S. J. Tester. Loeb Classical Library vol. 74. Cambridge, MA: Harvard University Press.
———. 1978. *De topicis differentiis*. Translated by Eleonore Stump. Ithaca, NY/London: Cornell University Press.
———. 1998. *De divisione liber*. Edited and translated by John Magee. Philosophia Antiqua, vol. 77. Leiden/Boston/Koln: Brill.
Bonaventure. 1885. *Lectures on the "Sentences" of Peter Lombard*, Book 2, Distinction 3, Article 1, Question 1. Pp 89–91 in *S. Bonaventurae Opera Omnia*, vol. 2, edited by Collegii a. S. Bonaventura, Quaracchi: Collegii S. Bonaventurae.
Brethren of Purity. See Goodman and McGregor 2009.
Brouwer, René. 2019. "Funerals, Faces, and Hellenistic Philosophers: On the Origins of the Concept of Person in Rome." Pp. 19–45 in *Persons: A History*, edited by Antonia Lolordo. New York/Oxford: Oxford University Press.
Brower, Jeffrey E. 2014. *Aquinas's Ontology of the Material World: Change, Hylomorphism, and Material Objects*. Oxford: Oxford University Press.
Burnett, Charles. 2005. "Arabic into Latin: The Reception of Arabic Philosophy into Western Europe." Pp. 370–404 in *The Cambridge Companion to Arabic* Philosophy, Peter Adamson and Richard C. Taylor. Cambridge: Cambridge University Press.
Butterworth, Charles E. 2005. "Ethical and Political Philosophy." Pp. 266–86 in *The Cambridge Companion to Arabic Philosophy*, edited by Peter Adamson and Richard C. Taylor. Cambridge: Cambridge University Press.
Calcidius. 2016. *On Plato's "Timaeus"*. Edited and translated by John Magee. Dumbarton Oaks Medieval Library, vol. 41. Cambridge, MA/London: Harvard University Press.

Casuto, Michael F. 2014. "Poverty." Pp. 577–92 in *The Cambridge History of Medieval Philosophy*, vol. 2, edited by Robert Pasnau with Christina Van Dyke. Revised edition. Cambridge: Cambridge University Press.

Catherine of Siena. 1980. *The Dialogue*. Translated by Suzanne Noffke, O. P. New York/Mahwah, NJ: Paulist Press.

Celano, Anthony. 2021. "Reasons and Actions." Pp. 336–44 in *The Routledge Companion to Medieval* Philosophy, edited by Richard Cross and JT Paasch. New York/London: Routledge.

Chittick, William C. 1989. *The Sufi Path of Knowledge: Ibn al-'Arabi's Metaphysics of Imagination*. Albany, NY: State University of New York Press.

———. 1998. *The Self-Disclosure of God: Principles of Ibn al-'Arabi's Cosmology*. Albany, NY: State University of New York Press.

Chisholm, Roderick. 1976. *Person and Object*, LaSalle, IL: Open Court Publishing.

Corbin, Henry. 2014. *History of Islamic Philosophy*. Translated by Liadain Sherrard with Philip Sherrard. London and New York: Routledge [orig. pub. Kegan Paul Intl., 2006].

Cory, Therese Scarpelli. 2013. *Aquinas on Human Self-Knowledge*. Cambridge: Cambridge University Press.

Cross, Richard, and J. T. Paasch, eds. 2021. *The Routledge Companion to Medieval Philosophy*. New York/London: Routledge.

Dawkins, Richard. 1976. *The Selfish Gene*. Oxford: Oxford University Press.

De Boer, Sander. 2012. "Radulphus Brito's Commentary on Aristotle's *De anima*." *Vivarium* 50: 245–353.

De Callatay, Godefroid. 2005. *Ikhwan al-Safa: A Brotherhood of Idealists on the Fringe of Orthodox Islam*. Oxford: Oneworld.

Descartes, René. 1984. *The Philosophical Writings of Descartes*. 2 volumes. Translated by J. Cottingham, R. Stoothhoff, and D. Murdoch. Cambridge: Cambridge University Press.

DeYoung, Rebecca Konyndyk, Colleen McCluskey, and Christina Van Dyke. 2009. *Aquinas's Ethics: Metaphysical Foundations, Moral Theory, and Theological Context*. Notre Dame, IN: University of Notre Dame Press.

Diagne, Souleymane Bachir. 2018. *Open to Reason: Muslim Philosophers in Conversation with the Western Tradition*. New York: Columbia University Press.

Druart, Thérèse-Anne. 1987. "Al-Farabi and Emanationism." Pp. 23–43 in *Studies in Medieval Philosophy*, edited by John F. Wippel. Washington, DC: The Catholic University of America Press.

Dunlop, Douglas M., ed. and trans. 1955. "Al-Farabi's Introductory Sections on Logic." *The Islamic Quarterly* 2: 264–82.

———. 1957. "Al-Farabi's Introductory *Risalah* on Logic." *The Islamic Quarterly* 3: 224–35.

———. 1957/59. "Al-Farabi's Paraphrase of the *Categories* of Aristotle." *The Islamic Quarterly* 4: 168–97 and 5: 21–54.

Epicurus. 1926. *The Extant Remains*. Edited and translated by Cyril Bailey. Oxford: The Clarendon Press.

Epstein, Brian. 2018. "Social Ontology." *The Stanford Encyclopedia of Philosophy* (Summer 2018 edition), edited by Edward N. Zalta. URL = <https://plato.stanford.edu/archives/sum2018/entries/social-ontology/> [originally published 2018; accessed: January 2021]

Evans, G. R. 2014. "Law and Nature." Pp. 565–76 in *The Cambridge History of Medieval Philosophy*, vol. 2, edited by Robert Pasnau with Christina Van Dyke. Revised edition. Cambridge: Cambridge University Press.

Fakhry, Majid. 2004. *A History of Islamic Philosophy*. 3rd edition. New York: Columbia University Press [original: 1970].

Farabi, Abu Nasr Muhammad al-. 1969. *Alfarabi: Philosophy of Plato and Aristotle*. Revised edition. Translated by Muhsin Mahdi. Ithaca, NY: Cornell University Press.

———. 1985. *On the Perfect State (Mabadi' ara' ahl al-madinat al-fadilah)*. Edited and translated by Richard Walzer. Oxford: Oxford University Press [reprinted by Great Books of the Islamic World, Inc. (Chicago, IL: KAZI Publications), 1998].

———. 2001. *Enumeration of the Sciences* (partial translation), in Alfarabi, *The Political Writings: "Selected Aphorisms" and Other Texts*. Translated by Charles E. Butterworth. Ithaca: Cornell University Press.

———. 2011. *The Political Regime* (partial). Translated by Charles E. Butterworth. Pp 36–55 in Parens, Joshua, and Joseph C. Macfarland, eds., *Medieval Political Philosophy: A Sourcebook*. 2nd revised edition. Ithaca, NY: Cornell University Press, 2011.

Ficino, Marsilio. 2002. *Platonic Theology*. vol. 2, books V–VIII. Latin text edited by James Hankins. English translation by Michael J. B. Allen. Cambridge, MA/London: I Tatti Renaissance Library, Harvard University Press.

Foltz, Bruce V., ed. 2019. *Medieval Philosophy: A Multicultural Reader*. London/New York: Bloomsbury Academic.

Frank, Richard M. 1978. *Beings and their Attributes: The Teaching of the Basrian School of the Mu'tazila in the Classical Period*. Albany, NY: State University of New York Press.

———. 1984. "Bodies and Atoms: The Ash'arite Analysis." Pp. 39–53 in *Islamic Theology and Philosophy*, edited by Michael E. Marmura. Albany, NY: State University of New York Press.

Fricker, Miranda. 2007. *Epistemic Injustice: Power and the Ethics of Knowing*. Oxford: Oxford University Press.

Gabriele, Matthew, and David M. Perry. 2021. *The Bright Ages: A New History of Medieval Europe*. New York: HarperCollins.

Galluzzo, Gabriele. 2013. *The Medieval Reception of Book Zeta of Aristotle's "Metaphysics"*, Vol. 1: *Aristotle's Ontology and the Middle Ages: The Tradition of "Met.", Book Zeta*. Studien und Texte zur Geistesgeschichte des Mittelalters 110/1. Leiden: Brill.

Gardet, L. 2008. " 'Ilm al-Kalam." *Encyclopedia of Islam*. Edited by P. Bearman, Th. Bianquis, C. E. Bosworth, E. van Donzel, and W. P. Heinrichs. Brill. Brill Online.

Gettier, Edmund L. 1963. "Is Justified True Belief Knowledge?" *Analysis* 23: 121–123.

Ghazali, Abu Hamid al-. 1980. *Deliverance from Error: Five Key Texts Including His Spiritual Autobiography "al-Munqidh min al-Dalal"*. Translated by R. J. McCarthy. Louisville, KY: Fons Vitae, no date [originally published as *Freedom and Fulfillment*. Twayne Publishers, 1980].

———. 1998. *The Niche of Lights*. Translated by David Buchman. Provo, UT: Brigham Young University Press.

———. 2000. *The Incoherence of the Philosophers*. Translated by Michael E. Marmura. 2nd edition. Provo, UT: Brigham Young University Press [1st edition: 1997].

———. 2016. *Love, Longing, Intimacy and Contentment* (*Kitab al-mahabba wa'l-shawq wa'l-uns wa'l-rida*): *Book XXXVI of The Revival of the Religious Sciences* (*Ihya' 'ulum al-din*). Translated by Eric Ormsby. 2nd edition. Cambridge: Islamic Texts Society.

Ghazzali, Ahmad. 1986. *Sawanih: Inspirations from the World of Pure Spirits*. Translated by Nasrollah Pourjavady. Lahore: Suhail Academy/London: Routledge & Kegan Paul.

Gohlman, William E., ed. and trans. 1974. *The Life of Ibn Sina: A Critical Edition and Annotated Translation*. Albany, NY: SUNY Press.

Goodman, Lenn E., and Richard McGregor, eds. and trans. 2009. *The Case of the Animals versus Man Before the King of the Jinn: An Arabic Critical Edition and English Translation of Epistle 22*. Epistles of the Brethren of Purity, 22. Oxford: Oxford University Press in association with The Institute of Ismaili Studies.

Gracia, Jorge J. E. 1984. *Introduction to the Problem of Individuation in the Early Middle Ages*. Washington, DC: Catholic University of America Press [2nd edition: Philosophia Verlag, 1988].

Gracia, Jorge J. E., ed. 1994. *Individuation in Scholasticism: The Later Middle Ages and the Counter-Reformation, 1150–1650*. Albany, NY: SUNY Press.

Gracia, Jorge J. E., and Timothy B. Noone, eds. 2003. *A Companion to Philosophy in the Middle Ages*. Malden, MA/Oxford: Blackwell.

Griffel, Frank. 2009. *Al-Ghazali's Philosophical Theology*. Oxford/New York: Oxford University Press.

Gutas, Dimitri. 1998. *Greek Thought, Arabic Culture: The Graeco-Arabic Translation Movement in Baghdad and Early 'Abbasid Society (2nd–4th/8th–10th centuries)*. New York: Routledge.

Hadewijch. 1980. *The Complete Works*. Translated by Mother Columba Hart O. S. B. Mahwah, NJ: Paulist Press.

Halkin, Abraham and David Hartman. 1985. *Crisis and Leadership: Epistles of Maimonides*. Philadelphia/New York/Jerusalem: Jewish Publication Society of America.

al-Hallaj. Husayn ibn Mansur. 2018. *Hallaj: Poems of a Sufi Martyr*. Translated by Carl W. Ernst. Evanston, IL: Northwestern University Press.

Harris, Nigel. 2020. *The Thirteenth-Century Animal Turn: Medieval and Twenty-First-Century Perspectives*. Cham, Switzerland: Palgrave Macmillan.

Hause, Jeffrey. 2018. "Merciful Demand: Fraternal Correction as a Form of Blame." *Oxford Studies in Medieval Philosophy* 6: 144–67.

Hirvonen, Vesa. 2021. "Emotions." Pp. 242–48 in *The Routledge Companion to Medieval Philosophy*, edited by Richard Cross and JT Paasch. New York/London: Routledge.

Hoffmann, Tobias. 2021. "Freedom." Pp. 317–35 in *The Routledge Companion to Medieval Philosophy*, edited by Richard Cross and JT Paasch. New York/London: Routledge.

Holmes, Robert L. 1999. "St. Augustine and the Just War Theory." Pp. 323–44 in *The Augustinian Tradition*, edited by pp. Gareth B. Matthews. Berkeley/Los Angeles/London: University of California Press.

Homerin, Th. Emil, trans. 2011. *Emanations of Grace: Mystical Poems by 'A'ishah al-Ba'uniyah (d. 923/1517)*. Louisville, KY: Fons Vitae.

Homerin, Th. Emil. 2019. *Aisha al-Ba'uniyya: A Life in Praise of Love*. Oxford: Oneworld Academic.

Hourani, George F., trans. 1961. *Averroes on the Harmony of Religion and Philosophy*. London: Luzac & Co. for the E. J. W. Gibb Memorial Trust [reprint 1976].

Hughes, Christopher. 2002. "Matter and Actuality in Aquinas." Pp. 61–76 in *Thomas Aquinas: Contemporary Philosophical Perspectives*, edited by Brian Davies. Oxford/New York: Oxford University Press.

al-Hujwiri, 'Ali ibn 'Uthman al-Jullari. 1959. *The Kashf al-Mahjub: The Oldest Persian Treatise on Sufism*. New edition. Translated by Reynold A. Nicholson. London: Luzac and Company.

Hyman, Arthur. 1987. "Maimonides on Creation and Emanation." Pp. 45–61 in *Studies in Medieval Philosophy*, edited by John F. Wippel. Washington, DC: The Catholic University of America Press.

Ibn Kammuna. See Perlmann 1971.

Ibn Rushd. See Averroes.

Ibn Sina. See Avicenna.

Ibn Tufayl. 1991/2009. *Hayy ibn Yaqzan: A Philosophical Tale*. Translated by Lenn Evan Goodman. 3rd edition. Los Angeles: gee tee bee, 1991; reprinted with new preface and bibliography, University of Chicago Press, 2009.

Ichikawa, Jonathan Jenkins, and Matthias Steup. 2018. "The Analysis of Knowledge." *The Stanford Encyclopedia of Philosophy*, edited by Edward N. Zalta. URL = <https://plato.stanford.edu/archives/sum2018/entries/knowledge-analysis/> [originally published in 2012, last modified 2018; accessed: January 2021]

Jacobs, Jonathan. 2021. "Law and Government." Pp. 377–93 in *The Routledge Companion to Medieval Philosophy*, edited by Richard Cross and J. T. Paasch. New York/London: Routledge.

Jackson, Sherman A. 2002. *On the Boundaries of Theological Tolerance in Islam: Abu Hamid al-Ghazali's "Faysal al-Tafriqa"*. Karachi/Oxford/New York: Oxford University Press.

Jaffer, Tariq. 2003. "Bodies, Souls, and Resurrection in Avicenna's *Ar-Risala al-Adhawiya fi Amr al-Ma'ad*." Pp. 163–74 in *Before and After Avicenna: Proceedings of the First Conference of the Avicenna Study Group*, edited by David C. Reisman with Ahmed H. al-Rahim. Leiden/Boston: Brill.

Jehuda Halevi. 1947. *Kuzari: The Book of Proof and Argument*. Translated by Isaak Heinemann. Oxford: East and West Library.

John Blund. 1970. *Tractatus de Anima*. Edited by D. A. Callus O.P. and R. W. Hunt. London: published for The British Academy by Oxford University Press.

John Buridan. 1984. *Quaestiones in De Anima (ultima lectura)*, book 2. In P. G. Sobol, *John Buridan on the Soul and Sensation. An Edition of Book II of His Commentary on Aristotle's Book on the Soul with an Introduction and a Translation of Question 18 on Sensible Species*, unpublished doctoral thesis, Indiana University.

———. 2001. *Summulae de Dialectica*. Translated by Gyula Klima. New Haven, CT: Yale University Press.

———. 2010. *Quaestiones super libros De generatione et corruptione Aristotelis*. Edited by M. Streijger, P. J. J. M. Bakker, and J. M. M. H. Thijssen. Leiden/Boston: Brill.

John of Salisbury. 1990. *Policraticus*. Edited and translated by Cary J. Nederman. Cambridge/New York: Cambridge University Press.
Kant, Immanuel. 1998. *Groundwork of the Metaphysics of Morals*. Edited by Mary Gregor. Cambridge: Cambridge University Press.
Kellner, Menachem Marc. 1982. "Maimonides's Thirteen Principles and the Structure of the 'Guide of the Perplexed'." *Journal of the History of Philosophy* 20: 76–84.
Kenny, Anthony, and Jan Pinborg. 1982. "Medieval Philosophical Literature." Pp. 11–42 in *The Cambridge History of Later Medieval Philosophy*, edited by Norman Kretzmann, Anthony Kenny, and Jan Pinborg. Cambridge and New York: Cambridge University Press.
al-Kindi. 2012. *The Philosophical Works of Al-Kindi*. Translated by Peter Adamson and Peter E. Pormann. Karachi: Oxford University Press.
King, Peter. 2000. "The Problem of Individuation in the Middle Ages." *Theoria* 66: 159–84.
———. 2004. "Metaphysics" Pp. 65–125 in *The Cambridge Companion to Abelard*, edited by Jeffrey E. Brower and Kevin Guilfoy. Cambridge: Cambridge University Press.
———. 2012. "Body and Soul." Pp. 505–24 in *The Oxford Handbook of Medieval Philosophy*, edited by John Marenbon. Oxford & New York: Oxford University Press.
———. 2018. "Marguerite Porete and Godfrey of Fontaines: Detachable Will, Discardable Virtue, Transformative Love." *Oxford Studies in Medieval Philosophy* 6: 168–88.
Klima, Gyula. 2002. "Man = Body + Soul: Aquinas's Arithmetic of Human Nature." Pp. 257–73 in *Thomas Aquinas: Contemporary Philosophical Perspectives*, edited by Brian Davies. Oxford/New York: Oxford University Press.
Klima, Gyula with Fritz Allhof and Anand Jayprakash Vaidya, eds. and trans. 2007. *Medieval Philosophy: Essential Readings with Commentary*. Malden, MA & Oxford: Blackwell.
Kretzmann, Norman. 1966. "Omniscience and Immutability." *Journal of Philosophy* 63: 409–21.
Kukkonen, Taneli. 2012. "Eternity." Pp. 525–46 in *The Oxford Handbook of Medieval Philosophy*, edited by John Marenbon. Oxford/New York: The Oxford University Press.
———. 2014. *Ibn Tufayl: Living the Life of Reason*. Oxford: Oneworld.
Lagerlund, Henrik. 2012. "Material Substance." Pp. 468–85 in *The Oxford Handbook of Medieval Philosophy*, edited by John Marenbon. Oxford & New York: Oxford University Press.
———. 2020. *Skepticism in Philosophy: A Comprehensive Historical Introduction*. New York & London: Routledge.
Lagerlund, Henrik, ed. 2018. *Encyclopedia of Medieval Philosophy*. Revised edition. Dordrecht: Springer [1st edition: 2011].
Laks, André and Glenn W. Most, eds. and trans. 2016. *Early Greek Philosophy VIII: Sophists, Part 1*. Loeb Classical Library, vol. 531. Cambridge, MA/London: Harvard University Press.
Lings, Martin, trans. 2004. *Sufi Poems: A Medieval Anthology*. Cambridge: Islamic Texts Society.

Lisska, Anthony J. 1998. *Aquinas's Theory of Natural Law: An Analytic Reconstruction*. Oxford: Clarendon Press.

———. 2012. "Natural Law." Pp. 622–42 in *The Oxford Handbook of Medieval Philosophy*, edited by John Marenbon. Oxford/New York: Oxford University Press.

Lottin, D. Odon. 1957. *Psychologie et Morale aux XIIe et XIIIe siècles*. Vol 1: *Problèmes de Psychologie*. 2nd edition. Gembloux, Belgium: J. Duculot.

MacCulloch, Diarmaid. 2009. *Christianity: The First Three Thousand Years*. New York: Viking.

MacDonald, Scott. 1999. "Primal Sin." Pp. 110–39 in *The Augustinian Tradition*, edited by Gareth B. Matthews. Berkeley/Los Angeles/London: University of California Press.

———. 2003. "Petit Larceny, the Beginning of All Sin: Augustine's Theft of the Pears." *Faith and Philosophy* 20: 393–414.

MacDonald, Scott and Eleonore Stump, eds. 1998. *Aquinas's Moral Theory: Essays in Honor of Norman Kretzmann*. Ithaca, NY: Cornell University Press.

McCarthy, Richard J., ed. and trans. 1953. *The Theology of al-Ash'ari: The Arabic texts of al-Ash'ari's "Kitab al-Luma'" and "Risalat Istihsan al-Khawd fi 'Ilm al-Kalam", with briefly annotated translations, and Appendices containing material pertinant to the study of al-Ash'ari*. Beirut: Imprimerie Catholique.

McGinn, Bernard. 1998. *The Flowering of Mysticism: Men and Women in the New Mysticism –1200–1350*. New York: Crossroad Herder.

———. 2005. *The Harvest of Mysticism in Medieval Germany (1300–1500)*. New York: Herder and Herder.

McGinnis, Jon and David C. Reisman, eds. and trans. 2007. *Classical Arabic Philosophy: An Anthology of Sources*. Indianapolis, IN: Hackett.

Madelung, Wilfred, ed., and Toby Mayer, trans. 2016. *Avicenna's Allegory on the Soul: An Ismaili Interpretation*. Institute of Ismaili Studies, Ismaili Texts and Translations Series, vol. 22. London & New York: I. B. Tauris.

Mahdi, Muhsin. 1984. "Remarks on Averroes' *Decisive Treatise*." Pp. 188–202 in *Islamic Theology and Philosophy*, edited by M. E. Marmura. Albany: State University of New York Press.

Maimonides, Moses. 1963. *The Guide of the Perplexed*. Translated by Shlomo Pines with an introductory essay by Leo Strauss. 2 volumes. Chicago/London: University of Chicago Press.

———. 1975. *Ethical Writings of Maimonides*. Edited by Raymond L. Weiss with Charles Butterworth. New York: New York University Press [Reprinted: New York: Dover, 1983].

Majcherek, Kamil. 2022. "The Medieval Problem of the Productivity of Art." *Philosophies* 7, no. 5: 101. https://doi.org/10.3390/philosophies7050101

Marenbon, John. 2003. *Boethius*. Oxford: The Oxford University Press.

———. 2007. *Medieval Philosophy: An Historical and Philosophical Introduction*. New York: Routledge.

———. 2013. *Abelard in Four Dimensions: A Twelfth-Century Philosopher in His Context and Ours*. Notre Dame: University of Notre Dame Press.

———. 2018. "Why We Need a Real History of Philosophy." Pp. 36–50 in *Philosophy and the Historical* Perspective, edited by M. van Ackeren, with L. Klein. Oxford: The British Academy by Oxford University Press.

Marenbon, John, ed. 2012. *The Oxford Handbook of Medieval Philosophy.* Oxford/New York: Oxford University Press.

Marguerite Porete. 1991. *The Mirror of Simple Souls.* Translated by Ellen L. Babinsky. New York/Mahwah, NJ: The Paulist Press.

Marmura, Michael E. 1979. "The Philosopher in Society: Some Medieval Arabic Discussions." *Arabic Studies Quarterly* 1: 309–23. Reprinted in Marmura 2005, pp. 409–25 [Citations are to the latter edition].

———. 1983. "The Islamic Philosophers' Conception of Islam." Pp. 87–102 in *Islam's Understanding of Itself*, edited by R. G. Hovannisain and S. Vryonis Jr.. Malibu, CA: Udena Press. Reprinted in Marmura 2005, pp. 391–408 [Citations are to the latter edition].

———. 1992. "Avicenna and the Kalam." *Zeitschrift für Geschichte der Arabisch-Islamischen Wissenschaften* 7: 172–206. Reprinted in Marmura 2005, pp. 97–130.

———. 2005. *Probing in Islamic Philosophy: Studies in the Philosophies of Ibn Sina, al-Ghazali and Other Major Muslim Thinkers.* Binghamton, NY: Global Academic Publishing.

Massignon, Louis. 1982. *The Passion of al-Hallaj: Mystic and Martyr of Islam.* 4 volumes. Princeton: Princeton University Press.

———. 1994. *The Passion of al-Hallaj: Mystic and Martyr of Islam.* Translated, edited, and abridged by Herbert Mason. Princeton: Princeton University Press.

Matthews, Gareth B. 2005. *Augustine.* Oxford: Blackwell.

Meister Eckhart. 1981. *The Essential Sermons, Commentaries, Treatises, and Defense.* Translated by Edmund Colledge, and Bernard McGinn. Mahwah, NJ: Paulist Press.

———. 1986. *Teacher and Preacher.* Edited by Bernard McGinn with the collaboration of Frank Tobin and Elvira Borgstadt. Mahwah, NJ: Paulist Press.

Montada, Josef Puig. 2005. "Philosophy in Andalusia: Ibn Bajja and Ibn Tufayl." Pp. 155–79 in *The Cambridge Companion to Arabic Philosophy*, edited by P. Adamson and R. C. Taylor. Cambridge: Cambridge University Press.

Nasr, Seyyed Hossein, with Caner K. Dagli, Maria Massi Dakare, Joseph E. B. Lumbard, and Mohammed Rustom, eds. and trans. 2015. *The Study Quran: A New Translation and Commentary.* New York: Harper Collins [references to the paperback edition: 2017].

Nederman, Cary J. 2014. "Individual Autonomy." Pp. 551–64 in *The Cambridge History of Medieval Philosophy*, vol. 2, edited by Robert Pasnau with Christina Van Dyke. Revised edition. Cambridge: Cambridge University Press.

Noone, Timothy. 2014. "Divine Illumination." Pp. 369–83 in *The Cambridge History of Medieval Philosophy*, vol. 1, edited by Robert Pasnau with Christina Van Dyke. Revised edition. Cambridge: Cambridge University Press.

Ormsby, Eric. 2008. *Ghazali: The Revival of Islam.* Oxford: Oneworld.

Parens, Joshua, and Joseph C. Macfarland, eds. 2011. *Medieval Political Philosophy: A Sourcebook.* 2nd revised edition. Ithaca, NY: Cornell University Press.

Pasnau, Robert. 2002. *Thomas Aquinas on Human Nature: A Philosophical Study of "Summa theologiae" Ia75–89.* Cambridge/New York: Cambridge University Press.

———. 2011. *Metaphysical Themes 1274–1671.* Oxford: The Clarendon Press, 2011

———. 2014a. "Science and Certainty." Pp. 357–68 in *The Cambridge History of Medieval Philosophy*, vol. 1, edited by Robert Pasnau with Christina Van Dyke. Revised edition. Cambridge: Cambridge University Press.

———. 2014b. "Form and Matter." Pp. 635–46 in *The Cambridge History of Medieval Philosophy*, vol 2, edited by Robert Pasnau with Christina Van Dyke. Revised paperback edition. New York/Cambridge: Cambridge University Press.

———. 2017. *After Certainty: Historical Reflections on Our Epistemic Ideals and Illusions*. Oxford: Oxford University Press.

Pasnau, Robert with Christina Van Dyke, eds. 2014. *The Cambridge History of Medieval Philosophy*. 2 volumes. 2nd, revised paperback edition. New York/Cambridge: Cambridge University Press.

Pelletier, Jenny. 2022. "Getting Real: Ockham on the Human Contribution to the Nature and Production of Artifacts." *Philosophies* 7, no. 5: 90. https://doi.org/10.3390/philosophies7050090

Perler, Dominik. 2012. "Scepticism and Metaphysics." Pp. 547–65 in *The Oxford Handbook of Medieval Philosophy*, edited by John Marenbon. Oxford & New York: Oxford University Press.

———. 2014. "Skepticism." Pp. 384–96 in *The Cambridge History of Medieval Philosophy*, vol. 1, edited by Robert Pasnau with Christina Van Dyke. Revised edition. Cambridge: Cambridge University Press.

———. 2018. "The Alienation Effect in the Historiography of Philosophy." Pp. 140–54 in *Philosophy and the Historical* Perspective, edited by M. van Ackeren, with L. Klein. Oxford: The British Academy by Oxford University Press.

Perlmann, Moshe, trans. 1971. *Ibn Kammua's Examination of the Three Faiths: A Thirteenth-century Essay in the Comparative Study of Religion*. Berkeley/Los Angeles/London: University of California Press.

Pessin, Sarah. 2013. *Ibn Gabirol's Theology of Desire: Matter and Method in Jewish Medieval Neoplatonism*. Cambridge: Cambridge University Press.

Peter Abelard. 1919. "Glossae super Porphyrium." Pp. 1–109 in *Peter Abaelards Philosophische Schriften I. Logica "ingredientibus"*, edited by B. Geyer. Münster: Aschendorff.

———. 1970. *Dialectica: First Complete Edition of the Parisian Manuscript*. 2nd edition. Edited by L. M. de Rijk. Assen: Van Gorcum.

———. 1995. *Ethical Writings*. Translated by Paul V. Spade. Indianapolis: Hackett.

———. 2001. *Collationes*. Edited and translated by John Marenbon and Giovanni Orlandi. Cambridge: Cambridge University Press.

Peter Abelard, and Heloise. 2007. *The Letters and Other Writings*. Translated by William Levitan. Indianapolis, IN: Hackett.

Peter of Spain. 2014. *Summaries of Logic: Texts, Translation, Introduction, and Notes*. Translated by Brian P. Copenhaver, with Calvin G. Normore and Terence Parsons. Oxford: Oxford University Press.

Piché, David. 1999. *La Condamnation Parisienne de 1277: Nouvelle édition du texte latin, traduction, introduction et commentaire*. Paris: J. Vrin.

Pink, Thomas. 2012. "Freedom of the Will." Pp. 569–87 in *The Oxford Handbook of Medieval Philosophy*, edited by John Marenbon. Oxford/New York: Oxford University Press.

Polloni, Nicola. 2020. *The Twelfth-Century Renewal of Latin Metaphysics: Gundissalinus's Ontology of Matter and Form*. Toronto: Pontifical Institute of Mediaeval

Studies/Durham: Institute of Medieval and Early Modern Studies, Durham University.

Porphyry. 2000. *On Abstinence from Killing Animals*. Translated by Gillian Clark. London: Duckworth and Co. [Reprinted: Bloomsbury Academic, 2014].

Quran. See Nasr et al. 2015.

al-Raziq, 'Ali 'Abd. 2007. *Islam and the Bases of Power*. Partial translation in *Islam in Transition: Muslim Perspectives*, edited by J. J. Donohue and J. L. Esposito. 2nd edition, pp. 24–31. New York: Oxford University Press.

Relihan, Joel C. 2007. *The Prisoner's Philosophy: Life and Death in Boethius's 'Consolation'*. Notre Dame: University of Notre Dame Press.

Rist, John M. 1994. *Augustine: Ancient Thought Baptized*. Cambridge & New York: Cambridge University Press.

Rizvi, Sajjad H. 2005. "Mysticism and Philosophy: Ibn 'Arabi and Mulla Sadra." Pp. 224–46 in *The Cambridge Companion to Arabic Philosophy*, edited by Peter Adamson and Richard C. Taylor. Cambridge: Cambridge University Press.

Rosemann, Philipp W. 1999. *Understanding Scholastic Thought with Foucault*. New York: St. Martin's Press.

Rudavsky, Tamar, ed. 1985. *Divine Omniscience and Divine Omnipotence in Medieval Philosophy*. Dordrecht: D. Reidel.

Russell, Frederick H. 2014. "Just War." Pp. 593–606 in *The Cambridge History of Medieval Philosophy*, vol. 2, edited by Robert Pasnau and Christina Van Dyke. Revised second edition. Cambridge: Cambridge University Press.

Saadya Gaon. 2002. *The Book of Doctrines and Beliefs*. Translated and abridged by Alexander Altmann. Revised edition. Indianapolis, IN: Hackett, 2002 [originally published, Oxford: East and West Library, 1946].

Safi, Omid, trans. 2018. *Radical Love: Teachings from the Islamic Mystical Tradition*. New Haven, CT: Yale University Press.

Schimmel, Annemarie. 1975. *Mystical Dimensions of Islam*. Chapel Hill: University of North Carolina Press.

Sells, Michael A., ed. and trans. 1996. *Early Islamic Mysticism: Sufi, Qur'an, Mi'raj, Poetic and Theological Writings*. Mahwah, NJ: Paulist Press.

Segvic, Heda. 2000. "No One Errs Willingly: The Meaning of Socratic Intellectualism." *Oxford Studies in Ancient Philosophy* 19: 1–45.

Spade, Paul Vincent, trans. 1994. *Five Texts on the Mediaeval Problem of Universals: Porphyry, Boethius, Abelard, Duns Scotus, Ockham*. Indianapolis: Hackett.

Spade, Paul Vincent. 1999. "The Warp and Woof of Metaphysics: How to Get Started on Some Big Themes." Unpublished manuscript, available at https://pvspade.com/Logic/docs/WarpWoo1.pdf [accessed: September 2022]

Stahl, William Harris, and Richard Johnson, with E. L. Burge, trans. 1977. *Martianus Capella and the Seven Liberal Arts*. Vol II: *The Marriage of Philology and Mercury*. New York: Columbia University Press.

Strauss, Leo. 1952. *Persecution and the Art of Writing*. Glencoe, IL: The Free Press [reprinted: Westport, CT: Greenwood Press, 1973].

Stroud, Barry. 1984. *The Significance of Philosophical Scepticism*. Oxford/New York: Oxford University Press.

Stroumsa, Sarah. 1998. "'True Felicity': Paradise in the Thought of Avicenna and Maimonides." *Medieval Encounters* 4: 51–77.

Stump, Eleonore. 2003. *Aquinas*. London/New York: Routledge.

———. 2014. "The Problem of Evil." Pp. 773–84 in *The Cambridge History of Medieval Philosophy*, vol 2, edited by Robert Pasnau with Christina Van Dyke. 2nd, revised paperback edition. New York/Cambridge: Cambridge University Press.

Stump, Eleonore and Norman Kretzmann. 1981. "Eternity." *Journal of Philosophy* 78: 429–58.

Taylor, Richard C. 2005. "Averroes: religious dialectic and Aristotelian philosophical thought." Pp. 180–200 in *The Cambridge Companion to Arabic Philosophy*, edited by Peter Adamson and Richard C. Taylor. Cambridge: Cambridge University Press.

Thomas Aquinas. 1950. *In duodecim libros Metaphysicorum Aristotelis expositio*. Edited by M.-R. Cathala and R. M. Spiazzi. Turin/Rome: Marietti.

———. 1984. *Questions on the Soul*. Translated by James H. Robb. Milwaukee: Marquette University Press.

———. 1996. *Commentary on the Book of Causes*. Translated by Vincent A. Guagliardo, Charles R. Hess, and Richard C. Taylor. Washington, DC: Catholic University of America Press.

———. 2005. *Disputed Questions on the Virtues*. Edited by E. M. Atkins and Thomas Williams. Cambridge/New York: Cambridge University Press.

———. 2014. *Basic Works*. Edited by Jeffrey Hause and Robert Pasnau. Indianapolis, IN: Hackett Publishing.

———. 2016. *The Treatise on Happiness – The Treatise on Human Acts: "Summa Theologiae" I-II 1–21*. Translated by Thomas Williams, commentary by Christina Van Dyke and Thomas Williams. Indianapolis, IN: Hackett.

Treiger, Alexander. 2012. *Inspired Knowledge in Islamic Thought: Al-Ghazali's Theory of Mystical Cognition and its Avicennian Foundation*. New York: Routledge.

al-Tusi, Nasir al-Din. 2005. *The Paradise of Submission: A Medieval Treatise on Ismaili Thought*. Edited and translated by S. Jalal Badakhchani. London/New York: I. B. Tauris in association with The Institute of Ismaili Studies, London.

van Ackeren, Marcel, with Lee Klein, eds. 2018. *Philosophy and the Historical Perspective*. Proceedings of the British Academy 214. Oxford: The British Academy by Oxford University Press.

Van Cleve, James. 1986. "Mereological Essentialism, Mereological Conjunctivism, and Identity Through Time." *Midwest Studies in Philosophy* 11: 141–56.

Van Dyke, Christina. 2014. "Mysticism." Pp. 720–34 in *The Cambridge History of Medieval Philosophy*, vol 2, edited by Robert Pasnau with Christina Van Dyke. 2nd, revised paperback editon. New York/Cambridge: Cambridge University Press.

———. 2015. "Aquinas's Shiny Happy People: Perfect Happiness and the Limits of Human Nature." *Oxford Studies in Philosophy of Religion* 6: 269–91.

———. 2017. "Self-knowledge, Abnegation, and Fulfillment in Medieval Mysticism." Pp. 131–45 in *Self-Knowledge: A History*, edited by Ursula Renz. Oxford: Oxford University Press.

———. 2018. "What has History to do with Philosophy? Insights from the Medieval Contemplative Tradition." Pp. 155–70 in *Philosophy and the Historical Perspective*, edited by M. Van Ackeren, with Lee Klein. Proceedings of the British Academy 214. Oxford: Oxford University Press.

———. 2019. "Medieval Mystics on Persons: What John Locke Didn't Tell You," Pp. 123–53 in *Persons: A History*, edited by Antonia Lolordo. New York/Oxford: Oxford University Press.

———. 2022. *A Hidden Wisdom: Medieval Contemplatives on Self-Knowledge, Reason, Love, Persons, and Immortality*. Oxford/New York: Oxford University Press.

Van Ess, Josef. 1982. "Early Development of Kalam." Pp. 109–23 in *Studies on the First Century of Islamic Society*, edited by G. H. A. Juynball. Papers on Islamic History 5. Carbondale and Edwardsville: Southern Illinois University Press.

———. 2006. *The Flowering of Muslim Theology*. Translated by Jane Marie Todd. Cambridge, MA, and London: Harvard University Press.

Watt, W. Montgomery. 1962. "The Logical Basis of Early Kalam." *The Islamic Quarterly* 6: 3–10.

Watt, W. Montgomery, trans. 1994. *The Faith and Practice of Al-Ghazali*. Oxford: Oneworld [originally published 1953].

Wei, Ian P. 2020. *Thinking about Animals in Thirteenth-Century Paris*. Cambridge: Cambridge University Press.

Wieland, Georg. 1987. "Plato or Aristotle – A Real Alternative in Medieval Philosophy." Pp. 63–83 in *Studies in Medieval Philosophy*, edited by John F. Wippel. Washington, DC: The Catholic University of America Press.

William of Auvergne. 1674. *De universo creaturum*, in *Opera Omnia*. Edited by Le Feron. 1674 [reprint 1963].

William of Ockham. 1983. *William of Ockham: Predestination, God's Foreknowledge, and Future Contingents*. Translated by Marilyn M. Adams and Norman Kretzmann. 2nd edition. Indianapolis, IN: Hackett.

Williams, Scott M. 2019a. "Persons in Patristic and Medieval Christian Theology." Pp. 52–84 in *Persons: A History*, edited by Antonia Lolordo. New York/Oxford: Oxford University Press.

———. 2019b. "When Personhood Goes Wrong in Ethics and Philosophical Theology: Disability, Ableism, and (Modern) Personhood." Pp. 264–90 in *Lost Sheep in Philosophy of Religion: New Perspectives of Disability, Gender, Race, and Animals*, edited by Blake Hereth and Kevin Timpe. New York: Routledge.

Williams, Scott M. ed. 2020. *Disability in Medieval Christian Philosophy and Theology*. New York/London: Routledge.

Wippel, John F. 1984. *Metaphysical Themes in Thomas Aquinas*. Washington, DC: The Catholic University of America Press.

———. 2002. "The Five Ways." Pp. 159–225 in *Thomas Aquinas: Contemporary Philosophical Perspectives*, edited by Brian Davies. Oxford/New York: Oxford University Press.

———. 2014. "Essence and Existence." Pp. 622–34 in *The Cambridge History of Medieval Philosophy*, vol. 2, edited by Robert Pasnau with Christina Van Dyke. 2nd, revised paperback edition. New York/Cambridge: Cambridge University Press.

Wolfson, Harry Austryn. 1976. *The Philosophy of the Kalam*. Cambridge, MA and London: Harvard University Press.

Index

Abbasid Caliphate 37, 246–7, 278, 280
Abelard, Peter 2, 10, 69–70, 72–3, 77–9, 114, 135, 267, 279
accidents 60–3, 71–3, 76–8, 81, 84, 87, 94–6, 99, 104, 106, 110–12, 120, 131, 134, 142, 158
active intellect 121, 155, 161, 220, 232
afterlife 37, 121, 140–1, 150, 161, 169, 171–9, 204–5, 207, 209, 215, 231–2, 238, 241, 250, 257; see also resurrection
'A'ishah al-Ba'uniyyah 8, 190, 283
Albert the Great 10, 83–4, 89, 205, 280–1
angels 75, 85–7, 96, 131, 134, 158, 160, 169, 172, 177
animals 68, 76–9, 81, 88–91, 95, 105, 110–12, 115–17, 131–2, 139–41, 146–8, 154, 159, 183, 204–10, 212, 214, 216, 237, 253–4, 258
annihilation 44, 100, 121–30, 165–8, 184, 191
Anselm of Canterbury: ontological argument 9–10, 21–4, 279
apophaticism 19, 164–5, 168
Aquinas, Thomas see Thomas Aquinas
'Arabi (Muhyi al-Din ibn al-'Arabi) 98, 280
Aristotle 5–7, 10–11, 18, 33, 35–6, 46–7, 57–60, 63–4, 67, 72–3, 76–9, 88, 91–9, 105, 108–12, 114–20, 131–2, 140–2, 148–1, 171, 183, 188, 198, 204–5, 214, 218, 229, 236, 269, 277, 279, 281
Augustine 4–5, 10–11, 33, 39, 45–7, 99, 144, 183, 197–203, 210, 212, 264, 277
authority 15, 17–18, 28–9, 38, 98, 122, 176, 216, 226, 258, 262–3, 273
Averroes see ibn Rushd
Avicenna see ibn Sina

Boethius 2, 4–5, 10–12, 60–1, 66–9, 71–2, 76, 99, 103, 113–15, 133–6, 267, 277, 281
Bonaventure 46, 85–8, 280
Brethren of Purity (Ikhwan al-Safa) 206–10, 212, 279

Bruno see Giordano Bruno
Byzantium, Byzantine 57, 250, 275, 278, 280, 282

Case of the Animals versus Man Before the King of the Jinn 12, 206–7; see also Brethren of Purity
Catherine of Siena 3, 8, 130, 163–4, 166, 282
causation, cause 5, 41, 53, 70–5, 83–4, 96–7, 101, 116, 131, 143–7, 182–91, 193, 198–9, 208, 215, 223–4, 239–40
certainty 23, 30, 33–41, 47, 118, 148, 195, 244, 249
Christianity 4, 11, 35, 38–9, 49, 103, 118, 122, 129–30, 133, 138, 140–1, 161–2, 164, 168, 172, 181–2, 193, 233, 251–2, 256, 258, 264, 277, 280–2
Cicero 4, 47, 132, 141, 233
citizens 48, 132, 216, 218, 223, 229, 232, 253
cognition 18, 33, 45–7, 55, 60, 108, 147, 157, 160, 205, 220, 243
compel, compulsion see freedom, of the will
Confessions 11, 198–203; see also Augustine
Consolation of Philosophy 11–12, 265; see also Boethius
creation 20, 52, 63, 74, 77–8, 122–3, 128, 149, 156, 165, 174, 183, 186, 190–3, 203–10

Deliverance from Error 11, 21, 37, 47, 97, 231, 237–8, 243, 248; see also Ghazali
democracy 215, 224–7, 234, 262
Descartes see René Descartes
disputation, as method of philosophy 12–16, 67, 86, 117, 278; see also philosophy

education 13, 17, 141, 144, 215, 219, 227, 252
emanation 74, 98, 160–1, 215; see also Platonism
environment 204, 209–10, 212

essence 59–64, 70–1, 73–7, 85–7, 90, 94, 99, 106, 120, 147, 171; God's see God, essence of
ethics 20, 24, 31, 133, 140–2, 148–9, 156–8, 181–2, 194, 209, 215, 219; see also virtue ethics
eudaimonia 150, 155, 160, 213; see also happiness

faith 7, 22–3, 35, 48–9, 98, 118, 123, 125, 147, 162, 171, 176–8, 182, 189–90, 232, 237–8, 245–50, 256, 261–2, 264, 273
fall: of the devil (Iblis, Satan) 169–70; of human beings 23–4, 38, 197
falsafa 7, 124; see also philosophy
Farabi (Abu Nasr al-Farabi) 10, 39–40, 64, 103, 107, 159–60, 215–32, 236, 241–3, 248, 252–5, 258–9, 262, 264, 279
Francisco Suarez 6, 283
fraternal correction 182, 212
freedom: of the will 35–6, 50, 97, 148, 166–8; of thought, expression, or speech 232–4, 250–2
first cause see cause
Five Ways 9, 21; see also Thomas Aquinas
foreknowledge, divine 240, 265
form 56–8, 61, 74–9, 82–6, 88–90, 92–4, 98–9, 105–7, 110–12, 115, 117, 119–21, 132, 145–6, 156–7, 171, 186, 189, 208, 214; see also hylomorphism; matter

Ghazali (Abu Hamid Muhammad ibn Muhammad al-Ghazali) 7, 11, 21, 30, 37–47, 52–3, 97–100, 124–9, 144, 148, 167, 173–6, 182–92, 210, 212, 230, 232, 236–9, 241–52, 265, 279
Giordano Bruno 5, 283
God 9, 11, 18–24, 29, 32, 37–8, 41, 44–9, 51–4, 60–4, 69, 77–9, 83–7, 96–100, 108, 121–30, 140, 146–9, 156, 158, 160–71, 175–7, 184, 186–93, 195, 201–2, 208–10, 220, 229–32, 236, 238–51, 255, 257, 260–2, 265; essence of 46, 98, 100–1, 108, 121–3, 129, 135, 149, 164, 173, 191
Guide of the Perplexed 19, 94, 96, 103, 158, 160, 173, 177–9, 181, 214; see also Maimonides

Hadewijch 129, 280
Hallaj (Al-Husayn ibn Mansur al-Hallaj) 123–5, 128–9, 138, 170–1, 279
happiness 23–4, 130, 139–40, 147, 150–5, 160, 168, 170, 181, 184, 199, 209, 213–16, 220, 222–3, 228–9, 232–3, 246, 254–8

Hayy ibn Yaqzan 12, 124–9, 207–10, 255–9; see also Tufayl
history of philosophy 2, 5–7, 16–17, 26, 251, 266–75; see also philosophy
human beings: nature of 18–21, 23–4, 28–9, 44–7, 59, 65–73, 77, 79–82, 105–12, 114–21, 131–3, 139–48, 151–61, 168–9, 171–6, 183, 195, 204–10, 214–20, 223–6, 229–32, 253–8, 264
human flourishing see *eudaimonia* and happiness
humility 143, 162–6, 171, 181
hylomorphism 57, 64, 91–2, 103; Universal hylomorphism 84–8, 93, 103; see also form; matter

Iblis 169–71; see also fall, of the devil
ibn Rushd, Abu'l Walid Muhammad (Averroes) 2, 155, 178, 231, 237–48, 250, 252, 264–5, 279
ibn Sina, Abu 'Ali al-Husayn ibn 'Abdallah (Avicenna) 2–3, 12, 64, 69, 107–11, 120, 124, 129, 160, 173–5, 230–2, 236–7, 241, 252, 279–80
Incoherence of the Philosophers 7, 41, 174, 236–8; see also Ghazali
individual 134–5; cause of individuality of 65, 71–5
intellect 34–5, 50–3, 110, 117–21, 146–7, 155, 160–1, 215, 218, 226, 232, 236, 242, 255–6
intellectual ascent and vision 22–3, 107, 127–30, 147–8, 208–9, 255
Isagoge 11, 67–72, 76–7; see also Porphyry
Islam 7, 12, 28–9, 33, 37–9, 46, 53, 57, 103–4, 118, 122–3, 140–1, 149, 161, 167, 172, 181–2, 187, 192–3, 206, 212, 220, 237–8, 241–50, 256, 259–60, 264, 275, 278, 280

John Blund 108–11, 280
John Buridan 4, 10, 33–7, 48–53, 89–91, 95, 114–18, 282
John Duns Scotus 16, 75, 103, 148, 281
Judaism 7, 26, 28, 38–9, 46, 57, 84, 103, 118, 140–1, 149, 161, 172, 182, 193, 238, 256, 259–61, 279–82

kalam (*ilm al-kalam*) 7–8, 11, 30, 94–100, 103
Kindi (Abu Yusuf 'qub ibn Ishaq al-Kindi) 141, 278
knowledge 19, 28–41, 47–8, 51–3, 55, 98, 179, 218, 222, 230, 236, 239–41, 245, 264–5

love 22–3, 122–3, 125, 129–30, 134, 153, 164–71, 182–3, 210–12, 226; for God 187–93, for neighbor 193–7, for self 183–6

Maimonides 2, 19, 94–7, 99, 103, 143–4, 158, 160–2, 173, 176–9, 181, 214–15, 218–19, 259–62, 280
Marguerite Porete 8, 12, 122, 164–8, 171, 181, 235, 282
matter 56–65, 73–9, 81–93, 102–3, 105–12, 116–19, 141, 146, 155–9, 171, 173–5, 222–4; first or prime matter 74–5, 83–4, 89, 92, 103, 116, 224; spiritual 85–7
Meditations on First Philosophy 23, 32, 43, 107; see also René Descartes
Meister Eckhart 164–8, 181, 282
metaphysics 20, 24, 57, 59, 64, 83, 96–8, 102–3, 106, 126, 138, 157, 215, 237, 241
Metaphysics, Aristotle's 10, 35–6, 77–8, 156
Mirror of Simple Souls 12, 122, 165–7, 235; see also Marguerite Porete
morphe see form
Mulla Sadra 6, 98, 283
Mutakallimun 94–7, 103–4; see also kalam
mystical union 100, 121–30, 163–9, 187, 212, 255–6
mysticism 8, 11, 44, 53, 57, 97–100, 103, 105, 121–30, 138, 141, 161–71, 180, 187, 212, 250, 255–6, 275

neighbor: love for (see love)
Niche of Lights 98–9, 124–6; see also Ghazali
Nicholas of Autrecourt 51–3, 97, 102
Nicholas of Cusa 4–5, 282
Nicomachean Ethics 35, 142, 151–3, 158, 188; see also Aristotle
nominalism see universals, problem of

Ockham see William of Ockham
Ockham's Razor 65
On Being and Essence 59–63, 74–5, 85, 87; see also Thomas Aquinas
On the Perfect State 107, 159–60, 215, 221–9, 243; see also Farabi
Ontological Argument for God's existence 9, 21–4; see also Anselm
Outlines of Pyrrhonism 45, 47; see also Sextus Empiricus

persistence 73, 105, 112, 115, 157
person 15, 105–7, 119, 131–6, 138, 140–2, 155, 159, 204–5
Peter Abelard 2, 69, 103, 135, 279
Peter of Spain 10, 280
philosophy 1–12, 16–18, 20–1, 24–6, 32–3, 46, 52, 74, 97–8, 112, 124, 133, 139, 141, 156, 161, 164, 171, 189, 203, 206, 212, 215, 227, 229–30, 236–7, 241–3, 251–3, 257–9, 264–72, 277, 279, 281–2
Plato 6–7, 10, 46, 57–8, 60, 63, 74, 98–9, 107, 150–1, 156–7, 171, 184, 189, 198, 213–14, 218–19, 225–7, 229, 233, 236, 253, 282
Platonism 4–5, 7, 11, 31, 56–8, 69, 74, 91, 97–100, 103–4, 107–9, 111–12, 119–21, 123–4, 130–1, 141, 147, 149, 156–8, 160–1, 171, 173–4, 176, 186, 189, 206–7, 210, 214–15, 220, 223–5, 229, 255, 262–4, 277, 279, 282
Plotinus 98, 160–1, 282
political philosophy 20, 24, 133, 156, 213–15, 258, 264; see also philosophy
Political Regime 216–22, 224–8, 253; see also Farabi
Porphyry 11, 71, 76–7, 79, 82, 103
powers, of the soul 19, 28, 52, 79–80, 89–90, 108–10, 127, 146–7, 217; of God 48–50, 63, 78, 86, 97, 146, 156
Pyrrho and Pyrrhonism 31, 45–7

quiddity see essence

rational animal see human being
rational principles 42–3
rational soul 52–3, 73, 76–7, 79–81, 108, 112, 119–20, 125, 132–5, 140, 143, 146–7, 156–60, 205–6
realism see universals, problem of
reality: structure of 11, 19–20, 24, 30–1, 65–8, 91–2, 102, 126–8, 156, 168, 176, 193, 229, 240
reason: as faculty of the soul 12, 18–20, 23, 28, 35–6, 41–6, 49, 98, 125–8, 134, 140, 143–4, 147–8, 151–4, 160, 165–7, 171, 173–8, 205–6, 209, 212, 216, 233, 240, 242–3
religion 17–18, 20, 28, 38, 96, 123–5, 140–1, 167, 173, 175, 181–2, 189, 216, 220–1, 229–33, 235–7, 242–6, 249–51, 255–62, 273; philosophy of 20–1, 189, 229, 265
Renaissance 5, 278–9, 282
René Descartes 6–7, 9, 23, 32, 43–6, 48, 50, 53, 106–7, 271, 283
resurrection 171–9, 181, 232, 238, 249
Revival of the Religious Sciences 37–8; see also Ghazali
Roland of Cremona 80, 281

salvation 18–19, 29, 204
science 5, 7, 20, 31–3, 35, 50–2, 56, 60–1, 91, 94, 97, 179, 219–20, 237, 241–2, 252, 255, 269–70, 272, 278–80
Scotus see John Duns Scotus

self 46, 98, 120–3, 126–30, 131, 153, 160, 163–71, 182–6, 193, 209–10, 261;
annihilation of 121–30, 164–8; knowledge of, love for see love, of self
Sextus Empiricus 31, 45, 47
Skepticism 11, 30–3, 37–8, 46–7, 50, 54–5, 148; global skepticism 40, 45–7, 50, 53–4
state: political 48–9, 183, 215–29, 232–3, 247–51, 253–4, 262, 264, 269
soul 12, 24, 37, 46, 49, 59, 78–82, 86, 88–90, 94–5, 105–12, 115, 117–22, 126–7, 129, 132, 134, 136, 140, 143–9, 154–62, 165–7, 171–8, 189, 201–4, 215–16, 221–2, 231–2, 238, 251; see also rational soul
Suarez, Francisco see Francisco Suarez
substance 51, 57, 59–64, 71–5, 77–9, 81, 84–90, 92–7, 99–100, 104–12, 115, 120, 124, 128, 131, 133–6, 146, 155–6, 161, 171, 216–18, 223, 231–2, 257
substance dualism 106–7, 111–12
Summa theologiae 8, 10, 14, 17–18, 20, 75, 88, 181, 279; see also Thomas Aquinas

Thomas Aquinas 3, 8–11, 14, 17–22, 55, 59–64, 74–5, 78, 80–1, 85–9, 99, 102–3, 106, 145–9, 155, 157, 162–3, 171–3, 177, 181–2, 193–7, 210, 212, 265, 277, 279–82
Tufayl (Abu Bakr Muhammad ibn Tufayl) 12, 124–9, 207–10, 212, 252, 255–9, 279
Tusi (Nasir al-Din al-Tusi) 21–2

union: mystical 100, 121–2, 124, 129–30, 141, 163, 167–8, 170, 232, 255
Universal Hylomorphism see hylomorphism, universal
universals: God's knowledge of 239; problem of 65–70, 267

virtue ethics 148–54, 156–8, 181, 194
virtue, virtuous life 28, 107–8, 122, 140–54, 157–8, 162–6, 181, 189–90, 193–5, 213–15, 218–19, 222–3, 226–9, 231–2, 234, 244, 259–60, 262

will: as faculty of the rational soul 35–6, 49, 96–7, 134, 147–8, 152, 159, 164–9, 171, 180–1, 234, 260–1; of God 48, 96–7, 130, 165–9, 171, 180, 220, 239
William of Ockham 16, 65, 69, 103, 115–16, 251–2, 265, 267, 272, 281–2